Non dilexerunt animam suam usque ad mortem.

The Latin, *Non dilexerunt animam suam usque ad mortem*, translates, "... they loved not their lives unto the death." Revelation 12:11

On The Cover: *Massacres at Salzburg* took place in 1528 when Prince-Archbishop Cardinal Matthaus Lang of Salzburg issued mandates sending police in search of Anabaptists. Many were captured and killed. This engraving illustrates the sufferings and sacrifices these Dissenters endured when their government, in conjunction with established religion, attempted to coerce and impose uniformity of religious belief. Hence, this picture is a reminder of the cost of religious liberty and the ever-present need to maintain the separation of church and state. We use this art to represent our Dissent and Nonconformity Series.

THE

EARLY ENGLISH DISSENTERS

IN THE LIGHT OF RECENT RESEARCH

(1550-1641)

VOLUME I

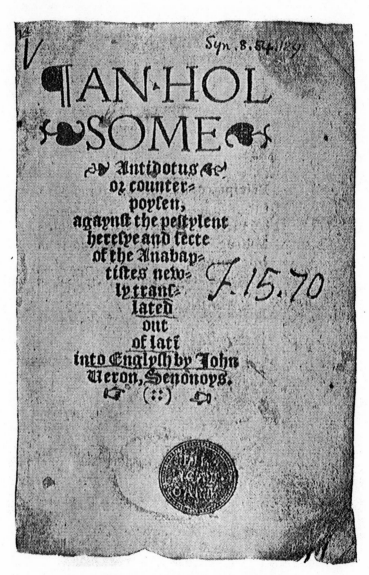

TITLE-PAGE. (*Facsimile.*) Date 1548.

See Vol. I., page 55.

THE

EARLY ENGLISH DISSENTERS

IN THE LIGHT OF RECENT RESEARCH

(1550-1641)

BY

CHAMPLIN BURRAGE

HON. M.A. (BROWN UNIVERSITY), B. LITT. (OXON.)

IN TWO VOLUMES
Illustrated

VOLUME I
HISTORY AND CRITICISM

Cambridge:
at the University Press
1912

he Baptist Standard Bearer, Inc.

NUMBER ONE IRON OAKS DRIVE • PARIS, ARKANSAS 72855

Thou hast given a *standard* to them that fear thee;
that it may be displayed because of the truth.
-- *Psalm 60:4*

Reprinted
by

THE BAPTIST STANDARD BEARER, INC.
No. 1 Iron Oaks Drive
Paris, Arkansas 72855
(501) 963-3831

THE WALDENSIAN EMBLEM
lux lucet in tenebris
"The Light Shineth in the Darkness"

ISBN #1-57978-894-7

TO
MY WIFE

PREFACE

HERETOFORE, even the best histories of the Church of England have been noticeably lacking in adequate information relating to our subject, while the average history written by Nonconformists is not unnaturally apt to be somewhat partial in its treatment. English Church history as a whole, however, cannot be said to be satisfactorily studied, unless the story of Dissent is fully and fairly presented. In the past, it is true, English Church historians may have felt that the record of organized separation from the Established Church was not of sufficient interest or importance to justify any detailed presentation. The modern student, however, who wishes as far as possible to know all the facts of English Church history, cannot be satisfied to remain largely in ignorance or doubt as to the salient points of Dissenting history.

To the student who desires, in particular, to know more of the story of early English Dissent, it is hoped that the present work may prove useful. As here presented, it is intended to be complete in itself for the period treated; but it is also designed as the first section of a larger treatise for which the author has been making investigations for a number of years. If completed as planned, the entire work will contain, besides a continuation of the historical and critical information to be found in these two volumes, an extended bibliography of between two and three thousand items, which has already been prepared as a supplement to Dr Henry Martyn Dexter's "Collections toward a Bibliography of Congregationalism", but which will be chiefly concerned with the literature of the English Anabaptists and Baptists before 1745.

On examination it will readily be seen that the present publication is not intended as an exhaustive history of English Dissent during even the period treated, but rather as an introduction to the study of that history and its literature. Furthermore the author has sought as much as possible to limit himself to the discussion of points which have not been previously treated, or which appear to have been handled with insufficient care. Accordingly some subjects that ought at least to be mentioned in a complete history will scarcely be referred to here, because on them more or less adequate work seems already to have been done.

In the following pages the author has also endeavoured to follow the trend of primary evidence, irrespective of his own preconceptions or of what has previously been written by others on the subject. His ideal has been to rely on secondary evidence as little as possible, and to amplify and correct the studies of earlier writers (including his own previous writings), in the belief that such further critical investigation was absolutely necessary, if the subject was ever truly to be understood. He therefore asks the reader to keep these necessary limitations and this ideal in mind, and to give him a patient hearing.

The author does not doubt that mistakes will be found in his work, but he has sought to make their number as few as possible, and here and elsewhere to correct any errors of the presence of which he has become aware. For any others which may be found, he asks the reader's indulgence. In one instance the title of a manuscript has been expanded without a statement to that effect, viz., "The second parte of a Register", mentioned on page 24. In a note on page 96 it is incorrectly asserted that the patronage of the Rectory of Achurch belonged to the Browne family at the time of Robert Browne's presentation. On the contrary Lord Burghley presented it to him, but the main point made in the note remains unaltered. Again, the death of Samuel Howe, or How, occurred in 1640, not in 1634 or 1635 as suggested on page 201. Definite evidence concerning that event is given in section XXIII of volume II. Contrary to what is said on pages 264–65 the Anabaptists' "Humble Supplication" to King James I evidently was printed in 1620. This point is at any rate asserted on the title-page of the edition published in 1662, though not found in the "Supplication" itself. On page 275 the name Isabel Toppe should read Israel Toppe (see Vol. II., pp. 248 and 257). On page 279 the author of "The Personall Reigne of Christ vpon Earth", 1642, has been given as John Archer, whose name appears in the work, but it seems that his real name may have been Henry Archer. Finally, I have recently discovered that Leonard Busher's last book to which reference is also made on page 279 was written in English and published in 1647, while he was still alive. It bore on the title-page the words: "Printed with priviledge of the heauenly kinge Christ Jesus the Messiah and onely son of the moste high God Matt: 28. 29. Gen 14. 18. 20. Anno Domini Syons style 1663. Romes style 1647." James Toppe's manuscript reply, of which the title has been given on the same page and the text of which the present author hopes soon to publish, was accordingly not written until about 1648. That treatise is fortunately not imperfect. Busher appears to have left Delft after printing his work, and one naturally wonders if at that favourable time he may not have returned to London, his native home. It should further be stated here, that any rare manuscripts or books to which reference is made in this work, but of which the present location is for special reasons withheld, will all be included in a later bibliographical volume, if adequate support can be secured, and there be definitely located.

Brief allusion should also have been made in the Introduction to the articles relating to various early English Dissenters in "The Dictionary of National Biography", in Dr James Hastings' "Encyclopædia of Religion and Ethics", and in the eleventh edition of "The Encyclopædia Britannica". Some of these articles have features of distinct value, but not a few invite revision in later editions.

Since the Introduction went to press, a copy of the English edition of Professor W. J. McGlothlin's "Baptist Confessions of Faith" has come into the author's hands. Though the work was only very recently published at Philadelphia, it has already been found advisable to enlarge and thus improve it. Such a book has long been needed, and this undoubtedly contains much useful information; but in various respects it is as yet disappointing, and as a whole can still hardly be said to compare favourably with Professor Williston Walker's volume on a similar subject, viz., "The Creeds and Platforms of Congregationalism," New York, 1893.

Three other books have lately been published which require mention in these pages. One of them is the Rev. William Pierce's edition of "The Marprelate Tracts", London, 1911, a painstaking and thorough work in which, however, the text has been unfortunately modernized. The second is the first volume of Mr Henry W. Clark's "History of English Nonconformity from Wiclif to the Close of the Nineteenth Century", London, 1911. This volume covers the period from Wiclif to the Restoration. In his prefatory Note (p. v) Mr Clark says that what "has been here attempted is not so much the discovery and presentation of fresh facts, but rather the bringing of the recorded happenings into the light of one general principle to be estimated and judged...the underlying idea is the testing of events as to their success or failure in manifesting a changeless spirit and ideal." Consequently, though Mr Clark has read widely and with some discrimination, his book does not contain such information as requires special mention here.

The third work to which reference should be made is the Rev. Walter H. Burgess's "John Smith the Se-Baptist Thomas Helwys and the first Baptist Church in England With fresh Light upon the Pilgrim Fathers' Church", London, 1911. This book, though a popular treatise, is of real historical value, as well as written in a pleasing style. On account of its late appearance and its subject-matter it requires rather extended comment.

With some qualifications and corrections Mr Burgess's work very well supplements a portion of the contents of the present book, in which it was found unadvisable to insert such a detailed presentation of the views and controversies of Smyth, Helwys, and Murton. On pages 212–19 and 239–69 also the early Anabaptist Confessions of Faith published respectively by Helwys' and by Smyth's followers are wisely given in good part, thus making their reproduction in the present treatise less necessary.

Mr Burgess's best services, perhaps, have been rendered on what for convenience may be called the genealogical side of his subject. Here he has achieved signal success. He gives a number of fresh details concerning the University life and later career in Lincoln of John Smyth (pp. 43–52), and various interesting points relating to the ancestry, station in life, and education of Thomas Helwys of Broxtowe Hall "overlooking Basford" in Nottinghamshire (pp. 107–17). Last but not least he proves that John Robinson, Pastor of the Pilgrim Fathers, was the son of John and Ann Robinson of Sturton le Steeple, Nottinghamshire, and had a brother William and a sister Mary; and that his wife, Bridget White, was the second daughter of Alexander and Eleanor White likewise of Sturton, both of the families represented being those of substantial yeomen (p. 317).

Of the details found in Mr Burgess's book not already or elsewhere mentioned in the present work, the following are perhaps among the most important: viz., that a fifth copy of John Smyth's "A Paterne of True Prayer", London, 1605, has recently been acquired by the British Museum (p. 54); that Smyth was "town lecturer" at St Peter at Arches, Lincoln, and is referred to as "clericus conscionator" before the beginning of his troubles there (p. 62); that Geoffrey Helwys, "'Merchant Taylor' and alderman of the City of London", was Thomas Helwys' uncle, not his brother as suggested on page 256 of the present volume (p. 289); that John Wilkinson was deceased by 1619 (p. 302); and that [John Murton], while a close prisoner in Newgate, "having not the use of pen and ink", wrote the Anabaptists' "Humble Supplication" of 1620 "in milk, in sheets of paper brought to him by the woman his keeper from a friend in London as the stopples of his milk bottle", which were later read "by fire" by this friend, transcribed, and preserved (pp. 308–9).

With the historical views maintained in the introductory and concluding chapters of Mr Burgess's book, and with a good many minor details other than those mentioned above, the present author finds himself unable to agree. The opinions advanced in those chapters are in general the traditional ones which have long been popular with writers of Dissenting history, and with which any student is already more or less familiar, only the influence of the early English Anabaptists is here more highly rated than has hitherto been customary,— and in the present writer's opinion somewhat exaggerated.

Naturally there are a number of minor inaccuracies in the volume, such as every researcher in this field is likely to make for years to come. Some of them need to be noticed here. On page 157 Mr Burgess asserts his belief that "I.H.", the author of "A Description of the Church of Christ", 1610, was a Familist. On the contrary there is practically no reason to doubt that he was Joseph Hall, later Bishop of Norwich, who was personally acquainted both with John Smyth and John Robinson. On page 226, at the suggestion of the Rev. Alexander Gordon, Mr Burgess gives a new reading for the word hitherto usually read as "Fryelers" in the title of one of Helwys' publications, taking it without question to be "Fryesers", i.e., according to his interpretation, Frisians. The correct reading, however, is certainly "Fryelers", for while an imperfect letter is used for the "l", it is not a broken "s", as a careful examination will plainly reveal. Furthermore, "Fryelers" ("Free-willers") is just the word required by the contents of the work, while Frisians is as manifestly out of place, to say nothing of the difficulty of finding the word Frisians in this imaginary word "Fryesers". On page 318 it is said that Henry Ainsworth's "A Seasonable Discourse or a Censure upon a Dialogue of the Anabaptists" "remained in manuscript for some years,..." This was not the case. The work was first printed in 1623 shortly after it was written, and the title of this edition may be seen on page 267 of the present volume. On page 322 Mr Burgess speaks of the exceptional interest attaching to the Bodleian copy of Edmond Jessop's "A Discovery of the Errors of the English Anabaptists", 1623, "because it has been profusely annotated with marginal notes in a contemporary hand", and supported by the purport of some of these annotations ventures to express the view (p. 327) that "in or about the year 1625" "attention was being paid [by the English Anabaptists] to the more limited meaning of the word 'baptize' in the sense of 'dip'." The present writer has consulted this copy of Jessop's work, and does not hesitate to say that practically all of the annotations therein contained were written after 1640. The dating has largely to be determined by the style of writing employed and by the use of one or two exceptional words which evidently began to be used about 1650 or just after. It may be well to call attention also to the fact that Mr Burgess has unfortunately incorporated in his book some of the blunders which occur in Dr B. Evans' " Early English Baptists ". For instance, on page 333 mention is made of Cornelius Aresto (Cornelis Claesz. Anslo), on page 334 of Thos. Denys (" thomas elwijs " [Helwys]), and on page 335 of James Joppe (James Toppe). Further, a mistake has clearly been made in associating this last name with that of a " certain John Joope" who " was a member of Henoch Clapham's Separatist Church...at Amsterdam in 1598 " (p. 335 note 1). But these are comparatively small blemishes in an otherwise excellent book, which will be welcomed by students as well as by the general reader.

Two further notable discoveries relating to the early English Dissenters have recently been made. For information regarding them the author is indebted to the courtesy of the Rev. F. Ives Cater of Oundle, to whom belongs the credit of having done more than any other person to elucidate the later years of Robert Browne's life. These most recent discoveries have been made by the Rev. R. M. Serjeantson, M.A., F.S.A.[1], who, it seems, following suggestions made by Mr Cater has succeeded in finding records relating to Browne's excommunication by William Piers, Bishop of Peterborough, about December, 1631, and also a nuncupative will of Browne's which was exhibited and proved in April, 1634, and in which he speaks of "my deare and loveinge wiefe Elizabeth Browne, who hath ever bine a most faithfull and a good wiefe unto me ",—an entirely unexpected and welcome statement. Thus we have at last definite evidence of the fact and time of Browne's excommunication, and of his ultimate reconciliation with his wife.

[1] In "A History of the Church of St Giles, Northampton", 1912, pp. 198–202.

In the course of his studies the author has been greatly indebted to many for courtesies shown him. In some instances he has had exceptional opportunities for examining unique treasures at first hand; and he now extends his hearty thanks to all those who have thus aided him. Among others he would specially mention Principal George P. Gould, M.A., of Regent's Park College, London; Henry Guppy, M.A., Librarian of the John Rylands Library, Manchester; Principal Sidney W. Bowser, B.A., of the Midland Baptist College, Nottingham; Canon John Watson, Librarian of York Minster Library; Professor Dr S. Cramer of the Mennonite Archives, and the assistants in the University Library, Amsterdam; Francis J. H. Jenkinson, M.A., Librarian of the University Library, Cambridge; Falconer Madan, M.A., Sub-Librarian of the Bodleian Library, Oxford; S. Wayland Kershaw, M.A., late Librarian, and Rev. Claude Jenkins, M.A., present Librarian, of Lambeth Palace Library; John A. Herbert, B.A., formerly Superintendent of the Manuscript Reading Room in the British Museum; Dr G. K. Fortescue, Keeper of the Printed Books in the British Museum; and Sir Edward Maunde Thompson, K.C.B., etc., late Director and Principal Librarian of the British Museum.

Recently, through the kindness of Messrs Sotheby, Wilkinson and Hodge, the author has enjoyed the very exceptional privilege of viewing and transcribing four printed leaves which up to that time probably no modern student had seen, containing the lost "Ten Counter Demands" of Thomas Drakes, concerning which Dr Edward Arber has said ("The Story of the Pilgrim Fathers", p. 242) that it "is apparently totally lost". The discovery of this tract not only modifies Dr Arber's statement, but also corrects an opinion expressed on pp. 191–2 of the present work. The entire text of this long-lost writing is now given, probably for the first time since its original publication about 1618 or 1619, in the volume of documents.

Excluding minor improvements, omissions, and additions (some of which have been made for the purpose of bringing the book up to date), the material here presented was offered under another title, in the autumn of 1908, as a dissertation for the B.Litt. degree at Oxford University. To the examiners appointed to report thereon, namely, Professor C. H. Firth and Dr Frederick J. Powicke, the author desires to acknowledge his indebtedness for various helpful criticisms and suggestions. To the former of these he owes thanks also for encouragement given by him as the author's supervisor for the B.Litt. course, as well as for commending his work to the Cambridge University Press. Finally, he wishes to express to the Secretary and Syndics of the Cambridge University Press his grateful appreciation of their willingness to undertake the production of the book, and of the attractive form they have given it; while for generous assistance in bringing about an early publication, he has to make further special acknowledgement to various persons, and in particular to his friends Dr J. Vernon Bartlet and Henry Guppy, M.A., and to Sir G. W. Macalpine.

C. B.

Oxford,
16 *December* 1911.

CONTENTS

VOLUME I

INTRODUCTION

CHAPTER VII

CHAPTER VIII

CHAPTER IX

CHAPTER X

CHAPTER XI

CHAPTER XII

CHAPTER XIII

CHAPTER XIV

APPENDIX A

APPENDIX B

Contents   xix

LIST OF ILLUSTRATIONS

(CHRONOLOGICALLY ARRANGED)

THE

EARLY ENGLISH DISSENTERS

IN THE LIGHT OF RECENT RESEARCH

(1550-1641)

VOLUME I

INTRODUCTION

I. AN ACCOUNT OF THE PRINTED LITERATURE ON THE SUBJECT (CHIEFLY MODERN AND GENERAL) WITH CRITICISMS

IT would be unnecessary and unduly tedious to give here all the modern general works that refer to this subject or to parts of it. Those who wish to become acquainted with an approximately complete list of such books or pamphlets published in England and America may consult Dr Henry Martyn Dexter's bibliography at the end of his *Congregationalism of the last three hundred years as seen in its Literature*, and the Rev. T. G. Crippen's *Bibliography of Congregational Church History*[1]. What is needed at present is not a mere bibliographical list, but a selected bibliography, with such criticism of each work as may serve to facilitate the researches of future students by showing what books are really worth consulting, and what are not.

Now some of the works to which reference is here made are, for our present purpose, of only slight importance. Such are for the most part mentioned by title only. They were generally produced in an uncritical period, or by writers none too exact, who contented themselves with rewriting what others had done before them, and with making but slight additions, which sometimes had better have been omitted. Other works are of such a popular nature as to contain little of special value for a critical study of the subject. General English Church histories have not been included in the list here given.

[1] *Transactions* of the Congregational Historical Society, for May 1905 (Vol. II., No. 2), and May 1906 (Vol. II., No. 5).

Two or three works concerning a portion of this field of investigation were written at an early date. Such were Gov. William Bradford's *History of Plymouth Plantation*, and Nathaniel Morton's *New Englands Memoriall*, Cambridge [N.E.], 1669. In 1681 Bishop Stillingfleet published a small quarto volume entitled, " *The Unreasonableness of Separation:* or, An Impartiall Account of the *History, Nature*, and *Pleas* of the Present Separation from the Communion of the Church of *England*", etc. This was at least twice reprinted and is a suggestive book.

It was not until 1700, however, that any general work of importance appears to have been published in defence of the Puritans or of any branch of separatists with whom we are at present concerned. In 1702 Cotton Mather brought out his now celebrated folio entitled, " *Magnalia Christi Americana:* or the Ecclesiastical History of New England, from Its First Planting in the year 1620 ", a book of decided historical value. Nevertheless, it contains a surprising inaccuracy relative to the text of the first covenant of the church at Salem drawn up in 1629, which is important enough to suggest that some critical care should be employed in reading the work. In 1710 James Peirce brought out his *Vindiciæ Fratrum Dissentientium in Anglia*, etc., which was translated and republished in 1717, and again in 1718, under the title, *A Vindication of the Dissenters, in Answer to Dr William Nichols's Defence of the Doctrine and Discipline of the Church of England.*

From 1698 to 1733 John Strype was publishing his numerous and voluminous writings concerning the Church of England and its dignitaries after, and during, the time of the Reformation. These works, of course, contain some references to the early English separatists, but while Strype was a more careful scholar than many of his day, it is well always to see the original documents from which he secured his information, for sometimes he gives abstracts instead of the actual texts of documents, and occasionally he makes statements without sufficient warrant. The dates he assigns to undated documents also should always be critically examined. During the years 1732–8 the Rev. Daniel Neal, M.A., published four octavo volumes entitled, *The History of the Puritans or Protestant Nonconformists*, etc., a work that has been republished several times. Though a very good production for that early period, and still of some value, it now needs a thorough rewriting. In fact, in my opinion, a far better result would be produced, if the whole subject should be independently studied from the source literature and the modern critical standpoint.

Up to this time (1738) the Independents in England and the Baptists had published nothing in the way of a history of their rise and growth. Some of the early leaders of the Particular (Calvinistic) Baptists in London, however, had fortunately left behind them a few documents relating to their early history, and containing a suggestion of facts of which even at the beginning of the eighteenth century the Baptist leaders themselves were not aware. These papers evidently had first been in the possession of Henry Jessey and William Kiffin and were probably transferred by Kiffin into the keeping of Mr Richard Adams, his successor in the church at Devonshire Square, who in turn placed them in the hands of Benjamin Stinton, son-in-law of Benjamin Keach and Keach's successor as pastor of the congregation in Horsley-Down. Adams perhaps suggested to Stinton the desirability of gathering further materials for compiling a history of the English Baptists. Whether this be true or not, Stinton soon began the task of neatly copying his manuscript collections into small volumes, probably all of quarto size. His first compilation of important documents was begun "in Ian: 1710–11", and until his death he seems to have been occupied in the work of transcription and in the arrangement of the material he had collected. He died, however, while still a comparatively young man on Feb. 11, 1718, and it is supposed that not long after some of Stinton's manuscripts came into the hands of Thomas Crosby, who was not a church historian, but, as he in one place styles himself "Teacher of the *Mathematicks* upon *Horselydown in Southwark*".

For some time, as Crosby tells us, he cherished the hope that he might find some one more capable than himself to complete Stinton's work, but in the meanwhile, he employed his leisure hours in arranging the historical material at his disposal, and in supplying as far as possible any portions of the history left unfinished by Stinton.   Finally, though with some misgivings, at the request of two Baptist ministers, Mr Edward Wallin and Mr William Arnold, who died respectively in 1733 and 1734, Crosby gave his historical materials into the hands of the Rev. Daniel Neal, M.A., "who had undertaken", he says, "to write an *History of the Puritans*; under which general name, I did apprehend the *English Baptists* might very well be included: And he had them [Stinton and Crosby's historical collections] in his hands some years".   What then was the natural disappointment of the Baptists and especially of Thomas Crosby, when, after the lapse of several years the whole history of their "rise and progress" was found to have been distilled into "less than five pages of his [Mr Neal's] third volume: and that too with very great partiality"!   This all too apparent slight may have caused Crosby to demand the speedy return of his manuscripts, and to commence at once the preparation for the press of a history of the English Baptists that would not only make a better impression on the unbiassed reader, but would at the same time correct the misstatements of the Rev. Daniel Neal.   At any rate, it is to be noticed that Neal's fourth volume and Crosby's first bear the same date, 1738.   Now, when Crosby began the printing of his work (which, he says, was made up chiefly from Stinton's manuscripts), he expected to publish only two volumes, but before the appearance of the second in 1739, he tells us, he had received so much important additional material (partly, or almost entirely, composed of collections made by Stinton, which evidently had for some reason not been in Crosby's possession before), that he felt obliged to publish it, in order that in the future he himself might not incur the censure of being "a partial historian". Accordingly third and fourth volumes appeared in 1740.   The work bears the title, THE | HISTORY | OF THE | *English Baptists*, | FROM | The REFORMATION *to the Beginning* | *of the Reign of King* GEORGE *I*, London, 8°.

Crosby had scarcely brought out his first volume, when the Rev. John Lewis, a clergyman of Margate, published his more scholarly and scientific "Brief History of the Rise *and* Progress of *Anabaptism* in *England.* To which is prefixed, Some Account of the Learned Dr. *Wiclif,* and A Defence of Him from the false Charge of *his,* and *his Followers,* denying Infant Baptism", 1738. Naturally Lewis's account differed radically from Crosby's, and furthermore, Lewis ignored Crosby's authority as an historian, and easily showed himself to be more than a match for Crosby. Nevertheless, though Lewis had, at the time of the publication of his pamphlet, been collecting materials concerning the English Anabaptists for nearly forty years, he had not at his disposal certain important documents with which the Baptists alone could have supplied him. Crosby of course replied to Lewis, and issued a scarce octavo pamphlet, entitled, "A BRIEF | REPLY | TO THE | Reverend Mr. *John Lewis*'s | Brief HISTORY of the RISE | and PROGRESS of ANABAPTISM | in *England*; | And to his | ACCOUNT of Dr. Wickliffe, | ...", London, 1738, 8°, pp. 44.

It must be admitted that Crosby's *History* is in many respects imperfect. Even Lewis knows the sources better than he. Further, Crosby's arrangement of the material is especially poor, the views expressed have not always been thoroughly thought out, and they are at least in one or two important instances very incorrect. Crosby's spirit, however, is excellent, and for nearly two hundred years his four volumes have been regarded with favour, and in certain quarters as almost inspired. Next after William Sewel's *History of the Rise, Increase and Progress of the...Quakers,* published in Dutch in 1717, and in English in 1722, Crosby's work is probably the earliest important apologetic history of any body of English separatists.

So successful in fact was Crosby that in 1770 Morgan Edwards brought out at Philadelphia a small volume entitled, *Materials towards a History of the Baptists in Pennsylvania, both British and German,* etc., and in 1792 a second called *Materials towards a History of the Baptists in [New] Jersey.* About 1790 appeared a small publication by John Asplund, entitled, *The Annual Register of the Baptist Denomination, in North-America,* and during the years 1793–1802 Dr John Rippon edited four volumes of a work bearing a similar title,

The Baptist Annual Register (by Dr Dexter wrongly ascribed to Asplund). In this work of Rippon's was first published Joshua Thomas's *History of the Baptist Association in Wales from the year* 1650, *to the year* 1790. Later (in 1795) Thomas's contribution was republished in pamphlet form.

These works that have just been mentioned contain nothing of special value concerning the period under investigation, but simply show how the historical spirit was spreading among the Baptists of America, as well as of England, before 1800. There is one important work, however, that must be mentioned here. This is Isaac Backus's *A History of New-England, With particular Reference to the Denomination of Christians called BAPTISTS*. The first volume appeared in 1777, the second in 1784, and the third in 1796. In general, Backus accepted Crosby's point of view, but he has the advantage of Crosby, in that having gathered his data himself he was better prepared to publish a consecutive and more accurate narrative. Backus is further said to have brought out *An Abridgement of the Church History of New England*, in 1804. His larger works have all been republished.

Thus like the Friends, or Quakers, Baptists early began to manifest an interest in the history of their origin,—an interest which with the recent organization of Baptist Historical Societies in England and in America is being renewed to-day. Following the works written in America there appeared in England in 1811 the first volume of Joseph Ivimey's *History of the English Baptists*, the second, third, and fourth volumes being published respectively in 1814, 1823, and 1830. This publication covers a period nearly one hundred years longer than that attempted by Crosby; but while Ivimey adds a good many points in the early portion of the history, he is not always so accurate as could be desired, and both he and Crosby are undoubtedly responsible for the prevalence of more than one error in the historical views of Baptists of to-day. Ivimey apparently was always a more genial, than critical, historian, but his last two volumes are of more importance than the first two.

Other historical works by Baptists, or concerning them, were published about this time. In 1811 a treatise by

H. Clarke is said to have appeared entitled, *A History of the Sabbatarians, or Seventh-Day Baptists in America*, and in 1813 a work in two volumes by D. Benedict was issued, entitled, *A General History of the Baptist Denomination in America, and other parts of the World*. In 1848 the latter was enlarged and republished in one volume of nearly a thousand pages. Adam Taylor also brought out his important *History of the English General Baptists, in two Parts*, in 1818. This work is now very scarce. Mr Taylor seems to have had somewhat greater historical ability than Stinton, Crosby, or Ivimey, but nevertheless he was unable to unfetter himself entirely from the trammels of the prevailing traditional views first expressed by Stinton and Crosby.

Just before and during a part of the period in which Ivimey was preparing his History, namely between the years 1808–14, was published Walter Wilson's work in four volumes, entitled, *The History and Antiquities of Dissenting Churches and Meeting Houses in London, Westminster, and Southwark*, etc. Wilson's extended MSS., probably containing much more material than was printed in the four above-mentioned volumes, are to be found in Dr Williams's Library, London.

In the "Collections of the Massachusetts Historical Society, *For the Year* 1794", Vol. III., published at Boston [Mass.], 1810, pp. 27–76, appears an edition of the remains of *Governour Bradford's Letter Book*. This is well worth the careful perusal of the student. In 1813, Benjamin Brook published his *Lives of the Puritans*. This work is in three volumes and is full of valuable information. Brook's MSS. rewritten by himself for a second edition are in the Congregational Library, London.

The year 1820 was the two hundredth anniversary of the landing of the Pilgrims, and various addresses, then delivered on that subject, were issued in pamphlet form. These, however, with other works relating to the Pilgrim Fathers printed before 1850, are chiefly of a popular nature and do not require extended mention here. With their publication seems to have begun the present wide-spread interest among Congregationalists in the history of their denomination, and from that time the literature relating to Congregational Church History has greatly increased.

During the years 1839–44 the first elaborate collection of material concerning the history and literature of the Congregationalists was published in three octavo volumes. The writer was Benjamin Hanbury, and the work entitled, *Historical Memorials Relating to the Independents, or Congregationalists: From their Rise to the Restoration of the Monarchy,* etc. This was a really learned book, and contained for the first time much material hitherto hidden away in old libraries. It is true Hanbury's style is not very pleasing, and some of his citations add little interest to the work, except in so far as they give the reader an idea of the tedious arguments employed in the early separatist controversial literature, but in spite of these faults Hanbury's three volumes are of a much higher order than the publications of Neal, Crosby, Backus, Ivimey, and other predecessors. Nevertheless, even Hanbury, the indefatigable, as he has been styled, left many interesting problems unsolved.

In 1841 Alexander Young brought out his *Chronicles of the Pilgrim Fathers of the Colony of Plymouth, from* 1602 *to* 1625, and in 1846 his *Chronicles of the First Planters of the Colony of Massachusetts Bay from* 1623 *to* 1636. The former of these contains Gov. William Bradford's work, otherwise practically unknown, entitled, *A Dialogue, or the Sum of a Conference between some young men born in New England and sundry ancient men that came out of Holland and Old England, anno domini* 1648. In 1841, also, George Punchard published his *History of Congregationalism, from about* A.D. 250 *to* 1616. A second edition appeared during the years 1865–81 rewritten and so much enlarged as to comprise five volumes. The first two volumes of the second edition contain little of real value and are popular in style. Punchard was no critic, and he, like some other writers, seems to have felt obliged to use a disproportionate amount of space in attempting to trace the origin of his denomination back to early Christian times.

Perhaps the first German contribution to Congregational history was made by H. F. Uhden in 1842, when he published at Leipzig a small octavo volume entitled, *Geschichte der Congregationalisten in Neu-England bis zu den Erweckungen um das Jahr* 1740.... A second edition of this work was translated by H. C. Conant and published at Boston in 1859 under the title, *The New England Theocracy. A History of the Congregationalists of New England,* etc. In 1845 Parsons Cook brought out a volume entitled *A History of German Anabaptism,...and embracing a view...of the historical connection between the present Baptists and the Anabaptists.*

About this time considerable interest was manifested in England in the history and literature of the English Reformation, and during the years 1846–54 the English Baptists through the agency of the Hanserd Knollys Society published ten volumes chiefly composed of reprints of early Baptist works with introductions. The two volumes of old church records are perhaps the most valuable to the historian, but most of the reprints, also, in spite of their modernized text, are useful. Some of the introductions are rather prolix and display too little critical insight. It is of course extremely doubtful whether a better choice of early Baptist works for reprinting might not have been made.

In 1846–7 were issued at Boston six volumes of the *Lives of the Chief Fathers of New England,* and in 1847 appeared Joseph Fletcher's four small duodecimo volumes entitled, *The History of the Revival and Progress of Independency in England since the Period of the Reformation.* Mr Fletcher seems to have done a good deal of reading, but unfortunately not in the earliest source literature, so that while his book is in places suggestive and well worth an examination, it perpetuates numerous errors of earlier writers and adds little to our knowledge of the subject.

In 1849 appeared J. Hunter's pamphlet, entitled *Collections concerning the Early History of the founders of New Plymouth,* an important little work in that it gave for the first time the name of the place where the Pilgrim church was organized. Hunter's pamphlet proved of such interest that it was rewritten and enlarged into a small volume of over two hundred pages, bearing the slightly altered title, *Collections concerning the*

Church or Congregation of Protestant Separatists, formed at Scrooby in North Nottinghamshire, in the time of King James I, 1854. The book is suggestive, and from the time of its publication interest in Congregational history has still further increased.

In 1850 Mr J. B. Marsden first brought out his work, twice reprinted, on *The History of the Early Puritans: from the Reformation to the opening of the Civil War in* 1642, London; and in 1852, *The History of the Later Puritans: from the opening of the Civil War in* 1642, *to the ejection of the Non-conforming Clergy in* 1662, London. About this time many small works especially pertaining to the Pilgrims and to the early Puritan churches in New England began to appear. In 1850, also, a pamphlet of twenty-eight pages is said to have been issued by S. Adlam, entitled, *The First Church in Providence not the oldest of the Baptists in America, attempted to be shown.* This may have started the controversy as to whether the church in Newport, or that in Providence, is the oldest Baptist church in America.

During this period one work followed closely upon another, so that only the most important can be mentioned. In 1851, R. Ashton published *The Works of John Robinson, Pastor of the Pilgrim Fathers, With a Memoir and Annotations,* in three volumes. Though the text is unfortunately modernized, the book is of much value. Mr Ashton was apparently the first scholar to notice that among the early English Brownists and Anabaptists in Holland the question of the proper mode of baptism was never discussed. In 1853 appeared W. H. Bartlett's *The Pilgrim Fathers, or the Founders of New England,* etc. This was reprinted in 1854. In 1855 J. B. Felt brought out one volume of *The Ecclesiastical History of New England,* etc.; in 1855–61 the *Records of the Colony of New Plymouth in New England* were edited by N. B. Shurtleff and D. Pulsifer in twelve quarto volumes. In 1856 the Massachusetts Historical Society issued a separate edition of Governor William Bradford's *History of Plymouth Plantation,* which had been previously printed in the Collections of the Society. A great improvement over this edition was secured in 1896 by the appearance of the splendid edition of the *History of the Plimouth Plantation Containing an Account of the Voyage of the 'Mayflower' Written by William Bradford One of the Founders and second Governor of the Colony Now Reproduced in Facsimile from the Original Manuscript With an Introduction by John A. Doyle*, London and Boston, and in 1900 after the return of the Bradford MS. to America by the publication of another edition at Boston by the State of Massachusetts. Still another American edition has appeared in the series of Original Narratives of Early American History edited by Dr J. F. Jameson of the Carnegie Institution at Washington. Of these different editions Mr Doyle's no doubt is decidedly the best, though not the most convenient in form. In 1858 J. S. Clark brought out a small volume entitled *A Historical Sketch of the Congregational Churches in Massachusetts.*

Other works followed in rapid succession. In 1860 two historical studies of interest appeared, namely S. G. Drake's quarto book entitled, *Result of some Researches among the British Archives for Information relative to the Founders of New England : made in the years* 1858, 1859 *and* 1860, Boston [Mass.], and *Open Communion and the Baptists of Norwich:...with an Introduction by the Rev. Geo. Gould.* This introduction by Mr Gould was the first really valuable critical piece of work produced by a Baptist concerning the long forgotten early history of the denomination. Mr Gould went to the originals for his information, and by so doing in comparatively few pages threw fresh light on various traditions concerning the rise of the present Baptist Denomination. His work strangely seems to have circulated among those who could not appreciate what he had to say. He was nearly two generations before his time. It was from a study of this book, that the discovery was made by President Whitsitt that the English Anabaptists did not practise immersion until about 1641.

In 1861 D. A. White published at Salem his *New England Congregationalism in its origin and purity; illustrated by the foundation and early records of the First Church in Salem*, etc., and in 1862 appeared the second volume of J. B. Felt's *Ecclesiastical History of New England*, etc. These were followed in

1863 by [Dr] John Waddington's book bearing the curious title, 1559–1620. *Track of the Hidden Church; or, The Springs of the Pilgrim Movement*, etc. This was Waddington's fourth published work, pertaining to Congregational Church history, his first on *John Penry* having been published in 1854. His second was entitled *Historical Papers [First Series]*, etc., and appeared in 1861. His third came out in 1862 under the title, "*Bicentenary Prize Essay. Congregational History. From the Reformation to 1662*". The success of this essay evidently led Waddington to undertake his large work on *Congregational History*. The first volume was published in 1869, and covered the period 1200–1567. This was followed at intervals until 1878 by three others, the second of the series appearing in 1874, and covering the years 1567–1700. Thus Dr Waddington in twenty-four years prepared an unusually large amount of historical material for the press. Nor is it only by the amount of his production that he is distinguished. With all their defects his works reveal a truly vast knowledge. Waddington's two worst faults as an historian are (1) his too apparent lack of critical and minute exactness (though his publisher and printer were possibly responsible for some minor errors, as, for instance, in dates), and (2) his almost constant practice of neglecting to give the exact location of the manuscripts to which he makes reference. Waddington's books, indeed, are filled with inaccuracies and small errors, which are just numerous and important enough to make the reader uncertain whether anything published by him is exactly as it should be. His work, therefore, to be of any value to-day would require thorough verification and rewriting, as may have been realized by Dr R. W. Dale years ago. Dr Waddington's strong point was his wide knowledge of the MSS. relating to his subject.

Returning to the year 1862 we find that it was during this and the two following years that Dr B. Evans published his *Early English Baptists* in two small volumes. With the exception of the Rev. George Gould of Norwich, Dr Evans is much the ablest of the early English Baptist historical writers, and he secured for his history documents that no one in England at least had previously published. These opened a whole new field of research, and furnished many important facts hitherto unmentioned and unsuspected. He had, too, the mind of a true historian, and saw clearly that he lived at too early a period to write anything approaching an adequate history of the English Baptists, but he also saw that the day was coming when such a work could be accomplished. Evans's work, however, excellent as it is in some respects, has its defects. The texts of the documents cited are chiefly in English, as they were translated by a Dutch professor, and so are not always expressed in correct English. The material secured from Holland is also not conveniently arranged, and the treatment of the political situation of the times is rather extended. Furthermore, Dr Evans's personal knowledge of the printed sources of early Baptist history seems to have been limited, and it is only in dealing with the translation of the Dutch manuscripts made for him, and in presenting other material furnished by Professor Dr Müller of Amsterdam, that he says anything especially new. Although Dr E. B. Underhill appears to have been the first Englishman in recent times to gain an idea of the contents of the Mennonite Archives in Amsterdam, Dr Evans deserves the credit of being the first to present translations of the texts of many of these early MSS. to the British and American public.

In 1867 H. S. Skeats brought out, and republished in 1869, *A History of the Free Churches of England from* 1688–1851. The book is popular and of little value in itself, but the idea of grouping the different bodies of separatists together is good. In 1868 Herman Weingarten of the University of Berlin published his work, well known in Germany, entitled, *Die Revolutionskirchen Englands,* etc. The first forty-five or more pages relate to the period before 1641, so that this work may be suitably mentioned here, though its contribution to our subject is small. The book also is long out of date. In 1874 Dr Leonard Bacon's work on *The Genesis of the New England Churches* appeared.

Two years later came out the first edition of Robert Barclay's admirable volume, entitled, *The Inner Life of the Religious Societies of the Commonwealth,* etc. This has been at least twice reprinted and is in some respects one of the best books that have yet been published relating to English separatism. In a sense, it must be admitted, it is a denominational (Friends' or Quakers') work, but it deals to a large extent with all early English separatists. The book manifests wide and critical reading on the part of the author and a considerable knowledge of the contents of certain libraries up to that time little investigated. Nevertheless, great as is Barclay's contribution to separatist history, his book shows that he was ignorant of the existence of many important works. He was fortunate, however, in having made the best use of various unique books, and in the expression of his conclusions he was at once impartial and critical. Some of these conclusions are of much value.

In 1879 appeared Mr Edward Arber's *An Introductory Sketch to the Martin Marprelate Controversy, 1588–1590* (No. 8 in the English Scholar's Library). The publication of this volume, of a subsequent work by Dr F. J. Powicke mentioned later, and of still another study published in the autumn of 1908 by the Rev. W. Pierce, entitled, *An Historical Introduction to the Marprelate Tracts*, London, makes it unnecessary for the present writer to deal further with the subject. These authors have rendered untenable Dr Dexter's opinion that Martin Marprelate was Henry Barrowe.

The year 1880 was notable in the field of separatist history on account of the publication of Dr Henry Martyn Dexter's epoch-making book entitled, *The Congregationalism of the last three hundred years as seen in its Literature*. This undoubtedly was the most learned work of the kind up to that time produced by an American scholar, and in the present writer's opinion surpasses even to-day in minute critical, detailed and vast knowledge anything that has been done in this line either by historians of the Church of England, or by English Dissenters. What might be called the period of the " Higher Criticism " of separatist history now really began, though for nearly fifteen years Dr Dexter's contemporaries seem to have thought that little more remained to be done in the way of writing a general scientific Congregational History. Dr Waddington's great work was at once superseded by the appearance of this single volume, which, though containing a good many errors of one kind and another, was nevertheless well packed with exact learning. In 1881 Dr Dexter also gave the American Baptists a shock of surprise by publishing *The True Story of John Smyth, the Se-Baptist*, a book pertaining to early English Baptist history, and so contrary to all accepted tradition that it excited no little comment. So quickly were the old-fashioned, uncritical, denominational histories made almost valueless.

Of course, it was soon seen that there were occasional points in Congregational history which needed still further attention. Accordingly a useful pamphlet was brought out in 1889 by Messrs Wm E. A. Axon and Ernest Axon, entitled, *Henry Ainsworth, the Puritan Commentator...(Reprinted from the "Transactions of the Lancashire and Cheshire Antiquarian Society"*, 1888.), Manchester, 8°, pp. 43–57 (41–2 blank). This incorporates the results of still earlier investigations concerning the subject made by Mr Ernest Axon, and gives some details of Ainsworth's life not generally known. In this way the attention of a wider circle of students was directed to the really reliable testimony relating to Ainsworth's death, which had previously been published in a leaflet by Mr Ernest Axon.

Thus the period of reconstruction began, but so well had Dr Dexter done his work, as has been said, that it was not until 1893 that any other extended contribution to general early separatist history was made. In that year Professor Williston Walker, then of Hartford Theological Seminary, and now of Yale University, brought out his admirable volume entitled, *The Creeds and Platforms of Congregationalism*, and in 1894, *A History of the Congregational Churches in the United States*. Of these two publications the former, though up to this time unfortunately little known in England, is indispensable. Indeed, the writer believes that it is one of the three or four best and most scholarly books relating to Congregational history yet published. It is unpartizan in tone, independent in thought, and replete with minute knowledge.

Professor Williston Walker's books have been followed in close succession by the publication of other important works. Among these may be mentioned Dr John Brown's *The Pilgrim*

Fathers and their Puritan Successors, 1895, a book especially pleasing for its literary qualities; by Dr Ozora Stearns Davis's pamphlet, entitled, *John Robinson Pastor of the Pilgrim Fathers His Life, Controversies and Personality Displayed in their Historical Connections*, 1897; and by Mr Edward Arber's illuminating and critical *Story of the Pilgrim Fathers*, 1606–1623 A.D.; *as told by Themselves, their Friends, and their Enemies. Edited from the original Texts*, published in 1897. This is an incisive, critical study, not always quite fair, and yet full of suggestion. The book certainly contains mistakes in spite of the author's "great desire...that there should be nothing in this Volume that the Reader may be hereafter compelled to unlearn", but it is nevertheless, in all probability, the most exact work on the subject that has yet been written.

In 1897 [i.e., Sept., 1896], President William H. Whitsitt of the Southern Baptist Theological Seminary, Louisville, Kentucky, also brought out his little book, *A Question in Baptist History: Whether the Anabaptists in England Practised Immersion before the year* 1641? *With an Appendix on the Baptism of Roger Williams, at Providence, R.I., in* 1639. This work defied Baptist tradition, and it has been thought that Dr Whitsitt indirectly through its publication lost his position. In this book he showed that he, and not Dr Dexter, was the original discoverer of the 1641 theory, and that Dr Dexter had really accepted and sustained the view which he (Whitsitt) had anonymously published in the New York *Independent* for September 2nd and 9th, 1880. President Whitsitt was at once vigorously attacked by various writers[1], but subsequent investigations have abundantly justified the most of his contentions. Concerning this discussion the following books may repay study, viz., two by Dr George A. Lofton, entitled, *English Baptist Reformation. (From* 1609 *to* 1641 A.D.), and *Defense of the Jessey Records and Kiffin Manuscript...*, both published in 1899, and two articles published in *The Baptist Review and Expositor* for October, 1905 and January, 1906, respectively, the first by the present writer, and entitled, *A Brief Exami-*

---

[1] Among these opponents was Dr John T. Christian, who wrote two books and numerous articles relating to the controversy.

nation *of the Gould Manuscript*, which in an improved and
corrected form is republished in this work; and the second
by Dr W. T. Whitley on *Four Early Separatistic Churches in
London.*

In 1899 the Congregational Historical Society was formed
and since April, 1901, has published *Transactions* and three
special pamphlets. In the *Transactions* some important material
has already appeared, which has well justified the existence of
the Society. Articles by the Rev. T. G. Crippen, the Rev.
F. Ives Cater, and the Rev. F. J. Powicke, M.A., Ph.D., will
especially repay examination.

In 1900 an interesting book was published from the pen of
Dr Powicke, entitled, *Henry Barrow, and the Exiled Church of
Amsterdam.* This work is popular, readable, and on the whole
far more scholarly in tone than the usual popular denominational
history. It does not pretend to present much fresh material,
but seeks chiefly to take account of what others had previously
gathered. The author is fair-minded and pacific in spirit, while
his critical ability is seen to good advantage in the final chapter
of Part II., where he examines and overthrows some of Mr Arber's
too hasty statements concerning Francis Johnson's congregation
at Amsterdam. If Dr Powicke had only been equally careful
to correct the mistakes of earlier Congregational historians,
his book as a whole would have a still higher value.

In 1901 Dr Alexander Mackennal brought out his *Sketches
in the Evolution of English Congregationalism Carew Lecture
for* 1900–01 *Delivered in Hartford Theological Seminary
Connecticut*, London, 12°. The work is popular, and its information is largely dependent on the researches of previous
writers. It is for our purposes, therefore, a book more important
in title than in content.

In 1905 appeared the Rev. J. H. Shakespeare's little volume
entitled, *Baptist and Congregational Pioneers*. This is a popular
book, unpartizan in tone, and written in a readable and attractive style. The author has made some study of the sources,
and has thus added to the value of his work.

In 1905, also, Dr Roland G. Usher published in the Camden Society series a useful book entitled, *The Presbyterian*

Movement in the Reign of Queen Elizabeth as illustrated by the Minute Book of the Dedham Classis 1582–1589 Edited for the Royal Historical Society from the MS. in the possession of J. F. Gurney, Esquire Keswick Hall, Norfolk. In this work one may notice the connection which a few of the early Barrowists had previously maintained with the Presbyterian movement. Future investigation ought to add materially to the minor results contained in the work.

During 1906 and 1907 two extended and important posthumous works appeared. One of these was begun by Dr Henry Martyn Dexter and finished and published by his son, the late Rev. Morton Dexter, entitled, *The England and Holland of the Pilgrims*, 1906. This is probably in its spirit the least partizan of Dr Dexter's publications. Like all posthumous books, however, it has the fault of not being thoroughly up to date, and it is to be regretted that Mr Morton Dexter did not further verify some of the statements made in the work. With a little investigation mistakes might have been avoided, and important material, which is not employed, might have been added. The account of Robert Browne, for instance, needs to be entirely rewritten. Some parts of the volume are naturally fresher and therefore more instructive than others, but regarded as a whole it is an unusually valuable book. It would be worth while to publish a second corrected edition. In the opinion of the present writer the best parts of the work, as it stands, are chapters four and five in Book II., concerning the literature of the early Puritans and their opponents; the whole of Book V., which treats of the Pilgrims in Amsterdam; and the Appendix giving the names of the Pilgrim company in Leyden, etc.

The other notable posthumous work, to which reference has been made, is Dr R. W. Dale's *History of English Congregationalism*, 1907, which was completed and published by his son Chancellor A. W. W. Dale. This is a popular and fair-minded book of nearly eight hundred pages, and is scholarly, well-written, and fairly up to date. The material, too, is well arranged and has been made very readable, by subdividing the chapters into short sections. Naturally Dr Dexter's minute scholarship is not to be seen here. The spelling of the citations has been modernized, and there is little or no addition to our knowledge of the source literature. The chief excellency of this work is that it puts into readable form, and in comparatively small compass, the scattered or disordered results of the studies of earlier writers. Another book which may be mentioned here, is the illustrated edition of Professor Henry C. Vedder's *A Short History of the Baptists,* first published at Philadelphia in 1891, and since revised and enlarged. Though only a popular work this is scientific in spirit, and generally up to date.

In November, 1908, the first number of the *Transactions of the Baptist Historical Society* was published, and since that time at somewhat irregular intervals other numbers have appeared. These have contained interesting and useful historical information, and have been well edited by the industrious Secretary, Dr W. T. Whitley. The Society has also brought out two volumes of *Minutes of the General Assembly of the General Baptist Churches in England, with kindred Records; Edited with Introduction and Notes* by Dr Whitley. Vol. I., published in 1909, covers the years 1654–1728, and Vol. II., published in 1910, the years 1731–1811. The material contained herein should prove of value to historians.

In 1909 Miss Winifred Cockshot of St Hilda's Hall, Oxford, brought out at London a popular work entitled, *The Pilgrim Fathers their Church and Colony...With twelve illustrations and a Map.* Miss Cockshot seeks to utilize the results of the most recent researches relating to her subject, but apparently has not herself attempted to do much research work. Though not always quite accurate, this is probably as good a popular history of the Pilgrim Fathers as has been published.

Mention should finally be made of Dr Frederick J. Powicke's *Robert Browne Pioneer of Modern Congregationalism,* Memorial Hall, London [autumn, 1910], a popular, but excellent little book, which deserves a wide circulation. Dr Powicke has made use of the latest researches concerning Browne, and has done his work with care and insight. Accordingly, his book is indispensable to those who are interested in Browne's career, and is undoubtedly the best life of Browne that has yet appeared.

Thus it will be seen that especially during the last fifty years some excellent work has been done in the field of separatist history. Indeed, before the middle of the nineteenth century it was practically impossible to do good critical work, for the eighteenth century was uncritical in spirit, and the persons who were most interested in separatist history could not easily gain access to much of the material they needed to consult. However, the few early English dissenting historians (and, with the exception of the earlier writers in New England, they were mostly Friends or Baptists) accomplished a good deal under disadvantageous conditions, and probably made no more mistakes than other historians of the period. Towards the middle of the nineteenth century access to interesting historical collections became more possible, and with the spread of the German critical temper, with improved facilities for research, and with an increasing interest in historical investigation, better work soon began to be done. This can easily be seen by examining the historical writings of Benjamin Hanbury, Dr John Waddington, Mr Robert Barclay, Dr Henry Martyn Dexter, Professor Williston Walker, Mr Edward Arber, President William H. Whitsitt, Dr F. J. Powicke, Dr R. W. Dale, and others.

Most of the writers just named have added something to our knowledge, and all of them have been much more exact in their expression than the earlier writers. Nevertheless much of the material that has been published even during the last thirty years has been derived from secondary rather than primary sources, and without the necessary critical examination, thereby perpetuating a good many errors of greater or less importance. In fact, until recent years neither a sufficient attack on the errors of tradition, nor a sufficient search to locate and utilize unknown or unused books and manuscripts had been made.

Some of the results of the writer's previous researches have been published under the following titles:

(a) *A "New Years Guift" an hitherto lost Treatise by Robert Browne The Father of Congregationalism In the form of a Letter to his Uncle Mr. Flower Written December 31st, 1588 (Old Style) and now first published. Edited with an Introduc-*

tion for the Congregational Historical Society, London, 8°, 1904 [January 1].

This treatise was the source from which Richard Bancroft, later Archbishop of Canterbury, took one of his citations for his famous 'Sermon preached at Pavles Crosse the 9. of Februarie,' 1588 [i.e. 1589]. The discovery of this document served to correct some mistaken opinions concerning Browne.

(*b*) *The Church Covenant Idea Its Origin and Its Development*, Philadelphia, 1904 [October], pp. 230.

This supplies a chapter in Congregational and Baptist history that has hitherto been overlooked, and might be termed a supplement to Professor Williston Walker's *The Creeds and Platforms of Congregationalism*. Like that work it seeks to preserve and make available the texts of important historical documents.

(*c*) *The True Story of Robert Browne (1550?–1633) Father of Congregationalism including various points hitherto unknown or misunderstood, with some account of the development of his religious views, and an extended and improved list of his writings.* Oxford and London, 8°, 1906, pp. viii, 75.

This attempts a reconstruction of Browne's life based on the discovery of new facts and of the two most extended MSS. of Browne's apparently still extant.

(*d*) *The 'Retractation' of Robert Browne Father of Congregationalism Being 'A Reproofe of Certeine Schismatical Persons* [*i.e.*, *Henry Barrowe, John Greenwood, and their Congregation*] *and their Doctrine touching the Hearing and Preaching of the Word of God' Written probably early in the year 1588 since lost, and now first published with a brief account of its discovery.* Oxford and London, 8°, 1907, pp. viii, 65.

(*e*) "*A Tercentenary Memorial* New Facts concerning John Robinson Pastor of the Pilgrim Fathers...With Facsimile Frontispiece." Oxford and London, 8°, 1910, pp. i, 35.

This announces the discovery of a manuscript hitherto unknown to historians, which contains citations from a lost writing by Robinson, and makes known for the first time among other points the church in which he officiated before he became a separatist.

II. COLLECTIONS OF PRINTED BOOKS AND MANUSCRIPTS THAT
SHOULD BE VISITED IN THE STUDY OF EARLY ENGLISH
DISSENTING HISTORY (WITH NOTES UPON THE STRONG
POINTS OF EACH LIBRARY)

Fortunately the source literature still extant on this subject
during the period in question is considerable. Manuscripts,
however, are exceedingly scarce, and on some points of interest
before 1582 there is very little direct information to be found.
Furthermore, the material to be consulted is so widely scattered that the student must be at some inconvenience before
he can personally examine it all.

The collections in the following libraries are among those
most abundantly supplied with the works of the earliest English
separatists and with the writings of their opponents.

1. The Library of the British Museum. This great library
is probably the richest of the world in literature, both printed
and in manuscript, concerning our subject. Among its manuscripts are some of priceless value. In its collections of books,
it is true, there were a good many important items wanting
fifteen years ago, but copies of a number of these have been
secured during the intervening years.

Among its manuscripts the following may be especially
mentioned :

(*a*) " M^r [Robert] Brownes aunswer to Mr Flowers
letter," written December 31, 1588 (O.S.), and published in
1904 under the title *A New Years Guift*.

(*b*) Robert Browne's letter to Lord Burghley of April 15,
1590, regarding his (Browne's) 'treatise' concerning 'the arts
& the rules & tearmes of Art.'

(*c*) Harleian MSS. 6848 and 6849, which contain a
large number of original papers, or contemporary copies of
them, relating to the earliest Barrowists.

(*d*) Volume I. of the Boswell Papers containing many
important and hitherto largely unused letters and documents

pertaining to the history of the English (separatist and non-separatist) Churches in the Netherlands during a good part of the period under discussion.

Among the printed books may be found:

(*a*) Practically all the first and later editions of the works issued by the English Family of Love as well as by their opponents.

(*b*) Most of the published works of the early Puritans, Brownists, Barrowists, English Anabaptists, and their opponents.

2. The Bodleian Library, Oxford. This library is extremely well supplied with printed books and pamphlets of the period. For nearly three centuries it has contained these books, and has therefore some important works of which no other library possesses a copy. There are also a few early manuscripts relating to the subject.

3. Lambeth Palace Library, London. This library like the two preceding is of the first importance, for though its collections are far less numerous than those of the British Museum and of the Bodleian, and though it has much less complete lists of the works of the various separatist leaders than either of these libraries, it is especially rich in unique or exceptionally scarce books, pamphlets, and manuscripts, which Archbishop Bancroft collected and left at his death as the foundation collection of what is now known as Lambeth Palace Library. Without this priceless collection of Bancroft's much of the early history of separatism would be entirely unknown to-day, or known only from the works of its enemies, or by tradition. The persecuted separatists dared keep but scanty records of their activities and views, and most of their books were soon destroyed, yet by the irony of history one of their greatest foes became the custodian of their productions, and founded the library that has preserved for three hundred years many an unknown fact of their history.

Among its treasures are:

(1) The three following writings of Robert Browne,—

    (*a*) *A Trve and Short Declaration* [1583 ?], printed pamphlet.

(*b*) *An answere to Mr Cartwrights Letter*, MS. [1584/5 ?].

(*c*) *A reproofe of certeine schismatical persons*, MS. [1588 ?].

(2) The recently rediscovered Papers of Henry Jacob of 1603–5, MS.

(3) An hitherto unnoticed letter of [Thomas] Helwys (Ellwes[1]) of September 26, 1608, MS.

4. The Mennonite Archives, Amsterdam. This library contains among its numerous treasures an unrivalled collection of unique Dutch, Latin, and English MSS. pertaining to the early English Anabaptist Congregations.

5. The Public Record Office, London. This contains important, unique manuscripts pertaining to the subject in hand. Here Dr Waddington found material relating to Richard Fitz's congregation. Here also is a petition of Francis Johnson and some of his followers to be allowed to emigrate to Canada, and there are other interesting items.

6. York Minster Library. This has two or three unique works of the early English Anabaptists, but it is neither so well provided with material pertaining to the subject, nor so accessible, as Lambeth Palace Library.

7. The University Library, Cambridge. While not so rich as the Bodleian in this particular class of literature, this library contains various important printed books of the period and one or two MSS., which will be mentioned later.

8. The Library of the House of Lords. This library has an undated manuscript petition of Helwys and Murton's congregation written in 1614.

9. Dr Williams's Library, London. This has many important printed books and one or two manuscripts relating to the present subject. Special mention should be made of the thick folio in manuscript entitled *The second parte of a Register*, the contents of which it is to be hoped may soon be published.

---

[1] Elwes.

10. Trinity College Library, Cambridge. This most beautiful and choicest of all the College Libraries of England has a good many printed books relating to the present subject including a copy of George Johnson's *A discourse of some troubles | and excommunications in the banished English Church at Amsterdam*, 1603.

11. Emmanuel College Library, Cambridge. This contains the only known copy of John Smyth's first published work, entitled, *The Bright Morning Starre*, 1603, also much of the general religious literature of the period under discussion.

12. The Congregational Library, London. The main collection of this library was made by Mr Joshua Wilson during a period covering many years. Like Dr Williams's Library it contains numerous important items.

There are also several works of interest for this period to be found in the libraries of Queens' College and of St John's College, Cambridge; in the Angus Library, Regent's Park College, London; in the Chetham Library, Manchester; and in the Library of the Inner Temple, London. The last of these possesses the hitherto unnoticed original of the letter by William Burghley to Archbishop Whitgift, dated July 17, 1584, formerly supposed to refer to Robert Browne, but believed by the present writer to refer to Edward Brayne. The Oxford college libraries; the John Rylands Library, Manchester; Sion College Library, and St Paul's Library, London, as yet appear not to be unusually rich in English separatist literature of the period at present under consideration.

In America the most valuable collections of material relating to our subject during this period are probably to be found in the Library of Harvard University, Cambridge, Mass.; the Public Library, the Atheneum Library, the Library of the Massachusetts Historical Society, and the Congregational House Library, Boston, Mass.; the Library of Yale University (Dexter Collection), New Haven, Conn.; the Lenox Library, and the Library of Union Theological Seminary, New York City.

III. NOTES RELATING TO THE CONTENTS OF THE FOLLOWING PAGES

1. The literature concerning the English Anabaptists before 1641 has been carefully examined, and what is believed to be an unusually complete list of such works is here presented.

2. The titles are given of certain books printed during the years 1550–1641, of which the writer has been unable to find a copy. These are mentioned in the hope that some of the works may be found, and to indicate a task that still needs to be undertaken.

3. The history of the early English separatist and independent congregations is critically reconstructed, and special attention is given to their interrelation, which tended toward the gradual evolution of a well-developed type of separatist church.

4. The early conventiclers at Faversham and Bocking, who since the time of Dr Gilbert Burnet have been known as either Anabaptists or separatists, were apparently only non-separatist Nonconformists of an unusual type.

5. Neither the so-called Baptist church at "Eyethorn," nor any other mythical early Baptist churches in England, existed as Anabaptist congregations before 1612, and indeed not until a much later date.

6. The name "Baptist" or "Baptists" appears never to have been applied before 1641 to those English people who espoused the cause of Anabaptism, and accordingly the name by which they were known to the public during this period has here been employed. The same rule has generally been observed with regard to Brownists, Barrowists, and Puritans, all of whom disliked the popular names given to them.

7. The difference in meaning between "Anabaptist" and "Catabaptist" is clearly given, in confirmation of Dr George A. Lofton's view expressed at the time of the so-called Whitsitt

controversy, that the prefixes in these words give no indication whatever of the mode of baptism practised by those to whom these names were respectively given.

8. The book entitled *The summe of the holye scrypture/and ordynary of the Christen teachyng/the true Chrysten faythe/*, 8°, published in 1529 or 1530, and at least three or four times reprinted, is here plainly shown not to be the translation of an Anabaptist work, as it has sometimes been mistakenly represented.

9. Several scarce early English translations of Continental books *against* the Anabaptists are here named, and their influence as a means of disseminating a knowledge of Anabaptist views, rather than the actual presence in England of English Anabaptists and Anabaptist books, is suggested.

10. The beginnings of later English separatism are not to be found in the migration of Continental Anabaptists to England, but rather in the congregations of Marian exiles on the Continent, or in the congregations which met together in London and elsewhere in England during Queen Mary's reign and later.

11. Richard Woodman, Anne Askewe, and William Tyndall, who have been claimed as Baptists, or possible Baptists, by over-zealous historians, are clearly proved not to have been such.

12. Evidence is given whereby we may know that Robert Cooche was not a member of an Anabaptist congregation about 1550 or 1551.

13. The views of Edward Wightman, the early Legatine-Arian or Seeker, are somewhat fully given from the record of his trial on November 19–December 5, 1611,—a trial record as yet almost unnoticed in England. That he was not an Anabaptist or Baptist, as has sometimes been represented, is made perfectly evident.

14. The views of William Sayer, are here, it is believed, first made known from a MS. of the date 1612. A letter of Archbishop Abbot relating to Sayer is also here given.

15. Good texts of various documents relative to the congregation of Richard Fitz are given in full, some of the mistakes of previous writers concerning this congregation are rectified, and the reason is stated why it cannot truly be considered the "first regularly constituted English Congregational Church of which any record or tradition remains", as claimed by Dr R. W. Dale. The history of Fitz's church is given in detail.

16.   Robert Browne, at an early stage of his career, may be truly called a pioneer of what *to-day* is known as Congregationalism, but a long period of evolution intervenes between him and present-day Congregationalists and Independents. His connection with the *first* Independents (or *first* Congregationalists) is likewise rather indirect. It is probable that Browne was never quite so rigid a separatist as he has sometimes been made to appear. For instance, he does not seem to have regarded the Church of England as a false Church, but only as an imperfect one. Barrowe and Greenwood, on the other hand, were strict separatists, and as they were popularly nicknamed "Brownists" (though, as they themselves claimed, utterly without foundation), their ideas concerning strict separatism seem to have been referred back to Browne, thus possibly making him in his earlier years appear to some of his contemporaries as a man of narrower spirit than he really was. As a matter of fact, Barrowe and Greenwood disclaimed (and as the writer believes, honestly) all connection with Browne. The Barrowists derived their ideas chiefly from Cartwright and his followers, as they asserted, and there now seems to be no reason for doubting their word. The author has specially sought to determine Browne's true place in the history of his time, and to give expression to a new interpretation of "A Booke which sheweth", which may aid us to a better understanding of his illusive hopes and ambitions. The theory is also expressed that he practised a certain type of Congregationalism during all the years spent at Achurch.

17. Some new light is probably thrown on the wife-beating episodes in Browne's life.

18. The "ancient" Barrowist church of Barrowe, Greenwood, and Johnson, is described from the primary sources, viz., the original Puckering MSS. from which the much used Baker transcripts in Harleian MS. 7042 were made. The results of recent researches relating to Barrowe and Greenwood are also discussed.

19. Two of the most extended and interesting manuscripts of John Penry apparently still extant are given in full in the volume of documents. One of these is an anonymous writing of his, which seems hitherto to have been unnoticed by modern historians, entitled *A short and true Answer*, etc., and the other is what in brief may be termed his Confession of Faith and his *Apology*, the location of which, though discovered by Dr John Waddington[1], has remained up to this time generally unknown. From these two documents we learn much more intimately what Penry's true views were, and that among his papers was "a diarie or daily obseruacion of myne [his] owne synnes", etc., which was intercepted and the entirely private contents of which, he feared, were to be used unjustly to assist in his conviction. Some interesting points in Penry's life are contained in the various Penry papers here presented.

20. Several varying texts are given of the covenant of the Barrowe and Greenwood congregation before its organization in September, 1592.

21. Some new light is thrown on Johnson's conversion to Barrowism.

22. Practically all the earliest Brownist and Barrowist leaders before they died made statements somewhat resembling "retractations", and Barrowe at the end, as indicated by his last words, seems to have wondered if he had been deceived in what he had taught his followers.

---

[1] Dr Waddington cited this work in part in his *John Penry*, 1854, but does not tell where the manuscript was to be found.

23. Sir Walter Raleigh's estimate of the number of Brownists as being 20,000 about 1593 is, upon good grounds, seriously questioned and rejected.

24. Certain evidence relating to Henry Ainsworth's early life (hitherto questioned by Congregational historians) is here admitted as trustworthy, while the true story of his death, it is believed, is told from the earliest published source. The exact title is also given of the first edition of Ainsworth's *A Censvre upon a Dialogve of the Anabaptists*, 1623, the existence of a copy of which has hitherto been unnoted by historians.

25. A list has been collected from George Johnson's " discourse " of the names of more than sixty persons who had been members of Francis Johnson's congregation before 1603.

26. Evidence is given that Giles Thorpe, contrary to Dr Dexter, never printed a book with the title, *The Hunting of the Fox, Part I*, and therefore obviously not in 1616, as he suggests.

27. The later history of the Ainsworth church is more fully told than hitherto.

28. The little known experiences of Sabine Staresmore are given in detail.

29. The story of John Canne in Amsterdam has been somewhat elucidated.

30. Stephen Offwood's position in Amsterdam has been made more clear.

31. An extended account is given of the congregation of London Barrowists after the departure of most of the members for Holland in 1593.

32. An attempt is made more definitely to locate the early Barrowist church "in the West of England".

33. The story of the Norwich Brownist (Barrowist) church from 1590 to 1603 is given with more fullness of detail than has been customary.

34. The problem as to the identity of the pastor of the congregation at Norwich has been successfully solved.

35. New points of interest are given with regard to William Euring and the Brownists of Great Yarmouth, and it is pointed out that the Brownist and the Independent (Puritan) congregations of that city had no connection whatever with each other.

36. The differences between the opinions of John Wilkinson and of other Brownists and Barrowists are carefully indicated, and mention is made of Wilkinson's dispute with John Murton in 1613, while both were in prison.

37. A new theory relating to the connection of Henoch Clapham with the Barrowists is here advanced, and an extended account is given of his strange career.

38. Some notes of interest are given concerning the early unsettled, wandering Brownists (Barrowists) who had deserted the orthodox Barrowists.

39. Various uncommon facts concerning the Family of Love are mentioned, and attention is first called to the only known manuscript copy in English of the *Psalmes & Songes brought forth through H.N.*, apparently translated as a Hymn Book for the English Family of Love.

40. The origin and views of the English Seekers (termed Legatine-Arians or the Scattered Flock before 1641) are given with some detail.

41. The first company of English Anabaptists of which we have definite information is here discovered not to be that of John Smyth, as has usually been supposed in recent years. A brief account of this first congregation is here presented.

42. Four copies are located of John Smith's (Smyth's) *A Paterne of Trve Prayer*, of which Mr Arber says (*The Story of the Pilgrim Fathers*, 1897, p. 133), " Every copy of this first edition of 1605 has apparently disappeared ".

43. The writer has discovered that John Smyth, in his character of Se-Baptist, is not so unique as has hitherto been

supposed. He was neither the only, nor even the first, English Se-Baptist.

44. Attention is called to an hitherto unnoticed letter of Thomas Helwys (Ellwes[1]), written on September 26, 1608, which describes the differences between John Smyth's congregation and that of Francis Johnson at Amsterdam. The letter proves that by September 26, 1608, Smyth's congregation was already in Amsterdam, and indicates that it had probably been there some little time. The letter further suggests that Smyth's congregation at first looked upon Johnson's followers as brethren, but gives no indication that Smyth's party ever joined Johnson's church.

45. Attention is also called to the fact that Smyth's congregation broke up into three, not into two, divisions. With the third division Leonard Busher may have associated himself.

46. Texts of a considerable number of important Dutch, Latin, and English MSS. pertaining to the earliest English Anabaptists are given in full. This is presumably the first time the original texts of most of these documents have been published in England.

47. This work also contains certain points, for the first time noted, concerning the printed English edition of the one hundred article confession of faith published by the remainder of John Smyth's congregation.

48. The discovery that Benjamin Stinton and Thomas Crosby made an error in fostering the belief that Thomas Helwys lived after May 10, 1622, enables the writer to prove beyond doubt that Helwys died before 1616.

49. A solution is suggested to the problem relating to the original edition of John Murton's *Truth's Champion*.

50. The exact title and probable date of the exceedingly scarce pamphlet, *A very plain and well grounded Treatise concerning Baptisme*, are made known. Dr Dexter apparently knew of no copy of this pamphlet.

---

[1] Elwes.

51. The problem of the letter signed " H. H.", heretofore usually ascribed to Thomas Helwys, is solved, and the probable meaning of its signature suggested.

52. The full title is given of *The Patrimony of Christian Children*, London, 1624, 4°. This was written by Robert Cleaver, " with the ioynt consent of Mr. Iohn Dod ". Dr Dexter seems to have known of no copy of this work.

53. Information is given concerning an hitherto apparently unknown Baptist minister at Tiverton in 1631, James Toppe, and also concerning an unnoticed MS. of his bearing the title, *CHRISTS MONARCHI*|*call, and personall Reigne vppon Earth: over* | *all the Kingdoms of this world,...* | *..*, written in controversy against Leonard Busher.

54. Various new points concerning Leonard Busher are offered for the first time[1].

55. A fresh chapter in the history of the Church of England has been prepared, giving some account of the English (Puritan) congregations on the Continent between 1579 and 1641. This description has been drawn from the hitherto little-noticed first volume of Boswell Papers.

56. The beginnings of Independency or Congregationalism, are not, as heretofore, traced to the Brownists or Barrowists, but to the Congregational Puritanism advocated by Henry Jacob and William Bradshaw about 1604 and 1605, and later put in practice by various Puritan congregations on the Continent, whence it was brought to America and back into England. Puritan Congregationalism accordingly did not have its source in separatism, nor was it separatist in spirit, but was constantly declared by its upholders as involving a separation only from the world, and not from the Church of England.

---

[1] I seem to have been followed in my researches in Holland by Dr W. T. Whitley, who in the *Transactions of the Baptist Historical Society* for April 1909 (pp. 107–113) has published an article entitled " Leonard Busher, Dutchman ", giving an English translation of a document upon which I base some of my information,

57. Through the agency of the Congregational Puritans, and especially Henry Jacob, John Robinson was won back from the ways of separatism before 1616 (certainly before 1618), while Jacob instead of being influenced by Robinson towards separatism according to tradition, can be readily shown never to have been a separatist from the Church of England.

58. The value of the Gould MS. is rediscussed, the important parts relating to our subject are given in full, and a reconstruction of these documents is undertaken, in so far as is necessary and possible, by the use of the best known historical data.

59. The solution of the problem concerning the Brownist-Anabaptist, Samuel Eaton, is given.

60. It is shown that the majority of the Puritan churches of New England did not even know what the church polity of the Plymouth Congregation was, and hence did not derive their views from the congregation of the Pilgrim Fathers. It is also pointed out that while the Plymouth church may at first have differed slightly from more professed followers of Henry Jacob, i.e. the Independent Puritans, it was, nevertheless, well leavened with "Jacobite" doctrine and seems ultimately to have become quite like the neighbouring Independent Puritan congregations. Hence American Congregationalism, as well as that in England, is to be traced back directly neither to Browne nor to Barrowe, but to the Independent or Congregational Puritanism of the Continent. American Congregational churches, then, did not originally separate from the Church of England, but have become separatist and as they are to-day in other respects, only by a gradual and almost unnoticed process of evolution.

61. A clear line of distinction is drawn throughout between separatists of whatever name and the Puritans. The separatists were not Puritans in the original sense of the word, and until this distinction is recognized, it will be practically impossible satisfactorily to explain certain phenomena to be found in early Dissenting history.

62. It is shown that there is reason to believe that the two earliest American immersionist Baptist churches at Newport and Providence, R.I., contrary to tradition, cannot have existed as such before 1647. It is also suggested that under these circumstances it looks as though the Newport church is slightly the older of the two, having apparently begun to practise immersion about 1648. The Providence church seems to have derived its baptism by dipping or immersion from the church in Newport in 1648 or 1649.

63. Attention is called to considerable new material relating to the early use of church covenants.

64. The fluctuations in the progress of English Dissent, as well as the unsettled state of dissenting ideals during this period, are noted.

I know *Machiavel* was wont to say, That *he who undertakes to write a History, must be of no Religion*:...

But, I believe, his *meaning* was much better than his *words*, intending therein, That *a Writer of Histories must not discover his inclination in Religion to the prejudice of Truth*:...

This I have endeavoured to my utmost in *this Book*; knowing as *that Oyle* is adjudged *the best* that hath *no tast at all*; so *that Historian* is preferred, who hath the *least Tangue* of *partial Reflections*.

(Thomas Fuller's "Church History of Britain", London, 1655,
"The Epistle Dedicatory" of the Tenth Book.)

FOREWORD

BEFORE entering upon the discussion of our subject it will be of advantage to define certain terms, the altered meaning of which after the lapse of three centuries requires a clear statement of their original signification. To-day the words Nonconformist, Dissenter, Independent, Congregationalist, Baptist, are all applied in popular usage to separatists from the Church of England. It may not be generally known that all these words have not always been so employed. The earliest Nonconformists, for instance, were not separatists, but often learned clergymen of the Church of England, who found fault with the clerical vestments, etc., and yet remained in the Church. The term Puritan appears to have been first used about 1566, and was correctly applied to Nonconformists as previously defined. The word Dissenter appears to have had a history similar to that of the word Nonconformist, only it seems to have been first employed after 1641. The terms Independent and Congregationalist have now come popularly to signify separatists, but as first used they, also, evidently were applied to nonseparatist Puritans, who, unlike those whom we may designate the elder Presbyterian Puritans, maintained that each congregation had the right to control its own affairs without interference from Classes and Synods, as well as from Archbishops and Bishops. The words Anabaptist (later Baptist), Brownist, Barrowist, on the other hand, have always been properly applied to separatists. With these distinctions fresh in mind we may turn to the discussion of our subject.

The years 1549–1641 were in every way momentous in the history of the English nation. Europe at that time was more or less in a state of upheaval. The first storms of the Reformation had left behind a long trail of unsettled conditions and bitter conflict. Nations that had long slept were beginning to awaken. The eventful but uncertain years of Henry VIII's reign were happily over, and the still more unsettled rule of Edward VI was coming to a close. The period that now began was one of great suspense, but was followed by another of unusual productiveness in letters and commerce, and ultimately in the development of English religious thought.

The English monarchs of this period were five in number,— Edward VI, Mary, Elizabeth, James I, and Charles I. Throughout this succession of years the personal views of the rulers had a powerful influence on general religious opinions and indirectly on the development of separatism. The Privy Council, also, in that day not only enjoyed the right of interfering in matters religious, but used it sometimes with good, sometimes with bad effect. Under Elizabeth new and unusually grave problems had to be faced. It seemed highly dangerous to allow any great diversity of religious views, especially as Rome might then again secure the mastery over the country. Accordingly, in suppressing the Roman Catholics the government felt it equally necessary to restrain all kinds of nonconformity and to demand uniformity in Church worship. The first task of Elizabeth was to unify the State, and in her opinion the quickest way to accomplish that end seemed to be to crush out all views inimical to the State religion. The Privy Council evidently determined to carry out this plan, and sometimes was probably even more truly responsible for persecution than the bishops, for more than once the Council must have instructed the bishops to do things which they might not otherwise have attempted. On the other hand, the Council occasionally curbed the spirits of too aggressive prelates.

This condition of affairs should be kept in mind when one speaks of the cruelty of the bishops of Elizabeth's reign. Some of them certainly were cruel at times, but even then they may have been inflamed to deeds of cruelty by order of the Privy Council, or by truly conscientious views. These possibilities are brought to mind because some of the bishops and archbishops have not always been dealt with any too charitably by modern Nonconformist historians. On the other hand Archbishop Abbot, who has been more favourably regarded because he was not so rigorous against the Puritans, appears to have been fairly eager in the pursuit of heresy. The fault evidently lay partly in a system in which religion was so ruled by politics that even an archbishop could not always do as he himself thought best, but must follow the dictates of politicians. Dr Powicke seems to have been the first Congregationalist to attempt to do the bishops of Henry Barrowe's time any degree of justice. Nor is this strange, for the contemporary reports of those who suffered are likely to make one think of some of the high Ecclesiastical dignitaries of that period as cruel and unreasonable men, but when allowance is made for the time in which they lived and the difficulties with which they had to contend, it appears that a more lenient view may sometimes be taken.

During the latter part of Elizabeth's reign the condition of the separatists improved, for none were put to death after the execution of Barrowe, Greenwood and Penry, and the remaining Barrowists were allowed to go into exile in foreign parts where they might live in peace. On the accession of James I conditions for a further reformation in the Church of England according to Puritan ideals appeared favourable, but the King had not been long on the throne before it became evident that he had no real sympathy with Puritanism and would be no tolerator of separatism. In the work of repressing Puritans and separatists an able instrument was found in the person of Richard Bancroft, who was raised from the position of Bishop of London to that of Archbishop of Canterbury. He, however, did not live many years and was succeeded by George Abbot, during whose primacy the cause of separatism certainly made some, though slow, headway.

On Feb. 2, 1626, Charles I became King, and in Sept., 1633, on the death of Archbishop Abbot, Dr William Laud was promoted to the primacy. With high hand Laud now began to overthrow whatever seemed to him to interfere with the prosperity of the Church of England. His manner of dealing with the Church of Scotland, as well as with Puritanism in England, however, eventually brought about his own downfall, and helped to dethrone his royal master. By this very work of repression the victory was temporarily secured for the cause he had sought to injure, and one may justly suspect that to him, and to some other bishops and archbishops who have held similar views, has also been due much of the continued development and success of English Dissent.

CHAPTER I

THE ANABAPTISTS IN ENGLAND BEFORE 1612

So far as can now be ascertained, a tendency towards separatism first made its appearance in England about 1550. Probably there was no uniformly continuous development of separatist views in the ensuing century. At times separation may even have been almost entirely crushed out, but it kept coming to life again in one form or another, and finally attained surprising growth in the period of the Commonwealth. Before and even during that time separatism must be regarded as in process of evolution. Into the final product were woven many elements, the combined contribution of Anabaptists, Puritans, the Family of Love, the English Seekers, Brownists, Barrowists, Franciscans or Johnsonians, Ainsworthians, Independents, and still other groups of later English reformers.

Before 1550, as the Calendars of State Papers plainly record, a few isolated Anabaptists had been found in England, but they seem to have been chiefly, or only[1], foreigners, and these were soon banished from the country or burned to death. Furthermore, the word Anabaptist even in these early times was evidently employed as a generic term to designate separatists, or indeed any persons of irregular or fanatical religious opinions. For this reason many mistakes concerning the early Anabaptists have been made.

[1] I am not yet certain, for instance, as to whether such Anabaptists of 1549, as "Michaele Thombe of London bocher" and "Johanna Bocher", otherwise known as Joan of Kent, mentioned in Davide Wilkins' "Concilia Magnae Britanniae", London, 1737, Vol. iv., pp. 42–44, were born in England or not. Their views were certainly of the Continental Melchiorite or Hofmannite type.

Before 1550, too, it appears that no Anabaptist books were printed in England, either in English or in any other language, and no English translations of the works cf Continental Anabaptists are known to have been published before the time of the Civil Wars. This may come as a surprise and disappointment to those who have hitherto supposed that the work, reported to have been translated by Simon Fish into English, entitled, "The sum≈|me of the holye | scrypture / & ordynary | of the Christen teachyng / | the true Chrysten faythe " / | ..., 8°, [fol. iv, xciii, 1529 or 1530], was an Anabaptist work[1].

It must first be admitted that some parts of the book relating to baptism, if taken without their context, might cause an uncritical reader to believe that the author of such passages must have been an Anabaptist, but if we make allowance for the interval of nearly four hundred years between the time of writing and our day, and observe how men at that period commonly expressed themselves on the subject of baptism, and if we then carefully examine other passages in the book of an evidently different tenor, we cannot help coming to the contrary conclusion that this work, in spite of its reputation among Baptists, was not written by an Anabaptist. If, further, we examine the contemporary opinion of the book as expressed by those who condemned it, it will be perfectly clear that its contents were not prohibited because it contained any taint of Anabaptism.

[1] Apparently there are only two copies of the first English edition of this work in existence, neither of them quite complete. The copy in the British Museum [Press-mark C. 37. a. 28 (2)] lacks the title-page, and the copy in the Cambridge University Library [Press-mark Syn. 8. 53. 9⁵] is slightly imperfect in the middle and at the end. From the two, one perfect copy might be made, the writer has good reason to believe, although it has hitherto been supposed that these copies were of different editions. There now seems to be no doubt that both copies are of the same edition. Several other slightly later editions in English may be found in the previously mentioned libraries. The book was apparently first published at Basle in 1523 and bore the title, "❡ La Summe de lescripture | saincte / et lõrdinaire des Chrestiẽs / | enseignant la vraye foy Chre≈|stienne:..." A copy of this edition may be found in the British Museum [Press-mark C. 57. a. 20]. The work was translated into Dutch, whence, it is supposed, it was translated into English.

In order to convince the reader of the truth of this assertion
all the necessary citations, favourable and unfavourable, may
be given, and the true gist of the author's statements carefully
extracted.   In the first place, he was certainly not an ordinary
Anabaptist, since he believed in original sin, a view not generally
held by Anabaptists.   He says on this point[1], "For we be therby
borne agayn / and they that were the chyldren of the deuell by
cause of the originall synne ar made the chyldren of God by
baptesme ".   Yet though he does not believe in original sin, he
says[2], "Nether hath the water of the fountaine more vertue in
hit sylfe then the water that rynneth in the ryuer of Ryne
[Rhine].   For we maye aswell baptyse in Ryne / as in the fount",
and he gives the following description of baptism[3], which on the
face of it, one must admit, looks decidedly as though the author
was an Anabaptist :—

Then when we be baptysed / we betoken that we wyll dye wyth
Chryst / we betoken I say / that we wyll dye as vnto the lyfe
passed as touchyng oure synnes and euyll concupiscences, and that /
as sayeth. S. Paul / we must walke in a newe lyfe, And therfore
be we plonged vnder the water, to thintent that by the maner of
spekinge / we shuld be here deed [*sic*] and buryed, as wryteth sainte
Paule vnto the Romayns Bretheren / saythe he / Esteme ye that ye
are deed as concernynge synne but a lyue vnto god, by Iesu Christ
our lord.   And in the same place, Ye are buryed wyth Christ by
baptesme into deth...[4].

That the author, however, is not speaking of adult, or
believers', baptism, but of that of infants, and yet in such terms
as Baptists of to-day suppose they themselves alone use, is seen
in the following statement[5], "And this haue we not gotten by
our good works for we haue yet don no good, when we were
baptysed ".

Among the passages most interesting in this discussion are
the following[6] :—

---

[1] Fol. ii, recto, of the first edition in English, 1529 or 1530.

[2] Fol. i, verso.   [3] Fol. ii, verso.

[4] With a few exceptions the abbreviations occurring in the *citations*
(though not in the titles of books or MSS.) throughout this volume have
been extended without any special indication.

[5] Fol. iiii, recto.   [6] Fol. v, recto.

And this is the grace the whych comyth to vs and is gyuen at the fount of baptesme.

But to thintent that we shulde not be vnkynde / therfore for this grace we do bynde our selues again [at Confirmation?] and yelde vs vnto hym, promysynge that we wyll serue hym / and denye the deuyll / and all his temptacyon / pompe, and counsell / and that we wyll serue Christ crucifyed for vs / and vpon this promyse receyue we our name / and god hath wryten vs as in a rolle for his Champyons and seruauntes / and so be we made propre to god.

This, if only casually examined, might not seem to refer to infants, and the following citation also at first sight appears to make certain the view that this work is that of an Anabaptist[1]:—

Beholde nowe thou seest well what thinge the baptesme betokeneth / & it is all one before god yf thou be .lxxx. yere olde / or twenty yere olde when thou receauest the baptesme, for god regardeth not howe olde thou art / but wyth what purpose and entencyon / and with what faythe thou receauest this baptesme and grace. He regardeth not whether thou be Iue or paynyme / man or woman / noble or vnnoble / byshop or cytezyn.

The following paragraphs, however, clearly indicate that the author is not an Anabaptist in spite of all that he has previously said which might suggest the contrary. Here the meaning is direct and clear[2]:—

And we be moche more bound vnto our promyse made at the baptesme, then any religyous vnto his professyon. For we make no promyse vnto man, but vnto god, and we promyse not to kepe the rule of a man but of the gospell, Thinke ye not therfore that it is a small thynge to be a Christen / when thou hast promysed to Iesu Christ to amende thy lyfe / & that thou wilt not lyue accordyng to the world / nor accordyng to the fleshe. It is a greate thyng to enterprise the christen faith, which so fewe people do knowe what thing it conteyneth / namely suche as here after the world do serue to be verey wyse & lettered.

But one myght say I haue nothing promysed to God / I was a chyld / let him kepe it that hath promysed for me. For this cause to thintent that no man shulde so say / it was sumtyme ordeyned that none shuld be baptysed before that he came to vnderstandynge and knowlege / to thintent that he myght promyse hym selfe / & forsake the deuyl, & that he myght know what thing he had promised If it were not that the children were feble & in peril of deth then thei must haue bin baptised

---

[1] Fol. vii, recto and verso.

[2] Fol. vii, verso,—fol. viii, verso.

Nowe allwayes albeit that we our selfe haue not promysed we be al egally bounde to obserue it, For if thou haddest dyed when thou were but a yere old / ...thou wylt saye ye / by the fayth of my godfathers and godmothers / and of holy churche. I say agayn, doest thou confesse that the faythe of thy godfathers & godmothers is so myghty that thou mayst therby be saued The same fayth is lykewyse myghty to subiecte the & binde the to that thing that they haue promysed for the vnder payne of thy dampnacyon, & losse of the helth wherfor thou must aswell kepe this that thy parentes haue promysed for the, as though thou haddest promised it thy selfe. The godfathers & the godmothers be bounde to warne the chyldren / and to helpe them that they be put to scole / to thintent that they may vnderstonde the gospell the ioyfull message of god with the epistels of S. Paule....

This author is in fact a Roman Catholic, who deplores the ignorance of many concerning the Pater Noster and the Creed[1],—"alas / ye shal fynde thousandes of auncyent persones that can not sey the pater noster & Crede in theyr mother tongue,...".

That this work did not appear to critical contemporaries to be written by an Anabaptist, is easily proved by examination of a "publick instrument" drawn up in 1530 by order of Henry VIII "in an assembly of the Archbishop of Canterbury [William Warham], the bishop of Durham", condemning the book with various others. The original of this document is in Archbishop Warham's Register, and the text is given in Davide Wilkins' "Concilia".[2] The criticism of "The summe of the holye scrypture" is rather minute and extensive. The portion of it relating to baptism, as given by Wilkins, reads[3]:—

The errours and heresies conteyned in. the boke called "The sum of Scripture.

The water of the fonte hath noo more vertue in it than hath the water of ryver.

The baptisme lyeth not in halowed water, or in other outward thinge, but in the faith oonly. 6. p. 1.

Men shulde not seeke their helthe in good works, but alonly in faith and grace. 1. f. 2.

The water of baptisme is noo thinge but a signe that we must be under the standard of the crosse. 12. p. 2.

---

[1] Fol. ix, verso.   [2] Vol. III., pp. 727–739.

[3] *Ibid.*, p. 730.

"The summe of the holye scrypture" seems to have been in considerable demand, for copies of at least three editions before 1550 are still in existence. It is not a work, however, that advocates separatism in the smallest degree, and there appears to be no evidence that it had any perceptible influence in that direction.

The subject of baptism seems to have exercised the minds of various other early writers, but while their works may also have set their readers' minds actively studying the matter, it is not therefore to be concluded that these authors were in the least infected with Anabaptist views. One of the works that might be mentioned here is William Tyndall's "The obe-diĕ|ce of a Christen man and how Chr|istĕ rulers ought to governe / | where in also (yf thou ma⸗|rke diligently) th⸗|ou shalt fynde | eyes to pe⸗|rceave | the | crafty conveyaũce of all [?] | iugglers." ["Marlborow [Marburg] in the lãde of Hesse The seconde daye of October. Anno. M.CCCCC. xxviij"] 8°. A later edition of this book was published at London in 1561. Joseph Ivimey saw a copy of this latter edition, or at least has a citation from it, but for some reason mistakenly calls the work "The obedience of all degrees proved by Gods worde", etc. Certain expressions in his citation from this work concerning baptism seem somewhat to have puzzled Ivimey[1]. But Tyndall, of course, had no intention whatever of advocating adult, or believers', baptism instead of infant baptism. Another scarce book that might be mentioned here is I.[ohn] F.[rith]'s "A myrroure | or lokynge glasse wherin | you may beholde the | Sacramente of | baptisme de⸗|scribed. | Anno. M.D. xxxiii, | Per me. I. F. | ...", London, 8°, 48 unnumbered pages. Frith, likewise, is opposed to Anabaptism, and also to adult, or believers', baptism as a general principle.

Not long after the publication of this work, in 1536 (?), appeared William Tyndall's "A Briefe de⸗|claration of the sacraments, expressing | the fyrst oryginall how they came | vp, ãd were institute with the | true and mooste syncere | meaning and vnder⸗|standyng of the | same...", 8°, fol. 40.

---

[1] "A History of the English Baptists :...", London, Vol. I., 1811, p. 93.

It may be remarked here that just such expressions as surprised Ivimey so much in Tyndall's "The obediē|ce" may be found in Archbishop Cranmer's "Catechismus", London, 8°, 1548, which though said to be the revised translation of a work by Justus Jonas, the Elder, must to some extent have been endorsed by Cranmer, as he at least sanctioned its publication[1]. Not even the most ardent Baptist historian would think of claiming either Jonas or Cranmer for Anabaptists! Yet the "Catechismus" has the following passages :—

Iesus Christe dyd institute baptisme, wherby we be borne agayne to the kyngdom of God. And you good children shal gyue dilygence, not onely to reherse these wordes, but also to vnderstand, what Christ ment by the same. That when you be demaunded any questyon herein, you maye bothe make a dyrecte answere, and also in tyme to come be able to teache your children, as you your selues are nowe instructed. For what greater shame can ther be, then a man to professe himselfe to be a Christen man, because he is baptised, and yet he knoweth not what baptisme is, nor what strength the same hath, nor what the dyppyng in the water doth betoken? wher as all oure lyfe tyme we ought to kepe those promises, which there we solemply made before God and man, and all oure profession and lyfe ought to agre to our baptisme. Wherefore good children, to thentent you may the better know the strength & power of baptisme, you shall first vnderstande, that our lorde Iesus Christ hath instituted and annexed to the gospel, thre sacraments or holy seales, of his couenant and lege mad with vs. And by these thre, gods ministers do worke with vs in the name and place of God (yea God himselfe worketh with vs) to confirme vs in our faith, & to asserten vs, that we are yᵉ lyuely membres of Gods trew churche, and yᵉ chosen people of God, to whome the gospell is sent, and that all those thinges belong to vs, wherof the promises of the gospel make mention. The first of these sacramentes is baptisme, by the whiche we be borne again to a new and heauenly lyfe, and be receaued into gods churche and congregation, whiche is the foundation and pyller of the trueth. The seconde is absolution or the authoritie of yᵉ kayes, wherby we be absolued from suche synnes, as we be fallen into after our baptisme. The thirde sacrament is the communion or yᵉ Lordes supper,...[2]

Wherfore good children when a man is baptysed, it is as muche to saye, as he dothe there confesse, that he is a synner, and that he

---

[1] See "Twelve Hundred Questions on the History of the Church of England," London, 1888, p. 135. The work from which Cranmer's "Catechismus" was translated was published anonymously at Nürnberg [in 1533]. Its title was "Catechismus oder Kinder predig".

[2] Fol. numbered ccxv, recto and verso—fol. numbered ccxiiii.

is vnder the rule and gouernaunce of synne, so that of himselfe he can not be good or ryghtuous. And therfore he commeth to baptisme, and there seketh for helpe and remedy, and desyreth God, first to forgyue him his synnes, & at length to deliuer him clerely from all synne, and perfectely to heale his soule from the sykenes of synne, as the physitian doth perfectely heale his patient from bodily diseases. And for his parte he promyseth to God againe, and solemply voweth, that he wyll fyght againste synne with all his strength and power, & that he wyl gladly beare the crosse, and al suche afflictions, as it shal please God to lay vpon him, and that also he wil be content to dye, y^t he may be perfectly healed and de-lyuered from sinne[1].

Fourthly by baptisme we die with Christ, and are buried (as it were) in his bloude & death, that we shoulde suffer afflictions and death, as Christe himself hath suffered. And as that man, whiche is baptised, doth promise to God, that he will dye with Christe, that he maye be deade to synne and to the olde Adam, so on the other part God doth promise againe to him, that he shalbe partaker of christes deathe and passion[2].

By thys which I haue hetherto spoken, I trust you vnderstand good children, wherfore baptisme is called the bath of regeneration, and howe in baptisme we be borne agayne and be made new creatures in Christe[3].

Ye shall also dylygently labour good children, to kepe and per-fourme those promises, which you made to God in your baptisme, and which baptisme doth betoken. For baptisme and the dyppyng into the water, doth betoken, that the olde Adam, with al his synne and euel lustes, ought to be drowned and kylled by daily contrition and repentance, and that by renewynge of the holy gost, we ought to ryse with Christ from the death of synne, and to walke in a new lyfe, that our new man maye lyue euerlastyngly, in rightuousnes and truthe before God, as saincte Paule teacheth saying. Al we that are baptised in Christe Iesu, are baptised in hys death. For we are buried with him by baptisme into deth, that as Christ hath risen from death by ye glori of his father, so we also shuld walke in newnes of lyfe. And this is the playne exposytion of ye wordes of holy baptisme, y^t is to saye, that we shoulde acknowlege oure selues to be synners, desyre pardon & forgyuenes of our synnes, be obedient & wylling to beare Christes crosse, and all kynde of afflyction, and at the last to die, that by death we may be perfectly deliuered from synne[4].

Besides that great light of the Church of England, William Tyndall (Tyndale), whom Baptists may have been glad to claim

---

[1] Fol. numbered ccxvii, verso—fol. numbered ccxvi.

[2] Fol. numbered ccxviii, verso.

[3] Fol. numbered ccxviii, verso—fol. numbered ccxix.

[4] Fol. numbered ccxxiii.

among those who favoured, or seemed to favour, their views, there are certain other well-known, but less prominent, characters of the Reformation period who have curiously appeared in Baptist histories as Baptists. One of these is Anne Askewe, who was burned at Smithfield in July, 1546. If the reader, however, will carefully peruse the text of her examinations as given by Iohan [John] Bale[1], he will readily perceive that she was not an Anabaptist, nor accused of Anabaptism. As to her heresy, she says she is of no sect, and that " thys is the heresye whych they report me to holde, that after the prest hath spoken the words of consecracyon, there remayneth breade styll."

In the period before 1550 there was at least one Englishman who was unjustly accused by his contemporaries of being an Anabaptist. Just who this individual was is not certainly known, but his initials were I. B., which are by some supposed to stand for John Bale. In Baptist histories he has not generally been noticed, probably because of the rarity of his book published in 1547, about the time that Bale was defending Anne Askewe. It is entitled, "A bryefe and | plaine declaracion of certayne | sentĕces in this litle boke folowing, | to satisfie the consciences of them | that haue iudged me therby to | be a fauourer of the Ana⸗|baptistes.|...", 8°, 40 unnumbered pages. This work contains another later title-page which reads, "❧ A BRIFE AND FAYTH|full declaration of the true | fayth of Christ, made by certeyne | men susspected of heresye | in these articles | folowyng.|..." That I. B., and these men susspected of heresy, who were of his own opinion, were not Anabaptists is shown by what is said on the subject of baptism in the section entitled, "To the reader", where I. B. says : " First thou shalt note that I am no fauourer of them [the Anabaptists] or theyr

---

[1] " The first examinacy⸗|on of Anne Askewe, latelye mar|tyred in Smythfelde, by the Ro⸗|mysh vpholders,..." [1546], 8° [Marpurg].

" The lattre examinacy|on of Anne Askewe, latelye mar|tyred in Smythfelde, by the wyc⸗|ked Synagogue of Antichrist, | ...", " 1. 5. 4. 7.", 8° [Marpurg].

Copies are to be found in the British Museum. Another edition of the two parts was in the Huth Library.

opinions, for that I shall playnlye declare that the scriptures whyche they aledge, make nothynge for their purpose And then, that I do in al that I may impugne them, by that I endeuour to establish & confyrme by the scriptures : the contrarye of their opinion.   For the fyrst thou shalt note, that the ground of their opinion is vpon the order that the Euangelist Mark kepeth in the rehersing of the wordes of Christ to his Apostles when he sent them to preach. Marke. xvi. Fayth saye they, dothe in the wordes of Christ go before Baptisme. Necessarye is it therefore, that he that shalbe Baptised do first beleue.   But the Infantes (which haue not the vse of reason) cannot vnderstande the fayth of Chryst (and much lesse embrace and professe it) wherfore, it cannot stande with the worde of God that Infantes should be baptised. No doubt (christen reader) it is not possible that any shoulde be acceptable before God, without fayth. For so writeth Paul to the Hebrues. xi. And truth it is also, that fayth must go before baptisme, none other wyse then in the cause proceadeth or goeth before the effect or thyng that commeth thereof,... But to inferre vpon this, that the Infantes and yong chyldren oughte not to be baptised : is far wyde from the true meanynge of these places of scripture ".

I. B. was, therefore, not an Anabaptist, but certainly he had been influenced by the Continental reformers, and if Bale was I. B., he was probably in Marburg on the Lahn at the time this work was published. I. B. was evidently a Nonconformist in the early sense of that word.

We may now turn to the early congregations at Faversham and Bocking, which appear to have begun to hold meetings about the time of the promulgation of the first Act of Uniformity in 1549.   Until comparatively recent times these conventiclers were supposed to have been English Anabaptists. This view seems first to have been expressed by Dr Gilbert Burnet, who in speaking of the congregation at Bocking, says, "These were probably some of the anabaptists, though that is not objected to them ". John Strype appears to have accepted this opinion, but unfortunately for the truth of this theory there is plenty of evidence which makes it perfectly plain that they were not

Anabaptists in any full sense. Dr Richard Watson Dixon[1], accordingly, thinks of them as being the first English separatists, a more natural view, but one which, also, in my opinion, is not quite sufficiently supported by the evidence still available. Without further information, therefore, we may express the opinion, that these early English conventiclers may best be known by some such title, and that, as a whole, they were merely Nonconformists (in the early meaning of that term) of a rather peculiar type.

The most reliable information at present known regarding these conventiclers is to be found in Harleian MS. 421 (fol. 133–34 verso) in the British Museum, and in the Privy Council Register at the Public Record Office. Most of the evidence from these sources is given in the volume of documents. From these old records the following points of interest have been gleaned :—

While conventiclers may have begun independently and almost simultaneously to hold meetings at Faversham in Kent, and at Bocking in Essex, the evidence we still possess suggests that small gatherings were first held at several places in Kent, or in Faversham, including one Cole's house in Faversham, and that some time between June 23, 1550[2], and Jan. 26, 1550/1[3], on account of impending persecution, the Kentish conventiclers removed to Bocking in Essex, where some Nonconformist interest probably was already known to exist.

At Bocking early in 1551 after the arrival of the Faversham party the conventiclers appear to have numbered over sixty persons. The names of a good many of them have been gleaned from the papers mentioned above, namely, John Grey; William Forstall; Laurence Ramsey; Edmonde Morres; one Cole of Faversham; Henry Harte; Thomas Broke; Roger Lynsey; Richarde Dynestake, clerk; George Brodebridge; Vmfrey Middilton [Humphrey Middleton]; Nicholas, or Thomas, Yonge

[1] "History of the Church of England", etc., Vol. III., Second Edition, Revised, pp. 206–11.

[2] See the published "Acts of the Privy Council of England", New Series, Vol. III., London, 1891, p. 53.

[3] *Ibid.*, p. 197.

of "Lannams" [Lenham ?]; one Vpcharde [Upcharde] of Bocking; one [Cuthbert?] Sympson; John Barrett [Barrey?] of Stamford, cowherd; Robert Cooke of Bocking, clothier; John Eglise, or Eglins, of Bocking, clothier; Richard Bagge, or Blagge; Thomas Pygrinde, or Piggerell; John Kinge; one Myxsto, or Myxer; one Boughtell; Robert Wolmere; William Sibley of "Lannams" [Lenham?]; Nicholas Shetterton, or Sheterenden, of Pluckley; John Lydley of Ashford; one Cole of Maidstone, schoolmaster; Thomas Sharpe of Pluckley; one Chidderton of Ashford; William Grenelande; and John Plume of Lenham. Among the leaders were Cole of Faversham, Henry Harte, George Brodebridge, Cole of Maidstone, Nicholas Yonge, and especially Humphrey Middleton and Cuthbert Sympson.

The conventiclers appear to have maintained rather varied views, only occasionally to have held their meetings, and not to have constituted any well-developed organization. The various opinions advanced by the conventiclers are noticeably Pelagian and anti-Calvinistic, and clearly differentiate them from the earliest Nonconformists, but nevertheless, in my opinion, do not prove that they were separatists in any modern sense. Accordingly, as has been suggested above, in the absence of a better descriptive term, we will merely denominate them early Nonconformist conventiclers. Here are some of the unusual views expressed in their gatherings:—

Cole of Faversham is said to have asserted that the doctrine of predestination was meeter for devils than for Christian men. Henry Harte, it is said, stated that God did not predestinate men to election or reprobation, but that their position in relation to these two states depended entirely upon themselves. It is also reported that Harte claimed that learned men were the cause of great errors, and that Cole of Maidstone had affirmed that children were not born in original sin. William Grenelande declared that to play at any game for money was sin. John Plume of Lenham deposed, that it was taught among other things in the congregation, that one ought not to salute a sinner or an entire stranger; that Humphrey Middleton had asserted that all men were predestinated to be saved; that it was generally affirmed in the congregation, that Predestination is a damnable doctrine; and finally, that Nicholas Yonge had said they would not communicate with sinners.

After the conventiclers had moved to Bocking a meeting was held at Upcharde's house one Sunday at twelve o'clock, where sixty or more people, including several residents of Bocking, were present, and discussed whether it were necessary to stand or kneel at prayer, and whether with their hats on or off,—a discussion which was concluded by the decision that such externals were unimportant. Apparently at this meeting in Bocking the conventiclers were arrested. Some of them, at least, were soon brought before the Privy Council, where they admitted that they had held their meetings "for talke of Scriptures", and had refused the communion [in the Church of England] for more than two years "vpon verie superstitiouse and erronyose purposes : withe Divers other evill oppynyons worthie of great punyshement". Accordingly some of their number were committed to prison, while others were released on bail, on the condition that they should appear before the Privy Council when called upon, and in case they had any further religious difficulties, that they should repair to their Ordinary. Whether the conventiclers continued to hold meetings after their release is not clear, but we know from John Foxe's "Acts and Monuments", that Humphrey Middleton and Cuthbert Sympson were both burned at the stake a few years later during the reign of Queen Mary.

One of those persons who have been incorrectly reckoned as Anabaptists in Baptist histories[1] is Richard Woodman. Several years ago I found a contemporary manuscript copy of Woodman's "Confession" hidden away in the Library of Gonville and Caius College, Cambridge[2]. It is clearly written and contains important material, the existence of which was evidently unknown to the writer of the article on Woodman in the Dictionary of National Biography. It appears herein that "Richarde Wodman" was "late of yᵉ parishe of Walebilton in yᵉ countye of Sussexe",

[1] Ivimey's "A History of the English Baptists", Vol. I., pp. 97–8, whose information is taken from Crosby's "The History of the English Baptists", Vol. I., p. 63.

[2] Press-mark, 233.

and that he had at the time he writes this confession already
been "prisoner in ye kinges benche" "one wholle yere the sixt
daye of Iune laste paste, for ye Testimonye of Iesus Chryste.
1552." He says he has been slandered as maintaining certain
opinions that he does not believe. He names various errors
held by religious men in his day, and gives an extended and
clear exposition of his own views. That Woodman was not an
Anabaptist is clearly manifested by the following direct statement[1] which shows his exact position :—

And Therfore I do here confesse & beleve y^t the custome vsed
in ye churche of god to chrysten yonge children ys moste godly and
agreinge to ye worde of god, and Therfore to be commendyde and in
any wyse to be retayned in Christes churche. And I do vtterly
dyssent frome ye Anabaptystes, wch hold ye contrary, howbeit I beleve
them to be saved by ye meryttes and mercy of god in christe. Also
I beleve y^t yf ye childe be baptysed in ye name of god ye father, y^e
sonne and ye holy ghoste (as Christe hath commaunded vs [)], that
then it is truly & sufficientlie baptysed (be ye mynister never so
wicked in lyfe or learnynge y^t doth baptyse it) for the effecte of
godes ordynaunce, doth not depende vpon the worthynes of y^e
mynister, but of ye truthe of godes promyses, and I do beleve y^t
those children y^t have bene, be, or shalbe baptysed of ye papisticall
mynisters, be truly baptysed, notw^thstandinge that ye minister be a
popishe heretyke. Howbeit this I do confesse and beleve y^t no
christian man oughte to bringe or sende his childe to the papistycall
churche to requyre baptysme at thaire handes. thaye beinge Anti-
christes mynisters, for in so doynge he doth confesse them to be the
trewe churche, wch is a grevous synne in the sighte of god,....

As to the life of David George [Joris] Ivimey has made
a curious mistake. Crosby had correctly given a brief story of
his life, and calls him an Anabaptist. Ivimey obtained his
information from Crosby, but mistaking his meaning, says that
George "died in London",—a most remarkable statement, as it
is quite contrary to the facts,—and adds also what is not in
Crosby and incorrect as well, "It is probable that David George
was a member of a church of foreign Baptists that was formed
in London in the former reign"[2]. This is a good example of
the careless way in which, it is to be feared, too much early
Baptist history has been written. It is well known that David

---

[1] On p. 37 of the MS.
[2] Ivimey's "A History of the English Baptists", Vol. I., p. 98.

George has long been considered an Anabaptist. For this opinion, however, there really seems to be very little foundation except in a generic use of that term, if we can trust the account of his life and death published in English at Basel in 1560. This pamphlet is entitled "Dauid Gorge / | borne in Holland /...", and gives a detailed life of George. He seems to have been a fanatic of the type of the late Alexander Dowie, but evidently exalted himself to an even higher position than Dowie ever attempted to claim. George certainly had nothing whatever to do with English Anabaptists,—the point with which we are chiefly concerned.

It has already been stated that before 1550 no works by English Anabaptists, or English translations of the works of foreign Anabaptists, are known. Furthermore, it is exceedingly difficult to believe that the books of Continental Anabaptists in their original form could have been read at all in England by the common people at that time, or, if they were read, would have had any influence on account of the strong English pre- judice against the very name Anabaptist. Nevertheless, the English public became acquainted with some of the leading views of Continental Anabaptists long before 1550, and about that time several books, most of them translations of continental works, or parts of them, *against* the Anabaptists, are known to have been published. The first appeared in 1548 under the title, "¶ AN · HOL| ↄ❧ SOME ❧ↄ | ↄ❧ Antidotus ❧ↄ | or counter≈|poysen, | agaynst the pestylent | heresye and secte | of the Anabap≈|tistes new≈|ly trans≈|lated | out | of latī | into Englysh by Iohn | Veron, Senonoys. | ☞ (::) ☜ " [" Im- printyd at London, by Humfrey | Powell, dwellyng Aboue Hol≈|burne Conduit."] 8°, pp. ii, 228, unnumbered[1]. It contains among other points of interest definitions of the words " Ana- baptist" and " Catabaptist " made by one of their most noted opponents at the time when the Anabaptists were first becoming

---

[1] This is said to be a translation of the first book of Leo Juda's enlarged edition of a work by Heinrich Bullinger, which Juda published at Zürich in 1535 under the title, "❧ↄ ADVER≈|SVS OMNIA CATA≈|BAP- TISTARVM PRAVA DOG≈|*mata Heinrychi Bullingeri lib.* IIII. *per Leonem Iudae aucti...*"

well known throughout Europe. In the so-called Whitsitt Controversy the question arose as to what was the distinction between these two words. It was claimed that Anabaptism meant simply rebaptism, but that Catabaptism meant rebaptism by immersion. Dr George A. Lofton disposed of this theory[1], but the exact difference in the meaning of these two words is possibly made a little more plain from their juxtaposition in the following citation on page 14 of this early work: "thys abhomynable secte. of yᵉ Catababtistys (for they ware called anabaptistys, because yᵗ they ware autors of rebaptization, or babtizyng agayne, and Catabaptistys, because, yᵗ they dyd speake and hold oppynyon, agaynst the baptisme of children)...". The prefixes " Ana " and " Cata ", therefore, in no way indicate the mode of baptism practised by those to whom these names were applied.

The next work in English against the Anabaptists was published at London in 1549, and is by "Mayster Iohn Caluine". The printer was "Iohn Daye". It is entitled, "A short | instruction for to | arme all good Christian | people agaynst the pesti͜| ferous errours of the | common secte of | Anabapti͜|stes ". [London.] 8°, 158 unnumbered pages. Dibdin incorrectly dates this 1544, evidently by a typographical error. The Preface to the Reader is headed, " ❡ Iohn Caluine to the ministers of the churches in the countie of Newcastel", and is dated, "From Geneua the fyrst of Iune. Anno Domini .M.D. xl.iiii." This work, therefore, seems to have been written with a special purpose to the churches in " Newcastel " in 1544, and is not, like some of the works translated, of little special significance in English church history. The seven main articles of belief of the moderate Anabaptists are separately given, and opposed from the orthodox point of view. To these are added two or three less generally accepted articles, which are also, in like manner, discussed. In 1551 "Ihon Veron" published two books, both probably translations of parts of Leo Juda's previously mentioned edition of Heinrich Bullinger's noted work against the Anabaptists, entitled, " ✑ | ADVER͜|SVS OM-NIA CATA͜|BAPTISTARVM PRAVA DOG͜|*mata Heinrychi*

---

[1] "English Baptist Reformation", Louisville, Kentucky, 1899, pp. 24-7.

Bullingeri lib. IIII. *per* | *Leonem Iudae aucti adeò ut pri-*
orem | *œditionem uix agnoscas.* | ...", Tigvri [Zürich.], 1535.
Both were printed in octavo at Worcester and may possibly
have formed two parts of one work, each part having a separate title-page. One of these books covers 44 unnumbered
leaves and bears the title, " ❡ A most necessary & frutefull |
Dialogue, betwene yᵉ seditious Libertin | or rebel Anabaptist, &
the true obedient | christiā, wherin, as in a mirrour or glasse |
ye shal se yᵉ excellencie and worthynesse | of a christiā magistrate:
& again what | obedience is due vnto publique ru|lers of al
thē yᵗ professe Christ | ..." The other covers 88 unnum-
bered leaves and has the title, "❡ A moste sure and | strong
defence of the bap⸴|tisme of children, against yᵉ | pestiferous
secte of the A⸴|nabaptystes. set furthe by | that famouse Clerke,
Hen|ry Bullynger : & nowe | translated out of La⸴|ten into
Englysh | by Iohn Ve⸴|ron Seno|noys. | ..." All of these
works are scarce.

By the publication of Confessions of Faith with articles
opposing the Anabaptists, as well as of works such as these
just mentioned, more than by any other means it would seem,
Anabaptism at first became known to the English people.
Whether the appearance of these works contrary to the intention of their publishers caused the spread of Anabaptist
views, or whether such books were published to ward off danger
caused by the actual spreading of Anabaptism among the
English, is not apparent. Suffice it to say that the first English
work favouring certain Anabaptist opinions was evidently produced about 1550 and was answered by "Wyllyam Turner" in
his little volume published in 1551, entitled, "A preseruati⸴|ue,
or triacle, agaynst the | poyson of Pelagius, lately | reneued, &
styrred vp agayn, | by the furious secte of | the Annabaptistes: |
deuysed by Wyl⸴|lyam Turner, | Doctor of Physick. | ...", 8°,
206 unnumbered pages. The author of the so-called Anabaptist
work, against which Turner wrote, and which probably was
never published, was one Robert Cooche (= Robert Couche or
Cooke) as is proved by the latter part of a Latin letter[1] dated

---

[1] In a collected volume of letters of John Parkhurst, Bishop of Norwich,
now in the University Library, Cambridge [Press-mark Ee. 2. 34 (20)].

Feb. 6, 1574 (Feb. 16, 1575, New Style), written by Bishop
Parkhurst of Norwich, and addressed to D[r]. Rod:[olphus]
Gualtherus, Tigurinus [i.e., of Zürich], of which the important
part of the text is given in the volume of documents. Cooche
is also mentioned in another earlier letter of Parkhurst to
Gualther, dated June 29, 1574[1], a part of which is likewise
given in the volume of documents.

Since Cooche's book, as Turner styles it, was probably never
printed, it is fortunate for us that Turner has cited in his
"preseruatiue" several quotations from Cooche's manuscript.
In fact, without Turner's book and the letters previously
mentioned, even the name of Robert Cooche might hardly
now be known, so that in Cooche's case, as in many others of
later date, we have to thank his opponents for preserving
almost all[2] that is now known of his life and character.

Early in his work[3] Dr Turner naively tells of his own
clerical aspirations and of how he happened to write his "preseruatiue", as well as of how Cooche (whom he does not call by
name throughout) came to write his book :—

But after that my lorde Arche byshop of Yorke, had ones geuen
me a prebende: I could not be quiet, vntill that I had licence
to reade, or preache. Whiche obteyned : I began to rede, and so
to discharge mi conscience. And because I dyd perceyue, that
diuerse began to be infected with the poysen of Pellagius: I deuised
a lecture in Thistelworth, agaynst two of the opinions of Pelagius :
namely against that childer haue no original sin, & that they oughte
not to be baptised. But within a few wekes after : one of Pelagius
disciples, in the defence of his masters doctrine, wrote against my
lecture. with all the cunnyng and learning, that he had. But lest
he should glorye and crake amonge his disciples, that I could not
aunswer him : and to the intent, that the venemous seede of his
soweyng maye be destroyed, and so hyndered from bryngyng forth
frute : I haue set out this boke, to aunswer hym, in the one of his
opinions :....

From this citation it seems likely that the two opinions

---

[1] *Ibid.* [Press mark, Ee . 2 . 34 (23)].

[2] A letter from Robert Cooche to Rodolph Gualter dated at the
Queen's Palace, Aug. 13, 1573, is given in "The Zurich Letters" (Second
Series), Parker Society, Cambridge, 1845, pp. 236-7. Some facts of
Cooche's life are also mentioned in a note.

[3] "A preseruatiue...", sig. a_{iii} recto.

advocated by Cooche were (1) that children are not tainted with original sin, and (2) that they ought not to be baptised. This book of Turner's is a reply only to the first, but he makes a promise, apparently never fulfilled, that when he has published his "Herbal", he will answer Cooche's second opinion also, a promise which later he qualifies[1] with the words, "yf it shall be thought expedient to the churche to do so." Turner has no love for his opponent's views, and yet he does not advocate persecution. He says[2]:—

This monstre is in many poyntes lyke vnto the watersnake with seuen heades. For as out of one bodye rose seuen heades: So out of Pelagius rose vp these seuen sectes: Anabaptistes, Adamites, Loykenistes, Libertines, Swengfeldianes, Dauidianes, and the spoylers. Sum would thincke: that it were the best way, to vse the same weapones agaynst thys manyfolde monstre, that the papistes vsed agaynst vs: that is material fyre, and faggot. But me thynk: seyng it is no materiall thynge, that we must fyght withal, but gostly, that is a woode spirite: that it were moste mete, that we should fyght with the sworde of goddes word, and with a spirituall fyre against it: elles we are lyke to profit but a litle in our besynes [business]... Then when as the enemie is a spirite, that is, the goste of pelagius, that olde heretike: ones welle laid, but now of late to the great ieperdie of many raysed vp agayn: the wepones, & the warriers, that must kyll thys enemie, must be spirituall. As for spiritual weapons: we may haue enow out of the store house, or armory of the scripture: to confound & ouertrow all the gostly enemies: be they never so many[.] But where, & from whence, shal we haue spiritual warriers ynow fit for this fyght? If that we had no mo enamies, but this alone, the fewer soldiers would serue:...we had nede of a great dele of mo souldiers, then al the scoles that are in this realme are able to set furth: if so many scoles haue bene put down of late, as the comon rumor reporteth....

The greater number of citations from Cooche's work are not extended or highly interesting, but from them and Turner's own remarks we get a very good idea of his views. At that time dipping, or immersion, of infants was the rule, for Turner says[3]: "And because baptim [baptism] is a passiue Sacrament, & no man can baptise hym self, but is baptised of an other: & childer may be as wel dipped into the water in y° name of

---

[1] "A preseruatiue...", sig. N$_{vi}$.   [2] *Ibid.*, sig. a$_{iii}$ verso—a$_{iv}$ recto.

[3] *Ibid.*, sig. G$_{viii}$ recto and verso.

Christ (which is the outward baptym and as myche as one man can gyue an other) euen as olde folke:...".

Turner also gives a very direct statement as to Cooche's views concerning original sin and the proper time for the administration of baptism[1]:—

is the matter of origynall synne no part of scripture? you do holde that there is none at all, and therefore that the childer nede not, nother ought to be baptysed, vntyll they be .xiiij yeare olde: before whiche tyme, they haue done many actuall synnes, whyche hadde nede to be wasshed awaye, wyth the bath of baptime....

As to Cooche's person and state in life, Turner has some amusing words[2]: "GOD neuer in his worde expressedly commaunded his Apostlles to suffer suche tal men as you bee to lyue syngle: therfor your curate doth wrong to suffer yow to lyue syngle."

The above mentioned letters referring to Cooche also give us a very good idea of his abilities and character. He finally abandoned his heretical opinions.

Thus we know the case of at least one Englishman of high position about 1550 who held two opinions maintained by the Anabaptists. Are we then justified in believing that his case was isolated, and that he did not belong to a congregation either of English or of foreign Anabaptists? Certainly, for Cooche is nowhere mentioned as a separatist, but as a member of the Church of England and under the charge of a curate!

From time to time until the last quarter of the sixteenth century foreign Anabaptists continued to come over into England, though in how great numbers it is now difficult to say. They do not appear to have been numerous, but as soon as they in any way manifested their faith, they were imprisoned and compelled to recant, or, if they refused, were hurried out of the country, or were burned at the stake. Those who were burned are reported to have been brave, and to have met their death joyfully to the astonishment of the beholders. From seeing their heroism some of the English may have been favourably impressed, but it is significant that the names of no genuine

---

[1] "A preseruatiue...", sigs. H_v recto and verso.

[2] *Ibid.*, sig. K_{vii} verso.

English Anabaptists before 1593 or 1594 seem to have been recorded[1]. To be sure various gatherings of the early Puritans were spoken of as Anabaptistical, and even Barrowe and Greenwood were ridiculed as Anabaptists, but these facts of course do not affect our argument, as it is generally well known to-day that the Puritans and the Barrowists were not Anabaptists, and that others besides Puritans and Barrowists were sometimes labelled with this term of opprobrium.

In 1555 was published a translation by Thomas Cotsford of a work by Ulrich Zwingli bearing the title, " The accompt re⸲| kenynge and confession of the faith | of Huldrik Zwinglius byshop of | Zuryk...", Geneva, 8°, pp. xxxii, 119.   This contains at the end, beginning with page 95, "An Epistle vvrit-|ten to a good Lady / for the comfort | of a frende of hers, wherin the Noua-| tions erroure now reuiued by | the Anabaptistes is con⸲|futed, and the synne a⸲|gaynste the holy | Goste playnly | declared ". I have somewhere seen what may prove to be the original English manuscript of this Epistle, or a contemporary copy of it, bearing the title, " An epistyll written wherin the novacions Error now newly | Revisid by the secte of Anabaptyst*es* / is Confuted & the tru dyffynyssen | of the syne Ageynst the holy gost playnly Declaryde—". The spelling suggests a North Country source, and the handwriting would indicate that the manuscript was written about the middle of the sixteenth century.

Likewise about 1556 was published the following work :— "⁋ Two bokes of the noble doctor | and B. S. Augustine thone entite|led of the Predestiu[=n]acion of sain⸲|tes, thother of perseueraunce vnto | thende, wherunto are annexed the | determinacions of two auncient ge|nerall Councelles, confermyng the | doctrine taught in these bokes by s. | Aug. all faythfully translated out of | Laten into Englyshe by Iohn Sco⸲|ry the late B.[ishop] of Chichester, very ne⸲|cessary for al tymes, but namely for | oures, wherin the Papistes & Ana⸲|baptistes haue reuiued agayne | the wyked opinions of the | Pelagiãs, that

---

[1] These first genuine English Anabaptists arose on the Continent, but one of them at least was in an English prison about 1597, as will be seen in Chapter IX.

extolled mās | wyll & merites agaynst | the fre grace of | Christ", 8°, fol. 123.

The indefatigable "Ihon Veron" in 1559, or about that date, published two more works bearing on this interesting topic. One dated 1559 has the following title, "❡ A moste | necessary treatise of free | wil, not onlye against the Pa⌇|pistes, but also against the Anabap⌇|tistes, which in these our daies, go | about to renue the detestable here⌇|sies of Pelagius, and of the Luciferians, | whiche say and affirm, that we | be able by our own natural | strength to fulfil the law | and commaunde⌇| mentes of | God. | ❡ Made dialoge wyse by *Ihon Ve⌇|ron*, in a manner word by | woorde; as he did set it | forth in his lectures | at Paules" [London], 8°, 188 unnumbered pages. The second work is entitled, "*A FRVTEFVL* | treatise of Predestinati⌇|on, and of the deuyne | prouidence of god, as far | forth as the holy scriptu⌇|res and word of god shal | lead vs, and an answer | made to all the vain and | blasphemous obiections | that the Epicures and | Anabaptistes of our | time canne make...". [London], 8°, 127 unnumbered pages.

About 1559 or 1560 the English Government seems for some reason to have been unusually disturbed concerning the Anabaptists, whether on account of the publication of so many books against them, or because of the actual spread of heretical views of one kind or another among the English people, it is difficult to say. At any rate in 1560 there was issued "A proclamation for the banishment of Anabaptists that refuse to be reconciled, 22 Septembris." One of them, of unknown name, about 1559 or 1560, seems to have written an anonymous work entitled, "The cōfutation of the errors of the careles by necessitie", evidently a treatise against the doctrine of Predestination. Whether it was a printed book or only a manuscript is not clear.

John Knox, then at the beginning of his famous career, undertook to answer "The cōfutation" in most thorough fashion, and published a good sized book in 1560 at Geneva against it, entitled, "AN ANSWER | TO A GREAT NOMBER | of blasphemous cauillations written by an | Anabaptist, and aduersarie to Gods eternal | Predestination. | *AND CONFVTED* | *By Iohn Knox,* *minister of Gods worde* | *in Scotland.* | Wherein the Author so

discouereth the craft and falsho-|de of that sect, that the godly
knowing that error, | may be confirmed in the trueth by the
euident Wor-|de of God. | [Device] | ...", 8°, pp. 455. This
work in either of its two editions[1] is rare.   In the Preface
Knox says that he has recently seen[2] " a book moste detestable
& blasphemous, conteinyng (as it is intiteled, The confutation of
the errors of the careles by necessitie[3])", adding, " with that
odious name do they burden all those that either do teach,
ether yet beleue the doctrine of gods eternall predestination
which booke written in the english tongue doeth contein aswell
the lies and the blasphemies imagined by Sebastian Castalio, and
laid to the charge of that moste faithfull seruant of God, Iohn
Caluine as also the vane reasons Pighius, Sadoletus & Georgius
Siculus, pestilent Papistes, & expressed ennemies of gods free
mercies.   The dispitefull railing of w° booke, & the manifest
blasphemies in the same conteined, togither with the earnest
requests of som godlie brethren, moued me, to prepare an
answere to the same :...".

In this book Knox has given so many and such extended
citations from his opponent's work that they furnish us with
a very complete idea of what the anonymous author of "The
côfutation" thought on the subjects of election, predestination,
etc., but since he apparently wrote nothing concerning baptism,
a subject so vital to the real Anabaptists, we hardly need here
to make further comment on Knox's work, though we could
not afford wholly to overlook it.

John Strype says[4] that in 1560 some Dutch Anabaptists who

---

[1] An octavo edition (pp. 443) was printed in London in 1591 probably
to prevent the English people from being infected with the opinions of the
Barrowists, who had been incorrectly given the nickname of Anabaptists.
This is apparently an unaltered edition of the text in so far as the wording
is concerned.

[2] P. 8.

[3] The Rev. J. H. Shakespeare in his "Baptist and Congregational
Pioneers", London, 1906, p. 16, curiously ascribes this work to John Knox,
though he may have intended to ascribe it to Cooche, but I know of no
evidence whatever that Cooche wrote it, and of course Knox did not
write it.

[4] "Annals of the Reformation", pp. 175–6.

had escaped to England tried to be admitted as members of the Dutch church in London, that their wish was not granted, and that again in 1564 there arose a contention in this church concerning the baptizing of infants, but that then also Anabaptist views were not welcome.   To consider that the Dutch church in London was an Anabaptist congregation at this time is, therefore, very inaccurate, and the present writer knows of no good evidence that it ever adopted any Anabaptist opinions.

It would seem that Anabaptism during the sixteenth century never appealed strongly to the English mind.   The name had too recently been associated with the fall of Münster and with events revolting to the sober-minded Englishman.   During that period one had to be an important personage to dare to hold Anabaptist views in England.   Even as late as 1567 "Iohn Iewel *Bishop* of *Sarisburie*" in "A Defence of the Apologie of | the Churche of Englande, | ...", said,—" Your Anabaptistes, and Zuenkfeldians, wee knowe not.   They finde Harbour emongste you in Austria, Slesia, Morauria, and in sutche other Countries, and Citties, where the Gospel of Christe is suppressed : but they haue no Acquaintance withe vs, neither in Englande, nor in Germanie, nor in France, nor in Scotlande, nor in Denmarke, nor in Sueden, nor in any place els, where the Gospel of Christe is clearly preached"[1].   To be sure, this is not quite exact in so far at least as Germany is concerned, but while a few isolated Anabaptists are reported to have been in England at this period, there appears to be no good reason for doubting that the Anabaptists were then generally unknown in this country.   However, about 1576 there seems to have been some fear prevalent that Anabaptism might spread among the English, for it is said that in that year a book was published, entitled, " Cuth.[bert] Mutton his confutation of the...sect of Anabaptistes : Wherein you may behold the perfecte humanity of Christ", 8°.[2]   About 1577 (?) Edmond Bicknoll also published his rare work entitled, "A Swoorde against | *swearing, contey-*|ning these principal | *poyntes.* | 1 That there is a lawful vse of an | oth, contrary

[1] P. 30.

[2] W. Herbert's "Typographical Antiquities", etc., Vol. II., p. 1135.   So far as I am aware, no living author has seen this work.

to the assertion of | the Manichees & Anabaptistes. | 2 *Howe
great a sinne it is to sweare | falsly, vaynely, rashly, or
customably.* | 3 That common or vsuall swearyng leadeth vnto
periurie. | 4 Examples of Gods iust and visible pu∢|nishment
vpon blasphemers,... | ¶ Imprinted at London for | *William
Towreolde*, by the | *assent of* Richard | VVatkins", 8°, 47 + i leaves,
chiefly in Black Letter. At least one other edition of this work
may be found in the British Museum.

After 1577 (?) for some years England was evidently not
especially troubled by Anabaptistical tendencies, though Robert
Browne in 1582 says[1] that he and his followers have been called
"Anabaptistes" because of their attitude towards magistrates.
However, no new books in English appear to have been written
on the subject until 1588, after Barrowe and Greenwood had
been imprisoned. Then Dr Robert Some, Master of Peterhouse
at Cambridge, inaccurately accused John Penry of holding
"many Anabaptistical, blasphemous and Popish absurdities"[2],
and in the following year, 1589, he seems likewise to have
included Barrowe and Greenwood among "the Anabaptistical
order "[3].

Again for more than twenty years comparatively little was
published in England about Anabaptists, and this fact argues
strongly that they had as yet gained no foothold on English
soil. In 1611, however, there came upon the scene one Edward
Wightman, a person who until the last decade, on account of a
lack of trustworthy information, has been much misunderstood,
and has been commonly termed an Anabaptist. It is true that
he held a few opinions maintained by the Continental Anabaptists, but together with these he advanced certain other
remarkable views, which make it advisable to consider his

[1] See the Rev. T. G. Crippen's edition of "A Treatise of Reformation
without Tarying for Anie", London, 1903, p. 27.

[2] In "A Defence of Svch Points in R. Somes Last Treatise, As M. Penry
hath dealt against :...", 1588, London, 4°.

[3] In "*A* | GODLY TREA-|TISE, WHEREIN ARE | EXAMINED
AND CONFV∢|ted many execrable fancies, giuen out and | holden, partly
by *Henry Barrow* and *Iohn* | Greenewood : partly, by other of the | Ana-
baptistical order.|...", 1589, London, 4°.

case in the discussion of the English Seekers in Chapter VIII.

William Sayer, on the other hand, who is brought to our notice in 1612, may perhaps be better presented here. In this year he was imprisoned in "the gaole for the Countie of Norff[olk]". Like Wightman he seems to have denied "the Godhead of Iesus Christe & of the holie ghost", but unlike him he does not appear to have looked upon himself as a prophet. Sayer disapproved of the baptism of infants, because they have no "actuall faithe"; he claims that it is lawful to carry arms and to fight with the same against the enemies of "the Church of the seperation from the Church of England"; that it is "vnlawfull to take an oath before any ecclesiasticall officer", or "to sue in any Criminall cause, before an ecclesiasticall magestrate"; that the king has no right to grant to Bishops or priests the rights of civil magistrates; and that the ministers of the Church of England are not lawfully called to their office since they are not called in scriptural manner.

Sayer was twice officially examined by John Jegon, Bishop of Norwich, just before, or about, November 25, 1612. He stood firm in his opinions and could not be persuaded to recant, although he was treated "in all mildenesse & lenitie", and "Great care had" been taken "for his better instruccion by often conference privately, & publiquely by learned & discreete divines."

Sayer's case appears to have greatly disturbed the Bishop of Norwich, who as a last resort wrote to Archbishop Abbot concerning it. The Archbishop replied in a letter dated, "Lambhithe Decemb: j. 1612." He speaks of Sayer as a desperate heretic, "who out of malice rather then out of vnderstanding mainteineth manie prophane & scismaticall opinions." The Bishop of Norwich seems to have suggested that "hee [Sayer] should burne as an Hereticque", but the Archbishop replies that such a severe course would "neuer be assented to" [by ecclesiastical law], unless Sayer should obstinately persist in denying the "Godhead of Christe, and of the Holie ghoste", in which case "the Lawe will [would] take holde of him, as it did this last yeare vpon Legate, and Wightman, to frie him at a Stake", a somewhat jubilant expression, it would seem, for Archbishop Abbot!

The present account is the first modern reference to Sayer that the author remembers to have seen.   It would be interesting to know how the case developed.   Certainly Sayer was not "fried" at a stake, but whether he recanted or not is at present apparently not known.   Copies of the original papers from which the information concerning this case has been gleaned are given entire in the volume of documents.

CHAPTER II

THE GRADUAL GROWTH OF PURITANISM AND ITS CON-
TRIBUTION TO THE DEVELOPMENT OF ENGLISH
SEPARATISM UNTIL 1581

HAVING seen that Anabaptism had practically no influence
on separatism in England before 1612, we may now glance back
at quite another current of religious opinion that began to
manifest itself shortly after the commencement of the English
Reformation. This was the old Nonconformity which later
developed into Puritanism.

From the time of Robert Baillie and his contemporaries
until comparatively recent years it has been the prevailing
custom among historical writers to ascribe the rise and growth
of separatism in England largely to the rapid spread of Continental Anabaptism. I myself formerly held this opinion, but
it now appears to me much more likely that the true source of
Brownism, as well as of Barrowism, is to be found in the so-called
old Nonconformity, in the London Protestant congregation of
Queen Mary's time, and in the views of many of the Marian
exiles, as well as in the maturer opinions of later Puritans.

Very little, I believe, has as yet appeared in English concerning the church organization of the Continental Anabaptists,
but in one of the best German works thus far written about
them[1], Dr Karl Rembert in a chapter entitled, "Tauferische
Gemeindeorganization in Jülich", names the following officials
who were perhaps usually to be found in an early Continental
Anabaptist congregation[2]:—"An der Spitze der Gemeinde

---

[1] "Die 'Wiedertäufer' im Herzogtum Jülich", Berlin, 1899. I do not
always agree with Dr Rembert's conclusions, but the work is in many ways
highly instructive.

[2] *Ibid.*, p. 404.

stand ein Aufseher, der den Titel 'Bischof' führte. Ihm lag die Leitung ob; seine Hauptthätigkeit bestand im Predigen, d. h. Auslegen der Schrift und im Taufen. Zur Seite standen ihm drei Diaconen, welche die Armen unter den Brüdern versorgten...." It will readily be seen that these officers were somewhat different from those of Brownists, Barrowists, and later English Anabaptists.

As soon as the Reformation in England commenced, there was naturally considerable interchange of thought between that country and Germany, the source of the Reformation, though Lutheran ideas seem seldom to have appealed particularly to the Anglican Church dignitaries. The views of the Swiss Reformers, and especially of Calvin, met with more appreciation in England. Even as early as 1536 there was published for the perusal of the English people a pamphlet of fourteen unnumbered octavo pages entitled, " ❡ A compēdious | letter which Ihon Pomeranè [Bugenhagius] cura⸗|te of the congre⸗| gation at Witten|berge sent to the | faythfull christen | congregati⸗|on in En⸗|glande." Of course this was not the only work of the kind. Many Continental books of Divinity must have been brought over into England at an early date, and their contents eagerly devoured by educated Englishmen. Sometimes the acceptance of the new views may have led to the imprisonment, banishment, or even death of those who adopted them. Thus I. B. [John Bale?] and "certayne men susspected of heresye" may have been banished in 1547, or earlier.

The idea of what may be termed a congregational church did not originate with Robert Browne. Long before he organized his "companie" in Norwich there had been congregational churches in England of certain types, but they were not exactly what we mean by the expression Congregational Church to-day, a society of separatists with a particular kind of church organization; and when Robert Browne advanced his own opinions, they naturally reflected to some extent views that had earlier been held by other English congregations.

In 1553, after the ten days' reign of Lady Jane Gray, Queen Mary came to the throne. During Mary's reign the adherents of the Reformed Church of England were placed in a most

trying position. Only those who were willing to accept Roman
Catholicism were safe. In this predicament the Reformation
leaders of the Church of England and the people who sympathized with them, we are told, were themselves "*separated
from the reste of the Lande, as from the world, and ioyned in
couenaunt, by voluntarie profession* [evidently much as were the
Scottish Reformers in time of special danger], *to obey the trueth
of Christ, and to witnes against the abominations of Antichrist,
As they also did euen vnto death, in the trueth which they sawe,
though otherwise being but as it were in the twylight of the
Gospell they had their wantes and errors...*[1]". It is said that
during Mary's reign several hundred people fled from the
country.

There was, however, a congregation composed of such
Protestant members of the Church of England that met in
and about London during the greater part of her reign. It
was finally betrayed into the hands of Bonner, Bishop of
London, about 1557 or 1558, by one Roger Sergeant, and a
very good idea of its services, etc., is to be obtained from
John Foxe's "Acts and Monuments"[2]. From certain depositions
therein contained we learn that the English service as expressed
in the second Prayer Book of Edward VI was used by this
church, which appears to have varied in numbers from twenty
to about two hundred, and to have greatly increased in size
towards the end of Mary's reign. On account of the danger of
persecution the congregation did not often meet in the same
locality. It is known, for instance, that meetings were held
"at Wapping at one Church's house, hard by the water side;
sometimes at" the house of Alice Warner, a widow and proprie-
tress of the King's head, Ratcliffe; "sometimes at St. Katherine's,
at" the house of a Dutchman named Frogg, who was a shoemaker; sometimes "at Horseleydown, beyond Battle-Bridge"

---

[1] Cited from a statement of Francis Johnson's published in Henry
Jacob's "A DEFENCE | OF THE CHVRCHES | AND MINISTRY |
OF ENGLANDE...", Middelbvrch, 1599, p. 13.

[2] "Fourth Edition : Revised and Corrected with Appendices, Glossary,
and Indices, by the Rev. Josiah Pratt, M.A.,...", London [1877 ?], 8°,
Vol. VIII., pp. 458–60, and 558–9.

" at a dyer's house, betwixt two butchers there "; and sometimes
" at the Swan at Limehouse".

The church seems to have come into existence " about the
first entry of queen Mary's reign", and " had divers ministers;
first, master Scamler, then Thomas Foule, after him master
Rough, then master Augustine Bernher, and last master
Bentham...(being now bishop of Coventry and Lichfield),..."
From this statement it is clear that the congregation was
not composed of Anabaptists, and also that they were not
separatists from the Church of England in any modern sense,
but only objected to Roman Catholic domination. As soon as
this was removed its pastor, and probably the people, returned
to the Church.

As to the services of the congregation Roger Sergeant
made the following deposition :—

Commonly the usage is, to have all the English service without
any diminishing, wholly as it was in the time of king Edward the
sixth; neither praying for the king nor the queen; despising the
sacrament of the altar, and the coming to church, saying that a
man cannot come to the church, except he be partaker of all the
evils there.

They have reading and preaching, and the minister is a Scotchman, whose name he knoweth not; and they have two deacons that
gather money, which is distributed to the prisoners in the Mar-
shalsea, King's-bench, Lollards'-tower, Newgate, and to the poor
that come to the assembly ;....

Sometimes the assembly beginneth at seven in the morning, or at
eight; sometime at nine; and then, or soon after they dine, and
tarry till two of the clock, and, amonges other things, they talk
and make officers.

Evidently some services were held " between nine and
eleven aforenoon, and from one till four at afternoon".

One William Ellerby, tailor, deposed, " that he hath been at
the assembly kept at Ratcliffe, at the King's-head, at the widow's
house there; where one Coste did read, in English, three psalms,
that is to wit, ' Confitemini', ' Magnificat', ' Nunc dimittis', upon
a Sunday, after even-song....which assembly lasted about half
an hour; some sitting at the table, some standing to hear the
said Scot, having three or four pots of beer before the said Scot
came to the assembly at Frogg's and went to the said play...".

In order to escape detection the members of this church

had to adopt measures of great precaution, as is perhaps best narrated in the deposition of Mrs Alice Warner,—

that upon a Sunday, six weeks agone, a certain company of Frenchmen, Dutchmen, and other strangers, and amongst them Englishmen, appearing to be young merchants, to the number of a score, resorted to her house of the King's-head at Ratcliffe; requesting to have a pig roasted, and half a dozen faggots to be brent. In the mean time the said company went into a back house, where they were two sundry times; the first time, between twelve and one, they were reading, but what, she cannot tell, whether it was a testament or some other book; and they tarried there about two hours. The second time was three weeks past, upon a holy-day, about the middle of the week; at which time they repaired to her house about seven o'clock in the morning, who had a fire and bread and beer within the said back house. And then this examinate, going abroad, did see the said multitude, and perceived that they also then did read, but what, she cannot tell; and the said multitude did tarry there from seven till ten before noon, and, at their departure, they laboured to this examinate that they might always have the said back house at their pleasure, to make good cheer at their repairing thither...And she saith that her maid said that she judged them to be the same that were first there; and how the said multitude called one another "brother," and did every one, to his hability, cast down upon the table money, which was two pence a piece. And this examinate saith, that she asked one of the said multitude, how the said money was disposed: answer being to her by him given, that it was to the use and relief of the poor. And this examinate thinketh it was a Frenchman, or some other outlandishman, because he spake evil English.

Among the narrow escapes from capture experienced by the members of this congregation, the following are especially mentioned:—

First, at the Black-friars, when they should have resorted to sir Thomas Carden's house,...

Again,...about Aldgate, where spies were laid for them; and had not Thomas Simson the deacon espied them, and bid them disperse themselves away, they had been taken...

Another time also, about the great Conduit, they, passing there through a very strait alley into a clothworker's loft, were espied,...

Another like escape they made in a ship at Billingsgate, belonging to a certain good man of Ley, where in the open sight of the people they were congregated together, and yet...escaped.

Betwixt Ratcliffe and Rotherhithe, in a ship called Jesus ship, twice or thrice they assembled, having there closely, after their accustomed manner, both sermon, prayer, and communion;...

Moreover, in a cooper's house in Pudding-lane,...

But they never escaped more hardly, than once in Thames-street in the night-time, where the house being beset with enemies, yet,...they were delivered by the means of a mariner, who being at that present in the same company, and seeing no other way to avoid, plucked off his slops and swam to the next boat, and so rowed the company over, using his shoes instead of oars; and so the jeopardy was despatched.

At Stoke in Suffolk there appears to have been a similar congregation[1] in or about 1558. These people were chiefly women, but there "were many", we are told, who seem to have covenanted by "giving their hands together", and to have concluded "by promise one to another, that they would not receive [the Mass] at all." To escape danger they finally fled to a place of safety. Of course it is understood that this congregation like that in London was composed of members of the Church of England who separated only from the Roman Catholic domination, and that it probably had no fixed or settled form of organization; but later reformers like Browne must have been aware of the proceedings of these earlier congregations whose existence and experiences had become known through the first (Latin) edition of Foxe's great work.

Of the English congregations on the Continent during Queen Mary's reign that with the affairs of which we are best acquainted was at Frankfort on the Main. A record of its troubles[2] was first published in 1574, twenty years after the events described occurred. Nevertheless, the story is told with great fulness and vividness, a record of discord and contention such as has seldom been depicted in the literature of modern church history. In fact, the quarrels in this congregation seem equal to, if not worse than, the troubles in Robert Browne's congregation in Middelburg, or the petty wrangling between George and Francis Johnson in the congregation at

[1] See Rev. Josiah Pratt's fourth edition of "The Acts and Monuments of John Foxe" [1877 ?], 8°, Vol. VIII., pp. 556-7.

[2] A Brieff discours | off the troubles begonne at Franck|ford in Germany Anno Domini 1554. Abowte | the Booke off off [*sic*] common prayer and Ceremonies/and conti⸗|nued by the Englishe men theyre/to thende off Q. Maries | Raigne/...", 1574, 4°, pp. ii, ccxv, i.

Amsterdam. It appears that four companies of exiles with their ministers arrived at Frankfort on June 17, 1554, and about a month later were granted permission to meet in the church used by the French congregation. In order that the service might not be too divergent from that of the French, responses to the Minister's reading, the litany, use of the surplice, "and many other thinges" that would seem "more then strange" to the Continental reformed churches, were omitted. In place of the English Confession the minister was to use one "off more effecte". After the Confession the people were "to singe a psalme in meetre in a plaine tune", and then after the minister had prayed "for thassistance off gods holie spirite", he was "to proceade to the sermon". "After the sermon / a generall praier for all estates and for our countrie of Englande was also deuised / at thende off whiche praier / was ioined the lords praier and a rehersall off tharticles off oure belieff / whiche ended the people" are "to singe and [*sic*] other psalme as afore. Then the minister pronouncinge his blessinge The peace off god / &c. or some other off like effecte / the people" are "to departe".

And as touchinge the ministration off the Sacraments sundrie things were also by common consente omitted / as superstitious and superfluous. After that the congregation had thus concluded and agreed / and had chosen their minister and Deacons to serue for a time: they entred their churche the 29. off the same monethe [July]......And for that it was thought the churche coulde not longe contynewe in good order withowte discipline / there was also a brieff forme deuised / declaringe the necessitie / the causes / and the order theroff / whereunto all those that were present subscribed / shewinge therby that they were ready and willinge to submitt themselues to the same / accordinge to the rule prescribed in gods holie word / at whiche time it was determined by the congregation that all suche as shulde come after / shulde doo the like / before they were admitted as members off that churche[1].

But some of those who subsequently came to Frankfort were more in favour of the service of the second Bock of Common Prayer used at the end of the reign of Edward VI and accordingly stirred up discord. Both parties finally agreed to submit the dispute to "5. notable men / Calvin / Musculus / Martir /

---

[1] "A Brieff discours | off the troubles...", pp. 7–8.

Bullinger / and Viret." " This condition was willingly accepted / and the couenaunte rated on bothe partes. A writinge was also theroff to testifie the promesse made off the one to the other. Moreouer thanks were geuen to god withe great ioye / and common praiers were made / for that men thought that daie to be thende off discorde. Besides this / they receyued / the communion as the sure token / or seale off their mutuall agremente / ...[1]".

Still the troubles continued and on the "laste off Feb.", " 1557" (Old Style) the Magistrate had to intervene, " and tooke order that all former offences shulde be vtterly extincte and buried in the graue off forgetfulnes. Wheruppon at the commaundement / and in the presence off this Magistrate / the parties ioined handes together in token that they were reconciled and were Good frinds and lovers...[2]". So by March 30 the new form of discipline had been subscribed by forty-two out of a total membership of sixty-two, but shortly after fresh troubles of a still more trying nature broke out. However, the election of officers under the " new discipline " was at length completed, and resulted in the choice of two ministers, six " Seniors " or elders, and four deacons.

For our purposes the articles in the old and new " Disciplines" concerning the admission of church members are of interest. In the " olde discipline " the section on this subject reads thus[3] :—

> The manner off receiuinge off all sortes off
> personnes into the saide congre‡
> gation.

Fyrste / everie one aswell man as woman which desireth to be

[1] *Ibid.*, p. 41. This is an interesting passage, as it may suggest the origin of the use of church covenants among later separatists. It is thus possible that they did not at first employ such covenants because they were used in the Apostolic or post-Apostolic churches, or even because they thought that the use of covenants was enjoined in the Bible. At any rate, this church covenant appears to have been nothing more than a compact between two parties in the congregation for settling past difficulties, and for making future disagreements between the members less likely.

[2] *Ibid.*, p. 87. In a somewhat similar manner Henry Jacob's Independent Puritan congregation in London was organized in 1616.

[3] *Ibid.*, p. 111.

receyued shall make a declaration or Confession off their faithe /
before the pastor and Seniors shewinge himselff fully to consent and
agree with the doctrine of the churche and submittinge themselues
to the discipline off the same.

The corresponding section of the "new discipline" is practically identical, with the exception of the addition of the
following words at the close, "and the same to testifie by
subscribing therto yf they can wryte". It is also to be noticed
that in the "new discipline" the final power is reserved in the
hands of the people and not of the ministers and elders.

These early Nonconformists, like the later Puritans, and like
Robert Browne, evidently did not believe in addressing questions
in baptism to infants, who could not think or speak, or in Godfathers and Godmothers. From this account we also learn that
in Queen Mary's time the German churches approved of having
one minister in a congregation superior in authority to any
others, that Calvin advocated two of equal authority in each
congregation, and that the Dutch church at Emden had three
ministers all of equal authority. There were other English
congregations in various Continental cities during Mary's reign,
as at "Arrowe" [Aarau] under Mr Leaver, at "Strausburgh /
Zurick / Densbrugh / and Emden", Basel, Wesel, Marburg on
the Lahn, and Geneva. There also seems to have been one at
Wittenberg.

The church at Frankfort on the Main, as we have already
seen, made use of an idea slightly suggesting the church
covenant idea of modern times, but it is much more plainly
manifested among the English exiles who published their
Confession of Faith at Wittenberg in 1554 under the title,
" ➋ THE HVMBLE | and vnfamed confessiõ | of the belefe
of certain poore banished | men, grounded vpon the holy Scrip⸗|
tures of God, and vpõ the Articles of | that vndefiled and
onlye vndoubt[edly ?] | true Christian faith, which [? the on⸗] | ly
Catholicke (that is to say vni⸗|uersal) Churche of Christ |
professeth. | ❡ Specially concerning, not only the | worde of
God, and the ministerye | of the same: but also the Church | and
Sacramentes | thereof. | Which we send moost humbly vn|to
the Lordes of Englãd, and al | the commons of the same. | …"

[Colophon.] "❧ From Wittonburge by Nicholas | Dorcaster. Ann. M.D.Iiiii. | [? t]he xiiii. of May."

This is an important work[1] and will repay examination. The Sacraments are defined "as substancial couenauntes & agrementes, whose nature is to declare vnto vs, some righte, title, priuiledge or gifte, that we haue or shal receiue thereby :...[2]"

The resemblance of a church covenant to a legal document is suggested in the following passage, which gives also an unusually clear presentation of the fundamental principle of such a covenant :—

In Ciuile causes the like order taketh place. Where a leace is made, it must not only be signed, sealed, & deliuered, but also receiued, and the partie put in possession : Not deliuered (I say) by euery man, but only by hym or his deputie, that hath authority to make or geue the leace : neither maye euery man receiue and ennioye it, saue only he, to whom it is made or geuen, or that hath ryght thereto. Agayne, a leace commonly is not made wythout condicions : whych if they be broken, doth not yᵉ farmer then forfeit his leace ?

And what meane we els by thys, but euen to shew that it is an horrible thing, & farre out of order, that whyle the Lord in this hys holy Sacrament [of the Lord's Supper] offreth vs so large a couenaunt of mercy, we shal thincke scorne, to kepe the condicions therof, and the rules that he hath prescribed vnto vs. No man doubtles (no not in Ciuile matters) would be so serued : wher like as it is no bargaine, till both parties be agreed, so cometh it to no perfect effecte, neither can it stand vnlesse the duties, condicions & promises be kept. Neuertheless this thing shal appeare muche more euident, if we compare the practise of these present miserable dayes, to the order of the Lord and his Apostles in the primitiue church, & lay the one agaynst the other. As for the perfourmaunce of the condicions on hys party, ther is no doubt : For wher as he couenanteth with vs in thys holy Sacrament, so to feede, nourish, & comfort our consciences, that he wyl euen seale vs vnto him selfe, set hys marke vpon vs, and take vs for hys own. He certifieth vs assuredly, that vpon such condicions, as we also vpon our allegiaunce, are bound to kepe (whych we must either do, or els become vnworthy Receauers to our damnation) we haue felowship with him,

[1] It is not an Anabaptist book as the Rev. J. H. Shakespeare, in his work "Baptist and Congregational Pioneers", pp. 37–8, mistakenly quotes the present writer as claiming.

[2] P. 54.

and are partakers of the same eternall lyfe, that he hym selfe hath purchased for vs in hys body and bloud [1].

It was not until after Queen Mary's death that Nonconformists began to secure a foothold in England. In the year 1561 appeared two works of great importance, as indicating the views with which many thoughtful Englishmen of Nonconformist inclination must have become acquainted during the next twenty or thirty years. Both were printed at London. One of them was published "according to the Queenes Maiesties Iniunctions", and was entitled: " The Confession of the | Faythe and Doctrine | beleued and professed, by the Pro⁘|testantes of the Realme of Scotlande, | exhibited to the estates of the same | in parliament, and by their pub⁘|licke voices authorised as a | doctrine, grounded vpon | the infallible worde | of God." The other is entitled "A CONFES-|*sion of Fayth, made* | by common consent | of diuers reformed | Churches beyonde | the Seas: with | an | Exhortation to | the Reformation of | the Churche". It contains the following significant paragraphs [2]:—

29   As concerning the true Churche, we beleue that it ought to be gouerned, accordyng to the policie, that our sauiour Iesus Christ hath established: that is: that there bee Pastours, Superintendes, and Deacons, to thende that the puritie of the doctrine maye haue his course, that vices maie bee corrected and repressed, and that the poore and afflicted maie bee succoured in their necessities: and that the assemblies maie bee made, in the name of God, wherein bothe greate and small maie be edified

30.   We beleue, that al true pastours, in what place so euer they be, haue equal power and aucthoritie vnder one onely soueraigne and onely vniuersall bishop Iesus Christ: and for this cause, that no Churche oughte to pretend any rule or Lordship ouer other.

31.   We beleue that none ought of his owne authoritie to thrust himselfe into the gouernement of the church, but that it ought to be done by election, for that it is possible, and God permitteth it.

When the Marian exiles returned to England they naturally hoped that their views might be well received, but they found society, and especially the Church, in a state of upheaval, and unwilling to give attention to any further changes in religious

---

[1] " ⊱ THE HVMBLE | and vnfamed confessiŏ | ..." [1554], p. 60.
[2] Fol. 109.

worship.   In spite of the new Act of Uniformity, however, Nonconformity was for some time prevalent, but "in March 1565, to make matters more secure, all the archbishop's licenses of preachers were called in, and licenses were granted only to such as proved conformable and amenable.   This, following upon the defeat of the champions [Sampson and Humphrey], was a paralysing blow to those whose religion centred round sermons from puritan [Nonconformist] divines, and who felt bound in conscience to abstain from worship where the surplice was worn.   To some of them this tyranny recalled the evil days of Mary; and remembering how then they had braved the authorities and met in secret in the heart of London itself, they began to do the same again, with the important difference that for their service they betook themselves not to the prayer-book but to the Genevan Order, a set of directions in outline for the conduct of services, which had been printed in English in 1550"[1].

It cannot have been long after March, 1565, that the Nonconformist ministers who had lost their licenses to preach began to try to find a way out of their difficulties.   About this time (1566 ?) the name Puritan first appears in English literature.   Bishop Grindal in a letter to Henry Bullinger, dated London, Aug. 27, 1566, says: "It is scarcely credible how much this controversy about things of no importance [i.e., the vestments, etc.] has disturbed our churches, and still, in great measure, continues to do.   Many of the more learned clergy seemed to be on the point of forsaking their ministry. Many of the people also had it in contemplation to withdraw from us, and set up private meetings; but however most of them, through the mercy of the Lord, have now returned to a better mind"[2].   Perhaps some such private assemblies were actually held as early as this, although such procedure was no doubt extremely dangerous.   Says Dr R. W. Dixon[3]:—"Soon

---

[1] W. H. Frere's "The English Church in the Reigns of Elizabeth and James I (1558–1625)", London, 1904, 8°, p. 127.

[2] "The Zurich Letters" (Parker Society [Vol. VII., first series]), Cambridge, 1842, p. 168.

[3] "History of the Church of England", Oxford, 1902, Vol. VI., p. 166. Unfortunately, Dr Dixon does not give his source for this information, and as yet I have been unable to discover it.

they [the Nonconformists] began to gather in larger numbers, and drew the attention of the authorities. A congregation, with Richard Fitz their minister, was surprised in the middle of this year (1567) and committed to Bridewell." "About a month later", that is, on June 19, a congregation of Nonconformists or Puritans, " to the number of a hundred", was discovered holding a private meeting at Plumbers' Hall, London, under the guise of a wedding. Seventeen or eighteen were taken prisoners and sent to the Counter. On the following day seven of the leading men appeared before the Lord Mayor, the Bishop of London, the Dean of Westminster, and " other Commissioners"[1]. They were "Iohn Smith, William Nyxson, William Wh.[ite, or Wight], Iames Irelande, Robert Hawkins, Thomas Bowelande [not Rowelande, as given by Dr Waddington and recently repeated by Dr Dale] *and* Richard Morecrafte"[2]. After their examination Dr Dixon thinks they were imprisoned in Bridewell, whither, as has already been stated, Fitz and his company appear previously to have been sent.

Besides the account of the examination of the leaders of the Plumbers' Hall society contained in "A parte of a register", one of the earliest definite statements concerning the congregation seems to be a reference in the well-known letter of Bishop Grindal to Henry Bullinger, dated London, June 11 (Latin text, June 9), 1568. The passage reads as follows:—

Our controversy concerning the habits, about which you write, had cooled down for a time, but broke out again last winter ; and this by the means of some who are more zealous than they are either learned or gifted with pious discretion. Some London citizens of the lowest order, together with four or five ministers, remarkable neither for their judgment nor learning, have openly separated from us ; and sometimes in private houses, sometimes in the fields, and occasionally even in ships, they have held their meetings and administered the sacraments. Besides this, they have ordained ministers, elders, and deacons, after their own way, and have even excommunicated some who had seceded from their church. And because masters Laurence Humphrey, Sampson,

---

[1] "A parte of a register", p. 23+, but only the Dean and the Bishop were Ecclesiastical Commissioners, as stated by Dr Dixon in a note.

[2] *Ibid.* See also "The Remains of Edmund Grindal, D.D.", Parker Society, 1843, pp. 201–16.

Lever, and others, who have suffered so much to obtain liberty in respect of things indifferent, will not unite with them, they now regard them as semi-papists, and will not allow their followers to attend their preaching[1]. The number of this sect is about two hundred, but consisting of more women than men. The privy council have lately committed the heads of this faction to prison, and are using every means to put a timely stop to this sect[2].

From this citation it seems that after a temporary lull (possibly caused by the discovery of Richard Fitz's church, as well as of the Plumbers' Hall congregation in the summer of 1567 and the imprisonment of their leaders) the controversy concerning the vestments broke out again. Bishop Grindal's letter does not make it clear through whose instrumentality this occurred, but a manuscript list (first discovered and examined by Dr Powicke several years ago in the Public Record Office[3]), the rearranged contents of which were published by him in an article entitled, "Lists of the Early Separatists"[4], makes that point perfectly plain. A copy of this worn and faded list is given, just as it stands, in the volume of documents. After a time the Plumbers' Hall prisoners had been set free. As long as they remained in prison quiet had evidently reigned, but soon after their release secret meetings again began to be held, and on March 4, 156⅞, seventy-two men and women were found in the house of James Tynne, goldsmith, within the parish of St Martin's-in-the-Fields. Among those taken were six of the first seven Plumbers' Hall leaders, while one of their number, Robert Hawkins, seems to have been

---

[1] This sentence does not in any way prove that the Plumbers' Hall congregation was truly separatist, for it is perfectly evident that its members did not separate from the State Church on the ground that the very conception of such a Church was fundamentally false, but only retired from it temporarily in order to avoid popish corruptions in the Church, which might, they felt, be noticed even at the preaching of such good men as Humphrey, Sampson, and Lever. These corruptions they hoped would soon be removed to their satisfaction.

[2] "Zurich Letters" (Parker Society, first series, Vol. VII.), pp. 201–2; Latin text at the end of the volume, p. 119.

[3] S. P. Dom., Eliz., xlvi (46).

[4] In the "Transactions" of the Congregational Historical Society (Vol. I., pp. 141–158).

B.   6

retained until April 22, 1569, or after his release to have been retaken at another time before that date.   Of those taken on March 4, 156$\frac{8}{9}$, eleven men and several unnamed women were either retained, or released and again imprisoned, while the rest, with the possible exception of Randall Partridge of Old Fish Street, were apparently set at liberty.   Partridge, as we shall learn later, became a separatist.   Finally, on April 22, 1569, twenty-four men, eleven of whose names appear to be new, and the seven previously mentioned unnamed women, were freed by Grindal.   In the list of men released on this last mentioned date are found the names of all the first seven Plumbers' Hall leaders except that of Richard Morecraft.   The list is given in full in the volume of documents, together with a promise to conform made by the Puritan preacher, William Bonham, who with Nicholas Crane had been one of their ministers[1].

The question whether the Plumbers' Hall congregation was truly separatist or not, is one of some delicacy, though I think it can now be definitely answered.   In the first place, it should be said that Daniel Neal regarded this congregation not as separatist, but as Puritan, nor do any of the best historians of the Church of England, whose works the author has examined, consider it a separatist church.   Dr Waddington even seems not to have done so, but to have differentiated between the Plumbers' Hall congregation and that of Richard Fitz.   Dr Powicke, however, has taken the view that the Plumbers' Hall congregation and Fitz's were one and the same, and Dr Dale has followed him.   A careful examination of the previously mentioned citation from Archbishop Grindal's letter, the date of the English text of which is June 11, 1568, and of the various manuscripts relating to the subject, convinces me that Dr Powicke and Dr Dale have herein been misled.

As a further proof of this contention that the Plumbers' Hall society was not composed of separatists, we find Dr Powicke himself admitting[2] that the two preachers of the

[1] See "The Remains of Edmund Grindal, D.D.", Parker Society, 1843, pp. 316–19.

[2] See "Lists of the Early Separatists", pp. 144 and 147.

congregation, William Bonham[1] and Nicholas Crane, were Puritans, not separatists, at this time, and that both of them were concerned in the Presbyterian movement of 1572. Remembering these facts and the lack of sympathy, as well as the fierce opposition, which the older Puritans constantly manifested towards separatism, it is impossible for us to believe that such preachers, as long as they remained Puritans, could have become the ministers of a separatist church. We justly conclude, therefore, that the Plumbers' Hall congregation was composed of Puritans, and that it did not truly separate from the Church of England[2].

As the previously mentioned citation from Grindal's letter, however, at first sight appears so opposed to this view, we will examine it more carefully. Grindal there, to be sure, as far as mere words are concerned, says plainly enough of the members of the Plumbers' Hall congregation, that they " have [had] openly separated from us; and sometimes in private houses, sometimes in the fields, and occasionally even in ships, they have [had] held their meetings and administered the sacraments...have [had] ordained ministers, elders, and deacons, after their own way, and have [had] even excommunicated some who had seceded from their church." If this were all the evidence on this point, we would not find it difficult to conclude at once that the Plumbers' Hall congregation was truly separatist, but as we have already seen, there is over-

[1] On May 1, 1569, just after the release of the Plumbers' Hall prisoners "William Bonam precher" was brought before Mr Thomas Hinck, Vicar-General of Bishop Grindal, and compelled to promise that he would not be present at, or preach before, any private assemblies contrary to the established religion. The text of his promise is given in full among the papers relating to Richard Fitz's congregation in the volume of documents. Bonham, of course, was a Puritan, not a separatist.

[2] The ablest historians of the Church of England appear to be unanimous on this point, as has been said in the text, nor, in my opinion, is their conclusion on this point in any way invalidated by the fact that they make little or no reference to the separatist "Privy Church" of Richard Fitz. Dr R. W. Dixon ("History of the Church of England", Oxford, 1902, Vol. VI., p. 177) well says that these early Puritans of the Plumbers' Hall congregation "had no more notion than Sampson and Lever of separating from the Church" of England.

whelming testimony to the contrary, and it should further be remembered that all the activities mentioned in this letter, even including such ordinations, could have taken place without separation.   In fact, in the later independent, non-separatist, Puritan congregations on the Continent ministers were thus re-ordained.   To Grindal, indeed, Puritan independency must have seemed as near a state of separation as he could well imagine, but in the light of all the facts known to-day it is sufficiently evident that the Plumbers' Hall congregation, as a whole, was in reality only an independent Puritan congre-gation modelled after the London Nonconformist congregation of Queen Mary's days, which did not separate from the Church of England as a State Church but merely from Roman Catholicism in the Church.   Further, this Plumbers' Hall congregation of 1567, it will be noticed, used the Genevan Order of service, as the congregation in Queen Mary's time had used the second Prayer Book of Edward VI, and therefore like it was not a Congregational, or separatist, church in the modern sense.

Some of the meetings of the Plumbers' Hall congregation, as suggested in a note by Dr Dixon[1], are without doubt mentioned in the following passage from John Stowe's "Memo-randa[2]" under the date 1567, i.e., 156$\frac{7}{8}$, where one congregation which met in different places appears to be spoken of as many congregations (= meetings of one congregation ?):—

About that tyme were many congregations of the Anabaptysts in London, who cawlyd themselvs Puritans or Unspottyd Lambs of the

[1] See "History of the Church of England", Vol. vi., pp. 175–6, note.

[2] "Three Fifteenth-Century Chronicles with Historical Memoranda by John Stowe, the Antiquary, and contemporary Notes of Occurrences written by him in the reign of Queen Elizabeth", Camden Society, New Series, Vol. xxviii., by James Gairdner, 1880, p. 143.   It will be noticed that one Brown and his followers, called "Brownings", are mentioned in this passage.   "Brownyngs" certainly suggests the Brownists.   It looks very much as if Stowe, while examining these notes at a period after 1583, mistook this Puritan Brown for Robert Browne, and added the words in parenthesis.   Otherwise these "Memoranda" appear to be fairly trustworthy records made by Stowe *about* the time at which the events described occurred.

Lord. They kept theyr churche in ye Mynorys with out Algate. Afterwards they assomblyd in a shype or lyghtar in Seynt Katheryns Poole, then in a chopers howse, ny Wolle Key in Thamse strete, wher only the goodman of the howse and the preachar, whose name was Brown (and his awditory wer cawlyd the Brownyngs), were comyttyd to ward ; then aftarward in Pudynge Lane in a mynisters hows in a blynd ally, and vij of them were committyd to ye Countar in ye Poultrye. Then aftar, on ye 29 of February, beyng Shrove Sonday, at Mountjoye Place, wher ye byshop, beyng warnyd by the constables, bad let then [them ?] alone. Then at Westmystar, the 4 of Marche, and in a goldsmythis house nere to the Savoy, the 5 of Marche, wher beynge taken to the nombar of 60 and odd, only 3 were sent to the Gatehous[1]. In many othar placis were and are the lyke. On Estar day at Hogston in my Lord of Londons mans house to ye nombar of 120, and on Lowe Sonday in a carpentars hous in Aldarman bury. It is to be noated that suche as were at eny tyme comitted for suche congregatynge were sone delyvered withoute punishemente.

In the "Calendar of Letters and State Papers relating to English Affairs, preserved principally in the Archives of Simancas. Vol. II. Elizabeth 1568–1579", London, 1894, there are three or four other passages evidently relating to these independent Puritans :—

About a week ago they discovered here a newly invented sect, called by those who belong to it "the pure or stainless religion." They met to the number of 150 in a house where their preacher used a half a tub for a pulpit, and was girded with a white cloth. Each one brought with him whatever food he had at home to eat, and the leaders divided money amongst those who were poorer, saying that they imitated the life of the apostles and refused to enter the temples to partake of the Lord's supper as it was a papistical ceremony. This having come to the ears of the city authorities, they, in accord with the Queen's Council, sent 40 halberdiers to arrest the people. They found them meeting in the house and arrested the preacher and five of the principals, leaving the others, and have appointed persons to convert them.—London 16th February 1568[2].

[1] Seventy-two men and women were taken on March 4, 156⅞, in the house of James Tynne, goldsmith, as may be seen in the volume of documents, but this passage from Stowe for some reason gives the date incorrectly as March 5. This citation, however, may rightly suggest that only three of the seventy-two captives were then imprisoned, and that as captures were frequent, only a few were imprisoned in each instance.

[2] P. 7.

Another letter written on Feb. 28, 1568, says[1]:—

I wrote to your Majesty that a new sect had been discovered; people who call themselves of the pure or apostolic religion, and that a houseful of them had been found, and six of them arrested. Another of their meeting places has been found, and six of the principal members of this congregation, too, have been arrested. I am told by a well-informed Catholic that he is certain there are 5,000 of them in this city alone.

The following further reference to the Puritans occurs in a letter written on March 14, 1568[2]:—

Orders have been given to release the people who call themselves members of the pure or apostolic religion, on condition that within 20 days they conform to the religion of the State or leave the country.

Still another reference appears under the date June 26, 1568[3]:—

In spite of the threats made to the sect called the Puritans, to prevent their meeting together, I am informed that recently as many as 400 of them met near here, and, although a list of their names was taken, only six of them were arrested, in order to avoid scandal and also because they have their influential abettors.

How long the Plumbers' Hall congregation existed before and after June 20, 1567, is not definitely known. Mr Frere says it had met for a month when it was discovered[4], but unfortunately this statement seems to be based only on the supposition, that at this early date the church of Richard Fitz and the Plumbers' Hall congregation were one and the same, —a supposition, the truth of which can be seriously questioned on account of evidence at hand, while it cannot be proved because of the dearth of further evidence. My present impression is that even in 1567 Fitz's church was separatist, and distinct from the Plumbers' Hall company. As to the length of time that the Plumbers' Hall congregation existed after the summer of 1567, it may be said with safety, that it certainly continued its activities for two years and a half[5], probably until 1572, and perhaps even longer.

[1] P. 11.   [2] P. 12.   [3] P 43.
[4] "The English Church", London, 1904, p. 127.
[5] Grindal in a letter of Jan. 4, 1569/70, complains of the continued activity of Bonham and Crane, and urges the imprisonment of at least

One point must be noticed at greater length before we leave the previously mentioned citation from Grindal's letter to Bullinger, dated (English text) June 11, 1568.   Before this time, Grindal says, there had been a secession from the Plumbers' Hall congregation, and the seceders had been excommunicated. Is it possible to ascertain who these seceders were, and why they seceded ?

Fortunately the answer to this question, I think, can be made in the affirmative.   It has already been made sufficiently evident that this congregation was not separatist, but independent Puritan, so that it would be impossible for one accurately to speak of its members as seceding into the Church of England, for its members had never separated from the State Church.   Therefore, it is manifest, that when Grindal says that some had seceded from the Plumbers' Hall congregation and been excommunicated, he cannot mean that some had returned to the services of the State Church.   On the contrary, the seceders were apparently some of the congregation who felt that even an independent Puritan position was not satisfactory, and that not only a change in the names of church officers and in vestments was needed, but that not even the second Prayer Book of Edward VI, or the Genevan Order of service should be used ; in other words, that no invention of man should find a place in church worship.   They therefore "seceded", to use Archbishop Grindal's phrase, in order to secure such worship as they desired.   Of course, this move on their part was returned by the counter-move of excommunication.

It is not easy to tell whether this secession occurred during the first or the second imprisonment of the Plumbers' Hall congregation, or even during the period intervening between them.   Fitz, and possibly some of his church, may have been in prison for all these months, and only in Bridewell may the members of the two congregations have come into contact with

twelve of the "most desperate" of the congregation in the common gaols at Cambridge and Oxford, and perhaps of some others in London prisons ("The Remains of Edmund Grindal, D.D.", Parker Society, 1843, p. 319).

each other.   Under circumstances like these some of the
Plumbers' Hall congregation may have begun to sympathize
with the separatist movement, though there was probably little
favourable opportunity to manifest their inclinations until after
April 22, 1569, when the thirty-one Plumbers' Hall conventiclers were set free.   The names of some of the seceders,
at least, are probably to be discovered by a comparison of the
names contained in the Plumbers' Hall lists with the names
appended to the petition drawn up in 1571 by Fitz's congregation, with which, I take it, the seceders united.   Of the
names of the 27 members who signed the petition of Fitz's
church, adding thereto those of Richard Fitz, Thomas Bowland,
John Bolton, Giles Fowler, and Randall Partridge, four of
whom are mentioned in the text of the document (making 32
names in all), we find only eight or nine mentioned in the
Plumbers' Hall lists, namely, John Bolton; Thomas Bowland;
Randall Partridge; Edde, or Edye, Burre, or Burris; John
Kynge, or Kinge; Jhon, or John, Leonards; Elizabeth Bamford,
or Balfurth; Elizabeth Sclake, or Slacke; and probably Eliza-
bethe Leanordes.   There are also four sets of two names each
(which may be made from the lists of the Plumbers' Hall
congregation and the list of the separatist " Privy Church "),
whose similarity suggests relationship of some kind between
their owners, as Robert Sparrow and Harry Sparrowe; Jone
Evanes and Annes Evance; James Ireland and Joane Ireland;
and Margarette Stockes and Helene Stokes.

After the addition of the seceders to the " Privy Church " of
Richard Fitz, church officers soon appear to have been chosen.
Fitz retained his position as minister, while Bolton was elected
elder, and Bowland deacon.   Whether Fitz was given his liberty
about the same time that the Plumbers' Hall prisoners received theirs is not evident, but he certainly died in prison.
Bolton and Bowland were later imprisoned for a third time, but
the date of their capture is not at present known.   Bolton[1] seems
in some way to have been persuaded to recant publicly at

---

[1] See John Robinson's "A | IUSTIFICATION | OF | *SEPARA-
TION* ", 1610, 4⁰, p. 54, and H.[enry] A.[insworth]'s " COVNTER-
POYSON ", 1608, p. 39.

Paul's Cross. Thereupon, he was excommunicated by the church, and he afterwards hanged himself. Fitz, Bowland, and Giles Fowler were evidently kept close prisoners until they died. Most of the congregation, however, appear to have been set free, and in spite of the imprisonment of their leaders lived on. Their activities are possibly referred to in a letter of Bishop Cox to Henry Bullinger, dated Ely, July 10, 1570[1], and probably described in the following passage from a letter of Bishop Horn to Henry Bullinger dated, August 8, 1571[2]:—

There are not however wanting some men of inferior rank and standing, deficient indeed both in sagacity and sense, and entirely ignorant and unknown, who, since they do not yet perceive the church to square with their wishes, or rather vanities, and that so far from agreeing with their follies, the wind is rather directly contrary, for this cause some of them desert their posts, and hide themselves in idleness and obscurity; others, shaping out for themselves their own barks, call together conventicles, elect their own bishops, and holding synods one with another, frame and devise their own laws for themselves. They reject preaching, despise communion, would have all churches destroyed, as having been formerly dedicated to popery; nor are they content with merely deriding our ministers, but regard the office itself as not worth a straw. And thus, as far as lieth in them, they are too rashly and precipitately accessory to the wretched shipwreck of our church, and are doubtless retarding not a little the free progress of the gospel. They themselves, in the mean time, wonderfully tossed about by I know not what waves of error, and miserably borne along, I know not whither, on the various gales of vanity, are reduced to the most absurd ravings of opinion. They therefore cut themselves off, as they say, from us; or rather, like Theudas, they depart with their own party, and act just like persons who, perceiving the wind somewhat against them, so that they cannot directly reach the point they aim at, refuse to reserve themselves for a more favourable breeze, but leaping out of the ship, rush headlong into the sea and are drowned.

A letter of Bishop Cox written to Rodolph Gualter as late as Feb. 12, 1571/2, seems to show that the "Privy Church" was still in existence and active[3]:—

We are undeservedly branded with the accusation of not having performed our duty, because we do not defend the cause of those whom we regard as disturbers of peace and religion; and

---

[1] "Zurich Letters" (Parker Society, first series, Vol. VII.), p. 221.
[2] *Ibid.*, pp. 248–9.   [3] *Ibid.*, p. 237.

who by the vehemence of their harangues have so maddened the
wretched multitude, and driven some of them to that pitch of
frenzy, that they now obstinately refuse to enter our churches,
either to baptize their children, or to partake of the Lord's
supper, or to hear sermons. They are entirely separated both from
us and from those good brethren of ours; they seek bye paths;
they establish a private religion, and assemble in private houses, and
there perform their sacred rites, as the Donatists of old, and the
Anabaptists now;...

Perhaps it was about this time that the members of the
"Privy Church" sent a written appeal to Queen Elizabeth in
behalf of England and signed with the names of twenty-seven
persons. The Queen seems to have handed the document
over to the Bishop of London as it bears the words "B. of
London. Puretans", and from the fact that the words "in white
Chappell streate" are written in the margin beside the first
column of signatures, it is probable that the homes of some of
the church-members, or perhaps one of the places where they
held their meetings, had been discovered, and that the members
were subsequently taken prisoners and the congregation sub-
dued or broken up. At any rate, I have as yet found no
evidence of its further continuance. Whether the two printed
papers of the church, which are now in the Public Record
Office with the appeal, were originally sent with it, is not
apparent.

Two questions need to be answered before we leave the
story of this separatist congregation of Richard Fitz: 1. What
were some of its principal views? 2. What right has it to
be called as by Dr R. W. Dale the "first regularly constituted
English Congregational Church of which any record remains"[1]?

1. The entire texts of the three extant papers of this
church are given in the volume of documents. Only the most
characteristic views, therefore, are here given. They are as
follows :—

(1) In the printed paper signed with Richard Fitz's name
the word "congregation" is not used, but the expression "the
priuye churche in London".

(2) This Privy Church had three main objects for which

---

[1] "History of English Congregationalism", London, 1907, p. 95.

BEyng thoroughly perswaded in my conscience, by the woorking and by the woorde of the
almightie, that these reliques of Antichriste be abominable before the Lorde our God,
And also for that by the power and mercie, strength and goodnes of the Lorde my God
onelie, I am escaped from y filthynes & pollution of these detestable traditions, through
the knowledge of our Lorde and sauiour Jesus Christ:
And last of all, in asmuch as by the worshyping also of the Lorde Jesus his holy spirite, I
haue ioyned in prayer, and hearyng Gods woorde, with those that haue not yelded to this
idolatrouse traditi, notwithstandyng the danger for not commyng to my parysh church.&c,
Therfore I come not backe agayne to the preachynges .&c, of them that haue receaued
these markes of the Romysh beast,

1. ℂ Because of Gods commandement, to go forewarde to perfection. Hebrew.6. verse.1?
2.Corinth.7. verse.1. Psalm.84. verse.7. Ephes.4. verse.15
Also to avoyde them. Roma.16. verse.17. Ephes.5. verse.11. 1.Thessal.5. verse.22.

2. ℂ Because they are abominations before the Lorde our God. Deut.7. verses.25.and.26
Deutero.13. verse.17. Ezekiell.14. verse.6.

3. ℂ I wyll not beautifie with my presence those filthy ragges, which bryng the heauenly
woorde of the eternall our Lorde God, in to bondage, subiection, and slauerie.

4. ℂ Because I would not communicate with other mennes sinnes. 1.John. verses.9. 10.
and.11. 2.Corinth.6. verse.17. Touch no vncleane thyng.&c. Sirach.13. verse.1?

5. ℂ They geue offences, both the preacher & the hearers. Rom.16 ver.17. Luke.17. verse.1

6. ℂ They glad and strengthen the papists in their errour, and argue the gospell. Ezekiel.13.
verses.22.and.12. Note this 21. verse.&c.

7. ℂ They do persecute our sauiour Jesus Christ in his members. Actes.9. verses.4. and.5
2.Corinth.1. verse.5.
Also they reiect and despyse our Lorde and sauiour Jesus Christ. Luke.10. verse.16.
Moreouer those labourers, whom at the prayer of the faithful, the Lorde hath sent furth
in to his haruest : they refuse, and also reiect. Math.9. verse.38.

8. ℂ These Popish garments .&c, are now become very Idolles in deede, because they are
exalted aboue the woorde of the almightie,

9. ℂ I come not to them because they shoulde be ashamed, and so leaue their Idolatrous
garments,&c. 2.Thessal.3 verse.14. Yf any man obey not our sayinges, note him.&c,

ℂ God geue vs strength styl to stryue in suffryng vndre the crosse, that the blessed woorde
of our God may onely rule, and haue the hyghest place, to cast downe strong holdes, to
destroy or ouerthrow policies or imaginations, and euery high thyng that is exalted a-
gainst the knowledge of God, and to bryng in to captiuitie or subiection, euery thought
to the obedience of Christ.&c. 2.Corinth.10 verses.4. and.5.&c, that the name and woorde
of the eternall our Lorde God, may be exalted, or magnified aboue all thynges. Psalm.
138. verse.2.

ℂ FINIS.

SEPARATIST COVENANT OF RICHARD FITZ'S PRIVY CHURCH. (*Facsimile.*)
Date between 1567 and 1571. See Vol. I., page 91.

it strove: "Fyrste and formoste", to have " the Glorious worde and Euangell preached...freely, and purelye. Secondly to haue the Sacraments mynistred purely...without any tradicion or inuention of man. And laste...to haue, not the fylthye Cannon lawe, but dissiplyne onelye".

(3) The second printed[1] paper of this church is what seems to be the separatist covenant of the congregation, though the term covenant is not used, and though the text is not expressed exactly in the terms of a covenant. The document is general and unsigned, but I imagine that every member of the church was supposed either to assent to or sign it, or other copies of it reserved for the purpose. After what I take to be the text of the separatist agreement or statement, nine reasons for separation are given with Scripture references, and at the end is a prayer for strength to continue to strive for the victory of the " word of our God ".

(4) The third and last document is a manuscript clearly written on one side of a good-sized sheet of paper, and is signed by 27 members. It is the previously mentioned appeal to Queen Elizabeth evidently written in 1571 (Old Style) stating the cause for the existence of the congregation and its reasonableness, and praying that she will follow the example of Jehoshaphat in [this] the thirteenth year of her reign by utterly overthrowing Roman Catholicism in England. The appeal manifests more spirit than the two other papers. It expresses the hope that " the word of our god may be set to raygne, and haue the hiest place, to rule & reforme all estates... to cut downe, to roote out, and vtterly destroy by the axe of the same his holy word, all monumentes of Idolatry, to wit, that wicked cannon law,...to destroy idoles temples & chapels which the papistes or infideles haue builded to the service of their godes." The congregation prays further that her Majesty may "send forth princes and ministers and geue them the booke of the Lord, that they may bryng home the people of god to the purity and truthe of the apostolycke churche ".

(5) This appeal also contains some interesting informa-

---

[1] This is not a manuscript as stated by Dr Dale ("History of English Congregationalism", p. 92).

tion concerning the Privy Church itself. It is here made plain that this "church" is only one congregation, and not more than one. Its minister Richard Fitz, its deacon Thomas Bowland, Randall Partridge, and Giles Fowler have all died in prison. John Bolton is not mentioned, nor does he sign the appeal. He had therefore probably recanted and been excommunicated before the document was written, but whether he had already hanged himself is doubtful, as such an incident might perhaps have been mentioned.

(6) Apparently the congregation met sometimes " in white Chappell streate", and it is described as "a poore congregation whom god hath seperated from the churches of englande [?] and from the mingled and faulse worshipping therin vsed". The appeal also says that "at this day [1571] we do serue the lord every saboth day in houses, and on the fourth day in the weke we meet or cum together weekely to vse prayer & exercyse disciplyne on them whiche do deserve it".

2. These are the main facts that we know about this congregation. What conclusion then may we draw from them as to Dr Dale's statement that this is the " first regularly constituted English Congregational Church of which any record remains"?

In the first place, the Privy Church certainly was separatist and congregational, but it was apparently congregational more by accident, so to speak, than because of the maintenance of any particular form of church polity on the part of its members. Also, as far as organization is concerned, was this Privy Church a regularly constituted English Congregational Church? This cannot be unconditionally answered in the affirmative. A regularly constituted English Congregational Church for the period before 1700, at least, was organized by means of a church covenant, but this congregation was not apparently familiar with that term, though it has been pointed out that the second printed document of the church is practically a separatist covenant. The real congregational church polity was only expressed later, and developed by slow evolution. This church has its part in that evolution. It was a pioneer congregation and undoubtedly made some advance over its predecessors, but not until later was organized the "first regularly constituted English Congregational Church." Richard Fitz's church was simply the earliest separatist congregation of which any considerable historical record has been preserved. Its ideal as manifested in the appeal to Queen Elizabeth appears not to have been a permanent separatist Congregationalism, but a national Church movement led by the Queen herself, her princes, and ministers, to "bryng home the people of god to the purity and truthe of the apostolycke churche", utterly to destroy and remove all relics of Roman Catholicism, and to set up what may be described as "the apostolycke churche". The congregation does not appear to have tried to formulate any church polity, or to show what constituted an apostolic church. Other matters took up their attention, and it was left to Robert Browne first to outline that religious Utopia which they longed to enjoy, but had no hope to realize.

Minute knowledge of the organizations both of Puritans and separatists at this early period is difficult to secure. Concerning the early English Classes there is considerable direct or indirect manuscript testimony still extant, but of the separatists of this period we know almost nothing. Now came the years of the publication of the "Admonition to the Parliament", and of the succeeding writings of Thomas Cartwright and Walter Travers. In 1575 Archbishop Parker died and was succeeded by Archbishop Grindal, who, had he been permitted by the Privy Council, would have allowed a good deal of variety in religious uniformity. That body, however, would not permit any tolerance on his part, and very well understood how to make him more arduous in the task of strictly enforcing uniformity. As his rigour increased the position of the Puritan leaders of course became more precarious, and requests for reformation of discipline more and more urgent. However, after the issue of Thomas Cartwright's "Second Reply" to Whitgift in 1577, there seems to have been a lull in published religious controversy between supporters of the orthodox Church of England and the Puritans and separatists until the appearance Robert Browne's first printed works in 1582.

CHAPTER III

ROBERT BROWNE AND THE ORGANIZATION OF THE FIRST ENGLISH CONGREGATIONAL CHURCH

I.

THE first Englishman of strong intellectual gifts to win distinction as a preacher of separatism and as the bold author of works which directly encouraged separation from the Church of England was Robert Browne. As we already know other English separatists had preceded him, but their influence is insignificant when compared with his. Even Richard Fitz, for instance, was practically unknown to the world until half a century ago, but the name of Robert Browne from 1582 to the present time has been a landmark in English church history, known not only in England, but also on the Continent and in America. While, however, in the past his life and real views have been much misunderstood or misrepresented, recent investigations have made possible a juster estimate of the man. He was in fact one of the most fearless and honest religious thinkers of a great age, who, though he himself receded from some of his early and more bitter opinions, left therewith such an impress on his contemporaries as to stimulate many to similar and even more advanced views long after he had returned to a comparatively conservative position.

It is not our purpose here to treat in detail all the events of Browne's life. Those who wish to know more of the recent discoveries concerning him may examine the four articles of the Rev. F. Ives Cater in the " Transactions " of the Congregational Historical Society[1], the present author's three pamphlets re-

[1] " Robert Browne's Ancestors and Descendants ", in Vol. II., No. 3, for Sept., 1905; " New Facts Relating to Robert Browne ", in Vol. III., No. 4, for January, 1906; "Robert Browne and the Achurch Parish Register", in Vol. III., No. 2, for May, 1907; and "The later Years of Robert Browne", in Vol. III., No. 5, for May, 1908.

lating to Browne[1], and Dr Frederick J. Powicke's "Robert Browne Pioneer of Modern Congregationalism", London, 1910. Only certain essential points in his career will be at present noted[2], and more particularly those that relate to the congregation which he organized, and to his general influence on, and position in, the religious history of his time.

While Browne was preaching in Cambridge in 1579, it should be remembered, he was not a separatist but a Puritan rapidly inclining towards separatism, and, though unwillingly, even had in his possession an Archbishop's license to preach. He was also offered the charge of a parish church in that town, but declined to accept it as he did not wish to be ordained by a bishop. His views at that time were undoubtedly advanced[3], but they became more pronouncedly so after Richard Bancroft, by instruction of the Archbishop of Canterbury, called upon him in his illness to take away his license. Browne promised Bancroft to preach no longer in Cambridge, but as he had heard of the prevalence of independent views (at Norwich?) "in Norfolke", he seems to have thought of going thither. His

---

[1] "The True Story of Robert Browne (1550?–1633) Father of Congregationalism including various points hitherto unknown or misunderstood, with some account of the development of his religious views, and an extended and improved list of his writings", Oxford and London, 1906, gives the most essential information. The other two pamphlets are: 'A "New Years Guift" an hitherto lost treatise by Robert Browne the Father of Congregationalism...', London, 1904, and "The 'Retractation' of Robert Browne Father of Congregationalism...", Oxford and London, 1907.

[2] The chronological scheme of Browne's life here presented is taken chiefly from the author's "The True Story of Robert Browne", 1906.

[3] In his admirable little book entitled "Robert Browne Pioneer of Modern Congregationalism", London, 1910, Dr Frederick J. Powicke states (pp. 19–21) the opinion, that Browne was a Congregationalist before he left Cambridge. In one sense he may have been, viz., in much the same sense in which any Puritan of the Cartwright type, also, may perhaps be called a Congregationalist. The same Congregational principles which Cartwright had advocated, Browne no doubt recommended at this time, as well as some still more advanced views, but I know of no saying of Browne's at this early period, which would justify us in believing that at Cambridge he enunciated such Congregational principles as would be recognized as satisfactory by the Congregational churches of to-day.

intention, however, was modified for the time by the sudden return to Cambridge of a former acquaintance, Robert Harrison, then of Norwich. The friends must already have had some ideas in common, and now they discussed together the religious difficulties of the time. Shortly after Harrison's return to Norwich, and no doubt with his approval, Browne followed him. This journey apparently took place in the summer of 1580. Longer talks now ensued wherein many questions pertaining to the condition of the Church were discussed, as for instance, what good was to be gained even from the preaching of Puritans in the Church of England, how faith was obtained, etc., etc. Harrison was with some difficulty largely won over to his friend's opinions, but he seems to have felt no little hesitation in giving up his liking for such Puritan preachers as the Rev. John More and one Mr "Robardes". Mr More was at this time the incumbent of St Andrew's, Norwich, which I have recently shown to have been practically a Congregational church in the Church of England[1]. Browne, too, no doubt attended services at St Andrew's and at first thought highly of Mr More, but later when he began to put his plans into practice, he found that More was not different from other Puritans whom he had regarded with less favour. Harrison was especially slow in detecting the defects in Mr More, and would have liked to see both him and Mr "Robardes" join in Browne's plan. Later, however, seeing that this was not to be hoped for, he loyally joined in with Browne, when perhaps about January, 1581, he began to gather his "companie" at Norwich. Among the earliest members was one Edward Tolwine[2].

[1] In "*A Tercentenary Memorial* New Facts concerning John Robinson", Oxford and London, 1910, p. 21. The same form of Congregationalism within the Church of England was very likely put into practice by Browne at Achurch, where the patronage, it will be remembered, belonged to the Browne family. In this sense Browne may perhaps be said to have really been a Congregationalist for about forty years of his life, and the old "Chapel House" would then only have been necessary for Congregational services during the period of his suspension.

[2] "The Prophane Schisme of the Brownists...", by Christopher Lawne and three others, 1612, 4°, pp. 18–9, has the following passage relating to Tolwine (see also p. 16 for Tolwine's first name) :—

Apparently not before the early spring of 1581 was complete separation undertaken. Even then the company in Norwich can hardly have numbered more than forty people, for when separatist doctrine was preached to them, some only were willing to follow Browne. Furthermore, after the congregation became separatist, still others who had adopted his latest views, were frightened by continued persecution and forsook the company. These included Robert Barker, Nicholas "Woedowes", Tatsel, Bond, and some others. Such losses seem to have made it evident that the congregation needed to be further organized, if it was to endure. So a day was appointed for the purpose and a covenant was drawn up. This church covenant was not a new invention of Robert Browne's as Dr Dexter seems to have supposed, for we know that the idea had been employed in England from the time of Queen Mary,

"THis old man (Father [Edward] *Tolwine*) being about fourescore yeares of age, the ancientist of their [the Brownists'] company [in Amsterdam], who saw the very beginning of the separation, hauing oft, of old, entertained master *Browne* into his house, where many consultations were held about this matter, before the resolution of renouncing communion with the Church of England was agreed vpon; before master *Iohnson*, or any of the *Franciscans* did dreame of this way, vpon the first separation of *Browne*, was much moued to follow him in this schisme; and when *Browne* went to dwell at Middleborough, resolued to have gone after him him [*sic*] thither; and to that end sold vp his liuing: but by the prouidence of God, before he was paid for the same, the man that bought it died suddenly,....And before he could againe take order for his iourney, he vnderstood of the great troubles among them of the separation at Middleborough; the dissolution of their compony [*sic*]; the departure of *Browne* from that place; and in fine, the departure of *Browne* from his profession also. But after this againe, the doctrine of *Browne* being taken vp and receiued by *H. Barrow*, and afterwards by *Francis Iohnson*, the mind of this old man was againe troubled by their books and writings; in so much that at length, after he had been long tossed vp and downe with the winde of their deceitfull doctrine, he left his old wife and friends, and came vnto Amsterdam, there to remaine with the *Brownists*, about some fiue or sixe yeeres agone...."

Father Tolwine afterwards came "to see the error of his schisme, and to forsake the same". We could wish that he had left some reminiscences of his experiences in separatism, as they would be invaluable to-day.

and in Scotland still earlier. The Continental Anabaptists also made use of such covenants, and some of them were better expressed and more fully developed than this of Browne's company, but it is now evident that the English and Scotch did not borrow the Church Covenant idea from the Anabaptists. Formerly, almost the entire section in "A Trve and Short Declaration", which describes the organization of Browne's congregation appeared to me to be intended to represent the text of the covenant, but now after further study that seems hardly probable, although some of the terms which are employed throughout the account are such as might have been used in a covenant. The covenant proper, therefore, as Dr Dexter believed, is evidently comprised in the first three sentences of the citation given below. The rest is merely a very exhaustive statement of how the first regularly constituted Congregational church on English soil was instituted. Of the organization of no other very early English church of this type have we so minute and complete a description :—

so a covenant vvas made & ther mutual consent vvas geuen to hould to gether.

There vvere certaine chief pointes proved vnto them by the scriptures, all vvhich being particularlie rehersed vnto them vvith exhortation, thei agreed vpon them, & pronounced their agrement to ech thing particularlie, saiing, to this vve geue our consent. First therefore thei gaue their consent, to ioine them selues to the Lord, in one couenant & fellovveshipp together, & to keep & seek agrement vnder his lavves & gouernment : and therefore did vtterlie flee & auoide such like disorders & vvickednes, as vvas mencioned before. Further thei agreed off those vvhich should teach them, and vvatch for the saluation of their soules, vvhom thei allovved & did chose as able & meete ffor that charge. For thei had sufficient triall and testimonie thereoff by that vvhich thei hard & savve by them, & had receaued of others. So thei praied for their vvatchfulnes & diligence, & promised their obedience[.]

Likevvise an order vvas agreed on ffor their meetinges together, ffor their exercises therin, as for praier, thanckes giuing, reading of the scriptures, for exhortation and edifiing, ether by all men vvhich had the guift, or by those vvhich had a speciall charge before others. And for the lavvefulnes off putting forth questions, to learne the trueth, as iff anie thing seemed doubtful & hard, to require some to shevve it more plainly, or for anie to shevve it him selfe & to cause the rest to vnderstand it. Further for noting out anie speciall matter of edifiing at the meeting, or for talcking seuerally there[t]ō, vvith some particulars, iff none did require publique audience, or if no vvaightier & more necessarie matter vvere handled of others. Againe it vvas agreed that anie might protest, appeale, complaine, exhort, dispute, reproue &c. as he had occasion, but yet in due order, vvhich Vvas then also declared. Also that all should further the kingdom off God in them selues, & especiallie in their charge & household, iff thei had anie, or in their freindes & companions & vvhosoeuer Vvas Vvorthie. Furthermore thei particularlie agreed off the manner, hovve to Vvatch to disorders, & reforme abuses, & for assembling the companie, for teaching priuatlie, & for vvarning and rebukeing both priuatly & openlie, for appointing publick humbling in more rare judgementes, and publik thankesgeuing in straunger blessinges, for gathering & testifiing voices in debating matters, & propounding them in the name off the rest that agree, for an order of chosing teachers, guides & releeuers, vvhen thei vvant, for separating cleane from vncleane, for receauing anie into the fellovveship, for presenting the dailie successe of the church, & the vvantes thereof, for seeking to other churches to haue their help, being better reformed, or to bring them to reformation, for taking an order that none contend openlie, nor persecute, nor trouble disorderedly, nor bring false doctrine, nor euil cause after once or tvvise Vvarning or rebuke.

Thus all things vvere handled, set in order, & agreed on to the comfort off all, & soe the matter vvrought & prospered by the good hand of God...[1]

From this passage we see how complete the organization of the congregation was for that early date, and how carefully all matters relating thereto had been thought out. At the time of organization Browne has been said to have been chosen pastor, and Harrison teacher, and it is possible that this was the case, though the writer in his study of the primary sources has not seen any direct statement that the titles of pastor and teacher were used at that time. It will be noticed that the members of the church prayed for the "watchfulnes & diligence" of their teachers, and, what seems a little unusual, "promised their obedience" to them, though opportunity was also to be given to the members of the congregation to "protest, appeale, complaine, exhort, dispute, reproue &c." The officers of this company as first fully organized apparently were not styled pastor, teacher, elders, and deacons, as might have been supposed, but "teachers, guides & releeuers". In "A Trve and

---

[1] "A Trve and Short Declaration", pp. 19-20.

Short Declaration" Browne does not speak of himself as pastor
until he describes "the Breach and Diuision which fell amongst
the companie" in Middelburg. Then he makes use of that
title several times. He never speaks of Harrison as teacher.

It was apparently after the company at Norwich had been
organized that Browne made journeys into the neighbouring
towns and country, evidently preaching fiercely against the
Bishops. About April 19, 1581, he seems to have been first
apprehended in the neighbourhood of Bury St Edmunds by the
Bishop of Norwich. This action was taken on the complaint of
"many godly [Puritan] preachers". His audience is said to
have numbered a hundred persons at a time and met, not with
the congregations of the Puritan preachers, but "in privat
howses & conventicles..., not without danger of some yll event".
He is reported by the Bishop to have taught "straunge and
daungerous doctrine, in all disordered manner", and to have
"greatlie troubled the whole Cuntrie, and broughte manie to
greate disobedience of all lawe and magistrates". However, the
"Chefest of such factions were so bridled, and the rest of their
followers so greatlie dismaied", that the Bishop had good reason
to hope that quiet would ensue.

No wonder the Puritans felt envious, for at least some of
Browne's hearers evidently were little more than Puritans at
heart, as is suggested by the fact that when Browne was in
prison at London, the "companie" were in favour of going
to Scotland, the home of Presbyterianism. He was obliged to
dissuade them from such a course. They then wished to go
to Jersey or Guernsey, where Cartwright and Edmund Snape
in 1576 had acted as advisers in completing the Presbyterian
organization of the churches in those islands[1]. Again Browne
had to urge his followers not to be in too great haste to leave
England.

Probably on the way back from his imprisonment in London
Browne again passed near, or through, Bury St Edmunds, and
about August 2, 1581, he was imprisoned once more by the

[1] See Mr E. le' Brun's article in the "Transactions" of the Congregational Historical Society (for May, 1907, pp. 110–13), entitled, "Puritans
and Presbyterians in the Channel Islands".

Bishop of Norwich. This time Browne is reported to have held
" priuate meetinges in such Close and secrett manner " that the
Bishop did not know how to stop them and had to write to
Burghley for " helpe in suppressinge him ", so that no further
harm might come to his Diocese, which he had mistakenly
imagined had already been brought into a state of repose.
Browne was now apparently once more imprisoned with other
leading members of the congregation, while the position of those
not in prison was made so precarious, that finally they all agreed
it was time for them to leave England.

Thus ends the first stage in the development of Browne's
congregation. It consisted largely of ardent criticism of the
bishops and of the condition of the Church of England, though
of course some constructive effort must also have been exercised
in organizing the " companie ".

II.

The next stage of Brownist separation is to be studied at
Middelburg, Zealand, whither the congregation appears to have
removed about January, 1581/2. This was the experimental
stage, the period of trial and failure, but also of literary pro-
ductivity on the part of Browne and of Harrison. Here
appeared Browne's now well-known work, composed in its
final form of three parts, bearing the general title, " A Booke |
WHICH SHEWETH THE | *life and manners of all true
Christians*, | and howe vnlike they are vnto Turkes and Papistes |
and Heathen folke. | ... Middelbvrgh ", 4°, 1582. In the first
section or work, " A Treatise of reformation without tarying for
anie,... ", Browne shows himself to believe in separation, not as
an end in itself, but rather as a means towards the ideal end
of producing a true Church of England, which should be un-
fettered by Prince, Privy Council, Parliament, or magistrate,
and the members of which should be raised to a state of all
possible perfection. He evidently was not thinking of permanent separation, but of using temporary separation as a
means of ultimately benefiting the condition of the State
Church, to which, no doubt, he hoped to return. He separated
because he believed that evil men should not be members of

the church, and if they might not be separated from it then he himself would separate, but it does not appear at all certain that he ever at that time contemplated such lasting separation as followed his action, has steadily increased in influence, and remains to this day a practically permanent element in English religious life.

The second section, which was probably written last of the three, " *A Treatise vpon the* 23. *of Mat|thewe* ", is the most scathing of all Browne's writings. Its purpose, as expressed in the latter part of the title, is to encourage people in " avoiding the Popish disorders, and ungodly communion of all false christians and especially of wicked Preachers and hirelings". Its direct influence is therefore towards separation, and people are even urged, if possible to flee from England, since the bishops are opposed to reformation of the Church, which is described as full of " Popishe disorders ". Browne as usual most savagely attacks the bishops. It is to be noticed that even Robert Harrison did not like this treatise but calls it " a pattern of all lewde frantike disorder "[1].

The third treatise has a separate title-page, much like the first, and is the most sober and constructive part of the work. Here Browne unfolds his views on Church Polity. Hitherto I have always considered that this section of " A Booke which Sheweth" was distinctly a work for (separatist) Congregationalists in the modern sense, and was, as it were, a (separatist) Congregational Church Polity, but after a very careful and critical examination of the book I have been to my surprise unable to find the slightest indication that Browne wrote this especially for the use of his own separatist congregation, or even for other separatist congregations like it. His idea seems to have been much broader than that. The work in reality unfolds what appears to have been his ideal of a true Church Polity for the use of the people of England in reforming the Church of England! It does not, therefore, offer an ideal for his own congregation alone, for separatists in general, or for a permanent

---

[1] See a citation from Harrison's letter to some one in London published in S. B.[redwell]'s "THE RASING | *OF THE FOVNDATIONS* | of Brovvnisme...", London, 4°, 1588 [1589], p. xii.

separation. This treatise may indeed be called the outline of a "spiritual and ecclesiastical Utopia", but it cannot properly be spoken of as a Utopia which Browne's church failed to realize, for it was never intended as a one congregation Utopia, or even as a general Congregational (separatist) Utopia.

In this general English ecclesiastical Utopia which Browne planned, Archbishops, Deans, Canons, and other unbiblical officials are to have no place, and even the odious name of bishop is not to be used. Everything is to be regulated by the people for the benefit of the people. Even the magistrates are to hold their positions only by the will and choice of the people. The people, and not the officers, constitute the church, they appoint the officers and on sufficient reason have the right at any time to remove them from office. A church is a single congregation which is under the immediate leadership of Christ and by his direct guidance is able in general to regulate its own affairs, though in especially important matters it may consult the opinion of other congregations, or of a Synod composed of members—not necessarily elders—of many churches. In each congregation those who are "forwardest and wysest" are apparently to be chosen by the people as elders, and the elders of a particular congregation acting in conjunction form the Eldership, whose duty it is to give redress and counsel. The people choose the other officers as well as the elders, but the elders ordain the pastor with imposition of hands, though such imposition is not absolutely essential. Browne mentions eight classes of officers, as those of Apostle, Prophet, and Evangelist, whom he groups in a division apart from the classes of "Pastour", Teacher, Elders, "Releeuers" or Deacons, and Widows. The elders collect the votes when the congregation is electing its other officers. Discipline is to be employed for the redress of abuses, but the expression "to give over to Satan" does not appear. The whole church is the ultimate authority in administering discipline, but the elders are to attend to minor cases. The above appear to be the principal views expressed in "A Booke which Sheweth".

The question may naturally be asked here, Would not the prosecution of such a plan only have involved all the people of

England in a species of separatism (even more marked than that of to-day), in which church-individualism would have been developed to such an extent that there would have been no church unity except in so far as each church would be under the direct control of Christ ? How then would these churches be any less separatist than are modern Congregational churches, or in other words, How can Browne have intended that there should be any State Church resulting from such a plan, or where in his scheme is any element of unification to be discovered ?

Such questions are pertinent, and certainly the answer is not too clearly delineated in the third treatise of " A Booke which Sheweth ". In fact, the realization of Browne's hopes for an ecclesiastical Utopia in England probably seemed so far distant at that time, that he had as yet not clearly thought out all the practical difficulties which would naturally arise in putting his views into practice. However, I think we can find in the three treatises of his first book taken together some elements which may aid us in answering the above questions.

In my opinion, Browne had no intention of instituting any permanent separation of all churches from one another. The idea of a State Church doubtless seemed to him as desirable as to any other English citizen. He would not destroy or secularize the churches because of any connection which they may formerly have had with Rome. He would undoubtedly have used the Parish church buildings, practically as they stood, for his congregational churches, as any Puritans of the time would probably have wished to do. He even mentions Synods as a justifiable means of settling unusual difficulties in the churches. Such Synods, of course, would have formed some bond of union between the different congregations, but in his congregational system Synods are not especially emphasized. We must, therefore, look further for a satisfactory solution of the problem.

It will be noticed that Browne makes little particular mention of the civil magistrate in the third treatise, but in the first, " A Treatise of Reformation ", he defines the relation of the magistrate to the Church in the following words[1] : " We knowe

---

[1] Rev. T. G. Crippen's edition, London, 1903, pp. 26–7.

that Moses might reforme, and the iudges and Kings which followed him, and so may our Magistrates : yea they may reforme the Church and commaunde things expedient for the same. Yet may they doo nothing concerning the Church, but onelie ciuile, and as ciuile Magistrates, that is, they haue not that authoritie ouer the Church, as to be Prophetes or Priestes, or spiritual Kings, as in all outwarde Iustice, to maintain the right welfare and honor thereof, with outward power, bodily punishment, & ciuil forcing of men.   And therfore also because the church is in a common wealth, it is of their charge : that is concerning the outward prouision and outward iustice, they are to look to it, but to compell religion, to plant churches by power, and to force a submission to Ecclesiastical gouernement by lawes & penalties belongeth not to them,..." . May it not be then, that even at this period, Browne felt that the power of the civil magistrate was one great force, which, *when properly limited,* might be used as a means of keeping the churches under state control, and so of ensuring in them a reasonable amount of unity in belief and practice[1] ?

After the breach between Browne and Harrison in 1583, Harrison undertook to expound his views in two books, which are, however, much less important than those of Browne.   One of them may have been produced to counteract the influence of Browne's publication, perhaps also to give peaceable people a more sober view of the opinions of early English separatism. The first of these two books was " A LITTLE | *TREATISE vppon the firste* | Verse of the 122. Psalm. | Stirring vp vnto carefull | desiring & dutifull labou*|ring for true church* | Gouernement. | ... | 1583."   In the following passage from the Epistle " To all our Christian Brethren in Englande,..."[2], Harrison gives an account of his experiences in separatism, and his reasons for writing this book :—

M Y state is known vnto manie of you...how that of certaine time...I haue striuen, and withstood the yoke of spiritual bondage in the worshippe of God,...From the which that I might bee

---

[1] Browne's view of the usefulness of civil magistrates is made more evident in " A New Years Guift ", as will be seen in the first note in the next chapter (IV.).

[2] Pp. iii–v.

deliuered (the Lorde God the searcher of heartes I take to recorde) that it haue bene myne onlie quarrel, and the cause of stirring me vp to do that, which I did. Concerning the whiche cause, I did not thinke it lawefull for mee (though I coulde haue escaped in tyme ynough) to withdraw my selfe into any other place, for myne owne liberties sake, vntill I had more openly witnessed the same cause. which when it seemed good vnto God, that I with some others should doo, by abyding imprisonment a certayne time : Then hauing offered our selues to suffer whatsoeuer our vexers should lay vpon vs, and espyinge nothing like to be done vnto vs, but to bee holden with lingering imprisonement, and that without libertie of communicating vnto others the instruction of the same cause, which we professed : we thought good rather to vndergoe some exile (as it were) for redeeming at least some libertie of worshipping God with safetie of conscience. which when we did, and diuers of our Brethren, which were willing to come vnto vs were restrayned : and we were per-suaded, that to returne vnto them thither, whereas by imprisonment we should againe be holden from them, would little auayle : I haue iudged that we haue bene debters to them to bestow vpon them some thing which might helpe to increase their spirituall courage and comfort. In which behalfe, when the expectation of me and diuers others rested vpon some, who in the ende did but slenderlie answere, and satisfie the same : Then I, which for my vnworthines and poore gifte, hadde thought neuer to haue set foorth any thinge publikely, yet was prouoked to indeuour my selfe, in some parte, as farr as the Lord should make me able, to satisfie that want, which I thought to be great. And I went about a piece of work touching Church gouernement. But partlie by sicknes, & partly by weying the cost of the print, and findinge it to be aboue my reache of abilitie : I was hindered, and haue let staye that worke, vntill the Lorde further inable mee.

In the meane tyme I thought good to write some other little treatse [*sic*] and I chose this 122. Psalme,...Agayne, sicknes and other causes cutting me short : I was constreined to ende at this time skarce finishing the firste verse....

Harrison has the following veiled reference to Robert Browne :—

And of late an other attempt haue bene giuen that waie by one of whom I must needs saie, that the Lord vsed him as a meanes to bringe the trueth to light, in manie points concerning the true gouernement of the Churche : who, I wish for the glorie of God, if it had ben his good pleasure, that he had stoode in integrity, without swaruing and leaninge to Antichristian pride, and bitternes. And for me to make thereof, may seme very hard, which am not so able therin to saue my self from the reproch of manie tongues, as I am to cleare my selfe of the deseruing the same...[1]

---

[1] Sig. D₂ verso.

Perhaps on account of the necessity of securing a new pastor to take the place made vacant by Browne's departure, the question of succession in the ministry seems to have been prominent in Harrison's mind when he wrote this book, for he says[1]:—

And moreouer, whereas they tie the Ordination of euerie Minister, as it were, vnto the girdle of other Ministers, that of necessitie it must at all times depende and staie vppon them : that is to laie a greater bondage vpon ye churches, then they are able to beare. For admitt there be onelie one church in a nation, and they want a pastour : must they seeke ouer Sea and lande, to gett a minister ordained by other ministers? But what if there shoulde be but only one apparent to vs in the world : shall that church for euer be depriued, after they haue once wanted a minister, for default of authoritie to call and ordaine an other? By this reason, euery church should not be perfect in it selfe, nor haue in it selfe meanes and power to continue by that measure of lines which the Lord haue measured out vnto it. And is it not a dishonour to Christ Iesus the head of euery congregation, which is his bodie : to say that his body together with the heade, is not able to be sustained and preserued in it selfe?

It appears from these citations that Harrison had been preparing for the press a work " touching Church gouernement", but that he had been constrained to give it up until a more favourable time. This undertaking he seems never to have carried out, although he published a small pamphlet of sixty-four pages in 1583 (i.e., before March 25, 1584) entitled, "Three Formes of Catechismes, conteyning the most principall pointes of Religion."

Before, or just after, Browne left Middelburg it seems probable that he also published "A Trve and Short Declaration". This is an exceedingly important autobiographical writing, and the preservation of a single copy of it has greatly helped in the final reconstruction of his life and in making plain his early aims. It clearly shows that his motives were good and awakens in the reader a sympathy for him in his troubles. This work shows further that Browne had developed strong separatist convictions before he left Holland[2].

Having examined the works of Browne and Harrison

---

[1] Sig. E$_2$ recto.

[2] This point should be kept in mind in order that it may be contrasted later with Browne's opinions as set forth in his "Retractation".

produced during the years 1582 and 1583/4 we may now briefly turn to certain points in the history of their church during that period. In the first place, it now appears unlikely that Browne's congregation on its arrival in Middelburg joined Cartwright's church, for, as we shall see later, Cartwright probably had not yet arrived in that city; or that after Browne's departure Harrison and the remnant with him joined it. It seems much more likely that Cartwright in his letter to Harrison[1] means that Browne's company had once been Puritans and members of the Church of England, but had become separatists, and that he had hoped they would now return to the Church of England by joining his congregation in Middelburg.

As to the explicit statement made by Dr R. W. Dale[2] that sixty of the company in Norwich came to Holland with Browne and Harrison, it seems more reasonable to believe that the Middelburg congregation, even at its maximum size, can hardly have comprised more than thirty or forty persons. In the first place, Harrison suggests that not all the church in Norwich went to Holland, but that "diuers" were "restreyned", and that the leaders, who had succeeded in reaching Middelburg, thought it would be of little use to return to England on their account. In the second place, the whole congregation in Norwich after so brief an existence and amidst ever increasing dangers can hardly have numbered more than sixty people. Again, Browne himself tells us that the congregation in Middelburg met in his chamber, which in his circumstances, one would think, could hardly have been large enough to accommodate so many. Finally, Browne never represents the congregation as at all large. He names the following persons in "A Trve and Short Declaration" as members of the Middelburg congregation,—Robert Browne (the pastor) and his wife; Robert Harrison, his sister, and probably his brother, William Harrison; Charles Munneman or Moneman (Moneyman?); John Chandler[3];

---

[1] Published in Robert Browne's "An Ansvvere to Ma:|STER CART-VVRIGHT HIS | *LETTER FOR IOYNING* with the English Churches: ..." [1585 ?], 4º.

[2] In his " History of English Congregationalism ", 1907, p. 125.

[3] John Chandler and his wife Alice became members of John Green-

and Tobie Henson. Most of these were Browne's opponents, and he gives the names of none of his supporters except that of his wife, but when he left Middelburg we know that there went "in companie with him 4, or 5 englishmen and their wives, and fameleis"[1]. Even such a slight withdrawal probably made a considerable decrease in the size of the congregation.

This estimate is of course contrary to the testimony of the following passage in Dr Edward Stillingfleet's "*The Unreasonableness of Separation...*[2]:—

When those who were called *Brownists*, from the freer Exercise of their *new Church way*, withdrew into the *Low-Countreys*, they immediately fell into strange Factions and Divisions among themselves. *A.D.* 1582. *Robert Brown*, accompanied with *Harrison* a *School-Master*, and about 50 or 60 Persons, went over to *Middleburgh*, and there they chose *Harrison Pastor*, and *Brown Teacher*. They had not been there *Three Months*, but upon the falling out between *Brown* and *Harrison*, *Brown* forsakes them, and returns for *England*, and Subscribes, promising to the *Archbishop*, *To live Obediently to his Commands*.

But Dr Stillingfleet's work was not first published until 1681, and no copy of the book from which he is supposed to have gathered his information has yet been discovered. Furthermore, even this source was not written until about fifty years after the events described. It will be noticed that Stillingfleet does not, like Dr Dale, say that 60 people accompanied Browne, but "about 50 or 60 Persons". This estimate appears to be nearer the truth than Dr Dale's, but even this is probably not perfectly accurate, though we might more easily accept it if we could be sure that the rest of the statements in the above-cited passage were correct. There are, however, at least two points in it to be seriously questioned, for we know from "A Trve and Short Declaration" that Browne's congregation

---

wood's congregation in London in 1587 and were taken prisoners on Oct. 8 of that year. John Chandler died in the Poultry Counter, London, before May, 1589, leaving his widow and eight children. She was released from prison on bail after his death.

[1] See "The True Story of Robert Browne", Oxford and London, 1906, p. 28.

[2] P. 48. The facts presented in this passage are taken from "Stephen Offwood's *Advertisement to* John De lecluse *and* H. May, p. 10, 39". This was published in, or probably not long before, 1633.

chose their officers in Norwich, not at Middelburg, and that Harrison was certainly not elected pastor while Browne was in Middelburg. These two inaccuracies are sufficient to make us question any other unwarranted affirmations in this passage.

The dissensions in Browne's church are already familiar to students, as well as the fact that Mrs Browne was at least partly their cause, but there is one point related to these troubles, which may not have been previously noticed, namely that the "ado" about Mrs Browne seems to have been concerned with "the povver & authoritie vvhich the Husband hath ouer the Wife"[1]. Here then in Middelburg evidently began Browne's matrimonial troubles, which appear to have embittered him during the greater part of his married life. In fact, there is a further passage in "A Booke which Sheweth"[2] which may throw considerable light on Browne's marital difficulties at Achurch. This section discusses the covenant between husband and wife and draws a distinction between what he calls the covenant of communion of marriage and the covenant of communion of government, and states that if one party in marriage insists on holding to a false religion the other may depart from the first and not be held in bondage.

One other point ought to be mentioned here, namely, that Harrison thought he had certain real grievances against Browne during the latter's sojourn in Middelburg. In a letter written to some one in London Harrison says with a good deal of bitterness[3]:—

In deede the Lorde hath made a breache amongst vs, for our sinnes haue made vs vnworthie to beare his great and woorthie cause. M. B.[rowne] *hath cast vs off, and that with the open manifesting of so many and so notable treacheries, as I abhorre to tell, and if I should declare them, you could not beleeue me. VVhich because this sheete and many moe would not suffice to rehearse, I will meddle with no particular thing, to declare it. Onely this I testifie vnto you, I am well able to proue, that Caine dealt not so ill with his brother Abel, as he hath dealt with me. Againe towards the ende of that letter, hee writeth thus. Also I would admonish you to take heede howe you aduenture your selfe to be a meane, to spread abroade any of that*

---

[1] In "A Trve and Short Declaration".

[2] Sig. K₂ verso.

[3] In S. B.[redwell]'s "THE RASING | *OF THE FOVNDATIONS* | of Brovvnisme", 1588, p. xii.

parties bookes, except it were more tending to the glorie of God then it is.   For in the first booke there is manifolde heresie: and the other vpon the 23. of Matthewe, is a patterne of all lewde frantike disorder, whoso haue eyes to see it.   And I do not doubt but that the Lord will yet driue him on to worse and worse,...

Undoubtedly there were two sides to this controversy and probably Browne as well as Harrison should be blamed for the troubles in Middelburg.   Indeed, if Browne had not written "A Trve and Short Declaration" one might be inclined to take sides entirely with Harrison, but in that little autobiographical writing Browne states his case so clearly and openly as to arouse sympathy for him in a contest in which, if he made mistakes, he had few to befriend him and help his cause.   George Johnson evidently did not sympathize with Browne's defence of himself, but people to-day will probably take Browne's part.   We may indeed deplore these internal dissensions in the church, and wish that they might have been avoided, but the Middelburg congregation like that of the Marian exiles at Frankfort, seems to have become a veritable hornet's nest.

III.

On leaving Middelburg, as is well known, Browne journeyed to Scotland, where he arrived early in January, 1583/4.   Here he seems to have remained for some months.   He still maintained his separatist ideas, for his "companie" is said to have "held opinioŭn of separatioŭn from all kirks where excommunicatioun wes not rigorously vsed against open offenders, not repenting", but though the Kirk interfered with the freedom of his movements, the King, apparently in order to spite the Kirk, for which he never had much liking, seems not to have molested him.   However, while Browne saw much of Scotland, he certainly spent some time in prison, for in writing his reminiscences of his Scottish visit in "A New Years Guift" five years later, he says: "in Scotland, the preachers hauing no names of byshops did imprison me more wrongfully then anie Bishop would haue done"[1].   That his imprisonment was not brief may perhaps be inferred from the aversion with which he speaks of the Presbyterians' "Lordlie Discipline".

[1] P. 27 of the edition published at Memorial Hall, London, in 1904.

Indeed, Browne may first have begun in Scotland really to dislike Presbyterianism. Before that time, to be sure, he had become aware that those who had caused his earlier imprisonments were Puritans. But now he began to understand what a fully developed Puritanism would mean, and to see that hidden under this gentle title lurked a tyranny less tolerant even than that of his old foes, the bishops.

As to Browne's success in disseminating his opinions in Scotland very little can be said. The Scotch mind was at that time even less prepared than the English for innovations in religion, and though King James speaks in the preface of his "ΒΑΣΙΛΙΚΟΝ ΔΩΡΟΝ", London, 1603, as if he was exceedingly sorry that Browne ever came to Scotland to sow his "popple" and to leave "schollers behinde" him, there appears to be no reliable evidence whatever that Browne's religious propaganda made any lasting impression in Scotland, and it is to be presumed that none of his followers found it worth while to remain in that country in order to complete any work he may have begun.

IV.

When Browne crossed the Scottish border on his way to Stamford, he must have felt that he was once more entering a free land. However, his stay in that town at this time was apparently brief. Whether he ever visited Norwich again is not known. Such a return would have been natural, for here, as we learn from the testimony of Robert Harrison, some of Browne's congregation had been restrained, and it is to be remembered that up to this time Browne still maintained his separatist principles. He therefore may soon have found his way to this ancient and historic city. It is quite possible too that from the remnant of the company in Norwich he first gained access to Cartwright's letter to Harrison after it had been circulating in other men's hands for five or six weeks. From here, too, he could have found the easiest approach to the sea-coast, in case he made a second journey "beyonde sea"[1].

[1] That Browne may have made a second voyage "beyonde sea" is suggested by the words, "For before my first voiag beyond sea, & sence

This seems to me now to be a more natural theory than that expressed five years ago in " The True Story of Robert Browne ", suggesting that he passed through London. The manuscript written in answer to Cartwright could easily have been sent to friends in London either by Browne himself or by members of the congregation in Norwich. However this may be, there is excellent proof, as is well known, that the Brownist congregation in Norwich had a continuous existence from 1582 until 1603, and probably later.

We may now return to a consideration of Browne's answer to Thomas Cartwright's letter to Harrison. In this Browne shows himself once more to have been fired with zeal for defending the cause which he had launched. He set laboriously to work, neatly and finely penning the folio sheets on which he wrote, until he had covered forty pages. To be sure, it seems that his views had grown a little less rigid, but still he defends the way of separation against " the ordinarie abused assemblies of false professors ", but denies that " we geue all the English

my last retourne ", which occur in " A New Years Guift ", p. 27, of the Memorial Hall edition published at London in 1904 ; and our information concerning its date is drawn from the fact that Browne, in stating to Stephen Bredwell his reservations relating to his subscription of Oct. 7, 1585, says, that his first child " was baptized in England he being beyonde sea " (See my " True Story ", 1906, p. 39). Mr Cater (" Robert Browne's Ancestors and Descendants " in the " Transactions " of the Congregational Historical Society for Sept., 1905, p. 155) assigns Feb. 8, 1584/5, as the date of the baptism of Browne's first child, Jone. Granting this to be correct, and knowing, as we do, that Browne was in Scotland in 1583/4, we must draw the inference that Browne had left England and probably the British Isles for a second time before Feb. 8, 1584/5. That Browne had returned to England with his wife in the autumn of 1584, and thence set out on his second voyage, I infer from the probability that his wife was with him in Scotland in 1583/4, and that she had her second child, Anthony, baptized at Stamford on May 10, 1585. He would hardly have allowed his wife to journey home alone from Scotland at that dangerous period of history. The truth of this theory of a second voyage depends very much on the correctness of the investigations of the Rev. F. Ives Cater. Should he have been mistaken as to the baptismal records of Browne's children, this theory might have to be abandoned. On the point of Browne's second voyage the reader should also consult Dr Powicke's " Robert Browne " [1910], pp. 39–40.

B.   **S**

assemblies, the black stone of condemnation ". The separation which Browne now advocated may, therefore, perhaps be termed conditional separation such as he might relinquish under changed conditions. The manuscript which he wrote is still preserved as it was apparently found at the press where this last of Browne's works published in his lifetime was printed. Save for some fading of the ink, it is in an almost perfect state of preservation, and still bears the marks probably made by the printer to indicate the ends of the various pages of the work as published. The manuscript is in Lambeth Palace Library[1] where it was practically lost on account of its not being entered in the index to the catalogue of manuscripts. It was first brought to the attention of students four years ago[2], and is entitled "An answere to M[r] Cartwrights Letter, for Ioyninge | with the English Churches". This work is particularly interesting to one who wishes to study the evolution of Browne's views, for therein he opposes certain of Cartwright's opinions[3] which later in his "Retractation" he adopted as his own. This answer with Cartwright's letter was apparently published without Browne's knowledge at London some time before May 16, 1585 under the title, "An ansvvere to Ma⸗|STER CART-VVRIGHT HIS | *LETTER FOR IOYNING* | with the English Churches:..."

On October 7, 1585, Browne made his subscription to the Archbishop of Canterbury, and though he had various reservations in mind[4] when he signed this document, it nevertheless appears to mark a turning point in his career, as is evident from subsequent events.

We may now direct our attention to the remnant of Browne's congregation which remained at Middelburg under Harrison's guidance. When Harrison died, or when the congregation at Middelburg was disbanded, is not exactly known. Harrison

---

[1] Press-mark, MS. 113 (12).

[2] In the author's "The True Story of Robert Browne".

[3] Cited in "The True Story of Robert Browne", pp. 34–5.

[4] But Browne can hardly have dared to mention any reservations to Archbishop Whitgift, contrary to the suggestion in "The True Story", p. 58, note.

certainly died before 1589[1], and from the fact that he published
no books after 1583, we may infer that he probably did not
live more than a year or two after the time of Browne's departure
for Scotland.   Indeed, Harrison's illness or death may account
for Browne's answering Cartwright's letter to Harrison in 1584
or 1585.   George Johnson[2] mentions the "pride of Mr Brovvnes
wife/and the other weomen in the banished English Church at
Middelburgh" as being "a great cause of disagreement betweene
Mr Harison and Mr Brovvn", and asks "whether it was not the
cause of Mr Harrisons death by inward griefe/who knoweth?"
"Yea some have so judged/and spoken", he adds.   Henry Ainsworth in his "Covnterpoyson", 1608, says[3]: "*Mr Harrison*
returned not vnto your church of England; but died at *Middleburgh* in this faith [of separation] that we professe".   The account
of Harrison in the Dictionary of National Biography, which
appears to be inaccurate concerning one or two points, suggests
that he died about 1585, a very good conjecture.

In 1603 nothing seems to have remained of Browne's congregation at Middelburg.   Says George Johnson[4], "remember
what is become of Brovvn and his company, who excommunicated them that rebuked pride among them/and Mr Brovvns
abusing his learning to dawb vp the same: not a man of them
remaineth faithfull: hath not the Lord svvept them avvay, as
a man svveepeth avvay dung, till all be gone?..."

V.

We now have before us an outline of the history of the first
Congregational church at Norwich and Middelburg.   Very
little is known about most of the English Nonconformist and
separatist congregations which preceded it.   Of these, we are
best informed concerning the congregation of the Marian exiles

---

[1] This is clearly indicated in the "Epistle Dedicatorie" of S. B.[redwell]'s
"THE RASING...", 1588, p. xii.

[2] In "A discourse of some troubles/...", 1603, p. 7.

[3] Mr Arber ("Story of the Pilgrim Fathers", London, 1897, p. 137)
claims that "This is quite a new fact" concerning Harrison.   This
passage, however, is quoted by Hanbury in his "Historical Memorials
Vol. I., p. 172.

[4] In "A Discourse", p. 20.

at Frankfort on the Main.   No account of the activities of this church, however, was published before 1574, so that Richard Fitz and his predecessors may have been little acquainted with its internal affairs.   Browne, on the other hand, must have been familiar with the record of its troubles, and, though his views on church polity evidently were not derived from that narrative, the very completeness of the organization of his own "companie" testifies to such a probability.

Compared with Browne's congregation in point of organization that of Richard Fitz was probably but as a shadow, and in point of the literary activity of its members it is hardly worth mentioning.   The only strong resemblance between the two churches appears to lie in the purpose which actuated their organization.   They were both composed of separatists, but certainly Fitz's congregation, as has already been seen, was not regularly constituted as a Congregational church of the present-day type.   Browne's church, on the other hand, stands out in a class by itself.   Browne at this early stage of his career may certainly be called a pioneer of *modern* Congregationalism, though a long period of evolution intervenes between him and the Congregationalists and Independents of to-day.

Browne, too, although he was considered unimportant in his own time, deserves a place among the literary men and religious leaders of his day, beside Richard Hooker, Walter Travers, and Thomas Cartwright.   Church historians and other writers in the past have found Browne a puzzle and have had little faith in his sincerity.   The Congregationalists even have said some hard things concerning him and have sometimes appeared ashamed to admit that he was in any way related to them.   To counteract such feeling Dr Dexter invented the ingenious theory that Browne became insane in later life,—a theory the falsity of which, it is hoped, has already been made sufficiently manifest.   Dr Leonard Bacon, it has been said, never could understand why the Congregationalists should claim Browne as their earliest pioneer.   As a matter of fact the connection is rather indirect, but of course history cannot be altered merely to accord with one's preferences.   And after all there is no need to be ashamed of Browne, for as a young man he was one of the keenest religious thinkers of his time. He undoubtedly was somewhat rash and impulsive in his earlier years, and he was a bold, fearless preacher, but he urged his congregation to more moderation in times of danger, and he was willing to suffer many imprisonments for his beliefs. He had also an honest, earnest spirit. The troubles of the period in which he lived were a heavy burden to his peace of mind, and he tried his utmost to do what he believed would help his country. Best of all, Browne learned from experience and gained wisdom with age, as who will not admit who observes the kindly spirit that characterizes his " Retractation " and " A New Years Guift "? No wonder Bredwell in 1588 could not understand him, for already the old Browne had vanished, and the new Browne was worthy of a larger place than either his contemporaries, or his successors were, or thus far have been, willing to give him.

CHAPTER IV

THE RISE OF THE BARROWISTS

BETWEEN the years 1586 and 1592 Nonconformist ideas became still more prevalent in and about London. Here, soon after his acceptance of the Head Mastership of St Olave's Grammar School, Robert Browne began to sow the seeds of Puritan discontent. Stephen Bredwell has recorded that Browne sometimes attended meetings in private houses and on one occasion at least preached before such an assembly, but it is improbable that he organized any congregation about London, though he is said to have preached to " certaine people " " in a Gravel-pit neare *Islington*"[1], and though his opinions certainly

---

[1] Ephraim Pagitt's " Heresiography ", fourth edition, London, 1647, p. 55. Very likely the " people " to whom reference is here made were the Barrowists, who probably began to hold their meetings in London late in the summer or early in the autumn of 1587. The ground on which Browne justified his private preaching is doubtless to be seen in "A New Years Guift ", written on Dec. 31, 1588. By this time Browne's views had become much clarified, and after formal separation he had found his way back into the State Church. For the Hierarchy of Archbishops and Bishops he had little or no more reverence than before, but his opinion of the importance of the civil magistrate had been much expanded and was much more clearly defined, as may be seen in the following citations from the Memorial Hall edition of "A New Years Guift ", London, 1904, pp. 30–32 :—

" If then it be demaunded who shal call & consecrat Ministers, excommunicat, depose & put downe false teachers & bad fellowes, & iudg in a number of ecclesiastical causes, let the word of God answere, which appointeth the cheifest & most difficult matters to be iudged by them of cheifest authoritie & guifts. & other matters of inferior gouernours Exod. 18. 22. 1 Cor. 6. 5. Rom/. 12. 3. If it be asked who be of cheifest guifts or ought to haue cheifest authoritie, I answere that the ciuil Magistrates haue their right in al causes to iudge & sett order, & it is intollerable præsumption for particular persons to skan of euerie Magis-

appear to have encouraged those who came in contact with him to be lax conformists, if not separatists. In fact, for some time after his departure from London Browne's influence seems to have been felt. We find, for instance, that Christopher Diggins of St Olave's parish, Southwark, where Browne lived for a time, deposed on April 3, 1593, that he had "not come nor repaired to any parishe Churche to heare devyne service these two yeres", i.e., since the spring of 1591, and George Knifton, one of the two elders in Johnson's congregation, also in 1593, directly ascribes to Browne the beginning of his Nonconformity.

trats guifts or authoritie or to denie them the power of iudging ecclesiastical causes..."

"If againe it be saied, that while men might take & refuse their ministers as they list, all factions & heresies might grow / I answere that the ciuil Magistrat must restraine that licentiousnes. But the way to restraine it is præscribed of God /. First that a number of vnlawful ministers being now descried & made manifest to the world, that the Magistrats if they can not remoue them, do yet quietly suffer the people to fall away from them, which if they do not suffer, there will be in tyme, ten fould more factions & diuisions then otherwise there should be,..."

"Thirdly that for auoiding heresies & strange opininions [*sic*], none be admitted or suffered to refuse or withdrawe them selues which hould not the doctrine of christianitie after some exacter forme of catechisme, & be also able to geiue a good reason of their religion & profession in all such matters /. And that therefore if they haue conference, readings or expositions, in priuate houses, the officers appointed for that purpose do serch & trie their opinions & doctrine & see their orders / & if nothing be erroneously & disorderedlie attempted, that they be suffered, yea though some smaller fault or error be committed or escaped, yet if a greater fault happen, that they be punishable accordingely.

"Lastly, that none be suffered to haue their voice or right in chosing church offices & officers but onely such as are tried to be sufficiently grounded & tried & to be able to geiue a reason of their faieth & religion / And that the ciuil Magistrats may if they will, be both present & directers of the choise, yet permitting anie man to make iust exceptions against them which are to be chosen[.] Further that they which are to ordeine, consecrate or pronounce them authorised, do it not in their owne name, but by voice & testimonie of the most of those wyser sort, whose consent & voices for the most part he hath gathered & doth shew. Also it skilleth not who do pronounc[e] & consecrate them whether Bishop or other, so that it be according to the forme aboue mencioned & the partie be a wise & good man /,..."

Browne, however, it will be noticed did not commend separation to him :—

[Knifton] saythe he hath had conference with M[r] Browne whoe perswaded him not to recive the Communyon and synce hath had conference with Barrowe with Greenewood and with Penry and was made Elder about half a yere since [in September, 1592] and that he misliketh Cartwrights plan [?] of Church goverment[1].

John Dayrell in " A TREATISE OF | THE CHVRCH. | VVRITTEN AGAINST | them of the Separation, commonly | called BROWNISTS. |... ", London, 1617, says,—" your *seperation* [probably referring especially to Francis Johnson's congregation] *is as auncient as Browne,* who first caused, or at least greatly furthered that seperation and schisme from our Church : where vpon you are called *Brownists*"[2].

In view of the work already done by Dr Dexter, Dr Powicke, and others, it is hardly necessary here to dwell upon the lives and activities of the Barrowist leaders. What now appears to need more attention is the story of the rise of the first Barrowist congregation. The principal original sources for the information needed are to be found in the various Barrowist depositions contained in the hitherto too little used Harleian MSS. 6848 and 6849[3] in the British Museum.

---

[1] Harl. MS. 6848, fol. 76 verso.　　　[2] P. 151.

[3] Mr Arber in prefacing his account of the history of Francis Johnson's congregation ("Story of the Pilgrim Fathers", London, 1897, p. 105) says :—

"Harleian MS. 7042 consists of the BAKER Transcripts from the Manuscripts (now lost) of the Lord Keeper of the Great Seal, Sir JOHN PUCKERING ; who died on 30th April 1596."

Fortunately for the historian this statement is not accurate. The MSS. of Sir John Puckering which Thomas Baker transcribed certainly are not lost, but form parts of Harleian MSS. 6848 and 6849, and though too little used by Dr Dexter, are mentioned by him again and again. Why he persisted in using the transcripts so frequently, when the originals or early copies of them were at hand, is a mystery. Mr Arber must have been led into making his erroneous statement by too closely following Dr Dexter. In the account here given of the early Barrowists the Baker transcripts are not used, and reliance is placed entirely on the Puckering MSS.

Dr Powicke has called my attention to the fact that Mr Arber in "An Introductory Sketch to the Martin Marprelate Controversy, 1588–1590",

From similar statements at the beginning[1] and at the close[2]
of a document contained in one of these manuscripts bearing
the title, "The Manner of thassemblie of the secret Conventicklers", etc., and also marked, "Certen wicked sect*es* &
opin*ions*. m*ar*che 1588 & 89 No. 3i. Eliz.", it is evident that
a congregation of secret conventiclers had been meeting in
London for a year and a half before that date. This information corresponds well with the report of an examination[3] of
twenty-one so-called "Brownestes" held on Oct. 8, 1587, in the
palace of the Bishop of London. They had been taken the
same day "at privat conventicles" in Henry Martin's house in
St Andrew's in the Wardrobe, and inasmuch as it was so difficult to hold private meetings in those days without detection, it
is probable that the congregation had not held many meetings
before that time. The conventiclers taken were [Nicholas]
Crane a Puritan minister already mentioned in connection with
the Plumbers' Hall congregation, Henry Martin, George Smells,
Edward Boyce, Anne Jackson, George Collier, Katherin Owin
[Onyon], Roberte Lacy, Thomas Freeman, Edithe Burry
[Burroughe], Mr [John] Grenewood preacher, Margaret Maynerd, "Alice Roe widow", Agnes Wyman, Roberte Griffith, John
Chaundler, Edmond Thompson, Henry Thompson, Roberte Red-
borne and Thomas Russell servants of Mr Boyce, and Peter Allen
servant of Mr Allen, a salter. The list ends with the words
"vacat Clement Gamble servante to Anne Iackson", and all the
words of this entry but "vacat" and "servante" have been crossed
out. There is also no number before Gamble's name, though
all the other names mentioned are numbered, so that he may
not have been considered a regular member of the company.

The meeting of this congregation may have resulted in
part from the Puritan activities of Nicholas Crane[4], who had
always been a difficult person for the civil and ecclesiastical

1880, not only uses the Puckering manuscripts in Harl. MSS. 6848 and
6849, but, strange to say, seems to know that they are the Puckering
manuscripts! See what Mr Arber says on pp. 35–40, 88–93, etc.

[1] Harl. MS. 6848, fol. 83 recto.   [2] *Ibid.*, fol. 84 recto.

[3] S. P. Dom., Eliz., Vol. cciv. (10) in the Public Record Office.

[4] A writing of Nicholas Crane's against subscription is given in
"*A parte of a register*". See "The Table" of Contents, p. iii.

authorities to deal with. To Crane's assistance, we may suppose, came John Greenwood, who, according to the manuscript list of prisoners of Oct. 8, 1587, was a "preacher depriued of his benefice in norfolke about 2 yeres past [i.e., about October, 1585], takin at the said privat conventicles in martins howse." Greenwood quickly became the leader of the company, while Crane, who may never have become a true separatist and was well advanced in years, seems to have retired into the background. It may have been the influence of Henry Barrowe that induced the little company more and more to become full separatists.

Hitherto, Greenwood has generally been said to have been arrested in the autumn of 1586, but we can now safely assign his imprisonment to October 8 of the following year. As leader of the congregation he was committed to the Clink, while George Collier and Margaret Maynerd were removed to Bridewell. As far as this list is concerned, it might appear that the rest were set free, but from a subsequent statement, still extant in manuscript, prepared about May, 1589[1], it becomes evident that Henry Tomson; Edward Boyce, or Boyes; John Chaundler; George Smells, or Smalls; Edithe Burry, Barrowe, or Burroughe; Alice Roe, or Roo; Nicholas Crane; and probably Roberte Griffin or Griffith, were also detained at that time, or if they were then set free, were subsequently retaken. Clement Gambell, or Gamble, "servante to Anne Iackson", for some reason, appears to have been at liberty, or missing, at the time of the examination of the rest of the congregation in the Bishop's palace. Perhaps he had escaped. If, as has been suggested, Gamble was not regarded as a whole-hearted Brownist, it should be said that he certainly seems to have attended the church meetings regularly for a year and a half after this examination, and was apparently retaken in March, 1588/9, when he gave evidence concerning the activities of the congregation and probably was at once given his freedom.

Of the persons examined (Nicholas) Crane, the Puritan preacher, is here described as having been "a student in Lawe in the inner Chauncery", and as having been made a minister

[1] Harl. MS. 6848, fol. 20 verso and 21 recto, in the British Museum.

"by 23 Grindall when he was Bushop of London". Crane does not yet seem to have become a real separatist, for evidently the most striking statement made by him was "that all the booke (meaninge the comon booke, is not gospell)", which is certainly a very mild statement. Indeed, I doubt if he ever advanced beyond the Puritan position. Margaret Maynerd, however, was of a different and bolder type. When examined she spoke without reserve, saying that "ther is no church in England", and that "she hath not bin at church theis x. yeres". The rest of the company appear to have said nothing especially offensive. The full text of the examination of these conventiclers is given in the volume of documents.

After the imprisonment of Greenwood the nine members who were set free were apparently left to shift for themselves, but three of them certainly retained their interest in the congregation. Other prisoners were taken from time to time as Henry Barrowe; Jerome Studley; Christopher Raper, or Roper; Roger Jackson; George Bryghte; Thomas Legate[1], (William[2]) Clerke, or Clarke; Alyce Chaundler; John Fraunces; Robart Badkinge; Wylliam Denford; Quyntin Smythe; John Purdye; and William Bromell[3]. Of the prisoners taken before May, 1589, John Chaundler, George Bryghte, Margaret Maynerd, Alice Roe, Roger Jackson, and Nicholas Crane, had died before that date, while Roberte Griffin, or Griffith, had been bailed, "being very sicke"[4].

It is possible that at first the congregation was not entirely composed of separatists, for William Clerke in his examination on April 2, 1593, says "he hath refrained to come to churche but halfe a yere, but hath held his opinions these fyve yeres", i.e., since the spring of 1588. The church covenant of this congregation seems to have been very simple. Clerke says that on his becoming a member he merely "made *promise to*

---

[1] This Thomas Legate I take to have been one of the three brothers Legate (the earliest English Seekers), who died in Newgate about 1607, as will be seen in Chapter VIII.

[2] See the deposition of William Clerke on Mar. 8, 1592/3 in the volume of documents.

[3] Harl. MS. 6848, fol. 20 verso and 21 recto.   [4] *Ibid.*

stand with the said Congregation soe longe as they did stand for the truthe and glory of god". In this statement any engagement of separation from the Church of England is rather implied than expressed, and yet it will be noticed later in this chapter, that the general policy of the congregation was certainly separatist before March, 1588/9, and probably in the main from the beginning of its history.

Several versions of the early covenant of this congregation are given in different depositions, and hence it probably had as yet no stereotyped form. It may be of interest to insert the various texts :—

1. As given by William Clerke (previously cited).

2. As given by "Iohn Barnes tayler", who evidently had been a member since the spring of 1588/9 :—

"Item he saith that at his first entringe into that societie he *made noe other vowe, but that he wold followe them soe farr forth as the word of god did warraunt him*".

3. As given by Quintin Smyth of Southwark, feltmaker, who apparently had been a member of the congregation since the spring of 1590/1 :—

"Item, he sayeth he did covenaunt with the Congregacion to walk with them in the lawes of god, soe longe as ther doinges should be approved by the word of god, and soe longe would forsake all other assemblies".

4. As given on April 6, 1593, by William Weaver " of Grayes Inne lane Shomaker", who had then been a member of the congregation for over a year and a half, that is, since about October, 1591 :—

"Item, he saieth that when he was ioyned to their congregacion, they caused him to vse words to this effect, that he should promise to walke with them, soe longe as the[y] followed the ordinance of Christ". In another deposition he says he "made a Couenaunte to the Congregation to bee of their Societie & refuseth to goe to the churche".

5. As given by Daniel Bucke probably in the spring of 1591/2 :—

"Beinge asked what vowe or promise he had made

when he came first to their socyetye he aunswhereth and saith that he made this protestation, That he wold walke in the waye of the lord and as Farr as might be warraunted by the word of god".

6. As given by Abraham Pulbery, who evidently became a member not earlier than March, 1591/2 :—

"Item hee saieth that hee hath made a promise to the Lord in the presence of his Congregacion when hee entred therevnto that hee would walke with them as they would walke with the Lorde".

Robert Aburne, or Abraham, who does not appear to have become a member of the congregation before September, 1592, evidently was not required to enter into covenant at all, for he says :—

"he this examinant, beynge amongest them [at Bridewell prison], was receaved and admytted into ther societie and congregacion, without eyther examinacion, or further enquirie of his conversation".

Fortunately the customs and views of this church are well known. The paper containing this information has been largely given in the volume of documents, and brief reference has already been made to it as bearing the title, "The Manner of thassemblie of the secret Conventicklers", etc. The material contained in this document is drawn chiefly from the confessions made in March, 1588/9, by Clement Gamble and one John Dove, M.A., the latter of whom appears to have gained entrance to some of the meetings of the congregation in order to see what their opinions were.

The principal points mentioned may be summarized and arranged as follows :—

I. AS TO THEIR MEETINGS.

In the summer the congregation met in the fields a mile or more outside London, where most of the members would sit down on a bank while several expounded the Bible to them. They would arrange in advance where to hold their meeting on the following Sunday, as for instance in some particular house, where they would assemble as early as five o'clock in the morning. Here they would remain all day (probably for fear of detection), engaging in prayer and exposition of the Scriptures. They would dine together, and afterward take a collection to pay for their meal. If the amount collected exceeded the sum required, some member would carry the remainder to those of the congregation who were confined in the prisons.

II. As to their Views.

1. *Of Prayer.*

They believed in the use of extemporary, but not of any form of read, or "stynted", prayer. They never used the Lord's Prayer, but evidently considered it only " A Patterne of Trve Prayer". As to their manner of praying John Dove quaintly says, " one speketh and the rest doe grone, or sob. or sigh, as if they wold wringe out teares".

2. *Of Church Government.*

" In all there metinges they teach that there is noe heade or supreme gove[rn]ment of the Church of god, but Christe, That the Queen hath no aucthoritie to appoyn[t] mynisters in the Church nor to set downe any govermente for the Church which is not directlie commanded in godes worde".

3. *Of the Ministry.*

Public ministers are not needed now that the office of apostles has ceased. Any private man (layman) who is a Brother (churchmember), whatever his calling, may preach.

4. *Of the Church of England.*

They condemn all attendance at any of the services of the Church of England including even public prayer and preaching, and they call its preachers "fals teachers & falce prophettes" "sent in the lordes anger to deceyve his people with lyes", "and all that come to our Churches to publicque praier or sermons they accompt damnable soules".

5. *Of Baptism.*

They hold it " vnlawfull to baptise Children [infants] emongest vs [i.e., in the Church of England] but rather Chewse to let them goe vnbaptized" until a satisfactory baptism (by a true preacher of the Gospel) can be secured, even though it come later in life. (They were in a sense therefore Catabaptists, but not Anabaptists. The Barrowists evidently did not attempt "a baptizing againe" as claimed by R. Alison[1], but were only opposed to infant baptism when it was in their opinion improperly administered.)

6. *Of the Administration of the Lord's Supper.*

Clement Gamble confessed that although he had attended all their regular meetings for a year and a half he never saw the Lord's Supper administered, and did not know where the ceremony took place[2]. It is possible, of course, that the celebration of the Communion only commenced after the arrival of Francis Johnson.

7. *Of Marriage.*

"for marradges if any of there Chirch Marry together some of there owne Brotherhood must marry them as of late A Cople were married in the fleet".

8. *Of Apostates.*

Any one of their secret Brotherhood who deserts them and returns to the services of the Church of England, even to public prayer and preaching, is condemned as an apostate.

9. *Of Delivering over to Satan.*

Such an apostate who continues, or is disposed to continue, worshipping in the Church of England, they summon and seek to win back by argument, but if they fail by this means they give him over to the hands of Satan (or excommunicate him), until he shall submit, and while the congregation is kneeling, the one who has pronounced the sentence of excommunication

---

[1] "A PLAINE | CONFVTATION OF | A TREATISE OF BROWNISME", London, 1590, sig. A₃ verso, where he says, "(Whervpon though the renuer of this schisme [of Donatists], Browne I meane, did not in plaine wordes require a baptising againe, yet their successors [the Barrowists] in their established Church attempted it [From margin. "Some of their owne companie haue confessed it."].)..."

[2] This statement may indicate that Gamble was not regarded as a real member of the church.

prays God to ratify that censure. It would appear that this was the first modern congregation in England to use the term "give over to the hands of Satan". Already before March, 1588/9, one Love had been given over to Satan, because he had deserted the brotherhood.

The story is also told in this document of one "Wydowe Vnyon" who belonged to the congregation, and had a twelve-year-old child which was unbaptized. Evidently the child had been so frightened by people in the Church of England, that it had come to believe it was in danger of eternal damnation if it should remain unbaptized. It is reported often to have besought its mother to allow it to be baptized, but Widow "Vnyon" was firm in her principles. Hearing of the case, the Chancellor of London is said to have caused the child "to be publiquely Baptised, at a sermon made for that purpose", in the summer of 1588, "and the mother ranne awaie for feare of punishmente". This widow seems to have been Katherin Onyon, who in a deposition of 1593 is recorded as being a "spinster dwellinge at Allgate", and whose name is reported by mistake in the list of Oct. 8, 1587, as "Katherin Owin".

On Nov. 19, 1587, Henry Barrowe visited John Greenwood in the Clink prison. This date stands as Nov. 19, 1586, in the first examination of Barrowe before the High Commissioners as published by him, but it is undoubtedly incorrect[1], and the mistake is probably due to a typographical error, though we should also remember that he wrote this account in prison about 1592, and only "as neere as my [his] memorie could cary".

In the first place, it is very probable that Nov. 19, 1587, and not 1586, is the correct date, since there appears to be no official record of Greenwood's being taken prisoner before Oct. 8, 1587. Furthermore, it is six weeks to a day from Oct. 8, 1587, to Nov. 19, 1587, which is the exact length of time mentioned by the captives[2] as having elapsed between the beginning of

---

[1] See "The Examinations of Henry Barrowe Iohn Grenewood | and Iohn Penrie / before the high | commissioners / ...", 4º [1593]. The acceptance of this view will require the alteration of some of the dates of Barrowe's examinations as given by Dr Powicke in his "Henry Barrow".

[2] Harl. MS. 6848, fol. 20 verso, where it is stated that Greenwood had been imprisoned in the Clink thirty weeks and Barrowe twenty-four weeks.

Greenwood's imprisonment and that of Barrowe, while it is indirectly specified elsewhere by the prisoners in manuscript that they were imprisoned in the autumn of 1587[1], and not of 1586. Barrowe was evidently a member of the congregation as early as Oct. 8, 1587, and probably from the time when the private meetings began to be held, which presumably was not much earlier than that date. Certainly he knew the "brethren" whom he saw at his first examination before the High Commissioners, wherein it was also said that the capture of his person had long been desired[2], i.e., we may suppose, for six weeks before Nov. 19, 1587, or since Oct. 8, 1587.

Barrowe's long imprisonment may have prevented him from ever assuming more than the position of a trusted adviser to the congregation, but it is also extremely doubtful whether at this early period even under the most favourable circumstances he would as a layman have taken the office of pastor or teacher among the conventiclers. Besides, it is known that Barrowe and Greenwood did not always agree. Barrowe, however, by writing and publishing works full of scathing invective against the Church of England and its ministry, became far more influential than any minister at that time connected with the separatists, and in this way made himself their true leader and the real formulator of their policy. Indeed, without him the congregation might have made little progress. With his aid it became widely known.

Barrowe certainly resembled Robert Browne in his impetuous zeal to reform the Church of England, but neither Barrowe nor Greenwood ever admitted that they had taken their opinions from Browne. In this, I think, they spoke truly. Browne and Barrowe never could agree, and we now know that there were bitter dissensions between them which were carried on in writing over a considerable period of time. That there had

---

[1] See Strype's "Annals", ed. 1731, p. 95. This Supplication was evidently written early in January, 1592/3 ("Annals", p. 96), and if Barrowe and Greenwood had then been imprisoned for five years, as is stated, they were, therefore, taken prisoners in 1587.

[2] See "The Examinations of Henry Barrowe Iohn Grenewood and Iohn Penrie", [1593,] as above.

B. 9

been such discord was a well known fact in the early sixteenth century[1], but it is strange to notice how utterly forgotten were these disagreements before the publication of Browne's "Retractation" in 1907. Barrowe was what might be termed an extreme Puritan. He detested the name of Brownist, partly no doubt because he was not a Brownist. Browne considered the Church of England to be imperfect and therefore needing reform; Barrowe termed the Church of England a false Church, which it was one's duty to desert. Browne became a separatist more because of pressure put upon him from the Archbishop and Bishops; Barrowe became a separatist in defiance of the wishes of the Church authorities. Even as to internal policy it is a familiar fact through Dr Dexter that Browne and Barrowe differed considerably. Browne appears, too, to have been disposed to give a little more power to the ordinary members of the congregation, than Barrowe, who, though his views on this point may have been exaggerated[2], nevertheless made more of the eldership than Browne.

One point in Barrowe's life may here be noticed, namely, that early in 1590 he must have been at least temporarily out of prison. This appears in a deposition of John Clerke, "husbandman of the parishe of wallsoken in the Countye of Norffolke", made early in April, 1593, wherein he says that he "was committed three yeares paste by the Sheriffes of London beinge taken in an assembly with Barrowes".

Of only one of Barrowe's early published writings is it my purpose to make mention here, namely that which gives his ideal of a church, published in 1589, and entitled "A True Description ovt of the VVorde of God, of the Visible Chvrch". The opinions here expressed are undoubtedly not entirely original, nor on the other hand do they at all closely agree with the earlier published views of Robert Browne. Barrowe was probably much more indebted to the account, already mentioned, of the troubles of the Marian Exiles at Frankfort on the Main, first published in 1574. This narrative certainly might have furnished him with abundant material out of which to construct

---

[1] See H. A.[insworth]'s "Covnterpoyson", 1608, p. 41.
[2] See Dr Powicke's "Henry Barrow", 1900, pp. 105–6.

his own particular ideas of church polity. A further comparison of these two works is suggested as a study that may repay the investigator.

During 1588 and 1589 the Martin Marprelate tracts made their first appearance, and for about three years produced great excitement in religious circles all over England. It is not our purpose here to give much space to this controversy. It had no direct connection with the Barrowists, although in indirect ways it undoubtedly furthered their cause very much. Dr Dexter sought to prove that Henry Barrowe was Martin, but to-day no thoughtful person accepts this view, and while some still think that either John Penry or Job Throgmorton was Martin, it appears hardly probable that at this late date the true Martin will ever be discovered. But whoever Martin was, he certainly was a Puritan, not a Barrowist, at the time he wrote the Marprelate tracts, for the Barrowists of 1588 and 1589 did not think of either Penry or Martin Marprelate as in any way belonging at that time to their congregation of separatists. This fact is clearly shown by a letter of John Greenwood's which was intercepted and came into the hands of Richard Bancroft, who, as is suggested by the contents of his library, as well as by two letters given in the volume of documents, devoted much time to studying the opinions and activities of Puritans, Barrowists, and Brownists. Says Greenwood in this intercepted letter[1] :—

Surely it were a notable worke, and no doubt might doe much good in these times, for some one that God had indued with sound iudgement and sharpe sight, to gather the maiors or antecedents, of all those scattered pamphlets of Penries or Martins &c. and put newe minors or conclusions vnto them: and . so in one little nosegay, but as bigg as an almanack, to turne them vpon them-selues, and present them vnto them, for an answere.

We may now return to the history of the Barrowist congregation, which at this period was growing considerably in numbers. About January, 1589/90, many of the congregation appear to have been taken prisoners. Even up to this time complete organization had not been effected, as is evident from a deposition

[1] [Richard Bancroft's] "A SVRVAY | OF THE PRETENDED | Holy Discipline...", London, 1593, p. 430,

of Roger Waterer[1]. It may have been at this "assemblie in a garden howse by Bedlein, wher Iames Forrester expounded, before ther Churche was setled", that so large a number were captured. The names of many of the prisoners (there were apparently fifty-two in all) are new, though fourteen mentioned in the two earlier lists relating to the congregation also appear in this; as John Francys, Robert Batkine [Badkinge or Bodkyne], Thomas Freeman, George Collier, Christopher Raper [Roper], Quintan [Quintin] Smyth, William Denford [Dentforde], Edeth Burrowghe [Burry], George Smels, Robert Jackson, William Clarke, Henry Barrowe, John Greenwood, and Edmond Thomson. The name John Sparowe reminds us of a member of Richard Fitz's congregation who had the same name and possibly was the same person.

The other names, including that of John Sparowe, are James Forester, Thomas Settel, John Debenham, Edmond Nicolson, Christopher Browne, Androe [Andrew] Smyth, William Blakborowe, Thomas Lemar [Le Mare], Thomas Michell, Anthonye Clakston, William Forester, Roger Waterer, William Burt, Christopher Bowman, Nycholas Lee, Robert Andrewes, William Hutton [Hawton], John Buser [Bucer], John Fissher, Richard Maltusse, William Fouller [Fowler], Richard Skarlet, Roger Rippine [Rippon], John Clarke, Rowland [Rowlett] Skipworth, George Knifton, Richard Hayward [Haywood], John Lankaster, Thomas Endford [Eyneworth or Kyneworth], Daniell Studley, Walter Lane, John Nicholas, William Dodson [Dodshoe], John Barrens [Barnes], John Cranford, Richard Wheeler, Thomas Canadine, thirty-eight in all.

Such a great increase in numbers must have had a cause, and inasmuch as Barrowe and Greenwood both appear in the list and are no longer reported in the Clink, but in the Fleet, I infer that they had been temporarily released from confinement, and had not been slow to take advantage of this opportunity for disseminating their opinions.

About April, 1590, fifty-nine Barrowists were in various London prisons, and they then addressed a petition to "Lord

----

[1] Harl. MS. 6848, fol. 51 recto.

Burleighe"[1]. In this document nine new names are given, John Gualter, Thomas Reave, Luke Hayes, Richard Umberfield, Edward Marshe, Anthonie Johnes, — Cooke, — Awger, and Thomas Stephens, the last having died in Newgate. Up to this time ten of their number in all had died.

Before the congregation was organized in September, 1592, we have little further information concerning its affairs. The membership, however, appears to have increased slightly, and many of the members who had been imprisoned in 1589 or 1590 were at liberty and present at the organization.

Those who desire to become still more familiar with the opinions of the early Barrowists should consult the contents of the various manuscripts published in the volume of documents, and especially two letters of John Greenwood written from prison in 1587 and Henry Barrowe's treatise stating and defending four causes of separation, texts of all three of which were fortunately discovered by the Rev. T. G. Crippen in 1905, and were published in the "Transactions" of the Congregational Historical Society for January and May, 1906. These "finds" of Mr Crippen bring to our notice the most important writings of Barrowe and Greenwood that have been discovered for many years, if not in modern times. Of these the treatise by Barrowe (not by Barrowe and Greenwood jointly, as Dr Powicke has suggested to the author) is decidedly the most important. It is entitled "Fower principall and waighty causes whie every on that knoweth god & acknowledgeth the lord Jesus, or seekethe salvation in him, ought spedelye without any delay to forsack those disordered and ungodlye & unholye sinagogs, & the false teachers of these tymes as they genarallye stand in England"[2].

---

[1] Lansdowne MS. 109, fol. 42 (No. 15), in the British Museum.

[2] The discovery of this manuscript makes it possible for the first time to gain a knowledge of this treatise. Furthermore, it gives, I believe, the earliest known statement of the *Four Causes*, which later were extracted from the rest of the text of this extended document, slightly altered and expanded in form, introduced with six prefatory remarks, termed "A Briefe Svmme of the causes of our separation, and of our purposes in practise", and defended and published by Barrowe in "A Plaine Refvtation of M. Giffards Booke", 1591. "A Briefe Svmme" was not produced jointly

This work was evidently written to persuade Puritans and others to separate from the Church of England. Here are two characteristic passages which undoubtedly made special impression on those who read the document, and help to identify it as a general treatise of Barrowe's, of which several copies were probably circulated, and which was evidently answered in manuscript by Robert Browne, as well as by George Giffard, and possibly, also, by others:—

The haynouse & fearfull enormities that insue of these ar Infinitt & cannot be sufyciently expresed ether by word or writing: but sumarylye, you shall find herbye christ Jesus denied in all his ofices, & so consequently not to be com in the flesh. You shall find herby the last will and testament of our savior christ abrogat, his pretious bodie and bloud torne & troden under feette of dogges and swine, christ Jesus throwne out of his howse & antichrist his enimie exalted above god & raygning in the temple of god as god[1].
but this I say to lett you see the haynous Dealying of the tolarating prechers, even those yt ar best estemed, and your own fearfull estate that ar misled by them. they as you see betray not onlye themselves and you but even christ Jesus hime self & his gospell into the hands of antichrist. for see howe these deceivers ioyn the word of god and Idollatrye together, the gospell of christ and bondage, christ and antichrist to gether in on temple. See what kynd of gospell & what kind of christ they geve yow: a christ without power to governe & kep his owne, a gospell without lybertie; or else whie ar you thus Intangled with begerlye rudyments &c; whie ar you thus in subjection to the traditions of men? thus mak they your christ an Idoll & you Idolaters. be therfor no longer deceved; christ putethe not up these Iniuryes; his father hathe delyvered into his hands all power in heaven & earth, & he will shortlye show himself with his myghtye angels in flaming fier, rendering vengance unto them that know not god, which ar disobedient to his gospell: alsuche shalbe punished withe ever lasting perdition from the presence of the lorde and from the glory of his power. then shall none of those pretensed titles of graces, word of god, gospell, christ Jesus, faith, comfort, &c. serve them; for he whos eies ar a flam of fier can not be deceved; no

by Barrowe and Greenwood as is evident from the title-page of Barrowe and Greenwood's "A Plaine Refvtation...", 1591 [ed. 1606], in which the contribution of each writer is shown to be quite distinct from that of the other. Dr Powicke is therefore probably incorrect in styling "A Briefe Svmme", "*The Earliest Separatist Manifesto*" ("Henry Barrow", Appendix II.), as well as in believing it to have been produced jointly by Barrowe and Greenwood.

[1] "Transactions" for January, 1906, p. 292.

secrett is hiden from his bright eies. Though they byld as highe as babell & digg as low as hell &c, he seeith ther hipocrisie & will disclose it, & will judg them by ther fruts, even the bitter & accursed fruts of ther disobedience. this word of god, gospell, & christ, which they use as a snar & a fayer stall to draw gaynes & Ignorant sowles unto them & therby to justify ther wickednes, shall judg and condemn them amongest the devells with all ther knowledg & inward graces &c. neyther can this fayth wrought by ther ministrie, wherby they subtilie draw the wholl multytud of ther hearers upon us; as who shold saye ye muste ether condemne all these & every on of them to be without faithe or Justifey our ministry by the efectts. alas we Judg not; we with Jerymey wishe even so be it: but ther is on that Judgeth them, even that christ they boste of Judgeth them, & his word Judgeth them allredye. ther is no true faythe but that which is builte upon the word & bringethe forthe fruts accordinglye. Allas, the word condemneth them, ther fruts condemne them, yea them selves, when the boock of ther consciens shalbe opened by the lyght of gods word unto them, shall condemne themselves. The multytud of gods enimies shalbe as one mane; he that spared not the angells, he that spared not the owld world, he that spared not his own people, cannot spar them[1].

[1] *Ibid.*, pp. 296–7.

CHAPTER V

THE BARROWISTS UNDER THE LEADERSHIP OF
FRANCIS JOHNSON UNTIL 1597

NEXT to Henry Barrowe the most influential person who joined Greenwood's congregation was Francis Johnson. He appeared on the scene just at the moment when a new leader was most needed to inspire the flagging energy of the persecuted separatists. In fact, the cause of English separatism had never yet had such a leader, for Johnson was a truly learned, as well as a conscientious, man. Like other men he had his faults, but his good characteristics have been largely overlooked in recent writings, and especially by Mr Edward Arber, who sums up Johnson's character in the following comprehensive sentence :—

We then come to this judgement as to FRANCIS JOHNSON. That by October 1602, he was a dead Christian ; that, by then, he was an utter disgrace to our sacred Faith ; and that what he afterwards said, preached, or wrote, is not deserving of serious attention, from a spiritual point of view[1].

Scathing criticism this, but is it not untrue as well as uncharitable, and hence for the historian of little value ? Johnson undoubtedly was a complex character, and the problems he had to face were equally complex, but he stood loyally by the cause he had adopted through good and bad report up to the end, and though at the last he slightly altered his views, he nevertheless made no deathbed recantation as Mr Arber, by a curious error, dramatically declares. Further, in spite of all the unkind remarks that were written and published about him, Francis Johnson never retaliated in any of his writings with bitter or harsh terms.

[1] "The Story of the Pilgrim Fathers ", London, 1897, p. 112.

In reality the career of Johnson is as varied as it is pathetic. For our purposes, however, it is necessary to allude only to those points in his life which are related to our subject. Late in the autumn of 1589 Johnson was expelled from the University of Cambridge and imprisoned a second time for his religious beliefs. How long this imprisonment lasted is not apparent, but it seems to have been of considerable duration. Some time in 1590 or 1591 he appears to have arrived in Middelburg, where he was soon offered the position of minister in the English church of the Merchant Adventurers, not of the Merchants of the Staple, as stated by Gov. Bradford, Dr Dexter[1], and other writers.

Among the Boswell Papers in the British Museum is a paper[2] entitled, " Extracts out of yᵉ Registre book of yᵉ English Congregacion at Antwerpe Anno Dominj 1597 [.] 80. 81. 82.", etc. These extracts explain how there happened to be an English congregation at Middelburg and tell how long it had been there. We learn that in 1579 Walter Travers became the minister of the Company of Merchant Adventurers of London then in Antwerp. Some time before Dec. 17, 1580, he made a visit to England, and on that date the congregation received a letter from him excusing his failure to return and recommending Cartwright as his successor. The " Companie " moved from Antwerp to Middelburg " in 1582. or in the beginning of 1583. Mʳ Thomas Cartwright being Minister hauing succeeded Mʳ Trauerse ". Cartwright, therefore, probably reached Middelburg after the arrival of Robert Browne's congregation and not before it, as has usually been supposed.

When Johnson became the English minister at Middelburg, it will thus be seen, his church had already existed over ten years. He had not been long in his new position, when he seems to have created considerable surprise by demanding that

---

[1] " The Congregationalism ", etc., New York, 1880, p. 263. This mistake of Dexter's is evidently derived from Gov. Bradford's " A Dialogue,... ", written in 1648, and published in Alexander Young's "Chronicles of the Pilgrim Fathers", Boston, 1841, p. 424. See the citation therefrom given later in this chapter.

[2] Add. MS. 6394, fol. 113–14.

all the members of the congregation should sign the text of the following document[1], which is practically a covenant, though not so termed in this copy made by Mr Ferrers :—.

> *Francis Iohnson* his articles, which he vrged to be vnder-
> written by the *Englishe Marchants* in *Middleboroughe*
> in *October*. 1591, withstoode by me *Thomas Ferrers*,
> then deputie of the Companie there./

Wee whose names are vnderwritten, doe beleeve and acknow-ledge the truthe of the doctrine and faythe of our Lorde *Jesus Christe*, which is revealed vnto vs in the Canon of the Scriptures of the olde and newe Testament.

Wee doe acknowledge, that *God* in his ordinarie meanes for the bringinge vs vnto and keepinge of vs in this faythe of *Christe*, and an holie *Obedience* thereof, hath sett in his Churche teaching and rulinge *Elders, Deacons,* and Helpers: And that this his *Ordinance* is to continue vnto the ende of the worlde as well vnder *Christian princes*, as vnder *heathen Magistrates*.

Wee doe willinglie ioyne together to live as the *Churche* of *Christe*, watchinge one over another, and submittinge our selves vnto them, to whom the Lorde *Iesus* committeth the oversight of his *Churche*, guidinge and censuringe vs accordinge to the rule of the worde of *God*.

To this ende wee doe promisse henceforthe to keepe what soever *Christe* our Lorde hath commaunded vs, as it shall please him by his holie spiritt out of his worde to give knowledge thereof and abilitie there vnto.

It should be noticed that this seems to be a Puritan and not a truly separatist document. Johnson was still a member of the Church of England when he drew it up, but by this congregation it must, nevertheless, have been looked upon with suspicion, for though the Nonconformist and Puritan preachers in the Church of England from the time of Queen Mary may occasionally have employed covenants, this congregation was evidently not familiar with such a written document as this, and its subscription was formally opposed by Mr Ferrers. In fact, such an impression did the imposition of this covenant make upon Ferrers' mind, that he appears to have procured a copy of it and at some later period to have sent it to Sir William Boswell, thus rendering a good service to history.

Johnson had evidently so emphasized the importance of subscribing these articles that Ferrers adds the two following

---

[1] Add. MS. 28, 571, fol. 169 recto, in the British Museum.

explanatory paragraphs. Probably Ferrers feared that Johnson would cause the church to appear to manifest a tendency towards separatism. Here is what Ferrers claims Johnson had declared concerning the articles :—

That for anie w*h*ich haue bene of this *Churche* and will not vnder-write these wi*t*h promisse (as God shall inhable them) to stande to the same and everie poynte of them, againste men and *Angells* vnto the deathe ; otherwise he may not be receaved as a member in this *Churche*.

And allso that any man once havinge adioyned him selfe to this *Englishe* churche in *Middleboroughe*, he cannot fynde any warrant by the worde of *God* ; [?] that after, the same partie is to adioyne him selfe to anye other *Churche*, either in *Englande* or els where : but there, as the *Discipline* is rightlie established, as in this *Churche.*/

In the following citation Richard Bancroft probably refers indirectly to the drawing up of this covenant and to the way in which Johnson was compelled to defend it[1] :—

Diuerse ministers well reckoned of heretofore for their learning : are lately fallen from *Cartwright*, and his secte, into another more new frenzy of *Barrowisme*. In a letter that was taken not long since : I find some points to this effect. The preachers of *Midleborow and Flushing*, haue both giuen ouer their vnlawfull callings. *M. Iohnson hath written a most learned discourse, concerning the striking of a newe couenaunt, with some conferences had in that country*[2]. It is also reported, and I am perswaded, by that which I haue seene, that the report is true : vz. that maister *Penry* is entered in like manner into this new kind of couenaunt. A matter, that would seeme very strange vnto me : but that I know the nature of schismatickes, to bee of such giddinesse : as that no one thinge will content them longe...

This passage evidently means that Johnson had not found it easy to impose his covenant or articles upon the church members and had met with unexpected and prolonged opposition from some of the congregation. Perhaps he had even been compelled to acquiesce in their wishes. The passage also suggests that the unnamed English minister at Flushing had likewise advocated

---

[1] In "A Svrvay of the Pretended Holy Discipline", London, 1593, p. 427.

[2] Perhaps Bancroft thought that "the striking of a newe couenaunt" was peculiar to Barrowism. We now know that such a view is not strictly true.

the drawing up of a covenant, and, on meeting with similar difficulties, had after a time resigned. As was characteristic of him, Johnson had evidently not despaired of his situation because of a rebuff, but had prepared a treatise (which probably was never published) in defence of his views. Before Bancroft wrote his "Svrvay" which appeared in 1593, Johnson had also become a Barrowist and relinquished his position, but whether this had happened before or after his departure for England is here not clearly indicated.

During his stay in Middelburg Johnson like all Puritans was in reality a vigorous opponent of separatism, and had been delighted to discover Barrowe and Greenwood's "Plaine Refvtation" while it was in the press some time before March, 1591/2. Governor Bradford has so well described this event and so carefully stated its traditional important effect on Johnson's life, that it is here given in full[1]:—

Mr. Johnson himself, who was afterwards pastor of the church of God at Amsterdam, was a preacher to the company of English of the Staple [not of the Staple, but of the Merchant Adventurers] at Middleburg, in Zealand, and had great and certain maintenance ["£200 per annum."] allowed him by them, and was highly respected of them, and so zealous against this way [of separation] as that [when] Mr. Barrow's and Mr. Greenwood's Refutation of Gifford was privately in printing in this city, he not only was a means to discover it, but was made the ambassador's instrument to intercept them at the press, and see them burnt; the which charge he did well perform, as he let them go on until they were wholly finished, and then surprised the whole impression, not suffering any to escape; and then, by the magistrates' authority, caused them all to be openly burnt, himself standing by until they were all consumed to ashes. Only he took up two of them, one to keep in his own study, that he might see their errors, and the other to bestow on a special friend for the like use. But mark the sequel. When he had done this work, he went home, and being set down in his study, he began to turn over some pages of this book, and superficially to read some things here and there, as his fancy led him. At length he met with something that began to work upon his spirit, which wrought with him and drew him to this resolution, seriously to read over the whole book; the which he did once and again. In the end he was so taken, and his conscience was troubled so, as he could have no rest

[1] In "A Dialogue, or the Sum of a Conference between some young men in New England", etc., published in Alexander Young's "Chronicles of the Pilgrim Fathers", etc., Boston, 1841, pp. 424–5.

in himself until he crossed the seas and came to London to confer with the authors, who were then in prison, and shortly after executed. After which conference he was so satisfied and confirmed in the truth, as he never returned to his place any more at Middleburg, but adjoined himself to their society at London, and was afterwards committed to prison, and then banished; and in conclusion coming to live at Amsterdam, he caused the same books, which he had been an instrument to burn, to be new printed and set out at his own charge. And some of us here present testify this to be a true relation, which we heard from his own mouth before many witnesses.

This story as told by Bradford is most interesting, though in the light of evidence already given from Bancroft's "Svrvay", 1593, it may require some slight reconstruction. From reading Bradford one would think that Johnson voluntarily gave up his position in Middelburg after he had been persuaded by Barrowe and Greenwood in person to abandon it, while on the contrary there now appears to be some reason for believing that under adverse conditions Johnson may have been prepared to relinquish the Middelburg pastorate before he ever saw Barrowe. Just what effect the reading of Barrowe and Greenwood's "Plaine Refvtation" had on Johnson is uncertain. I fancy now that in his disappointment at finding that the people in Middelburg would not readily follow him, and were making it difficult for him to maintain his position unless he would comply with their wishes, he finally determined to consult the leaders of the separatists in London, whose work he had so carefully read. Having carried out this plan he was quickly and fully converted to their position. However this may be, in less than a year from the time when he tried to impose his covenant on the Middelburg congregation he had become pastor of the London Barrowists.

He was now at last in a congenial atmosphere, although, as he somewhere tells us, he was not in entire accord with Barrowe. The arrival and initiative of Johnson thus afforded an opportunity at last for organizing Greenwood's congregation in an acceptable way, and in September, 1592, therefore, the church was instituted at the house of one Mr Fox in St Nicholas Lane, London, where there were present among others[1] :—

[1] See the Deposition of Daniell Bucke, Harl. MS. 6849, fol. 216 recto.

Robert Abraham	Edward Graue	Abraham Pulbery
Avis Allen	Iohn Grenewood	Ione Pulbery
Iohn Barnes	An Homes	Christofer Raper
Iohn Beche	Robert Iackson	Roger Rippon
An Bodkyn	Frauncis Iohnes	Ellyn Rowe
Christofer Boman	George Knyfton	Barbera Sampford
Mrs. Boyes	Nicholas Leye[Lee]	Mr. & Mrs. Thomas
Robert Bray	and his wife	Settell
Davy Bristoe	Thomas Lee	William Sheppard
Daniell Bucke	George Manners	George Smell
Arthur Byllet	William Marshall	Daniel Studley
William Collins	George Marten	Christofer Symkins
Margery Daubin	William Mason	Edmund Thompson
Christofer Diggins	Thomas Michell	William Weber
Thomas Digson	Elizabeth Moore	Henry Wythers
Peter Farland[Fair-	Iohn Nicholas	
lambe][1]	Katherine Onnyon	

The attendance at the meetings evidently varied from 60 to 100 during this period[2].

The officers of the congregation at its organization were,—
Francis Johnson, Pastor.
John Greenwood, Doctor or Teacher.
Daniel Studley
George $\begin{Bmatrix} \text{Knifton} \\ \text{Knyfton} \end{Bmatrix}$ $\begin{Bmatrix} \text{Knifeton} \\ \text{Kniveton} \end{Bmatrix}$ Elders.
Nicholas Lee
Christopher Bowman $\Big\}$ Deacons.

There are some important particulars given in various Barrowist depositions (cited in full in the volume of documents) concerning the beliefs and customs of the congregation. Among these the following may be mentioned :—

1. *As to the administration of baptism.*

Daniel Bucke describes the baptism of seven children by Johnson in the autumn of 1592 as follows :—

---

[1] Who in 1606 published "The Recantation of a Brownist". See Dr Powicke's "Lists", p. 151.

[2] Deposition of Robert Aburne, Harl. MS. 6848, fol. 41 recto.

they [the congregation] had neither god fathers nor godmothers, and he tooke water and washed the faces of them that were baptised: the Children that were there baptised were the Children of m^r Studley m^r Lee with others beinge of seuerall yeres of age, sayinge onely in thadministracion of this sacrament I doe Baptise thee in the name of the father of the sonne and of the holy gost withoute vsinge any other cerimony therin as is now vsually observed accordinge to the booke of Common praier...[1]

2. *As to the administration of the Lord's Supper.*

Daniel Bucke also gives the following minute description of Johnson's method of administering the Lord's Supper:—

Beinge further demaunded the manner of the lordes supper administred emongst them, he saith that fyve whight loves or more were sett vppon the table and that the Pastor did breake the bread and then deliuered to the rest some of the said congregacion sittinge and some standinge aboute the table and that the Pastor deliuered the Cupp vnto one and he to an other, and soe from one to an other till they had all dronken vsinge the words at the deliuerye therof accordinge as it is sett downe in the eleventh of the Corinthes the xxiiij^th verse[2].

3. *As to the mode of excommunication.*

Robert Aburne, or Abraham, describes the excommunication of Robert Stokes and George Collier at some length[3]:—

He saieth that they did vse to excommunicate amongst them, and that one Robert Stokes, and one George Collier[4], and one or twoe more[5] whose names he Remembreth not, wear excommunicated, for that they discented from them in opinion but in what poynte he Remembreth not, and that the said Iohnson thelder did denounce thexcommunicacion against them, and concernynge the manner of proceadinges to excommunicacion he saieth, that they the said Stokes and the Rest beynge privatelye admonished of their pre-

---

[1] Harl. MS. 6849, fol. 216 verso.

[2] Deposition of Daniell Bucke, Harl. MS. 6849, fol. 217 recto.

[3] Deposition of Robert Aburne, Harl. MS. 6848, fol. 41 verso.

[4] As Dr Powicke ("Lists of the Early Separatists", p. 155) points out, Aburne must have made a mistake here in stating that George Collier was excommunicated, for Thomas Settle, examined on April 5, 1593, two days later, mentions the excommunication of Stokes only, while Collier himself deposed that he would not attend the services of his Parish Church in order to regain his liberty.

[5] Philipp Merriman also seems to have been excommunicated about this time. See G. Johnson's "A discourse", p. 7.

tended errors, and not conforminge them selves, and by Witnes
produced to their congregacion, then the said Iohnson, with the
Consent of the whole Congregacion, did denounce the excommunicacion, and that sithence they weare excomunicated which was a halfe
yere and somewhat more sithence, they wear not admitted into their
Churche /.

4.　*As to marriage.*

Christopher Bowman, one of the two deacons, held the
opinion "that mariage in a howse without a mynister by
Consent of the parties and frends is sufficient"[1].

5.　*As to the Lord's Prayer.*

John Nicholas of Smithfield, Glover, in his deposition taken
on March 8, 1592, said "that the Lords prayer is noe praier for
that...Christ did not saie it as a praier"[2].

It might be added here that one of the members of the
congregation named Abraham Pulbury who had been "prest for
a souldier", was taken prisoner while carrying a sword. This
fact seems to have suggested to the authorities that the Barrowists possibly intended an insurrection if they secured sufficient
support, and several of the congregation, who had been imprisoned, were questioned on this point. All who were thus
examined deposed that, so far as they knew, the separatists had
no intention of disturbing the peace of the country.

Richard Bancroft in "A SVRVAY | OF THE PRE-
TENDED | Holy Discipline", London, 1593, has preserved
some important particulars concerning the early Barrowists[3]:—

you may assure your selues, that this latter schisme groweth on
very fast. In somuch, that as *Cartwright* and his brethren beganne,
eight or nine yeares since, to sett vppe, and put in practise, theyr
Geneuian discipline : so doe these newe vpstartes, beginne to erecte
in diuerse places, theyr Barrowish synagogues, and I knowe not what
cages of franticke schismatickes. One *Collins* a man amongest them,
not vnlearned (as it seemeth) doeth write in this sorte hereof.
*Ecclesia potenti eius dextra adiuta, &c. The church assisted with the
mightie right hand of God, hath chosen ministers: Maister Iohnson
for her pastor: Maister Greenwood for her Doctor: Maister Studly
and Maister George Knife[ton], for her Elders: Nicholas Lee and*

---

[1] Harl. MS. 6848, fol. 70 verso.　　　[2] *Ibid.*, fol. 61 recto.
[3] P. 429, but incorrectly printed 249.

Christopher Browne [Bowman] *for her Deacons. The other assembly also (wherevnto are added, Iohn Nicholas: Thomas Michell: Iohn Barnes, and some others with mee) with Gods assistaunce, will beginne out of hand, to create vnto it selfe ministers.*

From this passage it appears that in or before September, 1592, when Johnson's congregation was organized, there was also another company of separatists in London to whom after that date were added "Iohn Nicholas: Thomas Michell: Iohn Barnes, and some others with" William Collins[1], who likewise "with Gods assistaunce" intended shortly to institute another church. Apparently Collins was taking the leading part in this movement, and even Bancroft can only remark that he was "not vnlearned (as it seemeth)", surely an unexpected admission.

Like the London congregation of Queen Mary's time, Johnson's church did not often meet in the same place. For example, we learn from the depositions that they congregated in Mr Boyse's house in Fleet Street, in the wood by or beyond Islington, at the constable's house in Islington, at Roger Rippon's house in Southwark, in the field or wood near Deptford, in a garden house by "Bedlein", in the house of one Fox in St Nicholas Lane, in Nicholas Lee's house in Cow Lane, at Penry's house, in John Barnes' house in Ducklane, in a house at Smithfield by St Bartholomew's Hospital (?)[2], at Mr Bilson's house near Christchurch, in Daniel Bucke's house at Aldgate within the wall, in the house of "one Lewes in Stepney", and in a Schoolhouse in St Nicholas Lane[3], probably where George Johnson was schoolmaster.

The Barrowists evidently now began still further to increase in numbers. In the various depositions we are told the names, occupations, addresses, and age of many of the members, which it may be of value to give :—

---

[1] Collins was imprisoned in Sussex with Abraham Pulbery [Pulbury] about April, 1592. See Harl. MS. 6848, fol. 47 verso.

[2] See the depositions of Robert Abraham on April 3, 1593, and of Christopher Bowman on April 4, of the same year, in the volume of documents.

[3] In this schoolhouse Francis Johnson seems to have administered baptism to several children about Christmas, 1592.

Robert Abraham, or Aburne, Leatherdresser, and servant to Thomas Rookes, St Olave's, Southwark, about 26 years old.

John Barnes of Ducklane, Taylor, about 26 years old.

Arthur Billet "of llanteglos by Fowhey in Cornwell Scholler", about 25 years old.

Robert Bodkin of Gray's Inn Lane, Taylor.

Christopher Bowman of Smithfield, Goldsmith, about 32 years old.   Imprisoned 4 years, and again later.

Edward Boyes, Haberdasher, Fleet St., 33 years old[1].

David Bristow or Bristoe, Tailor, St Martin le Grand, 30 years old[2].

Henry Brodewater of St Nicholas Lane, Scrivener, about 29 years old.

Daniel Bucke of Southwark, Scrivener.

John Clerke, or Clarke, "of walsotkon in Norffolk husbandman", about 50 years old.   Imprisoned 3 years and more.

William Clerke of St Botolph's, a worker of caps, about 40 years old.

George Collier, "of the parishe of St Martens at Ludgate", Haberdasher, 38 years old.   Imprisoned for 5 years and never examined until that time had passed.

William Curland of Deptford, Shipwright, about 30 years old.

John Dalamore of Bath, "Brodeweaver", about 25 years old.

William Darvall, Carpenter, Shoreditch, 25 years old[3].

William Denford of Fosterlane, Schoolmaster, 50 years old.

Christopher Diggins of St Olave's in Southwark, Weaver, about 24 years old.

Thomas Emery, fellow-servant of William Giles.

Edward Gilbarte, servant of Isaac Frize, Trunkmaker, 21 years old.

William Giles, Taylor, servant to Mr Cheryatt of "walbroke", 22 years old.

Edward Grave of St Botolph's in Thames Street, Fishmonger, about 25 years old.

Richard Hawton, or Howton, Shoemaker, deceased before Apr. 3, 1593.

---

[1] Taken from Dr Powicke's "Lists of the Early Separatists".
[2] *Ibid.*   [3] *Ibid.*

Thomas Hewet " of St Martyns Le grand pursemaker ", born at Swanton in Leicestershire, about 30 years old.

John Huckes, Shipwright, born at Chatham, about 21 years old[1].

Francis Johnson, Minister, Pastor of the congregation, about 31 years old.

George Johnson, late Schoolmaster in St Nicholas Lane, born in " Richmonshire " " in the Countie of yorke ", about 29 years old. After his brother's imprisonment he sometimes preached before the congregation[2].

George Knifton, or Kniveton, " of Newgate market potecary ", about 24 years old.

William Marshall of Wapping, Shipwright, 32 years old. He attended Church as well as this congregation.

Richard Mason, brother of the following.

William Mason of Wapping, Shipwright, about 34 years old.

Thomas Micklefield, " Ioyner ", of St Mary Overy's parish, 33 years old.

Thomas Mitchell of London, Turner, about 30 years old.

John Nicholas of the parish of St " Pulchres ", London, Glover, about 36 years old. Imprisoned more than 3 years in the Gate House, Westminster.

Katherine Onyon, Spinster, " dwellinge at Allgate ", and is reported as willing to go to Church, but is unable to give sureties.

John Parkes, Clothworker, servant of " m^r Livesey his sonne ", 50 years old.

John Penrie, Clerk, about 30 years old.

Leonard Pidder, or Pedar, of " blacke Friers ", 30 years old.

Abraham Pulbury of the parish of " Crichurche ", " pursemaker by trade, but free of the Coupers ", about 24 years old.

Thomas Settle " late of Cowlane ", Minister ordained by Bishop Freake, about 38 years old.

Christopher Simkins of Aldersgate Street, Coppersmith, about 22 years old.

[1] *Ibid.*

[2] See the deposition of Robert Aburne, Harl. MS. 6848, fol. 41 recto.

George Smelles of "Fynchelane", Taylor, about 40 years old.

Quintin Smyth of Southwark, Feltmaker, about 30 years old.

William Smythe of Bradford in Wiltshire, Minister ordained by the Bishop of Coventry and Lichfield, and licensed to preach by the Bishop of Sarum, about 30 years old. He came to London late in January, or early in February, 1592/3, to confer with Johnson, Greenwood, and others.

John Sparrow, Fishmonger of London, 60 years old[1].

James Tailor.

Roger Waterer, late servant to Robert Pavye of St Martin's, Ludgate, Haberdasher, about 22 years old. Imprisoned three and a quarter years.

William Weaver of Gray's Inn Lane, Shoemaker, about 40 years old.

Henry Withers of Deptford Strand, Shipwright, about 27 years old.

To this list may be added the name of "Thomas Farret servant to William Greene of Aldersgate streete", who is mentioned in a paper[2] containing the names of eight "Sectaries" who conformed and were released on bail, the other seven being John Hulkes or Huckes, William Mason, William Curland, Edward Gilbert, Henry Brodewater, Thomas Mihilfield, or Micklefield, and Henry Withers, previously mentioned.

By a comparison of the various facts here given some interesting points are suggested:—

1. Most of the members were men under thirty-five years of age, very few were over forty years of age.

2. Certain shipwrights (principally of Deptford Strand) had been connected with the congregation, but most, if not all, of them conformed and were released on bail.

3. The members came from various places, a few even from towns somewhat distant from London.

Just about the time of the execution of Barrowe and Greenwood the Barrowists prepared at least two supplications and one petition. One of the supplications is given by John Strype in

---

[1] Taken from Dr Powicke's "Lists of the Early Separatists".

[2] Harl. MS. 6848, fol. 210. This list is given in full in the volume of documents.

the " Annals of the Reformation "[1].   The other supplication and
the petition are to be found in Harleian MS. 6848[2] in the
British Museum.   Of the latter two, complete texts are given
in the volume of documents.   From these petitions and supplications we may glean several facts concerning the history of the
congregation at this time.

1.   In the first place, we may infer from the frequent
capture of members of the congregation, that most of those
taken before the execution of Barrowe and Greenwood were not
imprisoned for long periods of time.

2.   These Barrowists, or Johnsonians, looked upon themselves as veritable successors of the " persecuted Church &
Martyres " of Queen Mary's reign.   In fact, they even went so
far as to hold their meetings sometimes in the same place where
the members of that church " were enforced to vse the like
exercise in Queene Maryes dayes ", and on March 4, 1592/3,
the members of Johnson's congregation were taken captive on
this very spot.

3.   It appears that in March, 1592/3, seventeen or eighteen
of the church had died in the London prisons " within these .6.
yeeres " (which statement suggests that the imprisonment of
members of the congregation began in 1587 not in 1586, as
has hitherto been supposed).

4.   In spite of the capture of fifty-six members on March 4,
1592/3, many of the Barrowists were " by the mercy of GoD
still out of theyr [persecutors'] handes ".

5.   By March 11, 1592/3, there were about seventy-two of
their number in the London prisons " (not to speake of other
Gaoles throughout the Land) ", of whom sixteen must already
have been imprisoned for some time.

Just how steadfast in their opinions Barrowe, Greenwood,
and Penry were at the end of their lives, is a question which
needs some investigation.   The loyal Congregationalist of to-
day is likely to look back at these men as martyrs for their
opinions, and such in a sense they certainly were, but this is not

---

[1] Vol. IV., ed. 1731, pp. 93–8.   The original of this document may
be Lansdowne MS. 75, fol. 42.

[2] Fol. 150 recto, and fol. 2–6.

saying that they were entirely and finally satisfied with the views for which they had suffered so much.

The Puritan, John Cotton, one of the most noted and respected divines of early New England, at any rate, did not believe so, for he tells the following story concerning them, which he claims is well authenticated[1]:—

And it is alike [*sic*] mistake, when he maketh M[r]. *Penry* one of his witnesses unto the death for Separation. I have received it from M[r]. *Hildersom* [*Hildersham*] (a man of a thousand) that M[r]. *Penry* did ingenuously acknowledge before his death, That though he had not deserved death for any dishonour put upon the Queene, by that Booke (which was found in his study, and intended by himselfe to be presented to her own hand:) nor by the compiling of *Martin Marprelate*, (of both which he was falsly charged;) yet he confessed, he *deserved death at the Queenes hand, for that he had seduced many of her loyall Subjects to a separation from hearing the Word of life in the Parish Churches. Which though himselfe had learned to discerne the evill thereof, yet he could never prevaile to recover divers of her Subjects, whom he had seduced: and therefore the bloud of their soules, was now justly required at his hands*[2].

[1] In his " The Bloudy Tenent, *Washed*, And made white in the blood of the Lambe :... *Whereunto is added a Reply to Mr*. Williams Answer, to Mr. Cottons Letter ", London, 1647, the last half, pp. 117–18.

[2] The case of Penry is somewhat perplexing, though it now seems probable that he was not really a witness " unto the death for Separation ", as we understand that term, in the sense of a perpetual revolt from a State Church as false in essence. Of Mr Hildersham's testimony here cited, I have no confirmation, and do not consider it sufficiently convincing. Penry, however, has left various writings which give us trustworthy expositions of his views, and especially his extended Confession of Faith and Apology, the original MS. of which I have rediscovered and consulted. In this manuscript occurs the following remarkable statement:—

" I detest all heresies, sectes and schysmes and errors whether new or old, by whomsoeuer they haue been inuented. as P u r i t a n i s m e, D o n a t i s m e, A n a b a p t i s m e, L i b e r t i n i s m e B r o w n i s m e, all the dreames and dotages of the famylie of loue, but especyally all Popery, ..."

This outspoken and comprehensive detestation Penry is quick to explain and qualify in what follows, as may be seen in the volume of documents. Evidently he still believes as much as ever in the Church of England as a national institution, he agrees with its principal doctrines, he does not call it a false church, but nevertheless he wishes certain abuses removed before he will again have anything to do with the State Church.

As the time of his execution drew near, Penry wrote a final letter to

Touching his other witnesse, to the death of M[r]. *Barrow*, this I can say, from the testimony of holy and blessed M[r]. [John] *Dod*, who speaking of this M[r]. *Barrow, God is not wont* (saith he) *to make choice of men, infamous for grosse vices before their calling, to make them any notable instruments of Reformation after their Calling.* M[r]. Barrow *whilest he lived in Court, was wont to be a great Gamster, and Dicer, and often getting much by play, would boast,* Vivo de die, in spem noctis, *nothing ashamed to boast of his hopes of his nights lodgings in the bosomes of his Courtizens. As his spirit was high and rough before his reformation, so was it after, even to his death. When he stood under the Gibbet, he lift up his eyes, and Lord* (saith he) *if I be deceived, thou hast deceived me*[1]: *And so being stopt by the hand of*

Burghley on May 28, 1593. In this he speaks of not being wholly able to accord in religious views with those who held the evidence against him, but if his life should be spared, he seems to have intended to do what he could "for the apeasing & quiet taking vp, of the differences in relligion between mee [him] & the Ecclesiasticall estate of this land". We are left to surmise how far the effort to appease would have carried him.

It should, however, be remembered that Penry to the end loyally clung to this Barrowist congregation, and encouraged the other members to do so, while his daughter, Deliverance, followed the Barrowists to Amsterdam. How Penry could consistently do all this may seem strange, but his case presents one of the problems which often meet the historian and embarrass him in drawing his conclusions. If the congregation in London was not really separatist, the situation would be much clearer. It should be added that the Barrowists thought of Penry as a "faithfull Martyr of Iesus Christ" (F. Johnson's "Certayne Reasons", 1608, 4o, p. iii).

Penry's Apology also appears to me to favour the view that he was in Scotland for a considerable period of time, and that he did not leave that country until the autumn of 1592. This opinion is further confirmed by the dates of the two letters published in the "sixt Addition" of Ephraim Pagitt's "Heresiography", London, 1661, 8o, pp. 271–275. The first was "Written from *Edinburgh* in *Scotland, Apr.* 30. In 34th. of the Queen [i.e., 1592]", and the second was "Written also from *Edinburgh* in *Scotland. March* 1. In 33th. of the Queen [i.e., 1591]." The dates of these letters entirely invalidate the opinions of the Rev. T. Gasquoine, B.A., expressed in an article in the "Transactions" of the Congregational Historical Society (for Sept., 1907), entitled, "The Last Years of Penry". After his arrival in London in 1592, Penry seems to have been constantly moving, as is indicated in his deposition of April 5, 1593.

[1] Hanbury in his "Memorials", p. 62, note "a", approves of the ingenious suggestion made by Thomas Wall in "More Work for the Dean", 1681, that Barrowe is here quoting Jeremiah xx. 7. I have no objection to that interpretation, if it meets with special favour, only I

God, he was not able to proceed to speake any thing to purpose more, either to the glory of God, or to the edification of the people.

M[r]. *Greenwood*...indeed of all the rest was the more to be lamented, as being of a more tender, and conscientious spirit: but this have I heard reported of him by the same credible hands, That if he could have been sundred from M[r]. *Barrow*, he was tractable to have been gained to the truth.

It was in this year 1593 that Sir Walter Raleigh, speaking in Parliament concerning the Brownists, stated his belief that there were " near twenty thousand of them in *England* "[1]. This estimate is absurd unless Raleigh included Puritans in it, but whether he included them or not, we can be practically certain that his opinion is of little value, and that various more accurate statements concerning the number of Brownists at later dates show that at no time before 1630, and possibly even before 1640, can there have been more than five or six hundred genuine Brownists or Barrowists in England, while the presence of even a smaller number would exceed reasonable probability.

The execution of Barrowe, Greenwood, and Penry undoubtedly had some effect on the attitude taken by the public towards the Barrowists. No more of them were put to death, but nevertheless the government seems to have been determined, if possible, to get rid of them. It is probable that after this all the leading men were kept in prison without cessation, though as will be seen in the next chapter, most of the other members of the congregation were soon given their freedom.

In 1596, in order to make their position more plain, the first

---

would observe that it does not disprove in the least that Barrowe meant what he said, nor does it in any way invalidate the testimony of John Dod, who must have been one of the most honest, peaceable, and gentle of the Puritans of that time, and may have been a witness of Barrowe's death. Dod's account, at any rate, appears to be the most reliable one we have of Barrowe's execution, for while we could wish for further particulars, it does not lack elements of credibility. What a different report it is from that circulated by " Miles Mickle-bound " and later by Governor Bradford, which even Dr Powicke is constrained to say "sounds rather apocryphal ("Henry Barrow")" !

[1] Sir Simonds D'Ewes "The Journals of all the Parliaments, During the Reign of Queen Elizabeth ", London, 1682, p. 517.

edition of the Barrowists' "Trve Confession" of Faith was issued. It is a thin, rather poorly printed, quarto of only a few pages, but is an important document, as it gives the principal opinions of the separatists of that period. I can find no reliable evidence that Henry Ainsworth had anything to do with this Confession[1], but the hand of Francis Johnson is clearly to be seen therein, and from it we get the earliest published expression of his views.

In the Preface the execution is mentioned of "one William Dennis / at Thetford in Northfolke", as well as the fact that "24 soules have perished in their [the Prelates'?] prisons / with in the Cittie of London / only (besides other places of the Land) & that of late yeeres [i.e., before 1593]". In the margin the names of these unfortunate people are mentioned as follows:—

In Newgate.

Mr [Nicholas] Crane, about sixty years of age.

Richard Jackson.

Thomas Stevens.

William Howton [Hawton].

Thomas Drewet.

John Gwalter.

Roger Ryppon.

Robert Awoburne [Aburne].

Scipio Bellot.

Robert Bowle.

John Barnes "beeing sic / vnto death / was caryed forth & departed / this life shortly after".

Mother Maner, sixty years of age.

Mother Roe, sixty years of age.

Anna Tailour.

Judeth Myller.

Margaret Farrer "beeing sick vnto death was caried forth / and ended her lyfe within a day or two after."

In Bridewell.

John Purdy [Pardy ?].

In the Gatehouse.

Mr Denford, about sixty years of age.

[1] It will be seen later that it is exceedingly improbable that Ainsworth was "teacher" of the congregation in 1596.

In the White Lyon.
Father Debenham, about seventy years of age.
In Woodstreet Counter.
George Bryty [Dingthie ?].
Thomas Hewet.
In the Clink.
Henry Thompson.
In the Poultry Counter.
John Chandler "beeing sick vnto death was carryed forth &
    dyed" within a few days.
In the Fleet.
Walter Lane.

As this previously mentioned Confession is given in Professor
Williston Walker's "Creeds and Platforms of Congregationalism", further mention of its contents seems to be unnecessary.

In 1597, when the leaders of the congregation no longer saw
any hope of gaining their release and of living undisturbed in
England or even anywhere else in Europe, they finally petitioned
to be allowed to emigrate to Canada. The story of how they
escaped from their expected fate, of how one of their vessels was
shipwrecked without any loss of life, and of how the exiles
returned to London and finally reached Holland, has been so
well told by Dr Dexter that there is no need of repeating it
here.

CHAPTER VI

THE BARROWISTS ON THE CONTINENT

NOT long after the execution of Barrowe, Greenwood, and
Penry all of the Barrowists except the leaders were apparently
released from prison, and seeing the helplessness of their cause
in England, resolved to accept a proffered exile in Holland[1].
The movement thither evidently commenced in 1593[2]. What
difficulties lay before them even in that peaceful country can
hardly have dawned on their weary minds as they set sail from
the land of their birth. Outcasts at home, they soon found only
a chilly welcome in the Low Countries. It is to be especially
noticed that they did not visit, or settle in, Middelburg. Earlier
separatists had not fared well there. The dissensions between
Browne and Harrison were still fresh in their memory, and the
later experience of Francis Johnson with Thomas Ferrers had
plainly manifested that even the slightest suspicion of a tendency
toward separatism was certain to arouse antagonism. For some
reason, also, the company did not at first go to Amsterdam.
Very probably they wished to hide themselves in some more
remote spot where fewer English people would cross their path
and seek to injure their prospects.

The earliest emigrants of the congregation to arrive in

---

[1] "An Act to retain the Queen's Majesty's Subjects in their due
Obedience" had been passed by Parliament between Feb. 19 and April 10,
1592/3 (See "The Statutes at Large From the First Year of King Edward
the Fourth To the End of the Reign of Queen Elizabeth", London, Vol. II.,
1786, p. 658). This act would suggest that the emigration of the
Barrowists may have taken place within three months after the latter
date.

[2] See Francis Johnson's "An Inqvirie and Ansvver Of Thomas
VVhite", 1606, p. 63.

Holland seem at first to have settled at Campen [Campin][1] and
about 1595 to have removed to Naarden [Narden], for Francis
Johnson writing in 1606 says[2]:—

> Here he excepteth onely against one of our Deacons, *Mr C.
> Bow[man]*. To whom about eleven yeares synce, the Magistrates
> of Narden did once (and not weekly, as this man intimateth) send
> a little money to be given to the poore of the Church: which he
> together with one of the Elders (*Mr. G. Knifton*) did accordingly
> bestow vpon such as they iudged to stand most in need....

In the same work Johnson gives the following interesting
description of the troubles of the congregation in the Low
Countries, while he and some of the other officers and members
were in prison at London[3]:—

> I.   About thirteen yeares synce [1593 ?], this Church through
> persecution in England, was driven to come into these countreyes.
> A while after they were come hither [1594 ?], divers of them [at
> Campen ?] fell into the heresies of the Anabaptists (which are too
> common in these countreys) and so persisting were excommunicated
> by the rest.   Then a while after that [1595 or 1596 ?] againe, many
> others [at Naarden ?] (of whom I think he speaketh here) some
> elder some younger, even too many, though not the half (as I
> vnderstand) fell into a schisme from the rest, and so many of them
> as continewed therein were cast out: divers other of them repent-
> ing and returning before excomunication, & divers of them
> after....
> For the excommunication in generall, it was in deed recalled:
> wherevpon *C. S.* [Christopher Symkins ?], one of the schismed here
> mentioned by him, wrote vnto me thereabout.   (And here the
> Reader is to know that my self with some others of vs, both of
> the officers and other brethren, were then prisoners at London,
> while these things fell out in the Church being in the Low
> countreyes[4].)

Francis Johnson, George Johnson, and Daniel Studley
probably reached Holland late in September, or early in
October, 1597[5]. Whether the congregation had settled in
Amsterdam before that time is uncertain, but within two weeks

---

[1] In H.[enoch] Cl.[apham]'s "A Chronological Discourse", London,
1609 [p. 3].

[2] In "An Inqvirie and Ansvver Of Thomas VVhite", 1606, p. 46.

[3] *Ibid.*, p. 63.   [4] *Ibid.*, p. 64.

[5] See George Johnson's "A discourse", 1603, pp. 112–13, and E. Arber's
"Story of the Pilgrim Fathers", 1897, p. 107.

after Johnson's arrival it must have moved thither, if indeed it
had not done so before, for then "a great house / and having
sundry romes to spare" was hired in Amsterdam for the use of
the church[1].

Henoch Clapham gives still further information concerning
the congregation at Campen and Naarden, namely that they
"were contented" while in these towns "to dwell in *Monasteries*,
and so did"[2]. From Clapham it also appears that the first
Barrowists did not sing psalms, but that when Johnson became
pastor he persuaded his followers not to neglect singing[3]:—

Franc. Iohnson (being aduised by one [Henoch Clapham ?] that
talked with him thereabouts in the *Clincke* at *London*) did presse
the vse of our[4] singing Psalmes (neglected before of his people for
Apochrypha;) wherevpon his Congregation publikely in their meetinges vsed them, till they could haue them translated into verse, by
some of their Teachers : Which barbarous successe, I am not
ignoraunt [of]. *M. Tho. Settle* in *Norffolke*, can with me witnesse
this, so well as some resident now in *London*.

Clapham also furnishes us with other particulars relating to
the Barrowists in London when Francis Johnson came to confer
with Barrowe in the Clink, and afterwards. He tells us that
Johnson and Greenwood were made respectively Pastor and
Teacher, or Doctor, "without any *Imposition of hands*", but
that when Johnson came to Amsterdam five or six years later,
he had a ceremony of imposition of hands performed over him
by the lay members of his own congregation[5].

The manner of taking the collection at the Barrowist
meetings in London, and later in Holland, is thus amusingly
told by Clapham[6]:—

And hereupon it was, that the Separists *did at first in their secret*

---

[1] George Johnson's "A discourse", p. 113.

[2] Henoch Clapham's "A Chronological Discourse", 1609 [p. 3].

[3] *Ibid.* [p. 36].

[4] Notice that Clapham seems to consider himself among those interested
in the matter. He may have been imprisoned with the Barrowists and
indeed may have participated in their meetings. He does not include
himself among Johnson's "people", however, though for a time the Barrowists may have believed him to be thoroughly in sympathy with them.

[5] Henoch Clapham's "A Chronological Discourse" [p. 31].

[6] *Ibid.* [p. vi].

*Conuenticles, appoynt their Deacons to stand at the Chamber dore, at
the peoples out-gate, with their Hats in hand (much like after the
fashion of a Play-house) into the which they put their* voluntary.
*But comming beyonde seas, where a man might haue seauen Doyts
for a penny, it fell out, howsoeuer their voluntary (at the casting in)
did make a great clangor, the* Summa totalis *ouerseene, the maisters
of the Play, came to haue but a few pence to their share. Whereupon,
a broad Dish (reasonable flat) was placed in the middest of their
conuention, that when the voluntarie was cast in, others might obserue
the quantitie. But this way serued not the turne, for a few doyts
rushing in vpon the soddaine, could not easily be obserued, of what
quantity it might be. Vpon this, the Pastor gaue out, that if (besides
giftes from others abroad) they would not make him* Tenne *pounds
yearely at least, he would leaue them, as vnworthy the Gospell. They
stickle, for feare of a fall; and* [William] Holder [Houlder] *the
Glouer must giue sixe Styuers a weeke for his part:* George Cl.[eaton]
*the Bricklayer, more Styuers for his part, by reason that he had good
doinges: and so others accordingly. The Glouer complaines of the
greatnesse of the Cesse, and therefore sayd; that hee would for*
England. &c....

Houlder accordingly became a "wandering starre."

According to Clapham the Puritan ministers ridiculed the
style of preaching adopted by the early Barrowists[1]:—

A third cause of the Ministers contempt, hath arisen from our
Syncerians, *who haue made it a very small matter, to preach vpon the
Scriptures: holding euery howers talke, A Sermon: Insomuch as, a
number would not goe to meate (if a few were present of their faction)
but there must be a kind of Sermon.*

Maister Barrowe *himselfe, euen to my selfe (telling him that
Maister* Penry *did vse that fashion of Preaching,) did exceedingly
dislike it; saying of that, and of some Pin-sellers and Pedlers that
then were put to preach in their Thursedayes Prophecie, that it would
bring the Scriptures into mightie contempt.*

Before 1609 Francis Johnson seems to have been nicknamed
the "Bishop of *Brownisme*", because "he exerciseth authoritie
ouer some [Barrowist] assemblies in *England* and elsewhere"[2].

The internal troubles and dissensions in Johnson's congregation before 1603, as is well known, are most vividly told by
his brother George in a work printed at Amsterdam in that
year, and entitled, "A discourse of some troubles / | and ex-
communications in the banished | English Church at Amsterdam. |
Published for sundry causes declared in the preface to the

---

[1] Henoch Clapham's "A Chronological Discourse", 1609, p. vii.
[2] *Ibid.* [p. 56].

Pastour | of the sayd Church. | ... ", 1603. The only copies of this work known to me at present are those in Trinity College Library, Cambridge; in the Chetham Library, Manchester; and in Sion College Library, London; but Archbishop Bancroft also had a copy in his own library, which unless it has been lost, should some day be found in Lambeth Palace Library. The text of the work breaks off abruptly at page 214, and we learn from Francis Johnson's "AN INQVIRIE | AND ANSVVER | Of Thomas VVhite", published in 1606, that this publication of his brother's was "but part of a book, printed before the rest was finished "[1], so that probably not more than 214 pages were ever issued.

From this work by George Johnson we learn among other things that Henry Barrowe left a sum of money to Francis Johnson's congregation "for a stock", i.e., a trust fund, and that before 1598–9 "monie" had been "sent from [the Barrowist church in?] London, [Harrison's congregation in?] Middelburgh, and [Peter Fairlambe and his supporters in?] Barbarie for the poore" of the congregation at Amsterdam[2]. It also appears that while the Barrowists were at Campen and Naarden before Johnson's arrival, an attempt had been made to provide certain officers for the church. One Mr Smith [William Smythe?] seems to have been their "teacher" for a time[3], and Mr [Matthew] Slade was chosen an elder in addition to Daniel Studley and George Knifton. There was but one deacon, Christopher Bowman. After Johnson reached Amsterdam still further changes among the church officers were apparently made. Not until then, it seems therefore, could Henry Ainsworth have been elected "teacher", and very likely he was not chosen until somewhat later.

---

[1] P. 61.   [2] "A discourse", p. 60.
[3] P. 214. See, however, a passage in H. A.[insworth]'s "Covnter-poyson", 1608, p. 41, which seems to be contrary to this view: "Mr. *Smith, Crud,* and some others, (which never were officers, much lesse pillars, in our church,) did indeed forsake their first faith, and died soon after ;..." Whereby I think he must mean, in the face of George Johnson's testimony, that Mr Smith was never an officer, i.e., "teacher", of the congregation *after Ainsworth became the colleague of Francis Johnson.*

George Johnson's book is valuable not only because of its scarcity, but also because of the many important details it contains. Nevertheless, the work does not make us admire its author, for in it he not only seeks to malign his brother by publishing to the world an account of the unhappy differences in his congregation, but also, as will soon be seen, reveals himself as a person of such narrow views as to repel the modern reader.

About 1594 Francis Johnson, who was then in the Clink prison, became a suitor to Mrs Tomison Boys [Boyes], a widow. At once objections were made by George Johnson and others interested, who said that she "was not a fitt match for him". Notwithstanding this opposition we are told that "Shortly after they proceded in marriage secretly". Immediately an unceasing uproar arose in the congregation concerning the unsuitable elegance of Mrs Johnson's apparel, etc. Was ever the Puritan spirit more quaintly manifested than in the following passage written by George Johnson, Schoolmaster!

These things following were reproved in Mris Tomison Iohnson the Pastors wife touching apparel,...

First the wearing of a long busk after the fashion of the world contrary to Rom. 12. 2, I. Tim. 2. 9. 10. 2. Wearing of the long white brest after the fashion of yong dames, and so low she wore it, as the vvorld call them kodpeece brests. Contrary to the former places, and also to I. Pet. 3. 3[.] 4. 5. 3. Whalebones in the bodies of peticotes Contrary to the former rules, as also against nature, being as the Phisitians affirme hinderers of conceiving or procreating children. 4. Great sleeves sett out with whalebones, which the world cal....Contrary to the former rules of modesty, and shamefastnes. 5. Excesse of lace vpon them after the fashion of yong Marchants vvives. Contrary to the rules of modesty. 6. Foure or five gould Rings on at once. Contrary to the former rules in a Pastors vvife. 7 A copple crowned hatt vvith a tvvined band, as yong Marchants vvives, and yong Dames vse. Immodest and toyish in a Pastors vvife. Contrary also to the former rules. 8 Tucked aprons, like round hose: contrary likewise to the former rules. 9. Excesse in rufs, laune coives, muske, and such like things: contrary to I. Tim. 2. 9, I. Peter. 3. 3, forbidding costly apparel. 10 The painted Hipocritical brest, shewing as if there were some special workes, and in truth nothing but a shadow. Contrary to modesty, and sobriety. 11. Bodies tied to the peticote with points, as men do their dublets to their hose. Contrary to I. Thes. 5. 22. conferred with Deut. 22, I. Iohn 2. 16. 12. Some

also reporte that she laid forth her heare [hair?] also Contrary to
I. Tim. 2. 9, I Pet 3. 3....

Touching her actions and dealings giving offence, whereof she
was likewise admonished, they vvere as follow

First she stoode gazing, bracing or vaunting in shop doores.
Contrary to the rules of modest behaviour in the daughters of Zion,
and condemned. Isah. 3. 16, 2 She so quaffed wine, that a papist
in their company said to another vvoman: You leave some, and
shew modesty, but Mris, Iohnson, shee etc. she doth not. This
behaviour condemned I. Thess. 4. 12. and in the places named
before. 3. She laide in bedd on the Lordes day till 9 a clock, and
hindered the exercise of the worde, she being not sick, nor having
any iust cause to lie so long: This contrary to the diligent care,
and redines, which should be in Gods servants Psal. 119. Isah,
58. 13 Ezec. 20. 12. Act. 20. 7. &c. 4. Her behaviour in all
stoutnes, and (as some said) disdaine: she also (as some compleined)
did not willingly visit the poore. This is contrary to humility, and
love...[1]

On the whole Francis Johnson seems to have had as
difficult a life as any separatist leader, but he could not be
entirely overthrown in spite of the carping criticism of his
enemies. One would think that he might have felt it his duty
to have answered his younger brother's book, but he remained
silent, though three years later, when he prepared his work
against Thomas White, who also had dealt none too kindly with
him, he wrote in this calm, dignified style of the fanatic, narrow-
minded, brother whose excommunication we cannot feel was
entirely unmerited:—

As for that he saith of the book aforesaid [*"A Discourse of
certaine troubles & excom. &c."*] *lying vnanswered,* we have divers
reasons for so leaving it. 1. It is but part of a book, printed
before the rest was finished: And to see the whole, might be of
speciall vse if an answer should be given vnto it. 2. Synce the
writing thereof, it pleased God to visite him with sicknes that he
died: And seing he is dead, we do so leave him: forbearing now to
write what we could. 3. He did not, like as this man, leave or
contrary our generall cause and testimony against the Church of
England: but held it so himself, as of late going into England
he was there taken and put in prison for this cause, where he died
vnder their hands...[2]

The pathetic end of George Johnson's life is described as

---

[1] "A discourse of some troubles", 1603, pp. 135-37.

[2] "An Inqvirie and Ansvver Of Thomas VVhite", 1606, p. 61.

follows in Richard Clyfton's "AN | ADVERTISE-|MENT |
…", 1612:—

The one vvas *George Iohnson* the Pastours brother, vvho dyed
at Durham : the manner of vvhose sicknes and death vvas signified
hither to his brother by vvriting from thence, by a friend of his
that vvas often vvith him, both before & in the time of his sicknes:
VVho vvrote hither, that he being in prison, bestovved the most of
his time, in finishing the book which before he had begunne, and
whereof some sheets are printed ; vvhich vvhen he had done, it
pleased God to visite him vvith sicknes unto death. At vvhich
time on his death bedde, he gave out (as he vvrote, & is well
knovvn) *verie heavie & great exclamations about his sinnes by the
Lord layd to his charge, calling unto God for mercie.* And *in this
sort* (sayth the Gentleman that vvrit the letter, & vvas present
there) *he continued by the space of an houre that I was with him,
shewing great trouble in minde, yet not without comfort in the Lord,
whose servant I doubt not but he dyed...*[1]

With the death of George Johnson the troubles of the
Barrowists temporarily subsided, though soon to recommence.
Of those which occurred during Francis Johnson's lifetime we
shall make little mention, as they have been treated at sufficient
length, though the writer believes somewhat unfairly and rather
too sensationally, in Mr Arber's " Story of the Pilgrim Fathers".
Points that have been less emphasized may more profitably
occupy our time.

We may begin with the life of Henry Ainsworth, who,
according to the brief but instructive monograph of Messrs Wm
E. A., and Ernest, Axon[2], was born in Norfolk, not in Lancashire,
as has sometimes been supposed. " He was a native of Swanton
Morley", it seems, "where he was born in 1570. His father,
Thomas Aynsworth, was a yeoman. After being three years
under the scholastic care of Mr Clephamson, he proceeded to
St John's College, Cambridge, but a year later transferred
himself to Gonville and Caius College. Here he was admitted
at the close of 1587, and remained three years " as a scholar on
the foundation ". It is not stated that he received a degree[3].

[1] P. 14.

[2] " Henry Ainsworth, the Puritan Commentator…(Reprinted from the
'Transactions of the Lancashire and Cheshire Antiquarian Society',
1888.)", Manchester, 1889, 8°.

[3] Pp. 44–5.

Before 1598 Ainsworth seems to have been in Holland[1], though it is not manifest how much earlier he arrived. He is said at first to have "entered into the service of a bookseller at Amsterdam as a porter"[2], and it has usually been claimed by modern historians that he was the author, wholly or in part, of "A Trve Confession" published by Johnson's congregation in 1596. As yet I know of no trustworthy evidence for this assertion. He is said, further, to have been very poor at this early period of his residence in Holland. Already he must have had an unusual knowledge of Hebrew. It is my opinion that Ainsworth did not become "teacher" of the Barrowist congregation in Amsterdam until Francis Johnson's arrival in the autumn of 1597, and possibly not until a little later. Before that time in Johnson's absence, as has already been stated, one Mr Smith [William Smythe?] had probably held that position, and accordingly, if any one beside Johnson and the elders assisted in producing the Confession of 1596, Smith, and not Ainsworth, would naturally have been that one.

During his lifetime Ainsworth published a considerable number of books, but these contain almost nothing relating to his personal history, and therefore little is now known of his life except what appears in a few scattered references in the works of other writers. These references, however, are worth citing. In the first place, there are the following interesting, but too little noticed and appreciated, points relating to his early life given in John Paget's "*AN* | ARROVV | *Against the Separation* | OF THE | Brownists...", Amsterdam, 1618. Says Paget[3]:—

[1] John Paget's "An Arrovv", 1618 (not 1617 as given by Dr Powicke) p. 119,—"How comes it that you who have lived more than 20. yeares as a neighbour vnto the Reformed Churches in these countries should be such a stranger vnto them and so ignorant of their estate and practise?" This citation indicates that Ainsworth was in Holland in or before 1598, but, in the presence of other evidence, it cannot be used to prove more than that.

[2] "Henry Ainsworth", as above, p. 45.

[3] Pp. 91–2. I know of no good reason why the statements made in this citation cannot be considered as trustworthy. If they were not true, they are of such a nature, that they would certainly have been denied.

Now you being such an Apostata [Apostate] as according to
your present profession have sundry times turned back vnto the
Idolatrous false Church, as hath bene by divers persons witnessed,
neither could *Mr. Iohnson* deny the same, when he ["Inqvir. of
Th. wh.(ite) p. 41. 42."] was most desirous to excuse you therein :
though it was obiected that you had turned your coate as oft if not
oftner then D. Perne :...Let it be well observed that you are thus
noted to have turned your coate & changed your religion *five* severall
times, namely, *first* being of our religion and a member of the
church of England you forsook that Church and separated : *Secondly*,
that being separated, you did againe in *London* being in the hands
of authoritie yeeld to joyne with the worship and ministery of the
Church of England : *Thirdly*, that after this you did againe slide
back vnto the separation and renounce the Church of England :
Fourthly, that after this when you were in *Ireland*[1] and in some
danger of punishment for your scandal, you did againe returne vnto
the communion renounced by you, whether fainedly or vnfainedly,
I leave vnto your self to consider : *Fiftly*, after this you change
your profession againe and fall back vnto separation, and stick now
presently in this Schisme :...

Then there is the true story of Ainsworth's death, a citation
concerning which from the earliest published source is, I think,
here given for the first time. This account, it will be noticed, is
quite in conflict with tradition[2], and yet it is hardly surprising

Paget in a case of this kind may have made mistakes as other men, but,
though a busybody, he certainly did not purposely tell untruths.

[1] This statement that Ainsworth went as a Brownist to Ireland is
suggestive, for in the next chapter we shall see that in 1594 there were
Brownists in Ireland. Ainsworth probably was one of these, and Governor
Bradford in "A Dialogue" (See A. Young's "Chronicles", 1841) says that
Ainsworth came to Holland from Ireland.

[2] The earliest version of the traditional, apocryphal accounts of Ainsworth's death that I remember to have seen, is the following, taken from
an undated eighteenth century document (Rawlinson MS. B. 158, pp. 141-2)
in the Bodleian Library :

"Hen : Ainsworth was a great Separatist (a Brownist I think) and Lived at
Amsterdame where he had a congregation, one euening goeing along the
streete he stumbled, upon a purse which taking up he found full of gold,
with a small bunch of keies hanging at it. He Carried it home ; and the
next day sent about the crier to know who had lost a purse, about such a
time, neer such a place, with Money in it ; hereupon the purse &c : was
chalenged by a Iewish woman, who came to him told the just quantity of
the money In it caried him to her house, and shewed him the boxes [?] to
which those keies belonged in fine,—convinced him that it was her purse

that the facts have not been familiar even to one so learned as the editor of the "British Weekly"[1], for there is apparently only one copy extant of the work in which this particular information is to be found. This copy is in the Bodleian Library, and is entitled, "CERTAIN NOTES | *Of* | M. HENRY AYNS-WORTH | HIS LAST SERMON. | *Taken by pen in the publique delivery by one of | his flock, a little before his death.* | *Anno* 1622. | ... | Imprinted 1630 ", 8°. The book was published by Sabine Staresmore, who briefly tells the story of Ainsworth's death by "that sore perplexing and tedious disease of the stone". The passage is so little known that it may be cited in full[2] :—

They were the instructions our late faithfull Teacher M. Aynsworth, delivered to us all, the last time he ever executed his ministery with us, which was at such a time as his bodye & naturall strength were so decayed, that he wanted (as ye know) ability to come up again, even that very Lords day in the afternoone as his usuall manner was, wherein his faithfullnes may be seen even to his last gasp, in striving to feed the flocke even when the hand of God was heavy upon him in that sore perplexing and tedious disease of the stone, of which in a few dayes after he dyed, yet since even in his strong paines (that sometime by reason of the extremity caused a stay of speach, to the griefe of the hearers and beholders) he was delivered of this, as the last fruit of his ministry, ...

A fuller and later medical report of Dr Nicolaus Tulpius on Ainsworth's case is cited in the previously mentioned pamphlet of Messrs Wm E. A., and Ernest, Axon (pp. 54–5)[3].

and Money, and so he gave it her ; shortly after the woman brought her husband to him, who from talking of the purse &c: began to discourse of their Religion: &c: Ainsworth prevailed so upon him, that the Iew had nothing more to say In defence of his party ; onely he asked Liberty to bring a Couple of their Rabbies to Argue with him ; which they did, and Ainsworth is said to haue pleaded his cause so well with them both out of the Scriptures, and their own Authors that they had nothing to say, but within three days Ainsworth was found poisoned."

[1] Who several years ago, according to the author's recollection, in reviewing the Rev. J. H. Shakespeare's "Baptist and Congregational Pioneers", plainly manifested that he did not know how Ainsworth died.

[2] Pp. x–xi.

[3] The first edition of the "Observationes Medicæ" of Dr Nicolaus Tulpius of Amsterdam was published in that city in 1641. What seems to be a second enlarged and improved edition, called "editio nova", was

With these facts of Ainsworth's life before us we may now briefly consider the rise of the Ainsworthians, or followers of

issued in octavo at Amsterdam in 1652. A copy of this edition is in the Bodleian Library and gives (pp. 173–5) the following description of the disease from which Ainsworth died :—

"*Ischuria lunatica.*

"HEnrico Ainsvvordo, Theologo Britanno, supprimebatur urina, quolibet fermè plenilunio : cum insigni angustiâ, & evidenti totius corporis incendio. Neque excernebatur illa iterùm ; nisi vel declinante lunâ ; vel exsolutâ brachii venâ. Verùm sanguinem toties mittere, quotiens Luna orbem suum complens, supprimeret ipsi lotium : non videbatur è re ægri. Qui propterea aliquotiens, tulit patienter, quod nequiit altrinsecùs evitari, malum.

"Cujus rarus, & inusitatus rumor, ut excivit varia, cùm nostratium, tum Britannorum Medicorum ingenia : invenit tamen neminem tam sagaci judicio : ut potuerit reddere genuinam, reciprocantis hujus periodi, rationem : nedum subiti, illius auxilii ; quod æger dictum, ac factum percepit, à sanguine ex brachio misso.

"Sola anatome, post obitum instituta, eruit illic feliciter veritatem in profundum demersam : & ostendit distinctè, quî angusta, renis sinistri, pelvis, excrevisset in eam amplitudinem, ut suppleret commodè vicem, vesicæ urinariæ. Quæ proptereà tam fuit vacua, quàm ren repletus.

"Quæ collectio urinæ, majoribus venis adeò vicina, procul dubio, in causa fuit, quod tam promptè fluxerit ipsi lotium, simulac feriretur brachii vena. Nam velut œnopolæ, spiritu suprà priùs emisso, facilè vinum infra eliciunt, ex repletis doliis : sic reserantur quoque renes, ubi vel minimum, spirituosi sanguinis adimitur tumidis brachii venis. Ex quarum incisione, vident propterea peritiores Medici, non tam sisti, quàm promoveri sæpè mulieribus, suppressa menstrua.

"Sed quid dicendum, de lunæ consensu ? quæ uti reliquis dominatur aquis : sic videtur quoque vim suam exseruisse, in lotium hujus venerabilis Theologi. Cujus urinam, in rene detentam, suppressit intumescens hoc sidus, longè faciliùs ; & dispersit suppressam fortè multo celeriùs, per vicinas venas ; quàm si delituisset in remotioris vesicæ, receptaculo.

"A quâ periodicâ, reciprocantis urinæ, revolutione, credibile utique est, provenisse, quas singulis pleniluniis, patiebatur, cùm febres, tum augustias. Quibus cum plerumque conflictabat, ad diem quintum ; antequam ex toto liberaretur. Sed sanguine, ex brachio, emisso, resolvebatur ilicò frænum, lotium supprimens. Quantumvis vesica præter hoc impedimentum, in se præterea contineret, duos insignes calculos. Uti quoque folliculus fellis, sed parvos, nigros, teretes, &, instar pumicis, raros.

"Quantum verò huic Theologo profuit, sanguis ex brachio detractus, tantum juvere alios, in simili, urinæ, suppressione, vel sanguis ubertim è naribus profluens ; vel frequens macularum, in habitu corporis, eruptio.

Henry Ainsworth. Up to 1610, though there always was more or less friction in Francis Johnson's church, the leaders seem to have been peaceably disposed toward one another. There had, however, been defections, and their enemies had been watchful. Nevertheless, Johnson appears to have silenced their critics by his previously mentioned " AN INQVIRIE | AND ANSVVER | Of Thomas VVhite | ... ", published in 1606, so that for several years no slanderous works against his congregation were printed. This silence, however, seems to have been only a lull before the storm, which began to break in 1609 and 1610, and which finally resulted in a permanent division between the followers of Johnson and the supporters of Ainsworth. The decision to separate was made by the Ainsworthians on December 15, 1610, and carried into effect on the following day[1], after a whole year of oral and written discussion between the parties, in which each side claimed that the other was at fault[2].

The trouble between Johnson and Ainsworth may have been first brought about by those who had circulated scandalous stories against some of the congregation. Johnson probably felt that malice was the cause of much that had been said, that it was unadvisable at any time to bring such matters before the whole church, and that he did not wish to trust to a popular vote, because he was not entirely convinced that the people with whom he had to deal would render a really just decision. This led him to maintain that not the whole congregation, but the elders only, were the church,—a conclusion which Ainsworth naturally claimed was quite at variance with the principles on which the church had been founded. A relic of this discussion is probably to be found in an extended and hitherto unnoticed manuscript of Johnson's, probably preserved by Richard Bancroft and now in Lambeth Palace Library[3]. It has no title, and if I

Quibus duobus auxiliis sanitatem suam aliquando recuperavit, Iuvenis quidam ; cui integros octodecim dies stagnaverat urina."

[1] Richard Clyfton's " An Advertisement ", 1612, p. 93.

[2] In addition to the preceding reference to Clyfton's "Advertisement", p. 93, see Henry Ainsworth's " *An* Animadversion to Mr Richard Clyftons Advertisement", Amsterdam, 1613, pp. 123–36.

[3] MS. 445, fol. 512+.

remember correctly, is anonymous, but it is undoubtedly Johnson's work, as claimed in the catalogue.

The number of those who seceded with Ainsworth is not stated, but it looks as if most of the officers as well as many of the church members remained with Johnson. Considerable reorganization must now have taken place. New officers had to be found to fill the positions made vacant in Johnson's church, and Ainsworth's congregation had to begin an independent existence. For two or three years both parties lingered on in Amsterdam. At first Johnson kept possession of the church building, but later the courts decided that Ainsworth's congregation was the church, as maintaining its earliest traditions, and gave them the church building. After this Johnson's congregation may have remained in Amsterdam for a time, but they were apparently unpopular, and the circulation of pamphlets full of scandalous aspersions probably made a longer stay impossible. We are not, therefore, surprised to hear of their intention to leave Amsterdam for Emden in May, 1612 or 1613[1].

It is reported in "The Prophane Schisme of the Brownists or Separatists", 1612[2], written by Christopher Lawne, and three others, that only one elder of Johnson's congregation, Jean de l'Ecluse, formerly a printer of Rouen, and once stated to be "a notable drunkard", "went with M. *Ainsworth*, when he carried away the Church from the Franciscans", while Jacob Johnson, who had been exiled in 1599, evidently took de l'Ecluse's place in Johnson's church. It is also said that the Franciscans sought to banish the Ainsworthians from Amsterdam, and that the minds of some of the old members had been so unsettled that they were uncertain to which section of the congregation they should turn. This feeling shows that the stories, which had been printed against Johnson and the elders, even if true, had not entirely shaken the church's faith in their former leaders. How many elders Ainsworth's congregation had, is uncertain. We know, however, that Giles Thorpe was a deacon about 1612

---

[1] In "A Shield of Defence", 1612, by John Fowler and two others, p. 33.

[2] P. 109

or 1613, and that by 1618 he had been made an Elder with de l'Ecluse.

A mistake made by Dr Dexter relating to the Barrowist troubles about this time needs to be corrected. In his Bibliography he mentions a book entitled "The Hunting of the foxe. part I.", which he says was published by Giles Thorpe in 1616. Mr Edward Arber partially follows Dr Dexter in mentioning[1] this work as a "? Printed" book, but changes the date to "about 1610", and speaks of the work as an "utterly lost" book. As a matter of fact Thorpe wrote a work entitled, "The Hunting of the foxe. part I." before or about 1612, but that it was never printed or published as a whole, or under that title, is plainly shown by the following passage from John Paget's "ARROVV", 1618, in which he is evidently referring to three pamphlets entitled respectively "Brovvnisme Tvrned The In-side out-ward", London, 1613, by Christopher Lawne; "The Prophane Schisme of the Brownists or Separatists", 1612, prepared by Christopher Lawne, John Fowler, Clement Sanders, and Robert Bulwarde; and especially "A Shield of Defence against the Arrowes of Schisme", Amsterdam, 1612, written by John Fowler, Clement Saunders, and Robert Bulwarde[2]:—

you [Ainsworth] speak of *disguised pamphlets that are come out of our congregation*: but the bookes which you seeme to ayme at, are such as for the matter of them are taken out of your offensive company, and do in part shew the disguised practises of your separation: for the persons that published them, they also were such as came out of your company, who leaving their schisme, which they once professed with you, were more fit to vvitnesse such things as they had heard and seene among you: for the helpers, which they had herein, they had (besides others) M[r]. Th.[orpe] now an Elder of your congregation also (but then a deacon) out of vvhose vvriting [From margin: "The Hunting of the foxe. part. I."] vvhich he communicated vvith them, they receyved sundry things vvhich they published, and many more vvhich should have bene published, had not their book bene misprinted contrary to their mindes: for the maner of printing and publishing one of those bookes, great injury hath bene done vnto them,...

After the separation between Johnson and Ainsworth in

[1] "The Story of the Pilgrim Fathers", 1897, p. 9.
[2] Pp. 333–34.

1610 Richard Clyfton became teacher in Johnson's congregation and apparently remained in that position until Johnson's death in 1617. Johnson seems to have carried out his purpose to go to Emden, and probably would have remained there until the end of his life, but one of the elders, Francis Blackwell, interested the congregation in a voyage to Virginia, which in some way miscarried and ruined the prospects of many of the members. It was this misfortune perhaps that brought Johnson again to Amsterdam where more work and charity might possibly be found. At any rate, Johnson was temporarily in Amsterdam in 1617[1] when he died. Evidently no union could be effected between him and the Ainsworthians, and after his death the congregation, which appears to have been composed of about 150 members started on their fateful voyage to Virginia.

Thus were the early separatists torn and rent by endless divisions. Says John Paget in "*AN* | ARROVV | *Against the Separation* | OF THE | Brownists", Amsterdam, 1618, a work which is principally directed against Ainsworth and his congregation[2]:—

O F those that separate from the Church of God, there are many sorts : Though the Brownists assume vnto themselves the title of Separation, and call themselves the Churches of the Separation, yet is not this title sufficient to distinguish them; Separation being common to so many.

Of the Brownists also there are sundry sects: Some separate

---

[1] See the Epistle "To the Christian Reader" of Francis Johnson's "A Christian Plea", 1617. This work is the very "death-bed Recantation" of Johnson's which Mr Arber ("Story of the Pilgrim Fathers", p. 129, note) says it "is certainly not". The writer came to this opinion independently of Dr Powicke, who takes the same view.

[2] [P. iii.] Heretofore it has been the custom both of Congregational and Baptist historians to give too little credence to statements made by the opponents of their beliefs, and also to choose from these statements those which pleased their fancy, and to omit others. Paget has been dealt with in this way, but while he certainly was a busy-body and a disagreeable man, I find no evidence that he was really bad, or even that his controversial statements as a whole cannot be trusted as much as those of persons opposed to him. From the enemies of the early separatists in reality may be gleaned some of the most valuable points in their history.

from the Church of England for corruptions; and yet confesse
both it & Roome also to be a true Church, as the followers
of Mr. Iohnson: Some renounce the Church of England as a
false Church; and yet allow private communion with the godly
therein, as Mr. Robinson and his followers: Some renounce all
Religious communion both publique and private with any member
of that Church whosoever, as Mr. Ainsworth and such as hearken
vnto him, being deepest and stiffest in their Schisme. The evil of
this separation is great: First, the mindes of many are troubled
and distracted hereby; even of such as do not separate, but have
some liking thereof;...Secondly, for those that separate but do not
yet joyne vnto them, or being joyned do withhold from actual
communion, living alone and hearing the word of God in no Church,
as some do;...Fourthly, for further and greater evilles into which
they are given up; it is apparant that three or four hundred of the
Brownists have brought forth more Apostate Anabaptists and
Arians sometimes in one yeare then ten thousand members of the
Reformed Dutch Church in this citie [Amsterdam], have done in
ten yeares or more,...

The history of Ainsworth's congregation for at least a dozen
years after his death is more or less directly connected with the
name of Sabine Staresmore. We may therefore turn our
attention to this individual who now so suddenly comes into
special prominence. Staresmore first appears as one of the
leaders at the organization of Henry Jacob's Independent
(Puritan, non-separatist) congregation at London in 1616, where
he entered into the regular non-separatist covenant. In 1618
Staresmore was betrayed into the hands of the Bishops by
Francis Blackwell, the previously mentioned elder of Johnson's
congregation who was then about to sail for Virginia[1]. By
1619 Staresmore seems to have been released, and was still a
member of Jacob's church, as is evident from a work, of which we
shall hear more later, published in that year, and entitled,
"THE | VNLAWFVLNES | OF READING IN | PRAYER. |
OR, | THE ANSWER OF Mr. RI-|CHARD MAVNSEL
PREACHER, | VNTO CERTAIN ARGVMENTS, | or Reasons,
drawne against the using, or commu-|nicating, in, or with the
Booke of Com-|mon Prayer (imposed to be reade for | prayer
to God) in the Parish | Assemblies of Eng-|land. | *WITH* | A
Defence of the same Reasons, by SABINE STARESMORE. | ...".

---

[1] Governor Bradford tells of this affair, and gives the text of two or
three letters of Staresmore.

Apparently sometime within the years 1619–1621 Staresmore "went to, Mr. [Nicholas?] Lee, and his people [the remnant of the Barrowist congregation in London] and desired of them Communion signifying to them" that he was of their opinions and "in the same Covenant" as a member of Henry Jacob's church, "& so got into theire Communion: But when they came to heare that Mr. S.[taresmore] had deceiued them: ther vvas a meeting appointed betvvene Mr. Lee and his people, & Mr. Iacobe and his people, at the vvhich Mr. Sta.[resmore] himselfe vvas presente and three other men vvhich aftervvards vvere members of our [Ainsworth's] Church vvhich testified vnto vs, hovv things vvas caried: so being come together, Mr. Iacobe their manifested as the truth vvas that they never intended separation from the Church of England: appearing to Mr. S.[taresmore]. I [A.(nthony?) T.(hatcher?)] for vvitnesse saying their sittes Mr. S.[taresmore] lett him gainsay it if he can: to the vvhich speech, hee had not one vvord to gainsay "[1].

Evidently about 1622 Staresmore went to Holland where he hoped to find a congenial church home. On arriving in Amsterdam, however, he seems to have sought to enter Ainsworth's congregation without further covenanting on the ground of having been a member of the "Ancient Church" in London under the charge of Mr Lee, and he had almost persuaded Ainsworth to admit him, when the three persons who had been in Lee's congregation and had attended the previously mentioned conference concerning his case, testified against him[2]. Staresmore, in spite of this opposition, continued to claim that Jacob's congregation were for "the most part separated" and must have been conditionally admitted as a member, but while it is well known that Jacob's church separated from evil and the world, it is equally well understood, as appears in the preceding extended citation, that they, like all Independent Puritan congregations, never intended separation

[1] A. T.'s "A Christian Reprofe against Contention", 1631, p. 5. The initials A. T. may stand for Anthony Thatcher, whose name appears in George Johnson's "A discourse", 1603, p. 63.

[2] *Ibid.*

from the Church of England, and did not mention such separation in their covenant. However, Staresmore may have meant that there were many men of separatist opinions in Jacob's congregation. This interpretation does not appear to be impossible.

Ainsworth died in 1622 soon after Staresmore's arrival, and evidently left two elders in charge of the congregation, namely Jean de l'Ecluse and Giles Thorpe, the latter of whom apparently died not long after. His place seems to have been taken by Henry May, who had long been a member of the church[1], but the offices of pastor and teacher were certainly left unfilled for some years, since John Paget says in 1635, "for many yeares together" the Ainsworthians "were without Sacraments, and had neither Lords Supper nor Baptisme administred in their Church, their children for many yeares remayning unbaptised, and sundry dying unbaptized"[2]. In other words, there was no pastor or teacher in the congregation until after the arrival of John Canne about 1630.

In 1622 or 1623 after Ainsworth's death, Staresmore and others who sympathized with him were cast out of the church. This action was taken on the ground that Staresmore had misrepresented his case and had caused the congregation incorrectly to believe that he was a separatist. Such a course, it must be admitted, was not entirely unnatural, if the facts were as represented, but it was unfortunate, as it involved the church in a division that lasted for many years. Staresmore was a man of persistent purpose, and not easily turned aside from attaining his object. Hence, almost every Sunday for some time, we are told, he and his followers continued to attend the church services, and to create more or less disturbance. Says A.[nthony?] T.[hatcher?][3] :—

to bring their porposes [sic] about, they came most Lords dayes, diuers years & troubled vs with great desturbance, may haue been

---

[1] He is mentioned as being a member of Johnson's congregation before 1603.

[2] In "*An* Answer *To the unjust complaints* of William Best", Amsterdam, 1635, p. 134.

[3] In his "A Christian Reprofe", 1631, p. iii.

the prouocations, which they haue vsed towards vs to provoke vs : so that wee may truely say, that as Paule had fought with beast [*sic*] at Ephesus, so haue wee at Amsterdam, fought with men of a beastlike condition,...

In 1623 Staresmore prepared and published a " Loving Tender ", consisting of sixteen questions and answers propounded to the congregation and asking for peace and moderation,—a request, however, to which little heed was paid. No copy of this work appears to be in existence to-day.

As the publication of this little book did not bring about the desired result, Staresmore evidently went to Leyden[1] about the beginning of the year 1623/4, and, as was natural, was welcomed into John Robinson's Independent Puritan[2] congregation without further covenanting. Soon after he returned to Amsterdam, and knowing that the churches of Ainsworth and Robinson had been to a certain extent in communion, he now expected to be received as a member of the remnant of that congregation under de l'Ecluse. What was his chagrin, when his request continued to be firmly refused ! The church now seems to have written to Mr Lee's congregation at London asking about Staresmore's standing there. The answer was first sent to Jean de l'Ecluse at Amsterdam who was to forward it to Leyden[3]. He appears, however, to have retained the answer for some time, and Robinson also after he had received it did not hasten to reply, as he hoped before so doing to see a peaceful settlement of Staresmore's difficulties. Finally, on

[1] Says A. T. in "A Christian Reprofe", p. 19, " first as I haue before showed when hee creept into Mr. Lees people into their communion, and after that cam ouer heare, and vvould haue had communion with vs : but hee seeing himselfe to haue resistance heare, after this hee vvent to Leyden, and creept into that Church, and so made of them a bridge to git in vnto vs..."   [2] See Chapter XII.

[3] In John Robinson's "A Treatise of the Lawfvlnes of Hearing of the Ministers in the church of England :...", 1634, pp. 68–9. This letter also indicates that a question had arisen in Mr Lee's congregation concerning a maid who had joined in the separatist covenant with the other members, and nevertheless had gone to worship with Mr " Iakobs people", whom Mr Lee's company in 1624 seem to have regarded as " Idolators in their going to the assemblies",—the question being, whether this maid should be retained as a member, or excommunicated.

April 5, 1624, Robinson wrote the letter which was published in 1634 at the close[1] of his "A Treatise of the Lawfvlnes of Hearing of the Ministers in the church of England". In this, it should be noticed, he entirely exonerates Staresmore and his wife in their relations to the church in Leyden. The letter was publicly read before the whole congregation and with their consent was sent to London. Still the church at Amsterdam was not satisfied, and accordingly a communication lamenting their weakness, and bitterly complaining of Staresmore was sent to Leyden. To this Robinson replied in a letter written on Sept. 18, 1624, stating that he thought Staresmore, in spite of his differences of opinion and for the common good, ought to be received as a member of the church at Amsterdam[2]. Membership, however, was still denied.

Finding that nothing could be accomplished with Jean de l'Ecluse and Giles Thorpe, or more probably with de l'Ecluse and Henry May, Staresmore and his followers decided to organize an independent Puritan, non-separatist, congregation of their own. This they effected shortly after by entering into covenant "to...walke in the trueth, so far as they see or vnderstand"[3]. Staresmore's new undertaking seems to have met with great success at first, and his followers soon became "a great company"[4], while de l'Ecluse's church remained weak as it had been even in 1624. The members of these two churches apparently lived near each other, but they had no pleasant relations with one another[5].

Evidently by 1630 the condition of Staresmore's company had changed very materially. The membership had greatly diminished, and this fact together with the circumstance that John Canne may already have become pastor of the remnant of Ainsworth's church, may have roused him once more to seek a union with de l'Ecluse. In this year accordingly he published another book, to which reference has already been made, and

[1] Pp. 65–77.
[2] Published in Staresmore's "Certain Notes *Of* M. Henry Aynsworth his last Sermon", 1630, pp. xxxiii–xl.
[3] A. T.'s " A Christian Reprofe", 1631, p. 16.
[4] *Ibid.*, p. 41.   [5] *Ibid.*, p. 40.

which he hoped would heal the breach, entitled, " CERTAIN
NOTES | *Of* | M. HENRY AYNSWORTH | HIS LAST
SERMON. | *Taken by pen in the publique delivery by one of* | *his
flock, a little before his death.* | *Anno* 1622. | ...", 8°. This work
contains three main sections, the first prepared by Staresmore consisting of a narrative of the troubles of the congregation, etc., and
notes taken of Ainsworth's last sermon; the second, "An Appeale
on Trvths Behalf", being one of the letters to which reference has
previously been made, written by John Robinson on Sept. 18,
1624; the third, "Certain Observations of that Reverend, religious and faithfull servant of God, and glorious Martyr of Iesus
Christ, M. Randal Bate, which were part of his daily meditations
in the time of his sufferings, whilst he was prisoner in the Gatehouse at *Westminster*." Randal Bate is otherwise an almost
entirely unknown character. John Cotton somewhere refers
to him, but here his views are very fully given, though unfortunately almost nothing appears concerning his life-history. He
was evidently an Independent Puritan of the "Jacobite" type,
and may have been a member of Jacob's congregation in London.

Staresmore's work was answered by A.[nthony?] T.[hatch-
er?], who published in 1631 the previously mentioned "A |
CHRISTIAN REPROFE | AGAINST | CONTENTION. |
Wherin is declared and manifested a just defence | of the Church,
against such slanders and reproches which SABINE | STARESMORE
hath layd vpon vs in his two bookes, the first | being 16. Ques-
tions, called A louing tender. The second is his | Preface and
Postscript befor and behind Mr. Answorths last | Sermon, and
making a pretence by that to sett it out as a | loue token, hee
breatheth out his malice against vs: | And lastly her is an
Answer to a Letter written | to Mr. Robinson, and sent to vs
with the | consent of his Church, which now | Mr. Staresmore
hath published | to the world. | *To these things an Answer is
giuen by* A. T.... ", 4°, pp. iv, 43.

In this work it is claimed that de l'Ecluse's congregation had
borne with Staresmore's views before he was ejected, and
probably would have been still more patient, if he had not been
"so bussie & vnrestty", that is presumably, in winning others to
his own way of thinking, which was contrary, of course, to the

general opinion of the church. It is also stated that Staresmore's company was now smaller than that of de l'Ecluse, and in fact had "allmost come to nothing". The following passage concerning this point is so illuminating that it may be given in full[1] :—

In deed nearliest in dwelling, but fardist of in affection as it may appeare, not only by this bitter Letter, but also to strangers, as occasionally they passe by their dwellings [i.e., of Staresmore's company] by whome it cometh to our eares, hovv bitterly they [Staresmore's followers] inuay against vs [de l'Ecluse and the Ainsworthians]; and what is the cause, because wee wil not receiue their new found vvayes of declining, and because wee dislike that they looke not better to the Lords vvatch in suffering their members to apostat : some declining to the Church of England, & their liuing, other going a great compasse to new England to communicat with the Church of England : and some that are in this Land professe to hear in the assemblies, as they have occasion; and I make no doubte, but they haue don it many times : and this their negligent watch hath affected [them ?] so, that from a great company they are allmost come to nothing or fewer then those vvhom they despies, and haue sayd concerning vs, that our contentions would break vs to peeces.

In 1630 it is probable that Staresmore was in England for a time. We arrive at this conclusion by a comparison of two passages from widely different sources which seem to refer to the same unusual incident. One passage is in A. T.'s " A Christian Reprofe ", 1631, in which the following words occur : " yet since hee [Staresmore] was cast out from vs, hee went and had communion with them [members of the Parish churches in England], and baptized his child with them also "[2]. The other passage is in the so-called Jessey Records (No. 1 of the Gould Manuscript, of which we shall hear more in a subsequent chapter), three paragraphs from the close : " Whilst M[r] Lathorp [John Lathrop] was an Elder here [in Jacob's church] some being greived against one that had his Child then [1630] Baptized in the Common Assemblies,...". However, if Staresmore was in England in 1630, it is probable that he was in Holland during both 1632 and 1633, as we shall see later. He was certainly in that country sometime in 1633.

[1] Pp. 40–41. [2] P. 20.

B.   12

According to the Jessey Records John Canne [Mr. Can] with some others went to Holland, i.e., Amsterdam, in or about 1630. Here he seems to have been quickly[1] chosen pastor of de l'Ecluse's congregation, and at once began to strengthen that forlorn church. Benjamin Hanbury in his " Historical Memorials "[2] mentions a work by Canne entitled, ' " The Way to Peace : or, Good Counsel for it. Preached upon the 15th day of the second Month 1632[-3], at the Reconciliation of certain Brethren, between whom there had been former Differences." 12mo.' Hanbury seems to me to have made a mistake in giving the date of this sermon as 1632/33. April 15, 1632, appears to be the correct date, not Feb. 15, 1632/33, nearly a year later, as Hanbury evidently supposed. Hanbury never saw this work, and Dr Dexter, like myself, had seen no reference to it in contemporary literature. However, it is probably mentioned somewhere either by Canne or by one of his opponents, though it may have circulated only in manuscript, or have been printed by Canne himself in a very small edition. It is certainly disappointing that the contents of this sermon are not known to-day, as we would undoubtedly find some interesting information therein, but the mere title perhaps gives us the most suggestive and important point of all, namely, that Canne may temporarily have succeeded in healing the long standing breach between de l'Ecluse and Staresmore,—a truly notable achievement.

As has already been stated, Staresmore was certainly in Holland for a time in 1633, since in a letter of Alexander Browne to Sir William Boswell, dated Rotterdam, Dec. 13 [1633], there is mentioned " one Stasmore a Brownist. who is discontented about the busines [of surreptitiously publishing certain Bibles]..."[3]

Peace, however, did not reign for long in the reunited Ainsworthian church, for de l'Ecluse was evidently dissatisfied

---

[1] This appears to be implied in John Paget's "A Defence of Chvrch-Government", London, 1641, 4°, p. 33, where he speaks of " Mr Canne " as being "rashly elected a Minister by the Brownists " in Amsterdam.

[2] Vol. I., p. 516.

[3] Add. MS. 6394, fol. 146 verso, in the British Museum.

with Canne's sudden exaltation to the pastoral office, and would not work harmoniously with him. In fact, "shortly after that election", we are told[1], Canne "was censured and deposed from his office by that half [of the congregation] that rejected him & renounced communion with him". Concerning these new troubles, says Henry Elsynge in a letter to Sir William Boswell, dated, Amsterdam, June 6, 1633 :—

There are very pretty differences now *in motion betweene the Brownists heere* [in Amsterdam], *they haue diuided their Brother-hoods, some goe along with Iohn D'ecluse, some with M*^r *Kan* [Canne], the two heads of that *diuided Bodye* of which indeede there are none willing to bee feete, or any other enferior members, they would all bee heads : *Iohn D'ecluse has deliuered vp to Sathan M*^r *Kan, & his Sectaries, & M*^r *Kan will shortly bee ready, to doe him & his, the like courtesie*[2].

In his work as pastor Canne had such success that by 1634 it was supposed that some even in Robinson's church at Leyden might say that the Word of God "*is Gods word if M*^r. *Canne shall preach it*: *but if another, that is a Minister in England preach the same it is none of Gods vvord* "[3].

Before Sir William Brereton, Bart., reached Amsterdam about 1634/35, there seems to have been still another change of leadership among the Brownists, for he says[4] :—

the Brownists [are] divided, and differing amongst themselves ; Mr. Canne being the pastor of one company, and one Greenwood, an old man, a tradesman, who sells stockings in Exchange...is the leader of another company.

This passage may indicate that de l'Ecluse had left Amsterdam, or was now dead, and that this Greenwood had succeeded to his position of leader among those who were opposed to Canne.

One of the Amsterdam Barrowists who gave up his separatism, and evidently joined the church of John Paget some time after Ainsworth's death in 1622, was one Stephen Offwood. Little or

---

[1] John Paget's "A Defence of Chvrch-Government", 1641, p. 33.

[2] Add. MS. 6394, fol. 142, in the British Museum.

[3] John Robinson's "A Treatise of the Lawfvlnes of Hearing of the Ministers in the church of England :...", 1634, p. xvii.

[4] "Travels in Holland...M.DC.XXXIV–M.DC.XXXV", Chetham Society, Vol. I., 1844, pp. 64–5.

nothing appears to have been known about him until recently, but
he evidently kept a boarding-house.   In 1633 Thomas Cranford
is mentioned as being one "who doth vsually eate at Stephen
ofwoods"[1], and in 1634 or 1635 Sir William Brereton speaks of
Offwood as being his host in Amsterdam[2].   It was also reported
in 1633 that "Stephen ofwood is certainely the man which
procures the printing of all the blew bookes..."[3] Henry Elsynge
in the previously mentioned letter to Sir William Boswell, dated
June 6, 1633, has the following reference to him[4]:—

Stephen Offwod my Host was once one of the [Barrowist] *Brotherhood,
but tis long since hee fell from it : but his wife & children continuing
still among them, hee has written a booke which hee directs to them, in
which hee layes the Brownists very open, & layes downe motiues &
reasons to his wife & children, why they should forsake (as hee termes
them) their abominac[i]ons : but that hee maye shew himselfe auerse
to the Church of England & the discipline therein setled & approued
of, hee has a Tract wherein hee shewes that the English of these
Churches heere, had very good reason to leaue the Church of England,
bringes in a short Narratiue of the Troubles of Franckfort, when the
English first endeauored in the beginning of Queene Maryes tyme, to
erect a Church there, & vpon that occasion, brings in likewise the...
opinion of Mr Calvin, Bullinger & others of our Booke of Common
Prayer : but that I feare your occasions, would not dispence with
soe vnworthy an Interruption, I had sent you the Booke....*

No copy of Offwood's work seems to be known to-day, and
this is the fullest description we have of it at present.   It was
apparently composed of two parts, the first devoted to his
family and the evils of Brownism, and the other, here called a
tract, showing the value and reasonableness of the English
Puritan (non-separatist) churches on the Continent.   The book
was evidently published some time between 1624 and 1630, and
at least two further references to it have come down to us.   In
one instance, it is referred to as Stephen Offwood's book against
the Brownists, and more particularly styled "*Heady & rash
Censures*"[5].   In the other reference, it is called an "*Advertise-*

---

[1] Add. MS. 6394, fol. 146 verso, in the British Museum.

[2] "Travels in Holland", Chetham Society, Vol. I., 1844, p. 57.

[3] Add. MS. 6394, fol. 146 verso.

[4] *Ibid.*, fol. 142.

[5] See John Paget's "*An* Answer *To the unjust complaints* of William
Best", Amsterdam, 1635, p. 87.

A TRVE AND
SHORT DECLARATION, BOTH OF THE
GATHERING AND IOYNING TOGETHER
OF CERTAINE PERSONS: AND ALSO OF
THE LAMENTABLE BREACH AND
DIVISION WHICH FELL
AMONGST THEM.

THERE Were certaine persons In England, of vvhich, some vvere brought vp in schooles, & in the Vniuersitie of Cambridge, & some in families & houshouldes, as is the manner of that co intrie. Some of these vvhich had liued & studied in Cambrige, vvere there koovvne & counted forvvard in religion, & others also both there & in the contrie vvere more carefull & zelous, then their frovvard enimies could suffer. They in Cambrige vvere scattered from thense, some to one trade of life, & some to an other: as Robert Broune, Robert Harrison, William Harrison, Philip Broune, Robert Barker. Some of these applied themselues to teach schollers: to the vvhich labour, R. Broune also gaue himselfe, for the space of three yeares. He hauing a special care to teach religion vvith other learning, did thereby keepe his scholers in such avve & good order, as all the Tounsemē vvhere he taught gaue him vvitnes. Yet the vvorld being so corrupt as it is, & the times so perilous he greatly missliked the vvantes & defaultes, vvhich he savve euerie vvhere, & marcked plainly that vvithout red esse, nether the parentes could long reioise in their children, nor the children profit so much in religion, as that their other studies & learning might be blessed thereby. Hereuppon he fell into great care, & vvas soare greeued vvhile he long considered minie thinges amisse, & the cause of all, to be the vvofull and lamētable state off the church. Wherefore he laboured much to knovve his duetie in such thiges, & because the church of God is his kingdom, & his name especially is thereby magnified, he vvholy bent himselfe to search & find out the matter of the church: as hovv it vvas to be guided & ordered, & vvhat abuses there vvere in the ecclesiasticall gouernment then vsed. These thinges, he had long before debated in himselfe, & vvith others, & suffered also some trouble about thē at Cābrige. yet novve on fresh he set his mind on these thinges, & night & day did consult vvith himselfe & others about thē, least he should be ignorant, or mistake anie off those matters. What so euer thinges he ffound belonging to the church, & to his calling as a mēber off the church, he did put it in practis. For euen litle children are off the church & kingdom off God yea off such faith Christ doth his kingdom consist, & therefore both in his schole he laboured that the kingdom off God might appeare, & also in those of the tovvne vvith vvhom he

FIRST PAGE OF ROBERT BROWNE'S "TRVE AND SHORT DECLARATION" [1583?].
(Size of original $7\frac{7}{16}$ in. $\times 5\frac{9}{16}$ in.) See Vol. I., page 107.

ment to John De lecluse *and* H. May "[1]. At this time Offwood
was averse to the Church of England as established, as well as
to the Brownists, and in the end he was also not especially
enthusiastic over Paget's church which was connected with the
Dutch Classis, for we are told that he soon began to complain
of the power of the Classis[2].

Canne appears to have remained with the Amsterdam congregation for about nine years without intermission. During
this period evidently he not only took entire charge of the
church without the assistance of elders, but also at the same
time ambitiously undertook " the care and charge of divers
other trades, as of a Printers work-house in one place, of a
Brandery or Aqua vitæ shop in another place, and specially
of an Alchymists laboratory in another place "[3]. He was a
vigorous separatist, and in 1634 boldly published a work
bearing the title, "*A* Necessitie of Separation *From the Church
of England*"[4], and in 1639 another entitled, "A Stay against
Straying". About 1640/41 Canne seems to have made a short
visit to England, and in the spring of 1641 we find him in
Bristol and other places, but he must soon (i.e., probably some
time in 1641) have returned to Amsterdam. He was certainly
not an Anabaptist at this time[5].

Robert Baillie sums up the later history of Ainsworth's
church in the following words[6]:—

Ainsworths's [*sic*] company, after his death, remained long without
all [i.e., in reality, the two chief] Officers, very like to have dissolved : yet at last, after much strife, they did chuse one Master
Cann for their Pastor, but could not agree, til very lately, upon
any other Officer, and even yet [in 1645] they live without an
Eldership, as they did before without a Pastor.

---

[1] See Dr Edw. Stillingfleet's "*Unreasonableness of Separation*", 1681,
p. 48.

[2] J. Paget's "*An* Answer...", p. 87.

[3] J. Paget's "A Defence of Chvrch-Government ", 1641, p. 152.

[4] Reprinted by the Hanserd Knollys Society in 1849 with modernized
text and with an Introductory Notice by the Rev. Charles Stovel.

[5] I hope to present my reason for this assertion in a succeeding
volume.

[6] In "A Dissvassive from the Errours Of the Time", London, 1645,
p. 15.

As for Sabine Staresmore, he seems not long to have been able to endure John Canne's ministry, and once more to have returned to England.   There is reason to believe that he was in prison in London in 1635[1].   On May 27 or 29, 1644, he was present at a meeting of Henry Jessey's congregation in London[2], and about 1647 was evidently alive, and perhaps still in London. He is mentioned in the second section of John Cotton's " The Bloudy Tenent *Washed* "[3], which was published in 1647, as being friendly to Roger Williams, and as having written a confutation of Cotton's letter to Williams.

[1] "Transactions of the Baptist Historical Society" for January, 1910.
[2] The Gould Transcript of Benjamin Stinton's "Repository", No. 4.
[3] In the [second section], p. 1.

CHAPTER VII

CERTAIN OBSCURE BARROWIST AND SEPARATIST CONGREGATIONS BETWEEN 1588 AND 1641

IT must not be thought that during the latter part of the sixteenth, and the first quarter of the seventeenth, centuries the spread of separatist opinions was accomplished only through the agency of the congregations of the few best-known leaders. No doubt, in various quarters of England similar movements were going on during all this period[1], but of them unfortunately we have but little information. Furthermore, there was a considerable number of separatists who in time became dissatisfied with their new views and either returned to the Church of England, or began to maintain still newer doctrines, as we shall see later in this chapter. It is our purpose now to trace some of these less known Barrowist or separatist congregations in England or Holland before and during 1641.

After the departure of Francis Johnson and what seems to have been a large proportion of his congregation to Amsterdam, some Barrowists appear to have remained in London. It is evident, however, that unless William Collins had succeeded in organizing the second Barrowist company in London, as had been intended, there cannot have been any fully organized Barrowist church there until some years later. And that no such church was instituted until after 1603 is made very probable, since George Johnson in his "discourse", published in that year, blames his brother Francis for having discouraged

---

[1] Before 1617 Brownists or Barrowists are known to have come from at least thirty-three counties. See "The Brownists in Amsterdam", in the "Transactions" of the Congregational Historical Society for September, 1905, p. 170.

the organization of the London company, and for having drawn over to Amsterdam any converted Puritan preachers who might have made suitable officers for the London Barrowists. He also says that the latter had wished to have one " Mr Cr." (certainly not Mr Crane, perhaps Mr Crud) for their teacher, but that Francis Johnson and Daniel Studley "made a iarre betweene the people and him", and "by their dealing" drove him away[1].

How soon after 1603 the London congregation was organized, and how much longer it existed, does not appear to be known, but it certainly was in existence in 1624, and also in 1632[2]. This congregation was probably not that which on Oct. 22, 1608, was described as " a nest or assemblie of Brownists dis-couered on Sonday about Finsburie, wherof Fiue or sixe and thirty were apprehended with theyre preacher one Trundle that vsed to exercise at christs-church "[3]. We can only be certain that one Mr Lee appears eventually to have been chosen its leader or pastor. We also know that the London Barrowists found it difficult to live in peace with each other, as is made plain in a work[4] published in 1612 where it is said, that " the companie of the *Brownists* remayning in London haue oft layed" "manifold curses" "vpon one another, one halfe de-uouring another at once".

We may, I think, conjecture with reasonable probability the identity of the above mentioned Mr Lee. It will be noticed on examining the deposition of Daniell Bucke (in the volume of documents), made on March 9, 1592/93, that he refers to Thomas Lee and Nicholas Lee, or Leye, as being members of the con-

[1] P. 44.

[2] See John Robinson's "A Treatise of the Lawfvlnes of Hearing of the Ministers in the church of England", 1634, pp. 65–77, where a letter is given which was sent by him to this congregation in London, dated, April 5, 1624. In the volume of documents see also the so-called Jessey Records (from the Gould Manuscript, an account of which is given later in this volume) under the date May 12, 1632.

[3] In a letter written by John Chamberlain to Mr Dudley Carleton at Eaton. S. P., Dom., James I, Vol. 37 (No. 25) in the Public Record Office.

[4] "The Prophane Schisme of the Brownists or Separatists", 1612, p. 63.

gregation, and the latter as being a deacon. Nicholas Lee first appears in the lists of prisoners and petitioners of 1590, but though Bucke mentions Nicholas and Thomas Lee (they may have been brothers) in 1592/93, it should be noticed that neither of them seems to have been taken prisoner. At any rate, they were evidently not called upon to make depositions, and they almost certainly would have been, had they been in prison, nor is either of them reported as having died in prison before the publication of the "Trve Confession" of Faith of 1596.

From these facts the inference may very naturally be drawn that the deacon, Nicholas Lee, as the only officer of the congregation who apparently had not been captured by the civil authorities, now took charge of the members of the church who were still free, and that when the members of the congregation who had been imprisoned were subsequently exiled to Holland, he was able to remain in London[1]. Being probably a layman and a deacon, he would not be expected to become the pastor of the congregation, and so other plans for the choice of a leader had been made from time to time before 1603, but when these plans had long been frustrated for one cause or another, it is possible that finally (i.e., at some time after 1603) he was elected to the pastor's office, in which Henry Jacob may have found him about 1616 on his (Jacob's) return to London. In A. T.'s previously mentioned work entitled, "A | CHRISTIAN REPROFE | AGAINST | CONTENTION. | ...", 1631, it will be remembered, reference is made to Mr Lee and his congregation in connection with "Mr. Iacobe and his people"[2].

As early as 1588 or 1589 we find that there were Brownists not only in and about London, but also that they had "sparsed of their companies into seuerall partes of the Realme, and namely, into the West, almost to the vttermost borders thereof"[3].

---

[1] Johnson's church in Amsterdam had only one deacon at first, as appears in George Johnson's statement in "A discourse", 1603, p. 151. This deacon was Christopher Bowman.

[2] P. 5.

[3] S.[tephen] B.[redwell]'s "THE RASING | *OF THE FOVNDA-TIONS* | of Brovvnisme", London, 1588, p. iv.

This statement is of special interest when taken in connection with the fact that as late as 1606 there appears to have been a Brownist or Barrowist congregation "in the West parts of England"[1]. No more definite location of this church is given, but we may possibly infer that it was in Wiltshire in or near the locality where "one *Mr Io. Ie.* and other his fellowes"[2] lived, who had "bestowed much labour in reading" the early Barrowist and Johnsonian writings. Perhaps Gloucester was the place intended in this obscure reference, but at present we can only conjecture, as Brownists are known to have come from so many places in the western shires[3].

To this church in the west of England Thomas White[4], Thomas Powell, and others to the number of twelve or thirteen joined,—a group which later seceded and retired to Amsterdam in order to organize a church of their own. Of the movements of the seceding company of Thomas White, Francis Johnson gives the following description[5]:—

When they had left the Church of England, as having an Antichristian Ministery, worship, confusion, &c. they first joyned in & to a Church in the West parts of England professing the same faith with vs [Barrowists]. A while after, they came over hither, & at first communicated with vs: but afterward (being about twelve or thirteen) they joyned themselves here as a body together, to walk in the same faith and way as we do; reputing and calling themselves a Church, distinct from vs.

This congregation had cherished the hope of becoming a separate church in England, but had failed to realize it, and in Holland their object in keeping separate from Johnson's

---

[1] Francis Johnson's "An Inqvirie and Ansvver Of Thomas VVhite", 1606, p. iii.

[2] *Ibid.*, p. 12.

[3] See "The Brownists in Amsterdam", pp. 170–71, in the "Transactions" of the Congregational Historical Society for Sept., 1905.

[4] See *Ibid.*, p. 162. White is here reported to have lived in "Sechtenfort", England. This is evidently intended for "Slaugtenfort", Wiltshire, in John Speed's "The Theatre of the Empire", London, 1611, the modern Slaughterford, Wiltshire. Mr Madan of the Bodleian Library agrees with me in this identification.

[5] "An Inqvirie and Ansvver Of Thomas VVhite his Discoverie of Brovvnisme", 1606, pp. 52–3.

church appears to have been partly to increase the number of Barrowist churches, and partly to overcome the feeling of some critics that Francis Johnson's congregation was ambitious to lead, and perhaps to absorb, the other separatist congregations[1]. It is made evident also from Johnson's work that before 1606 Thomas White had returned to the Church of England[2].

By 1594 the Barrowists, or separatists, had even made their way into Ireland, for Miles Mickle-bound[3] speaks "of one of them in Ireland", who wrote in that year to a certain Mr Wood, a Scottish preacher there. Henry Ainsworth was probably one of these Barrowists, and may even have written the letter just mentioned.

Another Brownist or Barrowist church in England was situated at Norwich, and a few points in its early history are still preserved. In the first place, George Johnson in 1603 speaks of this congregation as the Amsterdam church's "elder sister in the Lord"[4], so that it must have been in existence before 1587. This fact suggests that the nucleus of the church in Norwich was formed by some of Robert Browne's "companie", who had remained in England after his departure for Holland about five years before, and whom he may have revisited on his return to England in 1584. Even after Browne's subscription in 1585 the existence of the congregation appears to have continued, and some time between 1590 and 1593[5], while Father, or

[1] "An Inqvirie and Ansvver Of Thomas VVhite his Discoverie of Brovvnisme", 1606, p. 53.

[2] *Ibid.*, p. iii. He was married in Amsterdam on April 10, 1604, to the widow of John Philips.

[3] "Mr. *HENRY BARROWES* | PLATFORM. |...", [1611], 8°, sig. C$_{vii}$ verso.

[4] "A discourse", p. 89.

[5] "*[*A note of the accusation / which Mr. Hunt P.[astor] of the [Parish] Church at Chatsam [Chattisham, not Chatham] saieth against M. D. St.[udley] ‡ This fel out about 12. yeares since if not more. so long since is it / that he first shewed his vsurping and proud minde / ..."] That the said Mr. Daiuel [Daniel] Studley (when ‡ goodman Debnam was in prison at London, and two of the elders, the deacons, and he vvere in prison at Norvvich, euen then) did put by Tho. Ensner from the spirituall exercises, and the vse of that gift that God of his rich mercy had given

Goodman, John Debenham was in prison in London (i.e. about 1590 or 1591), we find that Daniel Studley, George Knifton, Matthew Slade, and Christopher Bowman visited the Brownists in Norwich. Their object may have been to escape persecution in London, where they had now become known, and at the same time to organize the Norwich church and unite it more closely with the London Barrowists. One Thomas Ensner, who evidently had not been chosen pastor, had been

vnto him : and did put in place for spirituall exercises one Bradshaw a man so openly and manifestly knovvn of evil behaviour, that he was of thai [*sic*] whole Church vtterly refused to be received as a member vnto that Church. For this his not private but open deede (writeth M. Huut [Hunt] to this Pastor) vve desier that Mr. Studley may be dravv[n] to confes his sin, to repent, and so amend. This vvas vvritten to the Past.[or] 1600. the 6. of the 3. Mon[th]."

(From George Johnson's "A discourse", p. 205.)

Johnson speaks of Mr Hunt as pastor of the church at Norwich and also of that at "Chatsham". My interpretation of these statements is given later in the text. See "A discourse", 1603, p. 205, text and note. For the suggestion that "Chatsham" was Chattisham, and not Chatham, I am indebted to Mr Falconer Madan of the Bodleian Library.

Notwithstanding Mr Hunt's removal, Brownism apparently still continued to be maintained in Chattisham. In the Visitation Book of the Archdeaconry of Suffolk for the year 1606 (which I examined through the courtesy of Mr L. G. Bolingbroke, now Registrar of the Diocese of Norwich) complaint is made against the then Vicar of Chattisham, the Rev. John Baker, that "he hath not reed [*sic*] all the Cannons", that "he doth impugne & speake against the rightes & ceremonies established in the church of England", that "he doth not vse the prescripte forme of Common prayer but readeth psalmes of his owne chosing neither doth obserue all the rightes & ceremonies prescribed in the said Booke", that "he hath administred the communion but once since christmas was xij monthes", that "he doth not vse the signe of the crosse in baptisme", that "he weareth no surples...", and that "he doth neuer denounce excommunicate persons. neither doth geue thankes for women after Childbirth". Baker himself was not accused of being a Brownist or Barrowist, but complaint is made directly against Elizabeth Barker, widow, that "there be often metinges at her howse to conferre about religion and that the said Elizabeth is a brownest", and on June 6th, 1606, the complaint is registered against George Barker, who was evidently her son, that "he is a brownist or sectary...". Probably Mr Baker had no intention of inspiring his parishioners to become separatists, but nevertheless his influence certainly tended in this direction.

directing the activities of the congregation before the arrival of the Londoners. The presence of Barrowists in the city soon came to the knowledge of the authorities, and some of the church (including Studley, Slade, Knifton, and Bowman) seem to have been taken captive. During the period of their imprisonment, Studley, who apparently had taken a dislike to Thomas Ensner, in an autocratic way, which suggests that the London Barrowists had already assumed oversight over the Norwich congregation, "put in place [of Ensner] for spirituall exercises one Bradshaw a man so openly and manifestly knovvn of evil behaviour, that he was of thai [*sic*] whole Church vtterly refused to be received as a member vnto that Church". This action of Studley's appears to have made trouble at Norwich.

Late in 1589 or early in 1590, it would appear, one Mr Hunt (whose Christian name we do not at present know) came to Norwich and joined the Brownist congregation. He had been Vicar of Chattisham, Ipswich, from about May, 1586, until about December 5, 1589, and had been deprived for Brownism[1]. He had evidently witnessed, or at least was thoroughly conversant with, the difficulties caused by Studley, and very likely had become pastor of the Norwich Brownists as a substitute for Ensner and Bradshaw. However this may be, the troubles among the local Brownists at that period seem to have been so

---

[1] I am indebted for this information, probably given here for the first time, to the kindness of the present Vicar of Chattisham, Ipswich, Rev. A. H. Stevens, M.A., B.Mus., who has supplied the following memorandum from the Parish Register, inserted under the date 1586 :—

"Mʳ Hunt   Memorandum—that from the 28ᵗʰ day of May 1586 until
Vicar—   April 1590 there was no register kept that can be found during which time Mʳ Hunt was Vicar of Chattisham, who was *deprived* for *Brownisme* whom Iames Armond Vicar of Chattisham succeeded being inducted 5ᵗʰ December *1589*."

This is the only record concerning Mr Hunt in the Chattisham Register. I have extended one or two abbreviations in Mr Stevens's text as sent to me.

It was probably Mr Hunt who began the Brownist or Barrowist movement in and about Ipswich. At least several of the Amsterdam Barrowists before 1617 came from Ipswich or its neighbourhood. See "The Brownists in Amsterdam" in the "Transactions" of the Congregational Historical Society for September, 1905, pp. 160–172.

bitter, that they were long kept in memory, and as late as 1600, Mr Hunt wrote about them to the exiled church in Amsterdam. In 1603 Mr Hunt is spoken of by George Johnson as if he was still pastor of the Norwich Brownists. At present it is unknown how long the congregation in Norwich existed after 1603.

It is perhaps possible that this church in Norwich is referred to in 1602 as being in Suffolk, and as maintaining the opinion that it was "vnlawfull to eat blood; and to flie [flee from persecution into a foreign country]". One Mr Woolsey, then prisoner in Norwich, seems to have been the chief advocate of the former doctrine, and to have recommended its adoption in the exiled English Church at Amsterdam. He claimed that Henry Barrowe and his church then at London had written letters to this congregation in Suffolk [Norwich?] supporting his views. The church in Amsterdam, however, did not pay much attention to his opinions, and a reply to him dated "*Amsterdam*, Mon. 12. 7. 1602" was written by "*Francis Iohnson* Pastor *Henry Ainsworth* Teacher *Daniel Studley Stanshal Mercer* Elders", "in the name and with consent of the whole Church". This letter was first published at London in 1657 under the title of "A Seasonable | TREATISE | FOR | THIS AGE: | Occasioned by a Letter written by | one Mr *Woolsey* prisoner in *Norwich*, to | the then [1602]-exiled Church at *Amsterdam*; in | which he endeavours to prove it unlaw-| ful to eat *blood, things strangled,* and *things offered to idols,* now in the times of the Gospel...". Perhaps Daniel Studley was in part referring to unusual doctrines like these when he spoke of the congregation in Norwich as being "a simple people"[1].

Another early separatist or Barrowist congregation appears in Great Yarmouth early in the seventeenth century, though the year of its origin and the length of its existence are still uncertain. The first definite notice of this company which has come to my attention is dated July 17, 1630. On that day separatists or Barrowists to the number of twenty-eight persons in all, were resident in Great Yarmouth, while two miles outside the city lived two other persons who sometimes frequented their

---

[1] George Johnson's "A discourse", 1603, p. 205.

meetings. The name of these Barrowists at Great Yarmouth are given in the volume of documents. A "poore Mariner" named William Uring[1] [Euring] seems to have been the leader of the congregation at this time, and on July 17, 1630, he was "in Norwich Castle and comitted to the Goale in Yarmouth". William Birchall and Thomas Caine, two other members, were then also in Yarmouth Gaol. The rest appear at that time to have been free. There can be little doubt that there was some connection, direct or indirect, between the Brownists of Norwich and of Great Yarmouth, but the Independent or Congregational Church in Great Yarmouth organized in 1643 was evidently *in no way* related to this congregation of Barrowists, or so-called Brownists. The Independent church was an independent Puritan congregation founded after the ideals of Henry Jacob, and especially of Hugh Peter, formerly of Rotterdam, and at first was composed mainly of members of the independent, non-separatist, Puritan congregation at Rotterdam, from which they had been dismissed. As regards William Euring it seems that he has been little noticed heretofore, and that his place of activity has not been known. He was certainly a separatist as early as 1619, for in that year he published (it is thought through the instrumentality of William Brewster at Leyden) "AN | ANSVVER | TO THE TEN | COVNTER DE-|MANDS| PRO-POVNDED BY |T. DRAKES, Preacher of| *the Word at* H.[arwich?] *and* D.[overcourt?] | in the County of| ESSEX "[2], and the contents of this treatise make it probable that he had been a separatist for some time, perhaps even for several years, before that date. He says that the separatists "some good space since" (that is before 1619) had propounded "7 *Demands*", to which Drakes prepared "*Ten Counter-demands*". Up to this point the con-

---

[1] Not "William Pring" as given by Dr John Waddington in the second volume of his "Congregational History", 1874, p. 281. During John Robinson's controversy with John Yates of Norwich in 1618 concerning laymen's use of "prophecy", William Euring seems to have acted as carrier between Norwich and Leyden. See the author's "*A Tercentenary Memorial* New Facts Concerning John Robinson Pastor of the Pilgrim Fathers", Oxford and London, 1910, p. 21.

[2] What appears to be an unique copy of this work is in Dr Williams's Library, London.

troversy had evidently been conducted in manuscript, not in print as Mr Arber seems to suppose. Euring accordingly cites extensively the text of the "Demands" and also of the "Counter-demands". He further makes it clear in the following citation, that at this time he was not in England, but probably in Holland:—

not onely I my selfe, but all of vs, that now are separated from you [in the Church of England], would much more willingly and gladly returne againe and labor to plant our selues againe in the meanest parte of England, to inioy peace with holinesse and to follow the truth in loue among our kindred and friends in our owne natiue cuntry, then either to continue where now many of vs as yet liue, or to plant our selues in Virginia or in any other country in the world, vppon any conditions, or hope of any thing in this lyfe whatsoeuer[1].

From Peter Fairlambe's "Recantation of a Brownist", published in 1606, it is made apparent that Brownists or Barrowists early disturbed the religious peace of "the English Marchants in Barbary". Fairlambe was in that country in October, 1599, and even before his arrival, he says, Brownists or Barrowists were there. Having been banished from England for maintaining Brownist opinions which he had long held, he also sought here to persuade others to accept his views. However, he afterwards gave them up, returned to London, and was received again into the Church of England by Richard Bancroft, who had just been made Bishop of London. Soon after Fairlambe went back to Barbary to undo the work he had formerly furthered. In this he met with success as he claims, and finally returned again to his native land. From this bare account we may safely believe that there were not many Brownists in Barbary before 1606, surely not enough for an organized church, but it is nevertheless interesting to see how rapidly and how widely separatist views spread even at that early period.

Among the Barrowists of this time John Wilkinson and his congregation at Colchester should especially be mentioned, for he long maintained his influence, and yet did not entirely agree with the orthodox Barrowists. Probably the earliest reference to him now known is contained in a deposition of Christopher

[1] P. 36.

Diggins made in April, 1593, where he says that he had seen "one of Barowes his bookes in the handes of one Iohn wilkenson"[1], and we may infer that from about this time dates Wilkinson's interest in separatism. We next find further reference to him in a letter of " Mat. Savnders and Cvth. Hvtten "[2], written on July 8, 1611, where the statement occurs that " *Iohn Wilkinson* and his disciples will haue Apostles". In other words, his church was of the Seeker type. In 1613 Wilkinson was " *a Prisoner in* Colchester, *for the Patience and Faith of the Saints*". During this imprisonment he wrote " A reproof of some things written by *John Morton* [*Murton*], and others of his Company and followers, to prove *That Infants are not in the state of Condemnation*; And that therfore they are not to be Baptised". After Wilkinson's death this manuscript seems to have been entrusted "for the publicke good" to the care of one William Arthurbury, who "considering how needfull it would be to be published rather than obscured" had it printed before Nov. 17, 1646, under the title, "THE | SEALED | FOVNTAINE | opened to the Faith- | full, and their Seed. | OR, | A short Treatise, shewing, that | some *Infants* are in the state of | Grace, and capable of the *seales*, | and others not. | Being the chief point, wherein the | *Separatists* doe blame the | *Anabaptists*. | By JOHN WILKINSON, *Prisoner* | *at* Colchester, *against* John Morton | *Prisoner at* London" ["Nou: 17 1646"]. This work is to-day almost entirely lacking in interest except for its scarcity.

There are apparently but few references to John Wilkinson in contemporaneous English literature. One of these is in John Murton's "A Discription", 1620, where he says :—

some of the *Brownists* acknowledging it lawfull for any Disciple, to Preach & conuert, but not Baptise: though others of them [From the margin: "Io. Wilk.(inson) & his followers"] holde; that Disciples of *Christ* though not in office of Pastor or Elder may conuert and Baptise also, vpon which they haue bene at deadly jarres these many yeares[3].

---

[1] Harleian MS. 6848, fol. 32 recto.

[2] In "The Prophane Schisme of the Brownists or Separatists", by Christopher Lawne and three others, 1612, p. 55.

[3] P. 162.

From this statement one might infer that Wilkinson was still alive in 1620, but from it one would hardly suspect that he was a Seeker. Nevertheless, there is a persistent recurrence of the assertion that he held the specially characteristic opinion of the Seekers concerning the coming of new Apostles or Prophets, and Edmond Jessop in 1623 even seems to claim that he regarded himself as one of these honoured messengers. He was not, of course, an Arian like Wightman or Sayer. Jessop suggests further that Wilkinson died before 1623[1].

The religious unrest of the times succeeding the execution of Barrowe and Greenwood is indicated by the fact that those who left the Church of England had great difficulty in agreeing with one another in their new beliefs. In foreign countries, whither Englishmen had gone for purposes of business, this unrest is specially manifest. Such travellers certainly did not all become Brownists or Barrowists, but in the atmosphere of greater freedom they undoubtedly became more liberal than would have been the case, had they remained in England.

One of the reputed early converts to Barrowism was Henoch Clapham, or, in " Northbrittishe forme", " Cleypam". As he did not adhere, however, to the opinions which he was perhaps erroneously supposed to have adopted, not much attention has been bestowed upon him. Furthermore, Clapham's writings are all scarce, but in his various works he has left a good deal of biographical material which it may be profitable to examine. With regard to his early life we learn that about 1585 he gave up " the vayne exercise of Poetrie " and began to devote himself "(by Gods goodnes) to sad and sober studies; and so, about som 14. yeares since [i.e., about 1591]", he says, " carying letters of commendation from *Cambridge* to [" Wickam "[2]] the Bishop of *Lincolne* then at his Mannour of *Bugden*, I of him

---

[1] See Jessop's "A Discovery of the Errors of the English *Anabaptists*", London, 1623, p. 77: "There was also one *Iohn Wilkinson*, another ancient stout Separatist, who with diuers that followed him, held the same [opinion] likewise [viz., that he was a new specially called apostle], drawing it from the same ground, as a necessary consequence thereof, who also came to naught."

[2] "Antidoton", London, 1600, p. 6.

was ordained *Presbyter* (and that in his Librarie without Chappel-ceremonie) Doctor *Iermine* the Poser, and the Chappel-clarke onlie standing by, ...".

"To the terme *Clercke.* I am neither an *Amen-clercke* nor a *Pen-clarke*, and therefore I conceaue he meaneth thereby a *Clergie-man* as the word *Clericus* is ecclesiastically vsed. Such a one indeed I was by the former Ordination, but *Clericus sine titulo*, such a one as was vntitled to any particular place (but as a Sheepheard at randome to helpe where I could) ..."[1]

For two years in Lancashire he now "publikely ministred", that is, during 1591 and 1592, but as he loved his liberty and yet did not like, as he says, to "practise contrarie to my [his] perswasion, (as many deceitfully haue done)", he was forced to leave England. Previously, however, I believe he may have been imprisoned in the Clink with Francis Johnson and other Barrowists about 1592/93[2]. Certainly he came into close touch with them in some way about that time, though he does not seem to consider himself ever to have been one of their number. "First into the Low-countries I went", he says, "Afterwards into Scotland. After that againe into the Low-countries. Then again into Scotland: And once againe into the Low-countries. Then again into Scotland: And once againe into Netherland, &c. Sometimes haled by this faction, sometimes pulled by that faction...I kept me euer fast vnto the maine point, that is, vnto the foundation of the Gospell"[3]. The last time he was in Holland was evidently in 1597 and 1598, when we suddenly find him to be the minister of what he calls "that poore English

---

[1] "Doctor ANDROS | His Prosopopeia an- | swered,...", 1605, p. 4.

[2] In his "A Chronological Discourse", London, 1609, [p. 36,] Clapham has these suggestive words touching this point: "*Franc. Iohnson* (being aduised by one [Clapham ?] that talked with him thereabouts in the *Clinke* at *London*) did presse the vse of our singing Psalmes (neglected before of his people for Apochrypha;)..." The word "our" may suggest that Clapham with other Puritans was imprisoned with the Barrowists, in which case it may have been advisable to hold their religious exercises together.

[3] "Antidoton", p. 6.

Congregation, in Amstelredam "[1]. In another work of his
published at Amsterdam in 1598, entitled " THE SYN, |
AGAINST THE HOLY | GHOSTE:...", he mentions the
names of some of his congregation whom he styles " his faithfull
Brethren (a poore Remnant of the ever visible Catholike and
Apostolicke Church) Abraham Crotendine, Iohn Ioope[2], Hugh
Armourer, Christopher Symkins, Thomas Farrat[3] [?Farrar],
Abraham Wakefeild &c."[4] In another place in the same work[5]
he speaks of the " funerals " of his " excellent frend Mistris
Anne Ogle "; and of " his beloued Tho. whicks and Ri. Carter ",
whom he does not expect to see again. It should be kept in
mind that this church was not separatist, as will appear more
clearly in the next paragraph.

Of the persons here named it is interesting to note that
Christopher Symkins had been a loyal member of Greenwood's
congregation after October, 1591; that early in March, 1592/93,
he was taken captive " in the wood by Islington "; and that he
was examined on April 5, 1593, when he refused " to come to his
parishe Churche ", and said he was " ioyned to their [Barrowist]
congregacion from whence he will not departe "[6]. Symkins

---

[1] "THEOLOGICAL AXIOMS | OR CONCLVSIONS : | ...", 1597,
title-page.

[2] In 1599, after Clapham's departure from Amsterdam, John Joope
published a single chapter taken from an extended MS. of 26 chapters
written by Clapham. This independent publication Joope entitled " The
Discription of a trve visible Christian ", etc.

[3] Thomas Farrat (not Farrar) is undoubtedly here intended. The
name is elsewhere given as Thomas Farret. He is described in the spring
of 1593 as a " servant to William Greene of Aldersgate streete ". Previously he had attended meetings of the London Brownists and had been
taken prisoner. However, as he showed himself willing to conform, he
was soon released on bail. Later he evidently went over to Holland and
may have joined the Barrowists there. In that case he must have become
discontented and have taken part in the schism in which Christopher
Symkins and others were concerned, and thus, like him, is to be found
among Clapham's little company in 1598.

[4] [P. 2].   [5] [P. 21].

[6] See Symkins' deposition made on April 5, 1593, in the volume of
documents.

probably accompanied the other members of the church to Holland in 1593 and remained satisfied for a time, but he seems to have been one of the "many others", mentioned by Francis Johnson, who after "divers" of the congregation had fallen into the heresies of the Anabaptists and been excommunicated, "fell into a schisme from the rest" (led perhaps by Henoch Clapham, who evidently did not favour separatism), and continuing therein were "cast out". Johnson speaks of "*C.*[hristopher?] *S.*[ymkins?] one of the schismed" as writing to him, and says he understood that not half of the congregation fell into this schism, and that divers repented and returned before excommunication was pronounced, while others did so later[1]. Symkins, however, evidently did not return, and accordingly in 1597 and 1598, or 1598 and 1599, we find him one of a little group of men "(a poore Remnant of the ever visible Catholike and Apostolike Church)" under the leadership of Clapham at Amsterdam. In this way we may perhaps see how Clapham came to be looked upon as an apostate[2], for though apparently not one himself in reality, he was able to draw others into a prolonged apostacy, which he, no doubt, thought would prove their best means of finding the true Church.

Whether Clapham had been in Middleburg before he came to Amsterdam is difficult to say, but he states that "our Englishe [Puritan] teachers at Midleburgh" wrote letters to the preachers in Scotland, whither he had gone for a time,

---

[1] *Ibid.*, pp. numbered 64 and 63.

[2] There were evidently three persons whom the early Brownists looked upon with special disapproval as apostates. Among these three Clapham was included. This is made evident in the following citation from John Smyth's "Paralleles, Censvres, Observations", 1609, p. 5:—

"I do therfor Proclame you [Richard Bernard] vnto the whole land to be one of the most fearful Apostates of the whole nation that excepting, VVhyte, & Clapham, you have no Superior nor equal that I know or remember, who have thus often confessed & witnessed much truth, & now not only have fallen from it,..."

Probably the Brownists had hoped too much of Bernard and Clapham, and were bitterly disappointed that neither of them finally advanced to the full separatist position. Thomas White seems really to have espoused separatism for a time.

telling them that he "was a Brownist etc.", in order, as he claims, "to lessen their loues there to me [him] and my [his] brethren". Then he adds: "Som preachers beleiuing yt: They insinuate it in their pulpits. I wished therupon a tryall to be taken of my faith. A Convocation was had Clapham cold not be conuicted neither of heresie nor errour"[1]. In another place he says further: "Som of yow [Puritans] sent word into Scotland / that I fell from your Sect / twise to the Bishops twise to the Brownists (4. lies at a clap)..."[2] Probably, therefore, he was never entirely converted to Brownist views.

However, Clapham was certainly not thoroughly orthodox, and he must have been a curious character. Under these circumstances, accordingly, it seems strange that so many works of his were printed, and especially as he had little of real importance to say. His only strong point was his independent position, for he undoubtedly differed somewhat from the ordinary Anglicans, Puritans, and Brownists. In fact, there were those who feared "*that* Cl.[apham] *would bring people to all the corruptions of the English Church, and finally to* Romes *church*"[3].

Clapham thus describes the religious unrest of the period in which he lived[4]:—

REformists in England caried of erst with true zeale for reparing the walls of Ierushalem, the praise of the whole earth: they in the heat of their labour ouer-caried in som speach (as, Such & such ecclesiasticall functions, ordinatious [ordinations], administrations &c. they are merely Antichristian, badges of the beast) others theyr zealous hearers herevpon (and in the fore-front of such, Mr Rob. Brovvne) taking such assertions for sound Theologicall axioms, do conclude thus: Then not only that, but all flovving from that, it must also be meerly Antichristian:...Wherevpon fearing the iudgment denounced against the Beast his people Revel. 14. 9. 10. 11. they seperate not only from visible euell, but also from visible good) as all Anti-christian. Having thus confusedlie seperated from Confusion, it remaines they begin all anewe, wherevnto Ministers must be no ministers vntill they have a newe Ordination from such separists,...wherevpon (which Donatus durst not attempt, nor yet Rob. Br.[owne]) Laymen...must Lay on hands,...Others

---

[1] "Theological Axioms", p. iii.   [2] *Ibid.* [p. 25.]
[3] "An Epistle Discovrsing vpon the present *Pestilence*....Reprinted with some Additions", London, 1603, 4º, p. iii.
[4] "The Syn, against the Holy Ghoste", Amsterdam, 1598 [p. 2].

go on furder saing, Is it possible to receive laufull baptisme,...from
the Ministers and apostacie of Anti-christ,...and so seeke out newe
baptisme,...reiecting frely and voluntarily the former:...
The not being Cathechized in this one poore begining of Christ, it
hath caused Many teachers to lay false grounds, whereyn [whereon ?]
others buildinge, there is no end of wandring. Some Ronninge [?]
not onlie into Mr Br.[ownes] first course, but also further and worse
then that further [*sic*]: yea so far, as diuerse I feare haue committed the horrible syn against the holy Ghost, Heb. 6. and 10.
That I labour to proue in the sequell, which I incommend [*sic*] vnto
your Brotherhood for a signe to the Catholike Church of my soules
syncerity:...

Clapham has a rambling and sometimes figurative style,
which in many places tends to obscure his meaning, as, for
instance, in the following passage[1]:—

MAny Spirits conceiued in the Canicular days / hatcht in the
wayning of the Moone / vnreasonable men and as yet repro-
bate to the faith / gone out from amonge vs / as being neuer truly
of vs / They abroade in Englande and elsewhere / (as Hollands
Nightingals / I meane frogs) go croaking abroade / to the diffama-
tion of all such as professe Christ in syncerity.

Some time after 1598 Clapham journeyed to England, where
his various publications had preceded him. He was not warmly
welcomed, and some Puritan preachers had evidently given
instructions that their followers should not read his books,
confer with him, or hear him preach[2]. Perhaps it was some of
these ministers, who in order to get rid of his presence "com-
playned" to the Bishop of London, "that he preached a doctrine
...past the boundes of their knowledge"[3], namely, that the
plague was not infectious, and that "*All that dyed of the plague
were damned, as dying without faith*"[4].

For teaching such doctrine Clapham was committed to
prison. Thirty-four weeks after his first commitment he
preached against the report that had been made of his opinions;
and on November 14, 1603, at the close of his sermon, he "was

---

[1] "Theological Axioms", p. iii.
[2] "An Epistle Discovrsing vpon the present *Pestilence*....Reprinted
with some Additions", London, 1603, 4°, p. iii.
[3] "Henoch Clapham His Demaundes and Answeres touching the Pestilence", 1604, p. ii.
[4] *Ibid.*, p. iii.

conveyed to the Clink prison" for eleven weeks, and after that was sent to the Gatehouse, where his release continued to be delayed. Finally, in 1605 he wrote his "Doctor ANDROS | His Prosopopeia an-|swered, and necessarily directed | to his MAIESTIE,...". On the title-page he still speaks of himself as "Prisoner in the Gatehouse at Westminster, adioyning London". Later, however, he was freed, and in October, 1607, is said to have been made Vicar of Northbourne in Kent, a position which he held until his death in 1614[1]. After 1605 two or three new works by Clapham appeared, and before that time he had published at least fifteen books, as may be seen in a list printed on the back of the last leaf of his "Doctor ANDROS", 1605,—a remarkable record for any man at that period.

We may here also mention some of those less known early Brownists who renounced their opinions, but who instead of returning to the Church of England, wandered still further away, and presumably sought to make converts to their particular views. Among them should be included those "vvandering brethren, (vvandering starres)" who, even before 1603, according to George Johnson[2], went "hither and thither / to and from England abiding in no certaine place". These were John Beacham, William Shepheard[3], John Nicholas[4], Richard Paris[5], David Bristoe[6], and William Houlder[7]. A few years later, we hear of Thomas Lemar[8] as the inventor of "The Monster of Lemarisme" "with seuen heads", composed, as was

[1] Arber's "Story of the Pilgrim Fathers", London, 1897, p. 99.

[2] "A discourse", p. 32.

[3] Shepheard was present at the organization of the Johnson congregation in September, 1592.

[4] John Nicholas was also present at the church organization in September, 1592.

[5] Paris had died before Dec. 16, 1606 (New Style), and on that date his widow married Thomas Gillis of Hampton at Amsterdam.

[6] Bristoe was present at the organization of the Johnson church in September, 1592.

[7] Houlder, or Holder, had died before January 28, 1606 (New Style), and on that date his widow married Richard Ardivey at Amsterdam.

[8] Lemar, or Le Mare, was one of the London Barrowists whose names appear in the lists of 1590.

claimed, of doctrines drawn from practically all religions then known; of John Hancock, who invented se-separatism, or separatism by one's self; and of Leonard Pidder[1], Henry Martin[2], and others with them, who had become Anabaptists.

Though there was not much opportunity for the unimpeded development of separatism in England during the first forty years of the seventeenth century, and although we know so little about the separatist movements of this early period, we have nevertheless just evidence enough to convince us that Brownism or Barrowism was being taught in many quarters of England during all these years. London, of course, always furnished its quota of separatists, and in 1621, as is well known, a congregation was "constituted" there "& carried on by one Mr Hubbert", or Hubbard, who having renounced his ordination in the Church of England, "took his Ministry from this Church, & with them went into Ireland, & there died". The congregation was evidently organized by a League and Covenant entered into by the members one with another, and at first may not have been strictly separatist. The church "returned into England, & kept close their Communion here about London", where Thomas Hancock, an unordained member, preached to them for some months. Afterwards John Canne was chosen pastor, and he remained with the church until he went to Amsterdam. Samuel Howe, who had been a member of John Lathrop's independent Puritan church, was next ordained their pastor, and served the congregation in this capacity for seven years. During the period of his ministry the church was "much harassed up & down in Fields & Woods". Howe was excommunicated by the Church of England, and seems to have died about 1634 or 1635. About 1641, one "Stephen More, a gifted Brother", who had been a deacon, was elected pastor. Up to this time, of course, the congregation had not manifested any Anabaptist tendencies. The account of this church preserved in "Numb: 23" of the Gould Manuscript (the text of

---

[1] Leonard Pidder, or Pedder, was a prisoner for Barrowism in the spring of 1593.

[2] Henry Martin was evidently a Barrowist before Oct. 8, 1587, and was taken prisoner on that date.

which is given in the volume of documents), and supposed to have been originally written by "old Mr Webb", carries the history of the congregation down to 1705 when by agreement it was dissolved.

At Gainsborough, or in that neighbourhood, about the years 1625–1629 there was evidently some Brownist or Barrowist interest, though perhaps no congregation. Hanserd Knollys says that while he taught in the "Free-School" of that village, he was told "of one called a *Brownist*, who used to pray and expound the Scriptures in his Family, whom I [he] went sometimes to hear, and with whom I [he] had Conference and very good Counsel"[1].

After the death of Henry Ainsworth and of John Robinson at least one of their followers (Thomas Brewer) returned to England and remained there. About this time (1626) we begin to hear of the Brownists in Kent. Among them we find Brewer and one Turner. The chief strongholds seem to have been in the neighbourhood of Ashford and Maidstone. Turner was a candle-maker, or chandler, of Sutton Valence. Concerning the Kentish Brownists Mr Arber has published the following interesting document[2]:—

JAMES MARTIN'S DETECTION OF BROWNISTS IN KENT.

SUNDAY, 17/27 SEPTEMBER 1626.

A Detection of certain dangerous Puritans and Brownists in Kent.

1. THOMAS BREWER, Gentleman, who writ a book[3] containing about half a quire of paper; wherein he prophesies the destruction of England within three years, by two Kings: one from the North, another from the South.

---

[1] "The Life and Death of...Mr. Hanserd Knollys", London, 1692, p. 5.

[2] "The Story of the Pilgrim Fathers", 1897, pp. 246–47. Dr B. Evans ("The Early English Baptists", Vol. II., London, 1864, pp. 55–57) mentions Brewer, and on page 55 quotes a reference to him as having been in 1626 "A zealous minister of the Baptist persuasion"! I make some comment on Dr Evans' account of Brewer in Chapter XI.

[3] At this point I have omitted a few words within square brackets and a comma probably inserted by Mr Arber.

The said BREWER coming, not long since, from Amsterdam, where he became a perfect Brownist; and being a man of good estate, is the general patron of the Kentish Brownists; who, by his means, daily and dangerously increase.

He, the said BREWER, hath printed a most pestilent book beyond the seas: wherein he affirmeth, That King JAMES would be the ruin of Religion. To the like purpose, he published a book or two more: which DAVID PAREUS, at Neustadt, shewed to a Knight, who told me of it.

2. One TURNER, a candle-maker or chandler, of Sutton Valence in Kent, preaches in houses, barns, and woods, That the Church of England is the Whore of Babylon, and the Synagogue of SATAN, &c. He hath many followers: and is maintained principally by the said THOMAS BREWER; whose Chaplain he seems to be.

3 and 4. One WINOCK and [one] CRUMPE at Maidstone, both rich men, as far as in them lies, maintain these Sectaries.

Witnesses of the Premisses are

Sir P. H.; Knight.
Master BARRELL, Preacher of Maidstone.
Master SIMONDSON, Schoolmaster of Maidstone, and
Master FISHER, of Maidstone.
With many more.

Testified by them, September 16 and 17, 1626.

JAMES MARTIN, M.A.
S. P. Dom. *Ch. I.*, Vol. 35, No. 110.

Brewer was imprisoned for over fourteen years, and lived only about a month after his release. He is said to have written "many excellent manuscripts". A posthumous work by him was published at London in 1656, entitled "Gospel Public Worship", &c.[1]

The number of separatists in London had considerably increased by 1631, for on June 11 of that year the Bishop of Exeter wrote the following plaintive words to the Bishop of London[2]:—

I was bold the last week to giue your Lordship informacion of a busye, and ignorant schismatick lurking in London, since which tyme I heare (, to my greife) that there are eleuen seuerall congre-

---

[1] "The Story of the Pilgrim Fathers", p. 247.
[2] S.P., Dom., Charles I, Vol. 193 (69).

gacions (as they call them) of Separatistes about the city ; furnished with their ydly-pretended pastors, who meet together in Brewhouses, and such other meet places of resort, euery Sunday ;...

This statement evidently had its desired effect, for in the following year various separatist, as well as independent Puritan, meetings in London were surprised, and some of those who attended them were taken to prison. Among those thus captured were certain persons who were discovered, as reported, "about Christes Church in London", and who appeared before the Court of High Commission on June 14, 1632. Of this number were John Cooke, James and Margery Cleaver, John Japworth, and Anne —. "One [of them] was a yong girl." They were sent to several prisons two by two[1].

A congregation of Brownists or Barrowists was also taken "at a Conventicle in a wood neare Newington in Surrey", on Sunday between June 7 and 14, 1632. Those who were captured and brought before the Court of High Commission on June 14, 1632, were one "Rawlins, Harvy, Arthur Goslin, Howland, Robert Bye, Iohn Smith, & others", also Andrew Sherle[2].

In spite of the fact that Archbishop Laud had done so much to repress the separatists, their congregations in and around London about 1641 appear to have been fairly numerous. One of these was discovered by the authorities in the afternoon of Sunday, Jan. 13 [?], 1640/41. The company were taken "in the howse of Richard Sturges where, they saied, They mett to teach and edifie one an other. in Christ". The capture was made "by the Constables and Church wardens of St Saviours", and evidently on Jan. 16, 1640/41, the prisoners were brought before Sir John Lenthall. Those taken were Edmond "Chillendon", Nicholas Tyne, John Webb, Richard Sturges, Thomas Gunn, John Ellis, "with at least Three score people more"[3].

During the year 1640, such separatists as Edward Barber,

---

[1] Rawl. MS. A. 128 in the Bodleian Library.

[2] *Ibid.*

[3] See a paper in the Library of the House of Lords, calendared under the date Jan. 16 1640/41.

Mark Whitelock[1], Enock Howat[2], Thomas Lambe and Francis Lee[3] appeared before the Court of High Commission. Lambe and Lee were from Colchester in Essex, a Brownist stronghold. The latter was sent to the White Lion. Lambe was committed to the Fleet for four months and a half and was then released on security, as his wife and family were without maintenance. He was ordered "not to preach, baptize, or frequent any conventicle" until his next appearance in court.

A brief description of various separatist gatherings held in London at this period is found in a pamphlet entitled, "THE | BROWNISTS | SYNAGOGVE | ...", 1641[4]. Of course it is improbable that the entire contents of this work are veracious, but there is, no doubt, some historical foundation for what is said, and the writer may possibly have personally visited the meetings which he here enumerates. At any rate, the pamphlet shows what impression the separatists made upon some of their contemporaries.

The first Brownist mentioned is one Richard Rogers, a glover who lived near Whitecross Street in "Blew-Anchor-Alley", in the suburbs of London. He is said oftentimes to have called a "Congregation as he termes it", and to have claimed that he spoke "nothing, but that which the spirit gives [gave] him utterance for".

Jeremy Manwood of Goat Alley, also near Whitecross Street, is said to have taught once every fortnight and maintained that separatists should "abhorre the Society of the wicked".

Edward Gyles is reported to have had a congregation or company in Checker Alley in the same general locality, and to have preached on the first day of each month. He had evidently denounced "the guilded Crosse in *Cheapside*", because, in his opinion, many people worshipped it as an idol.

A button-maker in Aldersgate Street, Marler by name, is

[1] See "Calendar of State Papers, Domestic Series,...Charles I, 1640", London, 1880, p. 385.

[2] *Ibid.*, p. 426.   [3] *Ibid.*, pp. 391 and 432.

[4] Since my account was written, the text of this pamphlet with a brief introduction has been published in the "Transactions" of the Congregational Historical Society for May, 1910, pp. 299–304.

said to preach once a week. He seems at some time to have expressed the opinion that any one may preach, whatever his calling, and that because the clergy are "droanes", there is all the more reason why a layman like himself should "show himselfe a laborious Bee".

John Tucke is said to hold meetings in Fleet Lane, and to maintain that the Book of Common Prayer is taken from the Mass Book.

Humphrey Gosnold has meetings near Tower Hill. He wears long hair, and has told "his holy assembly, that those Pipes, or Organs, which are set up in *Pauls* Church, and other places, make more noyse with their roaring, then all the Bulls of *Basan* did, when *Ogg* their King passed by them in tryumph".

Jonas Hawkins, a fisherman living in Chick Lane, urges separation.

John Brumley of Chancery Lane preaches twice a week.

Roger Kennet, a Yorkshireman, has gathered a company near the Royal Exchange. He evidently taught that salvation was limited to members of his own congregation.

Edward Johnson, a chandler, is reported as teaching a company in More Lane. He believes "that the home, field, or Wood wherein their Congregation meets, is the Church of God, and not the Churches we meet in [in the Church of England], because the good and bad come both thither, neither is it lawfull to have any society with the wicked".

John Bennet, who preached in Love Lane, Westminster, is said to condemn human learning.

George Dunny teaches a society of "seperated Saints" in the Minories.

Charles Thomas, a Welshman, holds a conventicle every two weeks in Warwick Lane. Those who prophesy or preach, he maintains, should be "devout men" "familiar with the Spirit".

Alexander Smith teaches a congregation in Shoreditch. He believes that no one who is not called thereto by the Spirit should preach. He is reported to have maintained that the Latin language, which was so much used by "Schollers, as

Bishops, Deanes and Deacons ", " stinkes like a peece of Biefe a twelve moneth old, yet new salted ".

Edmond Nicholson is said to teach in an alley in Seacoal Lane an assembly of " the Elect and pure in Spirit, chosen vessels of honour, and not of this world ".

Greene and Spencer, " the two Arch-Separatists ", are reported to preach in no regular place. Greene is called a felt-maker, and Spencer a coachman. They called an assembly upon Tuesday, Sept. 28, [1641 ?] in Houndsditch. One of them taught to this effect : " That the Bishops function is an Anti-christian calling, and the Deanes and Prebends, are the Frogs and Locusts mentioned in the Revelation, there is none of these Bishops (saith he) but have a Pope in their bellies, yea they are Papists in grain, and all of them vnleavened soules, & we have turned them over to be buffetted by Satan, and such like Shismaticall [*sic*] Phrases, as the evill Spirit moves him ".

The manner in which these London separatists generally held their meetings is vividly described as follows[1] :—

In that house where they intend to meet, there is one appointed to keepe the doore, for the intent, to give notice if there should be any insurrection, warning may be given them.

They doe not flocke all together, but come 2. or 3. in a company, any man may be admitted thither, and all being gathered together, the man appointed to teach, stands in the midst of the Roome, and his audience gather about him.

He prayeth about the space of halfe an houre, and part of his prayer is, that those which come thither to scoffe and laugh, God would be pleased to turne their hearts, by which meanes they thinke to escape vndiscovered.

His Sermon is about the space of an houre, and then doth another stand up to make the text more plaine, and at the latter end, he intreates them all to goe home severally, least the next meeting they should be interrupted by those which are of the opinion of the wicked, they seeme very stedfast in their opinions, and say rather then they will turne, they will burne.

It can readily be seen from what has been said of these Brownist congregations in London, that they could hardly be

---

[1] " The Brownists Synagogve ", 1641, pp. 5–6.

called churches, or even organizations.   They appear rather to
have been only informal gatherings of people who were beginning
to think for themselves, and to wonder whether the Church of
England was really of any value to them.   They were certainly
little aware of the fact that they were on the eve of one of the
greatest political and religious upheavals of modern times, but
they were, nevertheless, all silently helping to bring about the
Civil Wars and the establishment of the Commonwealth.

CHAPTER VIII

THE FAMILY OF LOVE AND THE ENGLISH SEEKERS

I. *The Family of Love, or Familists.*

AFTER what has been written concerning the Family of Love by Dr F. Nippold[1] and by Mr Robert Barclay[2], there seems little need to devote much time to that rather mysterious society. The Familists appear not to have been a body of separatists from the Church of England, or even from the Church of Rome, and yet they certainly held private gatherings, and at an early date were evidently confused with the Seekers, who especially after 1641 had a very important influence on the development of English separatism. In the popular mind the Family of Love also seems to have been erroneously regarded as a branch of the Anabaptists, and this fact gives added reason why the Familists should at least be mentioned in this work.

For an account of the life of Henry Niclaes, or Nicholas, who was commonly referred to in the late sixteenth, and early seventeenth, centuries as " H. N.", and whose initials were said by his followers to have a mystic meaning, one may turn to the previously mentioned article by Dr Nippold. This pays much attention to Niclaes' many books, which were originally written in Low German and most of which, if not all, were translated into Latin, French, and English, and gives an elaborate description of the Family of Love which he organized.

---

[1] In his article entitled, " Henrich Niclaes und das Haus der Liebe. Ein monographischer Versuch aus der Secten-Geschichte der Reformationszeit...Erster Artikel: Leben des Niclaes ", contained in the " Zeitschrift für die historische Theologie ", Gotha, 1862, pp. 323-94.

[2] In "The Inner Life of the Religious Societies of the Commonwealth" Third Edition, London, 1879, pp. 25-32, etc.

B.

14

It was about 1574 that the appearance of English translations of Niclaes' works began to disturb the then comparatively peaceful religious atmosphere of England. By 1579 they were being vigorously attacked. What appear to be exaggerated, if not unwarranted charges, moreover, were at that time and later brought against the Familists,—charges which until recent times clung tenaciously to their name. Queen Elizabeth did what she could to suppress this sect as it was mistakenly called, but her efforts seem to have failed, for the Family of Love was certainly well known in England as an existing society during the reigns of James I and Charles I.

At the present time the Library of the British Museum is well stocked with the English editions of the writings of "H. N." For any study of the organization of the Familists, however, three manuscripts are of exceptional importance. These are described as follows by Dr Nippold, and are to be found in the "Bibliothek der Maatschappy van Nederlandsche Letterkunde" at Leyden:—

1. Chronika (oder Cronica) des Hüsgesinnes der Lieften: Daerinne betuget wert de Wunderwercken Godes tor lester tydt, unde idt jene dat H. N. unde dem Hüsgesinne der Lieften wederfaren is.—Dorch Daniel, ein Mede-older mit H. N. in dem Hüsgesinne der Lieften, am dach gegeven. Psalm 46 ; 65. (53 cap. 160 fol.).

2. Acta H. N.—De Gescheften H. N. unde etlicke hemmelsche Werckinge des Herrn undt Godes, die H. N. van syner jöget ann wedderfaren zynt.—Dorch Zacharias, ein Mede-Older in dem Hüsgesinne der Lieften, am dach gegeven. Psalm 46. 4. Prov. 2. (25 cap. 70 fol.).

3. Ordo Sacerdotis—De Ordeningen des priesterlicken States in dem Hüsgesinne der Lieften, also H. N. desulve uth dem Munde unde Worde des Herrn, na idt waeraftige Wesen, sulvest geschreven, unde den Olderen unde Ministeren in dem Hüsgesinne der Lieften överandtwordet heft. Psalm 32. Prov. 1. Jes. 61. 1. Petr. 2. (27 cap. 70 fol.).

In England there are probably no manuscripts related to this subject as important as the last of these three, but I have come across several which are of considerable interest. One of these, which may be mentioned here, is apparently an unique copy of an English Familist Hymn Book, translated from one of the Dutch editions of "H. N.""s Hymns. This seems to have been intended for publication[1] and use at the private meetings of the English Family of Love. The work is entitled, "Psalmes and Songes / | brought-forth through H | N. when the Lorde touched hym | with the Rodd of his Chasteninge/ | and lett hym see that Horrible-dis|trŭction of all the Vngodlie / that | Ende of the Wicked-worlde: | makinge manifest eŭenso vnto hym | the new-daye of the Loŭe / that | kingdome of Godes heaŭenlie Fair⸗|nes [?] / the Lordlie-tocominge of | Christ / to the renewinge of | Earth | with Rightŭosnes. | ..." The manuscript is carefully written on paper[2], and though undated was probably prepared between 1574 and 1600.

After an introduction of twenty-eight pages come various Psalms and then follow fourteen "Songes" or hymns. Here is a portion of one of the Psalms :—

The Firste Psallme.

...O Lorde my harte qŭaketh / my Legges wex feble / Sorrowfullnes / Paine / Sufferringe / and Smarte oŭerfalleth [?] mee.

Eŭenso feare I / O Lorde / thy chasteninge /. For in thy reproŭeinge makest thoŭ my Sinnes knowen vnto mee / and thoŭ lettest mee see the Wicked thinges / which haŭe captiŭed mee.

Willt not thoŭ / O God / releace mee from the same? so byde I then in mysterie / and mŭste feare thy Hande all wayes.

But thoŭ / O lorde / arte one that woŭndeste / and makest hoall againe : helpe mee therfore eŭen as thoŭ arte wonte.

Lett that sichinge [searching ?] oŭt of the Deepnes of my harte come before the and wind not awaye thy mercy fŭllnes frome mee.

Among the hymns the following may be given as an illustration :—

A Songe after the tŭne:

The Daye appeareth in the Easte &c.

1 Awake O lorde nowe vnto mee /
   vnstoppe the Eares thine /
   my harte I tŭrne then to thee /
   herken to the Compleinte myne.

2 The heaŭines of my wickednes /
   bringeth my harte frome eas /

---

[1] But I do not think it was ever published.

[2] MS. 869 in Lambeth Palace Library. I give only the original text without additions or marginal notes.

<blockquote>
my Sorrowe mŭst I confesse /
If it moŭght O Lorde the please.
</blockquote>

3
<blockquote>
Witsafe [?] to mee to winde /
my Greef O Lorde beholde & see /
let not the Synnes mee blinde /
bŭt enlarge thy Grace oŭer mee.
</blockquote>

4
<blockquote>
O lorde beholde my heaŭines /
and the great sorrowe of myne /
geŭe mee y¹ Comforte in Distres :
in this my needye tyme.
</blockquote>

5.
<blockquote>
Eŭell hath aŭght my hartes lŭst /
and in sorrowe broŭght mee :
I longe for thy Deliŭerance iŭst /
lorde plŭck not that away to yᵉ.
</blockquote>

6
<blockquote>
Clens nowe O lorde my harte /
and geŭe to mee y¹ Spirite of rest :
the Eŭell it doth bringe my smarte /
and maketh also in mee tempest.
</blockquote>

There are in all ten stanzas of this hymn, but as translated none of them are of any poetical merit. Who would ever read them to-day except as curiosities of expression? One of the hymns (No. 14) is entitled, " A. Daunsing Songe ", but this also is as lacking in rhythm as the others.

Before 1600 the Family of Love can have attracted few converts in England, and even until 1620 and later it must have made slow progress. Edmond Jessop, however, about 1620 after he had become an Anabaptist, nearly fell into the meshes spread for him by the ardent followers of " H. N." He knew therefore from experience what the Family of Love was really like and what was taught its members. The following is Jessop's account of it :—

some others [other Anabaptists] (who being, as it were, distracted with these things) haue fallen to another (the most blasphemous and erronious sect this day in the world) commonly called by the name of *the Family of loue*, whose author was one *Henrie Nicolas*, or *H. N.* for so they will haue him called, that is (as they expound it) *Homo Nouus*, the new man, or *the holy nature*, or *holinesse*, which they make to be Christ, and *sin* they will haue to be Antichrist, because it is opposite to Christ. They say, that when *Adam* sinned, then Christ was killed, and Antichrist came to liue. They teach, that the same perfection of holinesse which *Adam* [had ?] before he fell, is to be attained here in this life ; and affirme, that all their Family of loue are as perfect and innocent as he. And that the resurrection of the dead, spoken of by Saint *Paul* in the 1. Cor. 15. and this prophesie, *Then shall be fulfilled the saying which is written, O death, where is thy sting? O graue, where is thy victory?* is fulfilled in them, and denie all other resurrection of the body to be after this life. They will haue this blasphemer *H. N.* to be the sonne of God, Christ, which was to come in the end of the world to iudge the world; and say, that the day of iudgement is already come; and that *H. N.* iudgeth the world now by his doctrine; so that whosoeuer doth not obey his Gospel, shall (in time) be rooted out of the world; and that his Family of loue shall inherite and inhabite the earth for euer, world without end; only (they say) they shall die in the bodie, as now men do, and their soules go to heauen, but their posterities shall continue for euer. This deceiuer describeth eight through breakings of the light (as he termeth them) to haue beene in eight seueral times from *Adam* to the time that now is, which (as he saith) haue each exceeded other; the seuenth he alloweth Iesus Christ to be the publisher of, and his light to be the greatest of all that euer were before him; and he maketh his owne to be the eigth, and last, and greatest, and the perfection of all, in and by which Christ is perfected, meaning holinesse. He maketh euery one of his Family of loue to be Christ, yea and God, and himselfe God and Christ in a more excellent manner, saying, that he is Godded with God, and codeified with him, and that God is hominified with him.

These horrible blasphemies, with diuers others, doth this *H. N.* and his Family teach to be the *euerlasting Gospel*, which the Angell is said to preach in Reuelation 14. 6. and himselfe to be the Angell, yea and the Archangell which is said to sound the great and last trump, Reuel. 11. 15. They professe greater loue to the Church of Rome, and to all her idolatries and superstitions, then they do to any Church else (whatsoeuer) except themselues. They wickedly abuse these words of Christ, *I must walke to day, and to morrow, and the third day I shall be perfected;* and say, that by *to day* is meant the time of Iesus Christ and his Apostles; and by *to morrow*, all the time of the religion of the Church of Rome; and by *the third day*, this their day of *H. N.* and his Family, wherein they wil haue Christ to be perfected. And they doe compare all the whole religion of the Church of Rome, to the law of *Moses*; affirming, that as God did teach his people by those shadowes and types till Iesus Christ came, so he hath taught the world (euer since) by the images, sacrifices, and filthy heathenisme of the Church of Rome, till this wretch *H. N.* came, and now he must be the onely chiefe teacher, Gods obedient man, yea his sonne, as they blasphemously call him; he (by his Gospell) must make all perfect. They will outwardly submit to any kind of religion, and to any idolatrous seruice whatsoeuer, pretending it is not the bodie that can sinne, but the soule. They will be Priests in the Church of Rome, and act their Seruice after their maner of deuotion; and as Satan can transforme himselfe into an Angell of light, so they can thrust themselues (likewise) to be publike Ministers and Preachers in the Church of England; yea into the Kings Chappell, and to be of his officers and messengers, so bold they are, euen at this present; and so close and cunningly they can carry themselues (being directed thereto by their Master *H. N.*) that yee shall hardly (euer) find them out. They will professe to agree in all points with the Church of England, as also with the Church of Rome, if they should be examined by them, onely this, they will not (lightly) deny their Master *H. N.* nor speake euill of him or his writings, if they should be put to it: and there is no way but this whereby to discouer them, I say, to put them to the deniall and abiuring of him and his writings, and to pronounce him a blasphemer, and his doctrine blasphemous; this they will hardly doe, vnlesse they be not yet his full disciples[1].

II. *The Legatine-Arians, or English Seekers.*

Somewhat closely allied to the Familists, but apparently distinct, though perhaps originally derived, from them, were the English Seekers. How early they arose is uncertain, but it seems probable that the three brothers Legate were their first representatives in England, and that they began to champion Seeker views about 1600, possibly even before that date. The Seekers believed that since Antichrist had ruled so long over the Church, no true church and true church-officers existed any longer in all the world, and furthermore that they could not be secured until God sent new apostles or prophets to ordain new elders and establish entirely new churches. They claimed also that it was undesirable for any man to seek to hasten God's own peculiar business,—an opinion, of course, which was particularly distasteful to those English separatists who saw no need of delaying the preaching of the Gospel and the organization of new churches. Among those to oppose the views of the Seekers were the English General Anabaptists, who as early as 1611 seem to have confounded them with the Family of Love, though the Familists so far as I am aware, never held the previously mentioned views

---

[1] Edmond Jessop's "A Discovery of the Errors of the English *Anabaptists*", London, 1623, pp. 88–91.

which were evidently peculiar to the Seekers. Inasmuch, however, as at a later period also the Familists and the Seekers were confused in the same way, we may cite the General Anabaptist, Thomas Helwys, on this point as apparently one of the first, if not the first, to make this mistake. He says[1]:—

wee passe by the most vngodly & vnwise Familists and scattered flock, that say he [Christ] is in the desert, that is no where to be found in the profession of the gospell according to the ordinances thereof vntill their extraordinarie men (they dream of) come. which shall not be, vntil there come a new Christ, & a new gospell.

Helwys is here, it seems to me, not describing the Familists, but only the Seekers, whom he here styles the "scattered flock", a name sometimes given to them before 1620.

At first the English Seekers seem to have been known as English Arians, or Legatine-Arians, after the name of the three brothers Legate. Henoch Clapham in his "Antidoton", published at London in 1600, apparently makes the earliest reference to them, when he says[2]:—

Touching our English Arrians, they deny all Baptisme and Ordination, till new Apostles be sent to execute those parts to the Gentiles, and *Elias* the Thisbite do come for that end vnto the Iewes.

Later, in 1608, in "ERROVR | On the Right hand"[3], Clapham also speaks of the English Seekers as Legatine-Arians. He does not confuse their teaching with that of the Familists, but he attributes to the Familists views which, though popularly ascribed to them, are only suggested or are certainly uncommon, if they ever appear, in genuine Familist publications. Edmond Jessop, who came very near joining the Familists, and who, therefore, well knew their teaching, only remotely hints at such opinions, and clearly differentiates the Seekers from the Familists. Jessop also does not use the term Seekers. In fact he gives the followers of the Legates no special name. The name Seekers is said to have been used by John Murton in 1617[4], but in 1620 in

---

[1] In "AN AD:|vertisement or admonition, | unto the Congregations,...", 1611, p. 51.

[2] P. 33.   [3] Pp. 28–34.

[4] See Robert Barclay's "The Inner Life of the Religious Societies of the Commonwealth", Third Edition, London, 1879, pp. 411–12.

"A Discription of what *God* hath *Predestinated*", he does not employ that term, though he answers their argument, that a true church cannot be organized before a prophet like John the Baptist or new apostles arise, by quoting the passage " that the least in the Kingdome of *God* is greater then he "[1]. The word Seeker came to be well known not long after 1640, but as yet I am not satisfied that the term was ever used before 1620, or even before 1640.

We may now turn to Edmond Jessop's account of the rise of the English Seekers[2]:—

there were (among others) three Brethren, ancient Separatists from the Church of England, liuing sometimes in the Cittie of London, their names were *Legat*, these held it stifly, that their must be new Apostles, before their could be a true constituted Church, and they drew it from this their ground, the one was called *Walter Legat*, who about twenty yeares since was drowned, being with one of his brethren washing himselfe in a riuer, called the Old Foord; Another of them called *Thomas Legat*, died in Newgate about sixteene yeares since, being laid there for the Heresie of *Arius*; The third called *Bartholomew Legat*, was burnt in Smithfield about ten yeares since, being condemned for the same Heresie of *Arius*, for they all held, and stood stoutly for the same also. These *Legats* had a conceit, that their name did (as it were) foreshew and entitle them, to be the new Apostles, that must doe this new worke; but you see what became of them.

Among the Legatine-Arians, or English Seekers, as has already been said, Edward Wightman should probably be included. Fortunately the original manuscript relating to his trial appears to be catalogued among the Ashmole Manuscripts[3] in the Bodleian Library. This gives a minute and accurate description of his views, and as yet has been little used[4]. The document is entitled, "The proceed[ings a(?)]t

[1] P. 161.

[2] "A Discovery of the Errors of the English *Anabaptists*", London, 1623, pp. 76–7.

[3] Ash. MS. 1521 (vii). Dr John T. Christian deserves the credit of having first called attention to this valuable MS.

[4] The writer of the article on Wightman in the Dictionary of "National Biography" does not mention this trial record, but draws his information from an account of the case, written by Bishop Neile twenty-seven years after Wightman's execution, and preserved in the Public Record Office, London.

Lichfield in .7. | Court dayes [against ?] Edward Wightman | in case of b[lasphemie & (?)] heresie", etc., and is dated 1611. The seven court days are specified as Nov. 19, 26, 29, and Dec. 2, 3, 4, 5 of that year. The record is written partly in Latin and partly in English. From it we may gain a very good idea of the character of Wightman, who is said to have been the last person in England to be burned at the stake solely on account of his religious beliefs.

Wightman had evidently been imprisoned for over half a year at least before his trial. He was first examined on April 18, 1611, again on May 6, as to certain "Articles ministred by his Maiestes Commissioners for causes ecclesiasticall", and still further on Sept. 9, Oct. 8, and twice on Oct. 29, of the same year. The first day's trial on Nov. 19 was held in the Consistory of the Cathedral Church of Lichfield in the presence, and by the permission, of Richard Neile, Bishop of Coventry and Lichfield. We learn that Edward Wightman was a draper of the parish of Burton upon Trent in Staffordshire in the diocese of Coventry and Lichfield, and that he was tried for heretical depravity, having written with his own hand and delivered to the king a certain book in manuscript covering eighteen leaves. This little work began with the words: "A letter Written to a learned man [? Anthony Wotton][1] to discover and confu[t]e the doctrine of the Nicolaitanes very mightely defended with all the learned of all sortes, and most of all hated and abhorred of God himself, because the Wholl world is drowned therein: And seeing he hath promised to answere he knewe not vnto What, and least he should allsoe deale with me as the men of that faccion haue done allready" etc. It concluded thus: "And say glorie be to God alone which dwelleth in the high heavens, whose good will is such towardes men that he will now at the last, plante peace on the earth, and lett all people say, Amen. By me Edward Wightman". It is to be hoped that this writing may some day be found.

[1] One Mr [Anthony ?] Wotton seems to have promised Wightman that he would read the book, and "giue him an Answere". See p. 2 of the trial record, but the work was eventually presented to King James I, and may have been ultimately intended for him.

On Nov. 26, the second day of the trial, the number of people who wished to be present was so great that the Bishop could not get into the Consistory, and he accordingly ordered the session to be held in the Chapel of the Blessed Virgin, which he entered between one and two o'clock in the afternoon. The third day's trial was held in the same chapel, the fourth in the Consistory.

From what was said on the fourth day it appears that Wightman was born in England and baptized in the Church of England, "And that from the tyme of his Infancy vntill within theis Two yeares last past he did hould and beleive the Trinity of persons in the vnity of the diety". The fifth and sixth days' examinations were held in the Consistory. The seventb day was appointed for the hearing of the sentence.

It is interesting to note that among those who took part in this trial was "magister Willelmus Laude Presidens Collegij divi Iohannis baptistae in Academia Oxoniensi." This may have been Laud's first experience with a heretic, and here perhaps he began to develop his mistaken views of the necessity of maintaining uniformity of religious belief.

Wightman's trial, it should be said, is simply, and, so far as the present writer can judge, impartially described. From this record, as already stated, we learn that Wightman began to hold new views about 1609, and from that time he had probably been more or less persecuted. His various opinions, as summed up in his sentence, were the following :—

That there is not the Trinity of persons (the Father, the Sonn, and the holy Ghost) in the vnity of the diety. That Iesus Christe is not the true naturall Sonn of God, perfect God and of the same substance, eternytie and Maiestie With the Father in respect of his Godhead. That Iesus Christe is onely mann and a mere Creature and not both God and man in one person. That Christe our Saviour tooke not humane flesh of the substance of the virgine Marie his mother. And that that promise The seede of the Woman shall breake the serpents head was not fullfilled in Christe. That the person of the holy Ghost is not God coequall coeternall and coessentiall with the Father and the Sonn. That the Three Creedes videlicet the Apostles Creed, the Nicene Creed and Athanasius Creed (contayning the faith of the Trinity, the diety of Christe and the holy Ghost) are the heresies of the Nicolaitanes. That yow the sayd Edward Wightman are that Prophett spoken of in the .18.th Chapter of Deutronomy, and the .3. & .7. Chapters of the Acts of the Apostles in theis wordes.   I will raise them vp a prophett, from amonge theire Brethren like vnto the, &c.   And that that place of Isay: Whose Fan is in his hand, are proper & personall to yow. And that yow are that person of the holy Ghost spoken of in the Scriptures, And the Comforter spoken of in the .16.th of S^t. Iohns Gospell in theis and the like words videlicet.   It is expedient for yow that I goe away for if I goe not away the Comforter will not come vnto yow, but if I depart I will send him vnto yow, and when he is come, he will reprove the world of sin, of righteousnes, and of iudgment.   And againe When he is come which is the spiritt of trueth, he will leade yow into all trueth.   And that those wordes of our Saviour Christe.   Of the sin of blasphemie against the holy ghost, which shall neuer be pardoned in this lief nor in the lief to come, are ment of yourself.   And that that place the .4.th of Malachie . of Elias to come, is likewise proper & personall to yow.   That the Soule doeth sleepe in the sleepe of the first death as well as the body and is mortall as towching the sleepe of the first death, as the bodie is, And that the soule of our saviour Iesus Christe did sleepe in that sleepe of death as well as his body.   That the Soules of the elect Saintes departed are not members possessed of the Triumphant Church in heaven.   That the baptizing of Infantes is an abhomynable Custome.   That there ought not to be in the Church the vse of the Lordes supper to be celebrated in the elementes of bread and wyne, And the vse of baptisme to be celebrated in the element of water, as they are now practized in the Church of England   But that the vse of Baptisme is to be administred in Water, only to Convertes of sufficient age of vnderstanding converted from infydellity to the faith.   That God hath ordayned and sent yow to performe your parte in the worke of the salvacion of the world, to deliver it by your teaching or admonicion from the heresie of the Nicolaitanes, which is the common received faith contayned in those .3. Invencions of mann (hec enim sunt verba tua) comonly called the Three Creedes, to witt, The .12. articles of the beleife, The Nicene Creed, and Athanasius Creed, which faith within theis .1600. yeares past hath prevayled in the World, as Christe was ordayned and sent to saue the world, and by his death to deliver it from sin, and to reconcile it to God, saving that it be not vnderstood that the lymitacion of .1600. yeares, reach to the tyme of Christe and his Apostles, but since their tyme.   And that Christianity is not truely sincerely and Wholly professed and preached in the Church of England but onely in parte,...

To show how fairly the Bishop treated Wightman in the trial and how tenaciously the latter held to his beliefs, it should be noticed that after he had responded to all the questions regarding his heretical opinions, the Bishop asked him still again on the fifth day, "Whither he hath made theis answers advisedly deliberatly and freely of his owne Accord without distraccion of mynde or any other distemperature. Dictusque Wightman respondebat My Lord, Why doe yow aske me such a Question, I thincke yow seeke to disgrace me thereby; I say, that vpon deliberate advise and consideracion and freely I haue made my sayd Answers, and I doe & will stand to them." Wightman, it is stated[1], was first brought to the stake at Lichfield on March 9, 1611/12, but on feeling the heat said he would recant. Two or three weeks later, however, he refused to recant "in a legal way", and was apparently burned during the month of April following. He is said to have died blaspheming.

In conclusion it should be added that the English Seekers do not appear to have been of much influence before the period of the Civil Wars and the Commonwealth. Then the Friends, or Quakers, undoubtedly arose partly as the result of the continued dissemination of Legatine-Arian, or Seeker, views.

---

[1] See the "Dictionary of National Biography".

CHAPTER IX

THE FIRST TWO ENGLISH ANABAPTIST CONGREGATIONS AND THEIR LEADERS

In 1590, it will be remembered, R. Alison[1] says that some of the early London Barrowists had confessed that they "attempted" "a baptising againe" "in their established Church". This statement, interesting as it is, is unconfirmed by any reliable information which has come to my notice. In fact, it is certain that they did not administer a second baptism, though they seem to have been willing, if necessary, to reserve the baptism of their children until a convenient opportunity for its administration presented itself. However, it is possible that there were some in the congregation before 1590, who desired even then to be rebaptized, but were not able to accomplish their wish.

It may be more than a coincidence, therefore, that later, when the Barrowists had for the most part emigrated to Campen in Holland, the prevalence of Anabaptist views of a Continental type became quickly manifest in the congregation, and resulted in the formation of the earliest group of English Anabaptists of whom we at present have any definite knowledge. This view, I am aware, is not the one which has been generally maintained by scholars in recent years, to the effect that John Smyth's congregation, organized in 1608 or 1609, formed the first group of English Anabaptists of which we have any satisfactory evidence. The incorrectness of this latter position has only been gradually forced upon me, as certain details relating to English Anabaptists before 1603 have been specially brought

---

[1] In "A plaine Confvtation of a Treatise of Brownisme", London, 1590, sig. A_3 verso.

to my attention. These details which at first appeared to have little significance on account of their brevity, and no apparent interrelation, can by necessity refer to only one movement[1], and when brought together, may be correlated and woven into the new view here presented. Doubtless, the fact that the few allusions to the Johnsonian Anabaptists are so meagre and so scattered, has kept them from being appreciated at their full value.

In the first place, we learn from Francis Johnson[2] that these Anabaptists were composed of "divers" members of his congregation; that before they adopted their new beliefs they evidently did not secede or separate from his church, but even for some time afterwards remained members of it; and finally that as they persisted in their views and probably gave no sign of returning to their former position, they were excommunicated. From various citations given in the early portion of Chapter VI concerning the Barrowists on the Continent we may also infer with safety that this Anabaptist movement occurred at Campen about 1594 through the influence of the Dutch Mennonites, and may have led to the removal of Johnson's congregation from Campen to Naarden.

No list of these Johnsonian Anabaptists is at present known, but we can be practically certain of the names of three of them, viz., Leonard Pidder[3], Henry Martin[4], and T.[homas?] M.[ichel, or itchel?][5]. To these may possibly be added the names of Thomas Odal, or Odell[6], and Thomas Lemar[7], perhaps also that

---

[1] No well authenticated English Anabaptist movement is known to have occurred before 1603 besides that connected with Francis Johnson's congregation about 1594.

[2] In "An Inqvirie and Ansvver Of Thomas VVhite", 1606, p. 63. This passage is cited in full in Chapter VI, p. 156.

[3] "The Prophane Schisme of the Brownists or Separatists", by Christopher Lawne, and three others, 1612, 4°, p. 56.

[4] *Ibid.*

[5] [Iohn Payne's] "Royall exchange :....", 1597, 4°, p. 45.

[6] [George Johnson's] "A discourse", 1603, p. 194.

[7] Thomas Lemar, or Le Mare, is mentioned in the Barrowist lists of 1590. In "The Prophane Schisme of the Brownists", 1612, pp. 55–6, he is represented as then holding at least one Anabaptist opinion.

of John Hancock[1]. Of this number we later find Thomas Odal, or Odell, in the Dutch-English congregation of Amsterdam, which had been formed by the union of the Smyth party with the Dutch Waterlanders, a branch of the Mennonites.

Were the Johnsonian Anabaptists rebaptized, and whence did they secure their new baptism? One might think, inasmuch as they remained for some time in the Barrowist congregation, that they were content merely to hold various Anabaptist views for a while without receiving a new baptism, or if they were not so content, that they applied to the Dutch Mennonites for it. In my opinion Henoch Clapham in a work published in 1600[2], has preserved in the following words the answer to this question. But for this passing remark of his we would probably never have known of this interesting event:—

Touching the Anabaptists, they stand not partaking in the matter (as doth the Brownist) but they exufflate or blow off our Baptisme, so well as Ordination,...And so, one baptizeth [From margin: "I knew one such, and sundry can witnes it."] himselfe (as Abraham first circumcised himselfe: mary, *Abraham* had a commandement; they haue none, nor like cause) and then he baptizeth other[3]....

Thus we learn of an unnamed se-baptist before 1600 who baptized himself and then others, as John Smyth did some years later. Furthermore, Clapham is evidently speaking of an English se-baptist, for, in the first place, Clapham had known him, and, in the second place, no Dutchman would have thought of baptizing himself, but would almost certainly have applied to the Dutch Mennonites for baptism. It is not easy to imagine who this first English se-baptist can have been, but an allusion made in 1611 suggests that he may have been one of three men, Leonard Pidder, Henry Martin, or Thomas Michel, or Mitchell[4]. In 1594 both Pidder and Mitchell were about thirty-one years

[1] John Hancock must have joined Johnson's congregation in Holland. In "The Prophane Schisme", 1612, he is mentioned. Then he was a se-separatist.

[2] "ANTIDOTON : | OR | A SOVERAIGNE REME-|DIE AGAINST SCHISME | AND HERESIE : | ...", 1600.

[3] P. 33. The mode of baptism here practised was undoubtedly sprinkling or pouring.

[4] "The Prophane Schisme of the Brownists", 1612, p. 56.

old. Martin's age I do not know. If Leonard Busher, who then was only twenty-three years of age[1], had been older, one might suspect him to have been the original se-baptist of history, but his age is decidedly against such a supposition. Indeed, it appears to be extremely doubtful, whether he was ever connected with these Anabaptists.

As to the views of the Pidder-Martin-Mitchell Anabaptists, we are carefully informed by John Payne in a work[2] published at Haarlem in 1597, of which the "Epistle" is addressed to "Mr. A. T.[3] wth [sic] others of my lovinge acquayntans in the Royall Exchange" at London:—

Gentlemen warned of the opinions of the
Anabaptists.

Fyrst our Englishe and Dutche here howld that Christ toke not his pure fleshe of the Virgiu [Virgin] Mary: and do denie her to be his naturall mother. Secondly that the Godheade was subiect to passions and to deathe wch [sic] ys Impassible. Thyrdly that the infants of the faythfull ought not to be baptysed. Fourthly that the soules do slepe in grave [sic] wth [sic] the bodies vntill the resurrection. Fyfthly that Maiestrates ought not to put malefactors to deathe. Sixtly [sic] they condemne all warrs and Subiects in armure in the feyld. Seventhly they denye the article of predestination : they denye the L.[ord's] day. And finally they savour moch of the opinions of fre wyll / and the merit of workes...[4]

John Payne also tells us[5] that about 1597 the members

---

[1] Busher was seventy-one years old in 1642. See a letter by him of that date in the volume of documents.

[2] "Royall exchange: | To suche worshipfull | Citezins / Marchants / Gentlemen | and other occupiers of the contrey as | resorte thervnto. Try to retaine / Or send back agayne. | The contents ys after the Preface. | Sene and allowed here. | [Device.] | AT HARLEM / | Printed wth [sic] Gylis Romaen. | M.D.XCVII", 4°, pp. 48, Black Letter.

[3] "Mr. A. T." may have been Anthony Thatcher, who is mentioned in George Johnson's "A discourse", 1603, p. 63, and who in 1631 probably published "A Christian Reprofe against Contention".

[4] P. 3.

[5] Pp. 21–2. "I wishe you beware of the dangerouse opinions of suche Englyshe Anabaptists bred here / as whose parsons in part wth [sic] more store of there letters dothe crepe and spreade amongest you in cittie and contrey. The wch perilouse herysies wherewth they be so lately infected / dyd not only procede of obstinacie in error / but of pryde and singularitie / wth the want of love and humilitie to kepe vnitie and peace amonge theme

of this earliest English Anabaptist company were sending letters over to England where they were circulated both in London and in the country, and suggests that, not content therewith, one of their number, i.e., T.[homas?] M.[itchell?][1], had journeyed to Norwich[2] evidently with the purpose of making converts. Here he had been imprisoned and was "shortly lyke to die". Payne had already warned "sum particuler freynds" against the Anabaptists. He now published his previously mentioned book for the purpose of influencing the English public against them.

It would be interesting to know if this earliest company of English Anabaptists endured for any length of time, and what ultimately became of them. Some of their number were known

selves when they came over. And as by my privat letters I have forewarned sum particuler freynds: so by this symple and forrayne labor / I intended a more generall: sithens I heard that one of this companie in Norwich intendeth to indure shortly an execution against hym. By wch premonishement I would gladly make you more carefull and watchefull to prevent the invisible sower of darnell a monge the good wheate..."

[1] P. 45. But if "T. M." stands for Thomas Michel or Mitchell, as is probable, he certainly was not put to death, but was evidently banished a second time, for Prof. J. G. de Hoop Scheffer in an appendix to his paper on "The Brownists in Amsterdam", originally published in Dutch in the Transactions of the Royal Academy of Science at Amsterdam for 1881, mentions on April 15, 1606, the marriage of Thomas Michiels of Cambridge (turner and widower) to Margriete Williams of Leicester ("Transactions" of the Congregational Historical Society for September, 1905, p. 163).

[2] Among those who appear to have been influenced by the earliest English Anabaptists was one John Neale. Neale seems to have become infected with Anabaptist doctrine at a very early period, i.e., at least as early as 1604, as may be inferred from the following record, which I came across in the Register of the church of St Peter Mancroft, Norwich, under the date, "Nouem: 19", 1608:—
"Iohn, the sonne of Iohn Neale, sayweauer, & Margaret his wife,...this Childe was borne at Amsterdam, or Leyden in Holland, & was not baptized (his father being an Anabaptist) till this yeare bringing his wife & Childe over to see Ioane Vale widdow, her mother, & other freindes, where the saide Margaret, (refuseing to goe ouer sea with her husband) discouered the not baptizing of the Childe, & craued to haue it baptized, the Childe being at this time, about foure yeres old."

B.   15

to be alive and holding Anabaptist views in 1611[1], but whether they formed an united body at that date is far from certain. If such had been the case, it might have been natural for John Smyth and his party to have consulted them and to have secured their baptism through them, but as is well known, Smyth baptized himself and then the rest of his party. Probably the opinions held by the Johnsonian Anabaptists were too unorthodox to suit him and his adherents.

Fortunately, a far greater number of historical details relating to the Anabaptist congregation organized by Smyth is to be found than can be gleaned concerning the foregoing company. In the first place, we may glance at the story of Smyth's life which is unusually interesting, not only because of his beautiful spirit and his early and pathetic death, but also because of his ever-changing views. He had been a pupil of Francis Johnson and therefore was probably matriculated at Christ's College, Cambridge. He took orders of Bishop Wickham, "prelate of Lincolne, when I [Smyth] was chosen Fellow"[2] of that college. That Smyth became a Fellow of Christ's College and then took orders, are facts which seem hitherto to have been too largely overlooked. We may now, therefore, justly infer that he was a person of considerable learning, as well as agree with Dr Powicke ("Henry Barrow", p. 245), that he presumably never held any benefice. Bishop Hall is a good witness of Smyth's ability, when he says, "Alacke, Master *Smiths* bringing up hath not beene so Swineheard and Shepheard like: He is a Scholler of no small reading, and well seene and experienced in Arts"[3]. In fact, Bishop Hall possibly looked upon Smyth as an abler man than John Robinson, for he says, " I Wrote not to you [Robinson] alone: what is become of your partner, yea, your guide? Woe is me, he hath renounced our Christendome with our Church: and hath wash't of his former water, with new"[4].

---

[1] "The Prophane Schisme of the Brownists or Separatists", 1612, p. 56.

[2] In his "Paralleles, Censvres, Observations", 1609, p. 102.

[3] In I. H.[all]'s "A Description of the Chvrch of Christ,...against certaine Anabaptisticall and erroniovs Opinions, verie hurtfull and dangerous to weake Christians...", London, 1610, p. 108.

[4] In I. H.[all]'s "A Common Apologie", London, 1610, pp. 6–7.

How long Smyth remained a Fellow at Christ's College, or why he left that position, is not at present known, but I have been informed by the courtesy of Dr John Peile, late Master of that college, that Smyth was with little doubt admitted a sizar in March, 1586; doubtless took his B.A. in 1589/90 (though that degree cannot be found); advanced to M.A. in 1593; and became Fellow in Michaelmas term, 1594, when he was ordained by Bishop Wickham. Smyth was chosen preacher of the city of Lincoln on Sept. 27, 1600, and on August 1, 1602, that position was granted to him for life[1]. But it was not Smyth's lot to enjoy the privileges of his office for long. In fact, within three months of the time of his appointment, namely on Oct. 13, 1602, "the vote" which gave him his position "was annulled, and he was deposed" "for having 'approved himself a factious man in this city [of Lincoln] by personal preaching, and that untruly against divers men of good place'"[2]. Before December 13 he appears to have threatened a lawsuit, if his stipend was not paid according to agreement, and even as late as 1603 he seems to have still maintained his right to the title of City Preacher, for that is what he styles himself in a little book published in that year. Of this work there is at present only one copy known. It is to be found in Emmanuel College Library, Cambridge, and is entitled, "THE | BRIGHT MOR-|*NING STARRE*: | OR, | The Resolution and | *Exposition of the 22. Psalme, preached* | publikely in foure sermons | at Lincolne. | By *IOHN SMITH* Prea-|*cher of the Citie.* | ... | Printed by IOHN LEGAT, | *Printer to the Vniuersitie of Cam-|bridge.* 1603. | And are to be solde at the signe of the Crowns in | Pauls Churchyard by *Simon Waterson*", 12°, pp. vi, 196.

On March 22, 1604/5, Smyth published his second work entitled, "A | PATERNE | OF TRVE | PRAYER. | A LEARNED AND COMFOR-|table Exposition or Commentarie vpon | the Lords Prayer: wherein the Doctrine of | the substance and

---

[1] See the Rev. J. H. Shakespeare's "Baptist and Congregational Pioneers", London, 1906, p. 129.

[2] *Ibid.*

circumstances of true | inuocation is euidently and fully | declared out of the holie | Scriptures. | *By* IOHN SMITH, *Minister and Preacher of the* | *Word of God.* | [Device] | *AT LONDON* | Imprinted by *Felix Kynston* for *Thomas Man,* and | are to be sold at his shop in Pater-noster row | at the signe of the Talbot. 1605 ", 4°, pp. viii, 182.

In 1897 when Mr Arber published "The Story of the Pilgrim Fathers", he said concerning this book, "Every copy of this first edition of 1605 has apparently disappeared". Fortunately Mr Arber was mistaken. A copy of this edition, unless it has been lost, has probably been in York Minster Library from the time of its publication, and since Mr Arber wrote his book three other complete copies of the first edition have been found. Of these, one is in the Congregational Library, London, having been made up of portions of two imperfect copies, thanks to the good fortune and vigilance of the present Librarian, the Rev. T. G. Crippen; another is in the Angus Library at Regent's Park College, London; and the third is in the author's collection. A second edition of this work was published in duodecimo in 1624. It also is scarce, but there are copies in the British Museum and a few other libraries.

It is to be noticed that at the time this work was printed in 1604/5 Smyth no longer calls himself City Preacher of Lincoln, but simply "Minister and Preacher of the Word of God", and that he was still a member of the Church of England, for he says in the Epistle "To the Christian Reader": "*I doe here ingenuously confesse that I am far from the opinion of them which separate from our Church, concerning the set forme of prayer (although from some of them, I receiued part of my education in Cambridge)*".

In "The Epistle Dedicatorie", addressed "To the Right Honovrable Edmvnd Lord Sheffield, Lord Lievtenant, and President of his Maiesties Councell established in the North ", Smyth gives us some interesting facts relating to the publication of "this Treatise..., which not long since", he states, "I [he] deliuered to the eares of a few, being then Lecturer in the Citie of *Lincolne*". What had induced him to publish the work, he says, was "partly the motion of some friends, partly and chiefly the satisfying of some sinister spirits [who] haue [had] in a manner wrested from me [him] that [position ?], whereto otherwise I [he] had little affection". Certain "vniust imputations and accusations" had evidently been brought against him, and these he had been compelled to answer "before the Magistrate ecclesiastical." The matter was finally brought for settlement before Lord Sheffield, who "wisely and charitably compounded the controuersie on both parts to the contentment of either of vs ;...", a very unusual result for that disturbed period.

Evidently not long after the publication of this work Smyth began to entertain doubts concerning the Church of England. Perhaps Francis Johnson, or some of his other separatist acquaintances, had seen the passage in his book cited above, and had called his view in question. However this may be, he fell into a state of doubt, which, he says[1], lasted " 9. Months at the least ". During this time he seems to have been for the most part at or about Gainsborough, for he says in referring to this period, " 1 [I] appeale to the towne of Ganesbrugh, & those ther that knew my footesteps in this matter "[2]. During these nine months, also, it would appear, he "was delivered twise from the Pursivant, & was sick allmost to death "[3] at the home of Thomas Helwys[4] at " Bashforth "[5]. He had further a "quiet & peaceable conference" at Coventry "with certayne Ministers " (Mr Dod, Mr Hildersham, and Mr Barbon) "about withdrawing from true Churches, Ministers, and VVorship, corrupted : VVherein 1 [I, i.e., he] receaved no satisfaction, but rather thought 1 [I, i.e., he] had given instruction to them "[6]. Shortly after this last incident Smyth became a separatist.

[1] See "Paralleles, Censvres, Observations ", 1609, p. 5.

[2] *Ibid.*, p. 128.   [3] *Ibid.*

[4] Thomas Helwys was a married man, and I have discovered that he was married to Joan Ashmore at Bilborough, Nottinghamshire, on Dec. 3, 1595 ("Nottinghamshire Parish Registers. Marriages ", Vol. vi., London, 1904).

[5] See "The last booke of Iohn Smith, Called the retractation of his errours, and the confirmation of the truth".

[6] See "Paralleles, Censvres, Observations ", 1609, p. 129.

The years 1604–1606 happened to be a period of considerable moment in Lincoln Diocese. The Puritan preachers there wrote an extended work relating to their grievances, entitled "An Apologie for those ministers that are troubled for refusing to Subscription and Conformitie". This they presented to King James I on December 1, 1604, and later abridged and published in 1605 under the title, "An Abridgment of that Booke", etc. This work pleads[1] for "Christian Libertie, *which Christ hath purchased for vs by his death, and which all christians are bound to stand for, that the service wee are to doe vnto God now is not mysticall, ceremoniall and carnal (as it was then) but plaine and spirituall*".

Smyth may possibly have had some part in the preparation of this work. At any rate, he probably saw the printed edition. Indeed, such a passage as that just cited may have helped to persuade him finally to become a separatist. He apparently took this new step about the beginning of the year 1605/6, together with many others who had gradually been coming to the separatist position in Gainsborough, Scrooby, Bawtry, Babworth, Worksop, Austerfield, and their neighbourhood. At first these people seem merely to have met together at convenient times as Puritan members of the Church of England. They were obliged, however, even then to endure various privations, and finally they decided to shake off the yoke of "antichristian bondage", and to organize a separatist church of their own. Therefore, "as the Lords free people, [they] joyned them selves (by a covenant of the Lord [which had perhaps been suggested to them by Smyth's old tutor, Francis Johnson]) into a church estate, in the fellowship of the gospell, to walke in all his wayes, made known, or to be made known unto them, according to their best endeavours, whatsoever it should cost them, the Lord assisting them"[2]. The place where the covenanting occurred is not stated.

It is true that this account is not exactly that of tradition, which following a statement in Nathaniel Morton's "New

---

[1] P. 34.

[2] Governor Bradford's "History 'Of Plimoth Plantation'. From the Original Manuscript", Boston, 1898, p. 13.

Englands Memorial ", published in 1669, has maintained that the covenanting occurred in 1602, but certainly Governor Bradford's own version, which is the best we have, indicates that the true time was about the beginning of the year 1606/7. On this point he says explicitly[1] :—

So after they had continued togeither aboute a year, and kept their meetings euery Saboth, in one place, or other, exercising the worship of God amongst them Selues, notwithstanding all the dilligence & malice of their aduerssaries ; they seeing they could no longer continue in that condition, they resolued to get ouer into Holland as they could. Which was in the year .1607. & .1608....

After the covenanting two distinct congregations were organized, which met separately on account of the distance between the various towns in which the separatists lived. One church met at Scrooby Manor House under the leadership of Richard Clyfton, the other at Gainsborough. Whether the Gainsborough company at first had a separate pastor is uncertain, but within a very short time, at least, John Smyth, who had become a member of this congregation, must have been chosen its pastor. Even at this early period Clyfton and Smyth did not always entirely agree, for it is known that before they left England differences had broken out between them, and a " conference concerning excommunication and other differences then betweene you [Smyth] & me [Clyfton] was held "[2]. The two churches nevertheless continued to be so closely related that when their troubles became unendurable, " by a joint consent, they resolved to go into the Low Countries, where they heard was Freedom of Religion for all men ". From Bradford's narrative it also appears that the separatists tried to leave England in the autumn or winter of 1607 but did not succeed until the spring of 1608.

Before their departure they evidently sent one of their number over to Holland to report the condition of the country, for Bishop Hall had heard while on a visit to the Continent, " that certain companies from the parts of Nottingham and Lincolne (whose Harbinger had beene newly in Zeland before

[1] Governor Bradford's " History ' Of Plimoth Plantation '. From the Original Manuscript ", Boston, 1898, p. 31.

[2] [Richard Clyfton's] " The Plea for Infants ", Amsterdam, 1610, p. 4.

me [him]) meant to retyre themselves to Amsterdam, for their full libertie "[1].

The two companies seem to have reached Amsterdam about the same time, and evidently intended to unite under the leadership of John Smyth, had he not "broached" certain "opinions, both erronious & offensive "[2]. Apparently Smyth's congregation from the beginning maintained a separate existence from Johnson's[3], while Clyfton's company may have joined Johnson's church and remained with it until the end of April, 1609, when John Robinson with most of the original members removed to Leyden[4]. At first, the members of Smyth's and of Johnson's companies appear to have been in communion with one another. Later this relation ceased.

During the year 1608 events moved rapidly, and various disturbing controversies arose, which finally resulted in the display of much bitterness and in the parting of old friends. Books began to be written and published which soon told to the world all their troubles, but which, it is to be feared, did little toward settling their many difficulties[5].

[1] In I. H.[all]'s "A Common Apologie of the Church of England:...", London, 1610 [p. 125].

[2] See J. Smyth's "Character of the Beast", 1609, p. 2.

[3] In this view I am supported by Dr Dexter's judgment as expressed in "The True Story of John Smyth", Boston, 1881, [p. 2] note 15, in which he corrects his former error.

[4] This point is suggested by the fact that Clyfton took Ainsworth's place as teacher in Johnson's congregation after December, 1610, and perhaps by a statement in John Dayrell's "A Treatise of the Chvrch", 1617, p. 155, where it is said: "It may be also M. *Robinson* that for this cause, you your selfe haue left both M. *Iohnsons* Church then and M. *Ainsworths* also."

[5] Up to this time more works in opposition to the Brownists had either been written or published than has commonly been supposed. Richard Bernard in his "Christian Advertisements", London, 1608, mentions a number of these writings several of which, I believe, are at present not known: "[P. xi] and yet Master *Gyshops* booke, Master *Bradshawes* challenge, Doctor *Allisons* confutation, certaine Ministers reioynder to Master *Smith*, with other moe are not answered..."
"[P. 32] What M. Doctor *Allison*, M. *Cartwright*, M. *Iames*, M. *Rogers*, M. *Henrie Smith* and others moe, haue iudged of them [the Brownists], their labours being extant I referre men thereto,..."

Smyth's third work was a little octavo book published in 1607 and entitled, " PRINCIPLES | and inferences | *concerning* | The visible Church ". Of this there are apparently only two copies extant, one being in York Minster Library, the other, I think, in the Dexter Collection in the Library of Yale University. The following are some of Smyth's opinions herein expressed:—

A visible communion of Saincts is of two, three, or moe Saincts joyned together by covenant with God & themselves, freely to vse al the holy things of God, according to the word, for their mutual edification, & Gods glory...[1]

All religious societies except that of a visible church are vnlawful : as Abbayes, monasteries, Nunries, Cathedralls, Collegiats, parishes.

The true visible church is the narrow way that leadeth to life which few find...

Other religious communions are the broad way that leadeth to destruction which many find...[2]

The outward part of the true forme of the true visible church is a vowe, promise, oath, or covenant betwixt God and the Saints : by proportion from the inward forme :...

This covenant hath 2. parts. *1.* respecting God and the faithful. 2. respecting the faithful mutually...

The first part of the covenant respecting God is either from God to the faithful, or from the faithful to God...

From God to the faithfull. Mat. 22. *32.* the sum wherof is expressed *2* Cor. *6. 16.* I wilbe their God.

From the faithful to God 2 *C*or. 6. 16. the summe whereof is to be Gods people, that is to obey al the commandements of God. Deut. 29, 9[.]

The second part of the covenant respecting the faithful mutually conteyneth all the duties of love whatsoever...[3]

Weomen are not permitted to speak in the church in tyme of prophecy...

If women doubt of any thing delivered in tyme of prophecy and are willing to learn, they must ask them that can teach them in private,...[4]

The officers of the true visible church are al absolutely described in the word of God...

These officers ar of two sorts : 1 Bishops, 2 Deacons *Phil.* 1, *1.*

The Bishops are also called Elders or Presbyters...

The Bishops or Elders joyntly together are called the Eldership or Presbyterie...

[1] P. 8.   [2] P. 9.
[3] P. 11, incorrectly printed P. 10.   [4] P. 14.

The Eldership consisteth of 3 sorts of persons or officers : viz. the Pastor, Teacher, Governours...[1]

It should also be said that about one third of the contents of this little treatise (pp. 21–30) is made up of a discussion of church discipline.

About May 22, 1607, one Edward James, "Master in the Artes and Mynister of GODs worde", published a work, of which as yet I have seen no copy, said to be entitled, "*A retraite sounded to certen brethren latelye seduced by the schismaticall BROWNistes to forsake the Churche*"[2]. This was evidently directed against the separatists at Scrooby and Gainsborough, and its date of publication points to the winter or early spring of 1606/7 as the probable time of their covenanting. Smyth in his "Paralleles, Censvres, Observations", 1609, significantly mentions a "Mr. Iames"[3], as an opponent "of the Seperation". No doubt this was Edward James, and Smyth had evidently seen his book.

Not long after Smyth had published the previously mentioned "litle methode" concerning church polity, he began writing another work, which appeared in 1608 under the title, "The Differences of the Churches of the seperation". In this he speaks with great respect of "the auncient brethren of the seperation" as having accomplished much to restore the Church to its primitive condition[4], and on the same page he also gives an unusual text of the church covenant of the separatists at Scrooby and Gainsborough, which is worth noticing. He says : "it is our covenant made with our God to forsake every evill way whither in opinion or practise that shalbe manifested vnto vs at any tyme"[5], and it is on the strength of this covenant that he justifies his many changes of mind. In fact, Smyth had already begun to feel that though the members of the "Ancient Church" had made much progress in determining the constitution of the primitive churches, there was work that still remained to be done touching "the Leitourgie Presbyterie & Treasurie of

---

[1] Pp. 17–18.

[2] See Mr Edward Arber's "Transcript of the Registers of the Company of Stationers", London, Vol. III., 1876, p. 153.

[3] P. 127.   [4] P. iii.   [5] *Ibid.*

the Church ", and he now states six opinions in which he differs
" from the auncyent brethren of the Seperation "[1] :—

1 Wee hould that the worship of the new testament properly
so called is spirituall proceeding originally from the hart : & that
reading out of a booke (though a lawfull eclesiastical action) is no
part of spiritnall [spirituall] worship, but rather the invention of
the man of synne it beeing substituted for a part of spirituall
worship.

2 Wee hould that seeing prophesiing is a parte of spirituall worship:
therefore in time of prophesijng it is vnlawfull to have the booke
[i.e., the Bible] as a helpe before the eye

3 wee hould that seeing singinging [*sic*] a psalme is a parte of
spirituall worship therefore it is vnlawfull to have the booke before
the eye in time of singinge a psalme

4 wee hould that the Presbytery of the church is vniforme : & that
the triformed Presbytetie [Presbyterie] consisting of three kinds of
Elders viz. Pastors Teachers Rulers is none of Gods Ordinance but
mans devise.

5 wee hold that all the Elders of the Church are Pastors: and that
lay Elders (so called) are Antichristiau [Antichristian].

6 wee hold that in contributing to the Church Treasurie their ought
to bee both a seperation from them that are without & a sanctifica-
tion of the whole action by Prayer & Thanksgiving.

These statements in themselves are remarkable enough, but
the work is crammed with still more astonishing views, such as
modern separatists would find it difficult to comprehend, and
much more difficult to put into practice. Probably this book
will always remain one of the curiosities of English religious
literature. In closing Smyth mentions certain questions which
he has not yet been able satisfactorily to answer. Among these
are the following[2] :—

VVhither in a Psalme a man must be tyed to meter & Rithme, &
tune, & whither voluntary [*sic*] be not as necessary in tune & wordes
as in matter ?

VVhether one Elder only in a Church be Gods ordinance &
whither if ther be chosen any Elder ther must be chosen more then
one ?

VVhither the seales of the covenant may not be administred,
ther being yet no Elders in office ?

The exact period when these questions were most disturbing
the separatists is determined by an hitherto unnoticed letter of

---

[1] P. v.   [2] [P. 34.]

Thomas Helwys in Lambeth Palace Library[1]. This is of the date Sept. 26, 1608, and is given in the volume of documents. In the letter it is made clear that Smyth's congregation did not believe in having " Pastors & Teachers ", but " Pastors only ". Helwys repeats : " we approve of no other officers in the ministry but of Pastors ". The letter is unsigned, but is marked "A note sent by [Thomas] Ellwes [Helwys] one of thelders of the Brownest Churche ", thus suggesting that the congregation already had Elders. The letter also shows that by Sept. 26, 1608, Smyth's church was well settled in Holland.

In an undated letter of " Hughe and Anne Bromheade " to their cousin, Sir William Hammerton, evidently written in the early autumn of 1608, about the time that Helwys sent the above-mentioned note, is the following quaint description of the services in Smyth's congregation[2] :—

The order of the worshippe and goverment of oure church is .I. we begynne with A prayer, after reade some one or tow chapters of the bible gyve the sence therof, and conferr vpon the same, that done we lay aside oure bookes, and after a solemne prayer made by the .I. speaker, he propoundeth some text owt of the Scripture, and prophecieth owt of the same, by the space of one hower, or thre Quarters of an hower. After him standeth vp A .2. speaker and prophecieth owt of the said text the like tyme and space. some tyme more some tyme lesse. After him the .3. the .4. the .5. &c as the tyme will geve leave, Then the .1. speaker concludeth with prayer as he began with prayer, with an exhortation to contribution to the poore, which collection being made is also concluded with prayer. This Morning exercise begynes at eight of the clock[e?] and continueth vnto twelve of the clocke the like course of exercise is observed in the aft[er]n[o]wne from .2. of the clocke vnto .5. or .6. of the Clocke. last of all the execution of the g[over]ment of the church is handled /

Thus far Smyth had not criticized the baptism of the separatists. This subject was probably brought to his eager attention some time in the autumn of 1608. Having become convinced that in the primitive church infants were not baptized, he came to the conclusion that he ought to be baptized again. The problem of the proper manner of administering baptism

---

[1] MS. 709, fol. 117. I am not certain that this letter is written in Helwys' own hand-writing, but it was evidently sent by him.

[2] Harl. MS. 360, fol. 71 recto.

seems never to have troubled his sensitive mind. His chief difficulty appears rather to have been where to find a suitable person to baptise him. The Mennonites did not at that time meet his requirements on account of their peculiar beliefs. To whom then should he turn for baptism, for he demanded an administrator whose own baptism had been such that no one could with fairness adversely criticize it? To his disappointment there appeared to be no such person in all the world. Even the Johnsonian Anabaptists for some reason did not suit him, though he seems to have followed their method of procedure in the administration of baptism by first baptizing himself and then his followers. This fact shows that Mr Arber made much too strong a statement when he wrote that "In the year 1608, JOHN SMYTH baptized himself; and so became the Se-Baptist of Church History"[1]. To be sure Smyth baptized himself late in 1608, or early in 1609, but, as we have already seen, he was neither the first, nor the only, Se-Baptist.

John Smyth, therefore, is not such an unique figure in church history as Dr Dexter and Mr Arber would have us believe. In so far as his se-baptism itself is concerned, he attempted nothing original, but how did he baptize himself? Fortunately the following contemporaneous statements when linked together leave us in no doubt that Smyth's se-baptism consisted merely of his sprinkling himself with water from a basin and probably pronouncing the customary baptismal formula :—

M[r] Smith, M[r] Helw:[ys] & the rest haveing vtterly dissolved, & disclaymed their former Ch:[urch] state, & ministery, came together to erect a new Ch:[urch] by baptism : vnto which they also ascribed so great virtue, as that they would not so much as pray together, before they had it. And after some streyning of courtesy, who should begin,...M[r] Smith baptized first himself, & next M[r] Helwis, & so the rest, making their particular confessions[2].

Now for baptising a mans self ther is as good warrant, as for a man Churching himself: For two men singly are no Church, joyntly they are a Church, & they both of them put a Church vppon themselves, so may two men put baptisme vppon themselves : For as both those persons vnchurched, yet have powre to assume the

---

[1] "The Story of the Pilgrim Fathers", London, 1897, p. 137.

[2] John Robinson's "Of Religious Communion Private and Publique", 1617, p. 48.

Church each of them foɪ himself with others in communion : So each of them vnbaptized hath powre to assume baptisme for himself in communion : And as Abraham & Iohn Baptist, & all the Proselites after Abrahams example, Exod. 12. 48. did administer the Sacrament vppon themselves : So may any man raised vp after the Apostacy of Antichrist, in the recovering of the Church by baptisme, administer it vppon himselɪ [himself] in communion with others :...[1]

Mr. Sm.[yth] anabaptised himself with water : but a child could have done the like unto himself, who cannot performe any part of spirituall worship : therefore Mr. Sm.[yth] anabaptising himself with water, did no part of spirituall worship : and consequently it was carnal worship, and service of the Divil. If he answer, that a child though he could cast water on himself, & utter such words as he heard Mr. Sm.[yth] speak withal ; yet could he not preach or open the covenant as did the Preists and Levits, Nehem. 8. 8. and as Christ himself did when he read in the synagogue, Luk. 4. Wherefore reading and preaching being joyned togither, as baptising with water & preaching : he that condemns the one outward action because a child can doe it, condemneth also the other by the like reason. And Mr. Sm.[yth] having thus written of children, and doon to himself ; the babes and sucklings whose soules he would murder by depriving them of the covenant promise and visible seal of salvation in the Church ; shal rise up in judgment & shall condemn him in the day of Christ[2].

With the preceding citations the following words from Bishop Hall's " A Common Apologie of the Chvrch of England : ... ", 1610, should probably be joined :—

shew you mee, where the Apostles baptized in a Basen[3].

From this group of quotations we may get a very good idea of how Smyth's congregation was organized, and of the manner in which he baptized himself and those who were willing to follow him.

As may well be imagined, Smyth was soon in the midst of a still more heated controversy. Mr Arber and others have given considerable attention to the works relating to it, and we have no time to mention them except in so far as they furnish us with the opinions and practices of Smyth's company. By thus boldly rejecting the baptism of the Church of England and seeking rebaptism Smyth does not appear to have displeased Bishop Hall, but he set all the Brownists and Barrowists by

---

[1] John Smyth's "The Character of the Beast", 1609, p. 58.

[2] Henry Ainsworth's "A Defence of the Holy Scriptures, Worship and Ministerie,...", Amsterdam, 1609, p. 69.   [3] P. 91.

the ears, and they became exceedingly active in striving to defend their cause, which Smyth seemed suddenly to have undermined. He was accordingly soon at work on his book directed against infant baptism, which he entitled, "THE CHARACTER OF THE BEAST", 1609, and which he finished writing on Mar. 24, 1608/9. In "The Epistle to the Reader" he goes so far as to claim that "al that shal in tyme to come Seperate from England must Seperate from the baptisme of England, & if they wil not Seperate from the baptisme of England their is no reason why they should seperate from England as from a false Church "[1], "though they may seperate for corruptions "[2]. In closing, Smyth speaks of believers' baptism as the "most evident truth that ever was revealed to me [him]".

It was soon manifest that if this last view was true, it would overturn the existing opinions of all Christendom, even including those maintained by the orthodox Church of England, by the Puritans, and by the Brownists and Barrowists.

Smyth maintained his position in the following manner. He says[3]:—

baptisme in Popery is false baptisme, & so in the Lords account no better then Pagan washing, being administred vppon infants a subject that God never appointed to baptisme :...
[In contradistinction from baptism of infants which Smyth looks upon as false in essence] the Scripture describeth true baptisme which is the Lords owne ordinance thus : The matter must bee one that confesseth his Fayth & his sinnes, one that is regenerate & borne againe : The forme must bee a voluntary delivering vp of the party baptized into the Name of the Father, Sonne, & Holy Spirit, by washing with water, Mat. 28. 19. Mat. 3. 6. Iohn. 4. 1. Act. 2. 41. & 8. 36. 37. compared with Roman. 6. 17. & Mat. 28. 20. & 18. 20. & Gal. 3. 27. & Roman. 6. 2–6. VVherein ther must be a mutual consent of both persons contracting together : & that this is so, the forme of baptisme retayned in popery yet, teacheth plainly : wher they say. Credis? Credo : Abrenuntias? abrenuntio : which other persons speak for the infant that cannot speak, therby declaring that ther must needs bee a mutual contract of both the parties contracting : This ordinance of the L.[ord] therfor is abolished both in the matter & forme, & an other straunge invention of man is in the rome therof substituted, which is not the L.[ords] & therfor a nullity,...[4]

<hr />

[1] P. iv.   [2] *Ibid.*   [3] P. 48.   [4] Pp. 50–1.

This passage and another on page 48 show that Smyth still believed in the use of a covenant in the organization of a Christian church. His strong attack on the position of the Barrowists seems to have affected some of them even before March 24, 1608/9, when he finished "The Character of the Beast", for he says:—

why may not you [Richard Clyfton] returne back againe into England, & take vp your former ministery, & renounce your Schisme which you have made? & so I heare that some are mynded to doe:...[1]

Of the works written in this controversy against the English Anabaptists so much has already been said, that mention need only be made of one, of which it appears no notice has yet been taken. It is a little duodecimo work of twenty-four pages written by Francis Johnson and published in 1609, entitled, "A BRIEF TREATISE | conteyning some grounds and | reasons, against two errours | of the Anabaptists : | 1. *The one, concerning baptisme | of infants. |* 2. *The other, concerning anaba-| ptisme of elder people. |* ... "

In Holland it has been thought that the se-baptism occurred in November, 1608. My own view is that before that date Smyth could hardly have had time to change his opinions so greatly. December, 1608, or January, 1608/9, seems a more likely time, and would also have given him sufficient opportunity before Mar. 24, 1608/9, to write "The Character of the Beast".

Another treatise from Smyth's pen was published later in 1609 before he changed his ideas on the necessity of observing a succession in the ministry. This work was entitled "PARALLELES, CENSVRES, OBSERVATIONS." It breathes no suggestion of any new, sudden change of mind, and all seems calm in so far as his relations with his congregation are concerned. Here, however, he makes no slight prophecy with regard to church buildings, when he says, "that as the goodly buildings of the Abbayes, Monasteries, & Nunries, are already destroyed, & made barnes, stables, swinestyes, jakes, so shal it be done with al the Idol Temples [i.e., church edifices in which images, etc., had stood] when the howre of their visitation shal come:..."[2].

[1] P. 61.   [2] P. 122.

Smyth's opinion of the value of the Church of England is nevertheless by no means so poor at this time as one might expect :—

I for my part do professe that in your assemblies [of the Church of England] I receaved the seedes of true faith invisible, which (if I had dyed not knowing the Seperation) should I doubt not through Gods mercy have been effectual to my justification & salvation in Christ *:...*[1]

From Bishop Hall[2] we learn that in Smyth's congregation of Anabaptists, women were allowed at the Lord's table, the Communion was celebrated in the evening, and the minister preached over a table. All these customs seemed remarkable to Bishop Hall, and he claimed that no warrant for any of them could be found in the primitive church!

Before March 12, 1609/10, Smyth was encountering further troubles, this time with some of his own congregation concerning succession in the ministry, and all those who did not agree with him promptly withdrew from the church[3]. This unexpected movement was apparently led by the Elders, who may have been Thomas Helwys, William Pigott, Thomas Seamer, and John Murton.

This unfortunate situation will be made more clear by the following citation from Smyth's "last booke" :—

Succession is the matter wherin I hold as I haue written to maister Bernard / that succession is abolished by the church of Rome / and that ther is no true ministery deriued from the Apostels through the church of Rome to England / but that the succession is interrupted and broken of : Secondly I hold as I did hould then / succession being broken of and interrupted / it may by two or three gathered together in the name of Christ / be renewed and

---

[1] "Paralleles, Censvres, Observations", 1609, p. 131.

[2] In "A Common Apologie of the Chvrch of England", London, 1610, p. 91.

[3] Up to the present time it has generally been supposed that the church took the very unusual course of casting Smyth out. It now appears from words in Smyth's "last booke", where he speaks of "maister Helwys his seperation / against which I have done nothing in writing hitherto", that Helwys and his followers took the more natural step of separating from Smyth. On the other hand, see also the contents of MS. B. 1351 in the Mennonite Archives, Amsterdam, given in the volume of documents.

assumed againe : and hearin ther is no difference betwixt maister
Helwis and me.   Thirdly maister Hel.[wis] saith that although ther
be churches alreadie established / ministers ordained / and sacraments administred orderly / yet men are not bound to Ioyne to
those former churches established / but may being as yet vnbaptized
baptise them selues (as we did) and proceed to build churches of
them selues / disorderly (as I take it) Herin I differ from maister
Helwis / and therfor he saith I Haue sinned against the holy ghost.
bicause I once acknowledged the truth (as M^r. Helwis calleth yt:)
here I, answer .3. things 1. I did never acknowledge it. 2. it is not
the truth.   3. though I had acknowledged it / and it were a truth /
yet in denying it I haue not synned against the holie ghost.   first
I did never acknowledge yt / that it was lawfull for priuate persons
to baptise / when their were true churches and ministers / from
where wee might haue our baptisme without synne / as ther are 40.
witnesses that can testifie : onlie this is It which I held / that
seeing ther was no church to whome wee could Ioyne with a Good
conscience / to haue baptisme from them / therfor wee might baptise
our selues : that this is so the lord knoweth / my conscience wit-
nesseth / and maister Helwis him self will not deny it.   secondly it
is not the truth that two or three priuate persons may baptise /
when ther is a true church and ministers established whence
baptisme may orderlie be had : For if Christ himself did fetch
his baptisme from Iohn / and the gentills from the Iewes baptised /
and if God be the God of order and not of confusion / then surely
wee must obserue this order now / orels di[s]order is order / and
God alloweth disorder.   for if M^r. Helwis position be true / that
everie two or three / that see the truth of baptisme may beginne to
baptise / and need not Ioyne to former true churches / wher they
may haue ther baptisme orderly from ordained ministers : then the
order of the primitiue church / was order for them and those times
onely / and this discorder will establish baptisme of priuate persons /
Yea of women from hence forth to the worldes end /....

About February, 1609/10, thirty-two of the Smyth party
(there appear to have been forty-three in all), finding themselves friendless in a cold world, appealed to the Waterlanders, a
section of the Mennonites, that they might be allowed to unite
with them, as those whom they were now willing to recognize
as the " true church of Christ ".   On hearing of this new and
somewhat surprising movement, Helwys' followers seem to have
had a conference with the Waterlanders, in order to prevent
them from receiving Smyth's company.   At this meeting, however, the English were not able to express their views in Dutch
with facility " for want of speach ".   Hence on March 12,

1609/10, they wrote a letter in English to the Waterlanders deploring their lack of knowledge of the Dutch language, and urging them to be slow in receiving Smyth and his associates into membership.

The troubles of the English Anabaptists were quickly known and reported to the world. Richard Clyfton in his "Plea for Infants and Elder People", Amsterdam, 1610, says[1]:—

And now againe, many of this new communion have separated themselves from the rest, holding the error about the incarnation of Christ. An other sort are excommunicate, namely M. Smyth & divers with him, for holding (as it is reported by some that were of them) that their new washed companie is no true church, and that there cannot be in a church the administration of baptisme & other ordinances of Christ, without Officers, contrarie to his former judgment, practise & writings, & yet resteth not but is inquiring after a new way of walking, (as the same persons affirme) breeding more errors, as is strongly suspected, and by his manuscripts partly appeares.

It has long been known that John Smyth's original church of Anabaptists was early divided into two sections led respectively by Smyth and by Helwys, but hitherto it seems largely to have escaped observation that already by 1610 his congregation had in reality separated into three, and not two, distinct parties. The above citation shows that the third company " had separated themselves from the rest, holding the error about the incarnation of Christ ", in other words, having accepted at least one of the opinions maintained by the Continental Anabaptists, which was not acceptable either to Smyth or to Helwys and Murton.

This third company of English Anabaptists I judge included Leonard Busher, who is spoken of in 1611 as belonging to a class of Anabaptists distinct from Smyth as well as from Helwys[2]. Associated with Busher may have been Swithune Grindall, Richard Overton, John Drew (who later united with

---

[1] Sig. *3 verso.

[2] In the following citation from a letter written by "Mat. Savnders' and "Cvth. Hvtten" on July 8, 1611, the different English Anabaptist sections of this early period may be quite clearly made out:—

"Master *Smith* an Anabaptist of one sort, and master *Helwise* of

the Waterlanders), and probably others with whose names we are not familiar to-day.

Those of Smyth's party who first applied for membership among the Waterlanders were the following thirty-two[1]:—

Hugh Bromhead.

Iervase Nevill[2].

Iohn Smyth.

Thomas Canadyne.

Edward Hankin.

Iohn Hardy.

Thomas Pygott.

Francis Pygott.

Robert Stavely.

Alexander Fleming.

Alexander Hodgkin.

Iohn Grindall.

Salomon Thomson.

Samuell Halton.

Thomas Dolphin.

Anne Bromhead.

Iane Southworth.

Mary Smyth.

Ioane Halton.

Ales Arnefield.

Isabell Thomson.

Margaret Stavely.

Mary Grindall.

Mother Pygott.

Ales Pygott.

Margaret Pygott.

Betteris Dickenson.

Mary Dickenson.

Ellyn Paynter.

Ales Parsons.

Ioane Briggs.

Iane Organ.

Later the number was considerably increased.

Latin communications now began to be sent to the Waterlanders by both parties. Smyth wrote with his own hand a twenty-article Confession of Faith for their perusal, while Helwys and Murton sent them a letter in Latin, protesting that the Waterlanders should not receive Smyth and his

another, and master *Busher* of another......to speake nothing of *Pedder*, *Henrie Martin*, with the rest of those *Anabaptists*..."

("The Prophane Schisme of the Brownists or Separatists" by Christopher Lavvne and three others, 1612, p. 56.)

Busher was evidently connected with the third section of Smyth's congregation, but whether before the separation may be questioned. I do not find his name in any of the Smyth papers. Pedder [Pidder], Martin, and their followers are looked upon as quite distinct from the three Smyth groups.

[1] MS. B. 1347 in the Mennonite Archives, Amsterdam.

[2] Nevill later renounced his Anabaptism.

followers, and a Confession of Faith in nineteen articles, in which they speak of themselves as the "true Christian English church".

Evidently some of the Waterlanders, who were favourably disposed to the English, suggested that if a union were to take place, they must first accept the Confession of Lubbert Gerrits and Hans de Ries. Accordingly an English translation of it in thirty-eight articles[1], entitled, "A short confession of fayth", was drawn up and signed by forty-three English persons. Two of the names at the bottom of the first column are practically illegible, and so many mistakes of one kind and another have been made concerning various names in the list, that it may now be given in full. Fourteen of the names (as indicated in the volume of documents) including those of John Smyth and Hugh [and Anne] Bromhead have been crossed out, which probably means that before the English were finally admitted to membership by the Waterlanders in 1615, those whose names are crossed out had either died, returned to England, or again changed their beliefs. The following is the list[2]:—

Iohn Smyth.	Garuase Neuile./
Hugo [?] Bromhead	Elizabeth Tomson
his wife x Iohn Grindall	Mother Pigott.
Thomas Cannadine [?][3]	Mary Smyth
Samuel Halton	Iane southworth
Thomas Pigott	Margarett Stavely.
Iohn Hardie	Isabell [?] Thomson.
Edward hankin [?]	Iane Organ.
Thomas Iesopp[4]	Mary Dickens.
Robert Staveley	Betteris Dickens.

[1] Arts. 19 and 22 (Dutch) were omitted (McGlothlin's "Baptist Confessions", London, p. 54).

[2] MS. B. 1352 in the Mennonite Archives, Amsterdam.

[3] Thomas Canadyne had been a member of Greenwood's congregation in 1590, and evidently migrated to Amsterdam with the other church members about 1593.

[4] Thomas Jessop is mentioned as a Brownist in the Records of the Ecclesiastical Court of York under the date, July 26, 1607 [?] (see Dr John Waddington's "Congregational History", 1567–1700, London, 1874, p. 163).

Allexander fleeminge [?]

Iohn Arnfeld

Fraunces Pigott

Thomas Dolphin

Salomon Thomson.

Alexander Hodgkin

Vrsulay Bywater

dorethie Oakland

Iohn ......

....

Dorottie Hamand.

Ellin [?] Paynter

Anne Broomhead

, Ales Parsons.

Ioane Houghton.

Ioane Brigges

Ales Pigott.

Margarett Pigott

Ales Arnefield.

Elizabeth White

Dorethie Tomson

Margaret Maurice

But while some of the Waterlanders were evidently in favour of a union with the English Anabaptists under the leadership of John Smyth, others were not, as may be seen in several letters sent in April, May, and July, 1610, in which any haste in the proceedings is discouraged, and it is suggested that the Mennonites in other parts of Holland, as well as in Amsterdam, and even in "Prussia" and "Germany", should be consulted concerning such an important matter, so that there might be complete peace and unity among them. Accordingly, for the purpose of giving as much information as possible to the congregations outside of Amsterdam, a Dutch translation of the "Epistle to the Reader" of Smyth's "Character of the Beast" appears to have been made. This is still preserved in the Mennonite Archives.

What happened to Smyth's followers after they had been deserted by Helwys and Murton, and after their application to the Waterlanders had been passed over, is not quite clear. It is probable that they kept together and held meetings of their own, but it is also apparent that they attended the services of the Waterlanders, as may be seen in the following passage from Helwys' "An Advertisement or Admonition", 1611[1]:—

when he [John Smyth] had himself but a little vnderstanding of your [the Dutch] language, and the rest of his confedracie, when

[1] P. 37.

some of them had not anie vnderstanding to be spoken of, and divers none at all, neither yet [in 1611] have : have, and do come to worshipp with you, being Barbarians vnto you and say Amen (els what do they there) not knowing whether you blesse or curse.

Thus the years 1610 and 1611 passed. Smyth produced no more controversial works, but during this period Helwys seems to have been constantly engaged in writing, for in 1611 and 1612 no less than four books were published by him, including a Confession of Faith of his congregation, to which we shall refer later. To this Confession of Faith Smyth's company apparently prepared as an answer a corresponding Confession, finally composed of one hundred articles. Probably this was originally drafted in English, but a Dutch copy must have been quickly drawn up for the satisfaction of the Waterlanders. At any rate, in the Mennonite Archives there are two slightly varying Dutch copies of this Confession. One of them consists of 101, and the other of 102, articles, but, with one exception, they apparently contain almost exactly the same text. The former is in quarto format, is evidently the earlier copy, and is not so nicely written. The second is in folio and beautifully executed. As later published in English, the Confession is probably in its best and final form in so far as the text is concerned, though some of the Scripture references may contain typographical errors. Of course the Dutch copies were not published, but were intended only for private examination and therefore have no "Epistle to the reader", as does the published English text. In general the second Dutch copy and the English agree, except for slight additions or alterations in the wording, and some changes in the numbering and arrangement of the articles[1].

[1] Most of these differences may be mentioned here. The order of articles 25 and 26 of the English edition is transposed in the Dutch; article 28 of the English forms article 30 in the Dutch; article 28 in the Dutch becomes article 31 in the English; article 30 in the English does not appear in the Dutch; the text of article 31 in the English after "Rom. 13" is evidently not in the Dutch; art. 32 in the English is art. 33 in the Dutch; art. 33 in the English is art. 31 in the Dutch; art. 34 in the English is art. 32 in the Dutch; art. 35 in the English is art. 34 in

Smyth had long been of consumptive tendency, and in the summer of 1612 he grew rapidly weaker and died at the end of August in that year. He was buried in the Niewe Kerk on Sept. 1. Not long after his death there was published by T.[homas ?] P.[ygott ?] a little volume consisting of three parts, including the previously mentioned Confession of Faith of one hundred articles prefaced by a short Epistle. The title-page of the only existing copy of this work, which is in York Minster Library, is wanting, but fortunately the whole of the text has been preserved. The first section is called " Propositions and conclusions, concerning true Christian religion, conteyning a confession of faith of certaine English people, liuinge at Amsterdam ". Then come " The last booke of Iohn Smith, Called the retractation of his errours, and the confirmation of the truth", and a short account by Pygott of " The Life and Death of Iohn Smith ". Smyth manifests a truly beautiful spirit in these last two sections, and a perusal of them probably made Bishop Creighton, while Regius Professor of Modern History at Cambridge, pay Smyth the unexpected tribute, that " None of the

the Dutch; art. 36 in the English is art. 35 in the Dutch with a few changes; articles 44 and 45 in the Dutch become art. 45 in the English; the Dutch text has an article 52 which apparently is not in the English, and which reads as follows :—

" 52.

" Dat Iesus Christŭs aldŭs is geworden een Middelaerdes [*sic*] des [*sic*] nieŭwen Testaments te weeten koninck prister ende propheet oŭer sijn gemeente ende dat de wedergeboornen aldŭs door hem geestelijcke koningen ende propheeten geworden sijn· apo. 1. 6. 1 Ioh. 2. 20 apo. 19. 20."

Then for some articles the numbering of the Dutch is one ahead of the English. Again the Dutch articles 59 and 60 become art. 58 in the English, and art. 59 in the English is art. 61 in the Dutch. Art. 64 (English)=art. 67 (Dutch); art. 65 (Eng.)=art. 66 (Dutch) except for a few words added at the end of the Dutch text; art. 66 (Eng.)=art. 68 (Dutch), and from here the numbering of the English articles is two behind that of the Dutch. The English article 79 has two or three more Scripture references at the end than the corresponding Dutch article; the Dutch article corresponding to the English article numbered 81 adds a few words; and finally the Dutch article 98 (Eng. 96) adds at the end the words: " maer of het nŭter tijt den gemeente geopenbaert is of niet daer en derven [durven] wy niet seeckers van seggen."

English Separatists had a finer mind or a more beautiful soul than John Smith"[1].

It must not be supposed, however, because this last work of Smyth's is called "the retractation of his errours", that he deserted his little, loyal company at the end. His retractation, on the contrary, was of a somewhat different order, and consisted rather in his giving up his censorious habits in controversy, and in no longer answering the works written against him, both because he knew they would only breed further strife, and also because he had no further means with which to publish his writings.

In fact, his whole attitude toward the world had been modified by hard experience. He now saw that it was a waste of time to be fighting about "the outward church and Ceremonies", and that such differences should "not cause me [him] to refuse the brotherhood of anie penitent and faithfull Christian whatsoever", a remarkably enlightened statement for his day. In this respect then he had changed greatly. He had not returned to the Church of England, or deserted his own little company, but he had begun to see that in all churches, and irrespective of church, there are good men, and that further separation, and the striving after greater perfection of church organization were not the chief points to be emphasized. T.[homas] P.[ygott] reports that Smyth on his death-bed said: "if I liue... I will walke with no other people / but you / all my daies: he desired his wyfe also so to doe / being perswaded that shee would: and wished that his children should remayne with us", —final messages, eloquent of the faith to which he still firmly clung.

Though the attempt of Smyth's congregation to join the Waterlanders in 1610 was frustrated, the hope that such a union would take place had not been given up by "Lubbert gerretsz", and on Jan. 17, 1612 (New Style), or Jan. 7, 1611 (Old Style), as he lay in bed very ill he summoned all the Waterland ministers, including "hans de Rijs / Ian münter [who owned the Cake-House] / nittert obbesz / cornelis albertsz / Claes claesz /...

---

[1] "Historical Lectures and Addresses", second impression, London, New York, and Bombay, 1904, p. 56.

genraecht [?] Koefoot", and in their presence among other matters expressed his earnest wish that they might receive the English applicants for membership as speedily as possible, in spite of the fact that he did not consider the se-baptism of Smyth or the baptism of his followers all that was to be desired.

However, no union was accomplished until some years later, and in fact the English do not appear to have renewed their application until Nov. 16, 1614[1]. Finally, on the following Jan. 20, 1615, after some further discussion they were admitted to membership and those who had not been baptized or re-baptized, were baptized by Hans de Ries. Such persons as Swithune Grindall, Thomas Odell[2], Richard Overton, and John Drew[3], were apparently received as members on, or soon after, Jan. 20, 1615. In 1620 one Thomas —— (evidently Thomas Pygott) was the preacher of the English congregation, and after June 8 of that year he was permitted to administer baptism and the Lord's Supper,—a fact, which shows that a relatively separate existence was allowed the English members. This state of affairs lasted until 1640 or 1650, when either so complete a union had been effected, or perhaps more probably, so many of the English had returned to their native land, that the further existence of any of them in Holland is very difficult, if not impossible, to trace.

[1] For this and other following particulars see Dr B. Evans' "Early English Baptists", 1862, Vol. I., pp. 220–24.

[2] Thomas Odell, or Odal, had once been a member of Francis Johnson's congregation, and then probably was first attracted by Anabaptist views. See George Johnson's "A discourse", Amsterdam, 1603, p. 194.

[3] "John Drewe" is mentioned as a Brownist in the Records of the Ecclesiastical Court of York under the date, July 26, 1607 [?] (See Dr John Waddington's "Congregational History, 1567–1700", London, 1874, p. 163).

CHAPTER X

THE CONGREGATION OF ENGLISH ANABAPTISTS UNDER
THE LEADERSHIP OF THOMAS HELWYS AND JOHN
MURTON

So far as is known, the first English Anabaptist congregation
to be settled in England was that led by Thomas Helwys and
John Murton, the members of which, after withdrawing from
Smyth and his adherents in 1609/10, remained about two years
in Amsterdam and then removed to London. It appears from
the several writings of Helwys, that he blamed the Mennonites
for what he terms Smyth's change of attitude towards the question of the necessity of observing a succession in the ministry.
Evidently most of the separatists sympathized with Smyth
rather than with Helwys, who then seems to have been the
leading thinker of his party. Of the four works written by
Helwys in 1611 and 1612 it is a little difficult to determine
exactly the order of publication, but at present the following
arrangement seems possible :—

(1) "*A DECLARATION [OF]* | FAITH OF ENGLIS[H] |
PEOPLE REMAINING AT AM-|STERDAM IN HOL-
LAND. | Heb. 11. 6. | Without Faith it is impossible to please |
GOD. Heb. 11. | Rom. 14. 23. Whatsoever is not off Faith is
sin. | [Device] | *Prynted*. 1611." This little book, like all of
Helwys' published writings, is an octavo. It consists of 24
unnumbered leaves and was probably printed in Amsterdam.

(2) "A SHORT AND PLAINE | proofe by the Word /
and workes | off God / that Gods decree is not the | cause off
anye Mans sinne or | Condemnation. | AND | That all Men
are redeemed | by Christ. | *As also.* | That no Infants are |
condemned. | Collos. 2. 8. | Beware lest there be anie man that
spoyle | you through Philosophie / and vaine | deceipt. | Psal.
119, 113. | I hate vaine inventions : but thy Law doe | I love. |

[Device.] | Printed *1611*." This consists of only 28 unnumbered pages. The Epistle "To the ladie Bovves" is dated "Iune 2. 1611."

(3) " AN AD⸗|vertisement or admonition, | unto the Congregation, vvhich | men call the New Fryelers [Freewillers], in the lowe | Countries. wrirten in Dutche. | Aud [And] Publiched in Englis. | VVherein is handled 4. Principall pointes | of Religion. | 1. That Christ tooke his Flesh of Marie, | haveing a true earthly, naturall bodie, | 2. That a Sabbath or day of rest, is to be | kept holy everie First day of the weeke. | 3. That ther is no Succession, nor privile-|ge to persons in the holie thinges. | 4. That Magistracie, being an holy ordi-|nancë of God, debarreth not anie from being | of the Church of Christ. | After these followes certen demandes | concerning Gods decree of salva-|tion and condemnation. | Pro. 9. 8. | Rebuke the wyse, and they will love thee. | Pro. 29. 1. | They that harden their neck, vvhen they | are rebuked shall suddenly be destroyed, and cannot | be cured | Printed 1611." This contains 96 pages, and was published especially for the instruction of the Waterlanders.

(4) "A SHORT | DECLARATION | of the mistery of iniquity. | Ier. 51. 6. | Flee out of the midst of Babell, and deliver | every man his soule, be not destroyed in hir | iniquity, for this is the time of the | lords vengeance, he vvill render | vnto hir a recompense. | Hosea 10. 12. | Sovv to your selves in right eousnes, reape | after the measure of mercie, breake vp your | fallovv ground, for it is time to seeke | the lord, till he come & raine | righteousnes vpon you. | [Device] | Anno 1612." This consists of viii + 212 pages. An autograph note by Helwys to the king, on the recto of the leaf preceding the title-page of the Bodleian copy, shows that when this last work was published in 1612, he was living in England at "Spittlefeild neare London". Spitalfields may, therefore, have been the first location in London of Helwys' church. The general tone of the note indicates that the author and his congregation were already having trouble with the authorities. When the first three of these books were written Helwys appears to have been in Holland.

From the four works we find that the following opinions were prevalent in Helwys' congregation :—

(1)   Baptism, not a church covenant, is the true "form" of a church.

(2)   Every separate congregation of people, whether it has officers or not, may "come together to Pray, Prophecie, breake bread, and administer in all the holy ordinances".

(3)   "a Church ought not to consist off such a multitude as cannot have perticuler knowledg oue [one] off another."

(4)   "the Officers off everie Church or congregacion are either Elders, who by their office do especially feed the flock concerning their soules,...or Deacons Men, and Wemen who by their office releave the necessities off the poore and impotent brethren concerning their bodies".

(5)   These officers "are to be chosen when there are persons qualified according to the rules in Christ Testament,...By Election and approbacion off that Church or congregacion whereoff they are members,...with Fasting, Prayer, and Laying on off hands,...And there being but one rule for Elders, therefore but one sort off Elders." This congregation also maintained that church officers may hold office only in the church in which they have been ordained to their respective offices. John Smyth held that "an Elder off one [true] Church is an Elder off all [true] Churches in the World".

(6)   Magistrates are to be highly honored as a means of taking vengeance "on them that do evill", and may even be members "off CHRISTS church", and retain their office. Smyth opposed this view.

(7)   An Anabaptist (of the Helwys type) may take an oath "for the deciding off strife".

Helwys would also make believers' baptism [by sprinkling or pouring] an absolute necessity for salvation, teaching that the contrary doctrine of infant baptism is sufficient reason for eternal punishment, so "that iff you had no other sin amongst you al, but this, you perish everie man off you from the highest to the lowest. iff you repent not",—which is probably as strong a statement of this doctrine as has ever been made.

Helwys, like Smyth, was an Arminian, or General, Anabaptist, who believed in universal redemption, i.e., that Christ died to save all men and not only certain elect persons, but in

his third publication he seeks to show that though he holds
this doctrine, he does not uphold "that most damnable heresie"
of Free-will, which was usually supposed to be the natural
concomitant of the former doctrine.

In his fourth work, Helwys appeals to King James I against
the Hierarchy of the Reformation, which he interprets to be the
second Beast in the Book of Revelation, and asks that his congregation may have freedom to worship by themselves without
disturbance from Archbishops, Bishops, and other high officials in
the Established Church. He certainly exaggerates the number
of separatists (he cannot mean Anabaptists) when he speaks of
" vs (that are thousands of the K. of great Brittans subiects)".
In this long, rambling work, Helwys attacks his opponents in
scathing terms. He speaks " of the Lord Bs. [Bishops] that are
not able to direct themselves from the waies of death, but are
perished every man, that ever bare that Office with those names
and power, if they repented not thereof, although they had no
other sinne: and they also that do now beare that Office with
those titles & power shall likewise all perish to everlasting
destruction, if they do not repent thereof, and cast it away:..."[1]

He also manifests considerable hostility toward that " much
applauded profession of Puritanisme. The which profession to
prove it is a false profession, yea and such a false profession, as
wee know not the like vpon the earth, wee shall not need to
produce anie testimony but your owne:..."[2]

Wee wil not follow you [Puritan preachers] in these perticulers,
except further occation be offered. But remember how you compare
your fellow Preists to *Circumcellions* or Fryers, goeing vp and downe
with the bishops bulls like beggers, to see where they can get enter-
tainment and see not al this while your selves, yea some of your
cheife spirits for working lying wonders, stand in the market place
to be hired from the East to the west, and to be transported from
North to South, wheresoever [wheresoever] you can get a good
Towne pulpit, or a privileged Chappel a great Chamber or dyning
parlor to administer in, how prophane soever the Towne or hous-
hold be, you wil not let to make them all partakers of the holy
thinges at first, before you knowe your shepe, or your shepe knowe
you, contrary to Christs owne words. Ioh. 10. 14...[3]

---

[1] "A Short Declaration of the mistery of iniquity", 1612, p. 73.
[2] *Ibid.*, p. 86.   [3] *Ibid.*, p. 98.

The Brownists or Barrowists receive little praise :—

You [Brownists] confessing your selves to be of the world before
you ioined your selves together in your voluntarie profession, by
a Covenant of your owne devisings (you being of the world) your
Condition was the same :...[1]

they [the Brownists' prophets] are false Prophets because they are
Elected and ordeined to their Office, by a congregation of infidels or
vnbelevers that are not ioyned to Christ, and have not put on
Christ by baptisme,...[2]

In closing Helwys states his belief that Christians should
not flee into foreign lands to avoid persecution. As he seems
already to have returned to England when this work was published, he must have been aware of the risk he ran in so openly
making his views known to the world. Indeed, he thereby
exhibited bravery as well as rashness, and as might have been
expected he became a martyr for his opinions.

In the Library of the House of Lords is a small piece of
paper, on one side of which is preserved "A most humble supplication of divers poore prisoners and many others the kinges
maiesties loyall subiectes ready to testifie it by the oath of
allegeance in all sinceritie, whose Greviances are lamentable,
onely for cause of conscience."[3] The supplication is neatly
written and addressed "To the right Honorable assemblie of
the Commons-house of Parliament", and is signed, "By his
maiesties faithful subiectes most falsly called Anabaptistes."
The handwriting may be that of Thomas Helwys. The petition states that the suppliants are willing to take the Oath
of Allegiance, but the Bishops will not let them. Bitterly
they complain: "kept have wee bene by them many yeres
in lingering imprisonements, devided from wives, children,
servantes & callinges, not for any other cause but onely for
conscience towardes God, to the vtter vndoeing of vs, our
wives & children." Then they supplicate that they may be
freed upon taking the Oath of Allegiance. The words "reiected

---

[1] "A Short Declaration of the misery of iniquity", p. 125.

[2] *Ibid.*, p. 126.

[3] See the Third Report of the Historical Manuscripts Commission,
p. 14. The paper is there dated "[1613]", but as Parliament only met on
April 5, 1614, its real date is clearly 1614.

by the comitee" are written in a scrawly hand at the close of the petition.

Now it is well known that Helwys' congregation returned to England some time in 1611 or 1612, so that when the supplication was written, the suppliants could not have been imprisoned much more than two or three years. No doubt even this period seemed to them like "many yeres". The date 1614 agrees well with the fact that John Murton, or Morton[1], was in prison in London in 1613[2], and we may reasonably surmise that if Helwys was not already dead, he also was a prisoner at the same time. However this may be, Helwys was certainly not living in 1616, for in that year Geoffrey Helwys, who was probably Thomas Helwys' brother, speaks in his will of Thomas Helwys as no longer being alive ("Dictionary of National Biography").

This early dating of Helwys' death is, of course, quite contrary to the account given by Thomas Crosby, who thought that he was living "in all probability" on May 10, 1622, and wrote on that date a letter signed "H. H."[3] To be sure, it might strike the reader as strange that one whose initials were "T. H." should sign them as "H. H.", but the case appears still more interesting when all the facts concerning this letter are known. In the first place, a copy of it is given in Benjamin Stinton's "A Repository of Divers Historical Matters relating to the English Antipedobaptists...1712", a transcript of which is now incorporated ("Numb: 7:") in the Gould Manuscript at Regent's Park College, London, and the letter is referred to in another of Stinton's anonymous manuscripts in the Gould Collection entitled, "An Account of Some | of the | Most Eminent & Leading Men | among the | English Antipædobaptists. | ...", which was first identified as Stinton's by the author about eight years ago. In this latter MS. on fol. 11. Stinton gives part of the account of Helwys which Crosby later published,

---

[1] Murton = Morton just as Crumwell = Cromwell.

[2] See the title-page and page 1 of John Wilkinson's "The Sealed Fovntaine" [1646].

[3] See "The History of the English Baptists", Vol. I., pp. 275–76 and 133–39.

but some one, possibly Crosby, has questioned Stinton's referring the letter of May 10, 1622, to Thomas Helwys, and has made a note on the verso of fol. 10 to the following effect:—

†No [Number]—for your No 7 has the Signature of H. H. whereas you call this person *Tho'* then it should haue been T. H. Q. was not H. H. Henry Haggar?

It is, of course, perfectly manifest that "H. H." cannot have been intended for "T. H." except through a very unlikely error, and at that early date it is equally improbable, if not impossible, that Henry Haggar could have been the person to whom allusion is made. Who then is this "H. H."? On turning to "I. P."'s[1] "*Anabaptismes* | MYSTERIE | OF INIQUITY | VNMASKED. | …", 1623, in which the letter in question was originally published[2], the whole difficulty was quickly solved, for the initials there signed, though not so clear-cut as usual, were certainly not "H. H." but "H. N." In order to be perfectly sure that this was the correct reading, the writer consulted Mr Robert Procter, then one of the most expert critics on the staff of the British Museum. He at once agreed that this new reading was the right one. Thus was the main difficulty quickly removed. But who then was "H. N."? None other, without doubt, than Henry Niclaes, father of the Family of Love or Familists, of whom some account has already been given, and who in those days were popularly, but incorrectly, thought to be a branch of the Anabaptists. Thus the only argument that has ever been advanced to prove that Helwys lived after 1616 may be readily dismissed.

By 1615, and possibly even as early as 1613, John Murton had become the leader of the Anabaptists in England. He is accredited about that time with being "a Teacher of a Church of the *Anabaptists* in Newgate"[3]. Of Murton's early life at present almost nothing is known. John Fenwicke, "Lievtenant

---

[1] I would suggest that the initials "I.P." may more probably be those of Iohn Paget, than those of Iohn Preston, as suggested by Dr Dexter.

[2] Pp. 1–11.

[3] I.[ohn] G.[raunt]'s "Truths Victory against Heresie", London, 1645, p. 19.

B.   17

Collonel" in the "Epistle Dedicatory" of his work entitled,
"CHRIST | Ruling in midst of his | ENEMIES; | ...", London,
1643, speaks of one Murton, who was among the "godly
[Puritan] ministers", who had been "expulsed" from "Newcastle
upon *Tyne*". This, however, cannot have been our John
Murton, who is known to have been a furrier of Gainsborough,
and who was twenty-five years old on August 23, 1608, when
at Amsterdam he married Jane Hodgkin of Worksop, then
twenty-three years old[1].

In 1615 Murton and his followers published a book entitled
"OBIECTIONS: | Answered by way of Dialo-|gue, wherein
is proved | By the Law of God: | By the law of our Land: |
And by his Maties many testimonies | That no man ought to be
persecuted | for his religion, so he testifie his alle-|geance by
the Oath, appointed by Law. | ..." Of this original edition
only two copies, both in the Bodleian Library, appear to have
been preserved in England[2], but the work was reprinted in 1662
under the considerably altered title, " Persecution for Religion |
JUDG'D and CONDEMN'D: | ..."[3] It seems probable that
when the work was written Murton was still in prison. In this
dialogue the author treats of some other matters besides persecution. For instance, the question is brought up as to who may
be considered a true administrator of baptism at a time when
the rule of Antichrist had so long prevailed in the Church[4]:—

C.[hristian] For answere to this : there are three waies professed
in the world, one by the Papists, and their several successors, professing succession from the Pope and his ministers : another by the
Familists and scattered flock. that none may intermeddle therewith
lawfully. til their extraordinary men come: another, wee and others
affirme that any disciple of Christ in what part off the world soever
commeing to the Lords way, he by the Word and Spirit of GOD
preaching that way vnto others, and converting / he may and ought
also to baptize them:...

---

[1] See the "Transactions" of the Congregational Historical Society,
Vol. II., No. 3, for September, 1905, p. 164.

[2] Another copy of this first edition is said to be in the Library of
Union Theological Seminary, New York.

[3] A modernized text of this pamphlet was published in the Hanserd
Knollys Society's edition of "Tracts on Liberty of Conscience", London,
1846, pp. 83–180. [4] Pp. 64–5.

The matter of fleeing from one's native country on account of persecution is handled in the following manner[1]:—

I.[ndifferent] I hope I shall testify to all / my spedie walking in the steps of these holie men / but one thing / there is yet which hath much hindred the growth of godlines in this kingdom / and that is that many so soone as they see or feare trouble will ensue / they flie into another Nation who cannot see their conversation / and thereby deprive many poore ignorant soules in their own Nation / of their information / and of their conversation amongst them.
C.[hristian] Oh / that hath bene the overthrowe of Religion in this land / the best able and greater part being gone / and leaving behind them some fewe / who by the others departure have had their afflictions and contempt increased which hath bene the cause of many falling back / and of the adversaries exalting / but they wil tell vs / we are not to judge things / by the effects / therefore we must prove that their flight [is] unlawfull / or we say nothing.

So far as can now be learned the original publication of this work made little impression on the English people. In fact, at that time the English Anabaptists were probably looked upon as of no importance, but when John Terry published at Oxford in 1617, "*THE* | REASO[NA-?]|BLENESSE OF WISE [AND?] | holy truth: and the absurditie | *of foolish and wicked* | *Errour.* | ...", he devoted considerable space to the general subject of the Anabaptists.

Another work entitled "Truth's Champion" is said to have been published by John Murton in 1617[2], and to have been twice republished by the General Anabaptists after the Civil Wars. It seems, however, that very little is now known about this book, and that no copy of the second or third editions is at present accessible. It has even proved impossible to ascertain the years in which these two later editions were published, but happily there are a few references to the third edition in the publisher's lists. From one of these we learn that this last edition was brought out by Francis Smith "at the Sign of the Elephant and Castle in *Cornhill*, near the *Royal-Exchange*", London, in or before 1678. The title and description of the

---

[1] P. 76.

[2] See Robert Barclay's "The Inner Life of the Religious Societies of the Commonwealth", Third Edition, London, 1879, p. 412 and note.

book as given in his list at the back of Thomas Grantham's "Christianismus Primitivus", 1678, is as follows:—

"*Truth's Champion*[1]*:* Wherein are made plain these Particulars, That Christ died for all Men. Of *Predestination,* of *Election, Free-will, Falling-away.* Of *Baptism,* of *Original-Sin.* The Copy of this Book was found hid in an Old Wall near *Colchester* in *Essex.* The third Edition."

In 1620 the English Anabaptists published a small octavo entitled, "A | DISCRIPTION | OF WHAT *GOD* | hath *Predestinated* | Concerning | MAN." Of this book at least several copies are to be found. It was apparently written by one person and is therefore with good reason ascribed to John Murton. This was, I think, the first edition of "Truth's Champion", and I do not now believe that Murton published any work in 1617. At a later period, the name "Truth's Champion" might very well have been given to "A Discription" as a suitable title. It will be noticed that "The Contents of the Booke" on the verso of the title-page of "A Discription" singularly resemble the above account of the contents of "Truth's Champion", being "1. *Of* Predestination. 2. *Of* Election, *and* Reprobation. 3. *Of* Falling away. 4. *Of* Free-will. 5. *Of* the Originall estate of Man. 6. *Of* The beginnings of CHRIST, or Foundation. 7. *And lastly,* An answ. to a little Printed writing of *Iohn Robinsons,* touching *Baptisme.*" Still more like the contents of "Truth's Champion" is the account of the contents of "A Discription" given on Sig. A₂ verso in the Epistle to the Reader, where it will be observed that the contents of the two books are identical, with the exception of two inversions in the order, being "1. Touching *Predestination,* 2. Of *Election,* 3. Of *Falling away,* 4. Of *Free-will,* 5. Of *Originall sinne,* and lastly, Of the entrance into *Christ* [i.e., Baptism]".

There is, I think, only one strong objection against Murton's "A Discription", 1620, being the first edition of "Truth's Champion", and even that is not quite insurmountable. Robert

---

[1] John Murton's work, which was twice republished under the title "Truth's Champion", may be in some way related to Richard Stookes' at present equally unknown book entitled, "Truths Champion, *or* Truths Companion", published in 1650 or earlier.

Barclay tells us that he saw a copy of the third edition of " Truth's Champion " about forty years ago, and on page 412 of " The Inner Life ", Third Edition, London, 1879, he gives from it a citation concerning the Seekers which does not occur in " A Discription ". This fact would make the view here advanced utterly impossible, were it not for the probability that the word Seekers was not used as early as 1620. My theory, therefore, is that this paragraph quoted by Barclay was added by the later editor of Murton's work to counteract the influence of a party that since 1640 had come to be known by that name and to have much more influence than it had before 1620. Barclay also says[1] that the initials J. M. appear on the title-page of " Truth's Champion ". These, of course, are not found in " A Discription ", but they may originally have been only written in ink on the title-page of the copy of the first edition " found hid in an Old Wall near *Colchester* near *Essex* ", where John Wilkinson, one of Murton's strongest opponents, lived.

The truth or falsity of this theory will be quickly manifested when a copy of the third edition of Murton's " Truth's Champion " is discovered[2], but it should be said in defence of the theory, that if Murton's " A Discription " does not prove to be the first edition of his " Truth's Champion ", the two works must be remarkably similar. In fact, it is almost impossible to conceive how one man could write two distinct works within three years of each other on exactly the same subjects.

In " A Discription " Murton gives the following opinion of the way in which a church should be organized[3]. In this it will be noticed he does not even mention a covenant, a fact which probably indicates that, if the earliest Anabaptist congregations in England employed some simple covenant formula, they must have laid very little emphasis upon it. With them baptism had evidently taken the place of the church covenant :—

[1] " The Inner Life of the Religious Societies of the Commonwealth ", Third Edition, London, 1879, p. 411.

[2] As this sheet goes to press, it looks as though the author may yet see a copy of " Truth's Champion ", in which case the reader shall know of any further results in a brief Appendix at the end of the volume.

[3] Pp. 154–56.

But first I will lay down a maine foundation, which being sufficiently proued, the euident truth shall plainly appear : and this it is; That the members and Churches of *Christ*, are so made : both by *Faith* and *Baptisme*, and not by the one only, which being true ; it will follow, that neither the Church & members of *Rome*, are members and Church of *Christ*, because *Faith* is neither required nor performed thereto ; nor yet any profession of people, that seperate from *Rome* as from no Church of *Christ*, retayning *Romes* Baptisme, and building new Churches without Baptisme.

That the members and Churches of *Christ.* are so made by Faith and Baptisme, euen by both, it is proued in *Rom.* 11. 20. &c....so that to be gathered into the name of CHRIST, by being made Disciples and baptised, is, to be made members of his body (which is his Church) of his Flesh, and of his bone :...*Thus* Christ made Disciples, wee must be the sonnes of God by Faith, and put on *Christ* by Baptisme...and wee are made partakers of *Christ*, by hauing the beginnings, which beginnings are *Repentance, Faith,* and *Baptisme,* other beginnings, or foundation can no man lay.

This work also makes it clear that these early General Baptists maintained that any private church-member might preach, make converts, and administer baptism[1]:—

I say it is a meere fixion, there is not the least shew in all the Testament of *Iesus Christ,* that Baptising is peculiar onely to Pastors, which might satisfie any man of reason ; neither can it bee proued that euer ordinary Pastor did Baptise. And it is most plaine, conuerting and Baptising is no part of the Pastors office : his office is, to feed, to watch, to ouersee, the flocke of *Christ* already the Church : his charge is to take heede to the flocke, and to feed the Church, and to defend them in the truth against all gainsayers : furthes [further] then which, no charge is laid vpon him by vertue of his office : That hee may Preach, conuert and Baptise, I deny : not, as another disciple may ; but not that either it is required, or he doth performe it by vertue of his office ; no proofe for that imagination can be shewed : and therfore it remaineth firme & stable ; euery Disciple that hath abilitie is authorized, yea commanded to Preach, conuert & Baptise, aswell and asmuch (if not more) then a Pastor.

It is interesting to note that the Anabaptists themselves printed and bound "A Discription"[2]. They must, therefore, have had a press of their own which they probably brought with them from Holland.

[1] P. 163.

[2] P. 176. "if any defects bee either in Printing or binding, (both which vnto vs are difficult) wee pray the one may bee passed ouer; and th' other may be amended..."

From the time of Thomas Crosby, and still earlier, it has been repeatedly asserted that another book defending Baptist views was published in 1618.   Even Dr Dexter accepted this statement as a fact, but unfortunately like most traditions it needs some correction.   Here is what Crosby says:—

In the year 1618. there came forth a book, vindicating the principles of the *Baptists* [Note: "*A plain and well-grounded treatise concerning baptism.*"].   This was translated from the *Dutch*, and is thought to be the first that was published in *English* against the baptizing of infants[1].

Of course we are all well aware to-day that other earlier works in English had been published on this subject, but Crosby is also apparently mistaken in the date of the pamphlet, and has not given the title quite correctly.   Indeed, it is now evident that he never saw this work, but for his information concerning it relied entirely on the statements of William Wall[2], and Thomas Cobbet[3].   As a matter of fact, except for the words, "Printed in the yeare of our Lord and Saviour *JESUS CHRIST*", the pamphlet is undated, and though Crosby expresses surprise that it was not answered until 1648, we on the contrary find that circumstance most natural, for it was evidently printed in that year (Old Style), when with the trial,

[1] "The History of the English Baptists", Vol. I., London, 1738, p. 128.

[2] "The History of Infant Baptism", Second Edition, London, 1707, p. 426.   Crosby evidently took the date and title of this pamphlet from Wall's account.   Wall says:—
"the first [book] that ever I heard of, that was set forth in *English*, upholding this Tenet [of Antipædobaptism], was a *Dutch* Book, called, *A plain and well grounded Treatise concerning Baptism*.   This was translated and printed in *English Anno* 1618. the 16th Year of King *James* the First".   Evidently, therefore, Wall himself had not seen this work.

[3] Thomas Cobbet of "*Lyn* in Nevv-England" answered this pamphlet in 1648 in his work entitled, "A just Vindication of the Covenant and Church-Estate of Children of Church-Members:...Hereunto is annexed a Refutation of a certain Pamphlet, styled, *The plain and wel-grounded Treatise touching Baptism*", London, 4°.   The fact that this "Refutation" is annexed indicates that "A just Vindication" had probably been completed when Cobbet first saw "The plain and wel-grounded Treatise", a fact which favours our belief that "A very plain and well grounded Treatise" itself was published in 1648, just before the publication of Cobbet's work.   Crosby was indebted to Cobbet for whatever else he says about this pamphlet.

condemnation and death of Charles I the reign of Christ on earth was fondly believed by some of the pious to be beginning.

In fact, the general appearance of this work is not such as to warrant us in believing that it was printed before 1640. It was evidently published after the licensing of the press became less rigorous, when pamphlets began to be printed in a somewhat different style from that which was customary in 1618. Of course, so far as appearance is concerned this work might have been printed in 1645 as well as in 1648. Indeed, the former date is suggested as a possible time of publication on one of the copies which the author has seen, but 1648 (Old Style) appears to be an even more probable date.

Though this pamphlet, therefore, does not properly belong within our period, yet because copies of it are so scarce, and because these mistakes concerning it have been made, its correct title may be given here. This reads as follows:—

"A very plain and well | grounded | TREATISE | CONCERNING | BAPTISME. | *Wherein it is very cleerly shown, and out of* | *good grounds demonstrated that* Baptisme *was instituted and* | *ordained by the Lord Christ, for those that believe and repent,* | *and was so taught and used by his Apostles, and observed and* | *followed by the Primitive Church.* | As also how that in processe of time the Baptisme | of Children in stead of true Baptisme was brought in | and received, and by divers Councels, Popes, and | Emperours commanded to be observed. | Marke 16. 26. | *He that shall believe and be Baptised shall be saved,* | *But he that will not believe shall be damned.* | Printed in the yeare of our Lord and Saviour | *JESUS CHRIST.*" [i.e., ? 1648 (Old Style)], 4°, pp. 39.

In 1620, it is also said, that the English Anabaptists published "An Humble Supplication" to King James I[1]. This may be true, but in modern times no copy of a printed edition of that year has been seen, and the edition published in 1662 does not give us any solid ground for believing that the Supplication was ever printed before that date. The edition of

[1] See "Tracts on Liberty of Conscience and Persecution. 1614–1661", Hanserd Knollys Society, London, 1846, pp. 181–231, where the edition of 1662 is reprinted in modernized text.

1662 merely says that it had been "presented, 1620", probably meaning in manuscript. Of course, this theory may not prove to be correct, but it is suggested because we now know that Crosby was not well acquainted with the source literature of his subject, and in fact probably never saw many of the works mentioned in his "History". The following statement in this Supplication seems to indicate that other Anabaptist congregations than that at London may have existed before 1620, but possibly the reference is to separatists in general:—

Our miseries are long and lingering Imprisonments for many years in divers Counties of England, *in which many have dyed and left behind them Widows and many small Children*[1].

On May 10, 1622, a letter, to which reference has previously been made, was written by an Anabaptist in London to some friends of his in the Church of England seeking to persuade them to become Anabaptists. The letter was intercepted and came into the hands of one "I. P." [Iohn Paget?], who had it published in 1623 in a volume already mentioned entitled, "*Anabaptismes* Mysterie of Iniquity Vnmasked". This letter, it will be noticed, is signed with the mystic initials "H. N.", that is, of Henry Niclaes, father of the Family of Love, and "I.P." prefaces the letter by stating that it was "indited" for an anonymous Anabaptist by a "principall Elder, in and of that Seperation", as "H. N." was popularly but mistakenly supposed to be. No doubt "I. P."'s view is at least in part correct, but it seems to me probable that the writer of the letter himself signed it in this way, in order to conceal his identity in case the letter was intercepted, while the signature "H. N." would be easily understood by those to whom his missive was sent.

The contents of the letter indicate that the writer held the views of John Murton. He gives no evidence of yet having any interest in the Family of Love except by the use of the signature "H. N." In closing the writer says that he sends

[1] See "Persecution for Religion Judg'd and Condemn'd", 1662, pp. 49–50. This pamphlet was reprinted in modernized text in the Hanserd Knollys Society's edition of "Tracts on Liberty of Conscience", London, 1846, pp. 83–231, of which "An Humble Supplication" occupies pages 181–231. In the edition of 1662 see p. 190 for the above citation.

"one booke to Master *Strowd*, one to Goodman *Ball*, one to Mistris *Fountaine*, one to *Roger Seely*, one to *Samuel Quash*, and one to" the person to whom the letter was directed, all of them being at that time members of the Church of England. The book sent was possibly John Murton's previously mentioned "A Discription", 1620, the last known publication of the early English Arminian, or General, Anabaptists. Of the six persons to whom this book was sent none appears to-day to be known, but there is a possibility that "Mistris Fountaine" was the wife of a Mr Fountain who is mentioned in "Numb: 4" of the Gould Manuscript[1], as being in 1644 a member of Henry Jessey's congregation.

We are told by "I. P." that the writer of this letter of May 10, 1622, had returned to the fold of the Church of England by 1623, and it seems highly probable, therefore, that he was none other than Edmond Jessop, who having renounced his Anabaptism, published at London in 1623 "A | DIS-COVERY | OF THE ERRORS | OF THE ENGLISH | *ANABAPTISTS.* | ...". Certainly his case admirably fits the situation.

Like many others of his time Jessop had evidently gone "from one forme of religion vnto another", and had finally become an Anabaptist, as he expresses it, "wandring vp and downe amongst the drie hils and mountaines, conceiuing comfort, when alas I [he] was far from it; and", says he, "the farther I wandred vp and downe in that Egyptian darknesse, the more intricate labyrinth of error and darknesse my soule was plunged into;...and especially when I walked with the Anabaptists,...all which time, though strangely deluded, yet was I kept by the power and prouidence of God from being seduced and led into that destroying and irrecouerable way of death before mentioned, namely, the Familists, though very nigh vnto it, hauing one foote entred therein, whiles I walked with the people aforesaid [i.e., the Anabaptists]." During this experience he says God laid "the rod of correction" upon him, evidently in the form of imprisonment, and by this salutary

---

[1] An extended account of this MS. is given later in this volume.

means, which served to induce deeper meditation, he was soon persuaded to reject his " former receiued opinions, as erronious and wicked", and at last to find peace in the Church of England. Now, therefore, in 1623 having gone through what he had come to consider an unfortunate and painful experience of uncertainty, he published this work to dissuade others from undertaking a similar course. The manner in which the English Anabaptists of that time administered baptism is not mentioned in this work, a significant fact, which undoubtedly indicates that dipping or immersion had not yet begun to be practised by them.

Jessop has nothing to say in praise of the English Anabaptists. On the contrary, he speaks of them as " this little silly sect of English Anabaptists..., who (poore people) though he [Satan] haue much possessed their minds with error, yet there is some hope that they will be reclaimed, because it appeareth plainly (with some of them) that they are caried thorough zeale, being meerly seduced by such as haue beene longest settled in the deceit"[1].

Still another book appeared against the Anabaptists in the year 1623,—an occurrence which seems to justify the belief that the cause of Anabaptism was making progress in England, or among the English, about this time. This third work was published by Henry Ainsworth and is entitled, "A | CENSVRE | UPON A DIALOGVE OF THE | Anabaptists, Intituled, *A Description of | what God hath Predestinated concer-|ning man,* &c. | ...", 4°, pp. iv, 64. Dr Dexter knew of no copy of the edition of 1623.

The publication of these books just at this date also indicates that people were beginning to awaken to the fact that something must be done to stop the spread of Anabaptism. In fact, according to a letter written on Sept. 4, 1622[2], even King James I and Archbishop Abbot were becoming anxious at hearing every day " of soe manie defeccions from our Religion, both to Poperie and Anabaptisme, or other points of Separacion, in some parts of this kingdome ".

[1] In the " Epistle Dedicatorie ", p. v.

[2] Add. MS. 6394, fol. 29–30, in the British Museum.

In 1624 appeared two other important answers to Murton's "A Discription". One was by John Robinson, a scarce work entitled, "A | DEFENCE | OF THE DOC-|TRINE PRO-POVN-|DED BY THE SYNODE | *AT DORT*: | *AGAINST* | IOHN MVRTON AND | HIS ASSOCIATES, IN A | Treatise intituled; *A Description* | *what God, &c.* | *WITH* | THE REFVTATION OF | their Answer to a Writing touching | *BAPTISM.*" This is a quarto consisting of iv + 203 pages. The other book bore the following title : "THE | PATRIMONY | OF CHRISTIAN | CHILDREN : | OR, | A DEFENCE OF INFANTS | Babtisme prooued to be consonant to | the Scriptures and will of GOD (against | the erroneons [erroneous] positions of the | ANABAPTISTS. | By ROBERT CLEAVER, with the | ioynt consent of Mʳ. IOHN DOD. | ...", London, 4°, 1624, pp. xvi, 90, ii, the first two, and last two, pages blank. This latter work is written in an admirable spirit, and since it is as yet practically unknown, the following citation from the "Preface to the Reader" may prove of interest[1] :—

Our daies susteine the assaults especially of the Papists, the Arminians, the Familists, and the Anabaptists, who following the Arminians in some opinions, and confirmed by their Arguments, goe before them in others, whence they haue growen very hurtfull and infestuous to many. Now for their sakes together with others, in a louing desire to reduce them, and for a preseruatiue to such as might be infected by them, we haue both priuatly according to requests beene prest, and ready to debate the matter, and now publikely to the view of the world, haue declared our selues in this argument.

Wee stand not vp against them in way of opposition, as Antagonists, or as challengers in a combate, but in pittie, and compassion

---

[1] Sig. B₂ recto and verso. In introducing the "Errata" the following quaint remark is made :—

"THe Reader is to be intreated with patience to beare with many faults committed, partly by the Scribe who was vsed in the transcription and writing out of the copy for the Presse, and partly by those which were imployed in the Print-house: as first in mispointing, Commaes being put for Colons ; Colons for Periods ; Periods for Interrogations, and contrarily: so that it is hard in some places to finde where a sentence, yea, or a section beginneth or endeth, whereby the sense is much obscured. Secondly, by misplacing of many Quotacians in the Margent ; and altogether leauing out of some such texts as are the foundations of maine arguments there vrged, ..."

at the sight of their miserable fals, we as friends call vpon them to recouer themselues, and rise vp againe from the danger of destruction, which they incurre by passing so cruell a sentence, and desperate doome vpon·many millions of Gods holy seruants, as haue dedicated their yong children to the Lord by Baptisme, that solemne and sacred Seale of his Couenant. If the matter be brought to examination and sifting, wee hope that nothing will be found herein, but that which will abide the touch-stone of the Word : but being men, and not hauing an Apostolicall spirit of infalabilitie, we dare not arrogate too much to out [our] selues : onely this wee can in the vprightnesse of our hearts affirme, that if ought haue passed our pen, that is not Orthodoxe, and currant : *fit quia latet veritas, non quod indulgetur errori:* Wee will not stand obstinately in the defence of any thing that shall appeare to be vnsound. It shall not be needfull for vs, as we thinke, to make any large Apollogie for the enterprising of this businesse, sithence the motiues that incited vs vnto it, and the end wee haue aimed at in it, will vndoubtedly worke a charitable construction of our writing, in all vnpartiall and iudicious persons, that duly apprehend the same : and therefore be informed (good Reader) that vnderstanding of the industry, and great paines of them that are deceiued in this point, to deceiue others : and that with diuers of good note in pietie, they haue preuailed too farre : and being intreated by some, to administer helpe, and assistance to themselues, and their endangered friends, we durst not violate the precept of the Apostle, inioyning vs to contend for the maintenance of the common faith.

CHAPTER XI

THE ENGLISH GENERAL, OR ARMINIAN, ANABAPTISTS
BETWEEN 1624 AND 1642

WE have already seen that before 1620 Anabaptist congregations may possibly have been organized in various counties of England, but before 1624 nothing definite is to be learned relating to them or even to the internal affairs of the congregation in London. From several letters preserved in the Mennonite Archives in Amsterdam (texts of which are given in the volume of documents), however, we gain considerable information concerning these churches during the years 1624 to 1630. It appears from the papers in Amsterdam, for instance, that before May, 1624, sixteen persons including one Elias Tookey had been excommunicated by John Murton's congregation in London, and had formed a church of their own in that city, but had not as yet ventured to ordain a minister. Tookey and his associates, we are told, decided to apply for union with the Waterlanders, perhaps hoping through them to secure proper ordination for whomsoever they should choose as a pastor. They accordingly sent a letter by messengers to Amsterdam to prefer this request. The Waterlanders cautioned them not to organize a separate congregation until they had joined a true Church. Thus far no word from Murton had come to the Waterlanders, nor had they been up to that time fully able to understand all that Tookey had said in his letter. They advised him, therefore, to be patient, and said that if Murton should send them adverse information, they would nevertheless be impartial in their judgment of both parties. They also wished further particulars concerning Tookey's opinions.

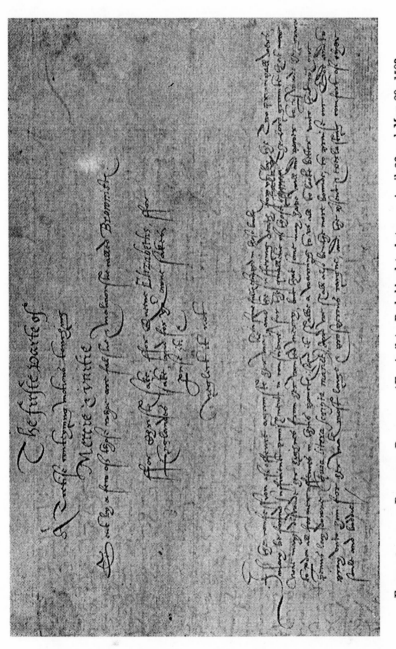

FIRST PAGE OF A BROWNIST PETITION. (*Facsimile*.) Probable date between April 26 and May 29, 1593.
For text of this treatise see Vol. II, pp. 113-25.

In compliance with this request Tookey wrote another letter in which the following points concerning his congregation appear.   Though not fully organized they celebrated the Lord's Supper, and probably baptism, through the agency of some lay member whom the congregation appointed. They did not believe in ordaining a minister without the assistance of properly ordained ministers.   They also did not hold that there was any excuse for them to flee into a foreign country on account of persecution.   The members had permitted two or three persons to remain in their communion who were not perfectly settled in their belief concerning Christ's deity,—a permission which had been granted, because these persons were peaceably disposed and believed that their salvation depended alone upon Christ.   This congregation like that of Helwys and Murton maintained that it was almost necessary for peaceable people in England to be willing to take such an oath as the Oath of Allegiance.   None of the members would become magistrates or carry arms, some of them taking this position for the sake of conscience, others for the sake of peace. The wish is expressed that the Waterlanders might write a few words to Murton and his people with the hope of establishing harmony between the two companies, and Tookey said that they themselves would strive as much as possible toward that end.   Many of Murton's followers, he said, were willing to be tolerant, and two of them especially had even been giving attention to the doctrine of succession, and desired to know if the Mennonites could give satisfactory proof that their beginnings could be traced back to the time of the Apostles.

When the Waterlanders received this fuller account of Tookey's views, they seem to have been less favourably impressed than at first with the advisability of a union with his company, and especially because the latter, though so few in number, were nevertheless not even united in their opinions concerning such a weighty point as the deity of Christ, any disbelief in which on their part, in case of the consummation of the proposed union, might bring the Waterlanders into trouble with the Dutch authorities, who were constantly on the look-out for heresy.   The Waterlanders were also disturbed by Tookey's ideas concerning the taking of an oath, and accordingly decided that they did not wish to think of any union until these objectionable views were altered.

Upon learning this decision Tookey wrote a letter on March 17, 1624/25, chiefly relating to the deity of Christ, and still urged the suggested union. The number of his company had now decreased to fifteen. By December 3, 1625, Hans de Ries wrote to Tookey that the Waterlanders had finally ceased to criticize his position with regard to the deity of Christ and would bind no one to dogmatic formulas, but expressed their strong convictions against the taking of an oath and the carrying of arms, and it was undoubtedly on account of their varying opinions concerning these last-named points that the two parties had not been united previous to Nov. 13, 1626. Before that date the membership of Tookey's company had increased to eighteen persons[1].

At the time when Tookey was excommunicated Murton was still living, and he was very likely alive on Mar. 17, 1624/25, but apparently between that date and November 12, 1626, he had died. I well realize that this was not the opinion of the late Rev. Morton Dexter[2], who thought that Murton was probably living as late as 1646, but this was clearly a mistake. Surely we cannot draw the inference that Murton was then alive merely on the ground that John Wilkinson's little work, relating to him and entitled, "The Sealed Fovntaine", was published in 1646! If Mr Dexter had opened this diminutive book and read its real title on page 1 as well as the Epistle of the editor, William Arthurbury, he would have quickly seen that the tract was written against Murton in 1613, and that it was printed in 1646 only as being in Arthurbury's opinion a useful little treatise, which deserved publication even though the author and his opponent were long since dead.

Even after Murton's death the breach between Tookey's and Murton's congregations had not been healed, but we hear

[1] See Dr B. Evans' "The Early English Baptists", London, 1861, Vol. II., p. 40.

[2] "The England and Holland of the Pilgrims", London, 1906, p. 385 note 6.

practically nothing more of Tookey or his followers.   Murton's company, likewise, after the death of their old leaders also entertained the hope of a union with the Waterlanders, and sent a Latin letter to them by two trusted messengers.   This letter, dated Nov. 12, 1626 (New Syle), states that there were five Anabaptist churches then in England,—namely, at London, Lincoln, Sarum, Coventry, and Tiverton.   At some of these places Anabaptists may have been persecuted even before 1620, as is suggested in the previously mentioned "Supplication" of that year.   If Tookey's company was still in existence, there is no reference here concerning it.   The members of the Anabaptist congregations had read the published Confession of Faith of the Waterlanders, and found that they agreed with them in all points except that of the oath, but they say that they also believe that the Lord's Supper may be celebrated every Sunday, that any church member, as such, may preach or administer the Communion or baptism in the pastor's absence, and that Christians may hold the position of magistrate and other worldly offices.   In 1626 the total number of Anabaptists in the five congregations in England was at least one hundred and fifty.

When the two messengers sent by the five English churches came to Hans de Ries, he asked them certain questions which he noted down with the answers given to them.   From these replies we learn that the five churches did not all have ministers, in other words, were not all fully organized, and consequently did not all have regular services.   Accordingly, when a congregation wished to celebrate Communion, it would wait until its turn came for the visit of a minister.   In fact, Murton's death may have left these churches without sufficient good leaders, and this may have been the chief cause for their seeking a union with the Waterlanders.

On Nov. 25, 1626, Hans de Ries wrote to the English congregations saying that their letter and the visit of their two messengers were most welcome, but that, on account of their opinions concerning the administration of the sacraments, the taking of an oath, and the holding of government positions, such a union as they desired was impossible.   Here, then, for the time the matter of a general union between the early English Anabaptist congregations and the Waterlanders seems to have been allowed to stand.

Mr Adam Taylor says that there " is some reason to believe that, in A.D. 1626, there was a general baptist church at Amersham, in Buckinghamshire"[1], and that " Tradition places the origin of the general baptist church at *Eyethorn*, in this county [Kent], towards the close of the reign of queen Elizabeth, about A.D. 1590". " For some time ", he continues, " the members of this society met for social worship in private houses: particularly at the house of one of their friends at Streetend. The owner of this house bequeathed a small annuity for the support of the cause; which like many similar bequests, has long been lost. In 1624, the number of the members was upwards of twenty;..."[2]

Dr B. Evans[3], also, speaks of the " Baptist church at Stoney Stratford" which dates " its origin", he says, " as early as 1625", and of one " Thomas Brewer, 'a zealous minister of the Baptist persuasion' ", who was arrested as early as 1626, being " a preacher among the Separatists in and about Ashford, in Kent".

We need pay but little attention to these statements, for we can be perfectly certain that the congregations mentioned were not Anabaptist at the dates given, or reference would have been made to them in letters preserved in the Mennonite Archives. However, there may have been separatist (Brownist or Barrowist) congregations in Amersham, " Eyethorn" and Stony Stratford in 1626, 1624, and 1625 respectively, from which General Anabaptist congregations were probably developed after 1640. As to Brewer, Fenner, Turner, and the other separatists at Ashford and Maidstone in Kent, about 1626, we now know that as late as 1638[4] they were not Anabaptists, but Brownists or Barrowists.

[1] "The History of the English General Baptists", Part First, London, 1818, p. 96.

[2] *Ibid.*, p. 281.

[3] "The Early English Baptists", Vol. II., London, 1864, pp. 54–7.

[4] "The Works of...William Laud, D.D." (Oxford, 1847–60, in 7 vols.),

In 1630 another attempt at union with the Waterlanders was evidently undertaken by the English General Anabaptists, and a letter was sent from the Waterland congregation in Amsterdam to the Anabaptist church at Lincoln, asking especially for further information concerning their views on the subject of excommunication, which had struck the Waterlanders as being rather narrow-minded. No beneficial result seems to have been secured by this correspondence. In 1634 the Lincoln Anabaptists appear to have been fairly numerous, and at that time had for their leader, one Johnson a baker[1].

On Sept. 13, 1630, the Waterlanders also sent a letter to the Anabaptist congregation at Tiverton stating among other things what attitude they would take toward a member of one of their churches who should hear a sermon in [the Church of?] England, and objecting to the English Anabaptists' defence of the use of the sword, etc. To this last mentioned letter James Toppe (not Joppe as printed by Dr B. Evans) and his wife Isabel responded in an undated letter supporting their position, and declaring it to be the fault of the Dutch, not of the English, that a union between them had not yet taken place. For the perusal of the Waterlanders, both of these letters were apparently translated into Dutch by Swithune Gryndall [Grindall][2], in May and June respectively, 1631. Anabaptist interest in Tiverton evidently continued unbroken as late as 1639, and probably later, for on October 10 of that year one John Fort, a clothier there, is mentioned as having been fined five hundred pounds for Anabaptism

Vol. v., Part ii., 1853, pp. 323, 331, 336, 347, and 355. See also Mr Edward Arber's "The Story of the Pilgrim Fathers", 1897, pp. 246–47, etc.

[1] "The Works of...William Laud, D.D.", Vol. v., Part ii., 1853, p. 326. "For Lincoln itself, my vicar-general certifies me, there are many anabaptists in it, and that their leader is one Johnson a baker;..."

[2] Swithune Grindall was a native of Tunstal in Yorkshire, and apparently came to Amsterdam in 1615 and joined the English-Dutch congregation. He was then 22 years old and is described as a "legatuurwerker". He married on May 2, 1615, Margriete Moritz of Scheckbye in Nottinghamshire, who was two years his senior. See the "Transactions" of the Congregational Historical Society, Vol. ii., No. 3, for September, 1905, pp. 167–68.

by the Court of High Commission[1]. On Feb. 22, 1640, the fine, which had evidently been paid in, was returned[2]. In another entry concerning Fort, as printed in the Calendar of State Papers, there is a query as to whether the name Fort is not really Topp[3]. This reading would accord so well with further information that I am inclined to believe that John Fort was none other than James Topp [Toppe]. That he was a clothier is a point of interest.

We thus learn for the first time the correct name of one of the prominent early English Anabaptists after the death of John Murton. Jacobus, or James, Toppe was apparently the recognized leader, and possibly the pastor, of the Anabaptist church at Tiverton. Very likely he was its organizer. Though little is known about him, it seems that he became in time a staunch millenarian, and lived until 1642 or later, about which time we hear of him as being engaged in a controversy with Leonard Busher.

This brings us to the career of "Mark, Leonard Busher", which we may now conveniently study. The earliest reference to Busher that I remember to have seen, is given in "The Prophane Schisme of the Brownists or Separatists", 1612[4], wherein he appears to be included among the English Anabaptists then residing in Holland, and is mentioned as holding different views from either John Smyth or Thomas Helwys. About 1613 he seems to have written his work entitled "Religions Peace", which was printed at London in 1614. When he wrote this tract, Busher was evidently in Holland[5], not in London as has generally been supposed. However, he naturally styles himself a "Citizen of *London*", since his home was there, and since he desired to indicate to King James and the Parliament, that although he was living in Holland, he was

---

[1] See "Calendar of State Papers, Domestic Series,...Charles I. 1640", London, 1880, p. 399.

[2] *Ibid.*   [3] *Ibid.*, p. 391.

[4] P. 56.

[5] As is shown in the following words (Hanserd Knollys Society edition, p. 31): "But when they come hither, or to some other free city or country, where (praised be God) is liberty of the gospel,..."

in exile and was really a loyal English citizen. The exact and complete title of the original edition of this treatise is not at present known, as no copy of it is apparently in existence to-day, and as certain changes seem to have been made in the title-page of the edition of 1646[1].

When Busher wrote this work, he was evidently persecuted and poor, but very desirous to publish his views against his opponents, for he says: "we that have most truth are most persecuted; and therefore most poore, whereby we are unable to write and print as we would against the adversaries of the truth"[2].

He had apparently already written another tract which he calls "a scourge of small cords, wherewith Antichrist and his Ministers might be driven out of the Temple of God. Also a declaration of certain false translations in the new Testament." This was evidently intended to be one book, for, says Busher, "I want wherewith to print and publish it"[3]. He also had sent a writing of his to John Robinson six months before he wrote "Religions Peace", but could obtain no answer from him[4], and even after a whole year's waiting, he tells us, he had still received no reply[5].

In "Religions Peace" Busher championed the cause of believers', or adult, baptism by dipping or immersion nearly thirty years before the Calvinistic, or Particular, English Anabaptists adopted it as the only correct manner in which to administer that ordinance. Busher maintains that Christians should "preach the word of salvation to every creature of all sorts of nations, that are worthy and willing to receive it. And such as shall willingly and gladly receive it", he says, "he [Christ] hath commanded to be baptized in the water; that is,

---

[1] The title-page of the edition of 1646 reads: "RELIGIONS | PEACE: | OR, | A PLEA for Liberty of | Conscience. | Long since presented to King *James*, | and the High Court of Parliament then | sitting, by *Leonard Busher* Citizen of *London*, | and Printed in the Yeare 1614. | ...", London, 1646, 4°, pp. ii, vi, 38. The edition of 1646 was reprinted by the Hanserd Knollys Society in a volume of "Tracts on Liberty of Conscience", 1846, pp. 1–81.

[2] Pp. 33–4.   [3] P. 34.
[4] Hanserd Knollys Society edition, p. 52.   [5] *Ibid.*, p. 52, note.

dipped for dead in the water.   And therefore the apostle saith, *Else what shall they do, who are baptized for dead, if the dead be not raised, why are they baptized for dead?*   And therefore he saith, *We are buried then with him by baptism, &c.*"[1]

In this work it would almost appear as if Busher was not pleading for any particular body of separatists, but on the contrary was only advocating a general separation from the authority of Archbishops and Bishops, and appealing for protection from their decrees.   He does not directly advocate Anabaptism, nor does he expressly oppose the baptism of infants, but from the above passage we may judge that he was at this time antagonistic to the latter and favourable to the former. The work is clearly written and unusually well thought out for that day[2].

After 1614 we do not hear of Busher again for many years, when on December 8, 1642, we find him still in Holland in the city of Delft.   On that date he wrote a piteous letter in Dutch to "Abram Derikson", saying that he has sent several letters to him without receiving any answer, and that he is a weak old man of advanced (71) years, now lying under his load (? of care and age) without any one to help him.   He asks that he may receive assistance, so that he may not remain in this lonely condition, but may be treated in a more brotherly fashion, since he, as well as Derikson, believes that Jesus is the Messiah.   He should, therefore, be treated as a brother, and

---

[1] "Tracts on Liberty of Conscience", etc. (Hanserd Knollys Society), London, 1846, pp. 59–60.

[2] It would have been practically impossible for a young Dutchman to have written such excellent English, and though Busher shows that he knows Dutch and was evidently in Holland when he wrote his works, he calls himself "your [King James I's] faithful and loving subject", and refers to "our land of Great Britain", etc.,—remarks which leave no doubt as to his nationality.   For these and other reasons stated elsewhere the author finds himself quite unable to agree with the conclusions advanced by Dr W. T. Whitley in his article entitled "Leonard Busher, Dutchman" ("Transactions of the Baptist Historical Society" for April, 1909, Vol. I., No. 2, pp. 107–113).   English, not Dutch, was Busher's native tongue, and whether his ancestry was Dutch or not, his name even as spelled at Delft in 1642 is English.

not in this unfriendly manner.   He hopes for an early answer,
and signs himself, "Your obedient servant [?] & desolate brother
in Christ, Mark Leonard Busher."

About this time, or a little later, we find Busher engaged in
the previously mentioned controversy with James Toppe concerning the second coming of Christ.   This controversy arose
in the following manner.   Toppe had been requested by a
friend to write a few lines "to proue Christes Monarchicall
reigne over all the kingedomes of this world".   His opinions
thus privately expressed came into the hands of "Mr. mark,
Leonard Busher" who was then living in Delft in Holland, and
who undertook to write an answer.   Therewith, he also wrote
a reply to a part of Mr John Archer's work on the same sub-
ject, issued at London in 1642 and entitled, "THE | PER-
SONALL | REIGNE OF | CHRIST | VPON EARTH. | In
a Treatise wherein is fully and largely | laid open and proved,
That *Iesus Christ*, toge-|ther with the Saints, shall visibly pos-
sesse a | *Monarchicall State and Kingdom* | *in this World.* | ...",
London, 4°, pp. ii, 54.

These replies together with Toppe's opinions Busher published, but at present no copy of the book seems to be known.
After the appearance of this work Toppe penned an answer
to it, which, though never printed, I have fortunately discovered in the original manuscript.   It is entitled, "CHRISTS
MONARCHI⸗|call, and personall Reigne vppon Earth: over |
all the Kingedoms of this world, Reu: | 11. 15. 17.   Dan: 7.
14. 27: | Or an Epistell to his Lovinge frind Mʳ. [mark, Leonard¹]
Busher In wᶜʰ is | allso shewed the tyme when [?] this kingdom
shall begin & [?] where it shalbe | ..."   This document is un-
dated, but was evidently written in 1642 or soon after.

Although the work is imperfect at the end, its discovery
is of considerable interest, as it gives the hitherto unsuspected
opinions of one who had been, and probably still was, a prominent
early English Anabaptist leader; as it furnishes us with information about a printed work of Leonard Busher's which up to this
time seems to have remained entirely unknown; and, finally,
as it is among the earliest manuscripts of the English General

¹ Interlined by Toppe.

Anabaptists still preserved. Where Toppe was when he prepared this document does not appear, but I presume he was at Tiverton.

Busher's name as given in the two manuscripts mentioned above, viz., "Mark Leonard Busher" and "Mr. mark, Leonard Busher", is certainly remarkable, but from Toppe's writing it is manifest that "mark" is to be separated from Busher's ordinary name, and I surmise that some time after his conversion to Anabaptism, following in a manner the example of the Apostle Paul, he may have given himself this new (New Testament) name. By so doing Busher may have thought he could the better conform his life to the Biblical pattern. The fact that he was still in Holland suggests that he may never have returned to England, but his controversy with Toppe shows that he had not forgotten his native tongue. Had he been a stronger and a younger man, he would certainly have fought in the Civil Wars for the Liberty of Conscience he had long before advocated.

As has already been indicated, the letters in the Mennonite Archives make it evident that the English Arminian, or General, Anabaptists after the death of Murton unsuccessfully sought for at least five or six years to be united with the Dutch Waterlanders. Apparently attempts at such a complete union failed even after 1630, but it is also probable that during the Primacy of Dr William Laud many of the English Anabaptists were suppressed, or compelled to flee out of England for safety. As such single persons emigrated to Holland, they undoubtedly applied individually for membership in the English-Dutch congregation at Amsterdam. Hence we find that on September 26, 1630, one Janneker (Jane) Morton was admitted to membership without further baptism, on the ground that she had formerly been baptized by Mr Smith (Smyth)[1]. This was certainly the wife of John Murton, and her application to the Waterlanders suggests the possibility of a temporary effacement of the English General Anabaptists in London, and a gradual reunion of the Smyth and the Helwys parties in the fold of the Dutch Mennonites.

[1] Dr B. Evans' "The Early English Baptists", Vol. i., London, 1862, p. 222.

CHAPTER XII

THE RISE OF THE INDEPENDENTS

THE rise of the Independents, or Congregational Puritans, has been much misunderstood. Scholars have generally thought of them as a direct outgrowth of Brownism or Barrowism, and have even confused them with separatists. It is gradually becoming more and more clear, however, that the *early* Independents, or *early* Congregationalists, were merely a certain type of Puritans, and not separatists from the Church of England, also that the Independents did not directly obtain their opinions from either Brownists or Barrowists. Besides this confusion in the past which has obscured the history of the early Independents, the dearth of material relating to them has rendered it an unusually difficult task accurately to trace their beginnings. However, with the help of the first volume of Boswell Papers preserved in the British Museum, which was only casually used by Dr John Waddington[1] and was apparently unknown to Dr Dexter, and also with the aid of certain other little known manuscripts, the origin of early Independency may now be made much more plain than heretofore.

We may begin our investigations with the career of Henry Jacob, under whose direct influence the *early* Independents, or Congregational Puritans seem to have originated. As is well

---

[1] See his "Congregational History", 1567–1700, 1874, pp. 287–305. Dr Waddington does not style these papers the Boswell Papers, though he mentions Boswell's name once or twice, and it was only about the beginning of 1909 that I became aware of the fact that he had used them at all. Dr Waddington's careless manner of indicating his sources is particularly aggravating in an instance like this.

known, Jacob first appears as a public figure about 1596 when he had "some speach with certen of the separation", i.e., Barrowists, "concerning their peremptory & vtter separation from the Churches of England", and "was requested by them" to give the reason for his defence of the State Church. If he would comply with their wish, they said, they would then secure a satisfactory answer to his argument, or renounce their separation. Accordingly Jacob gave them a brief note of his reasons which was sent to Francis Johnson then in the Clink prison in Southwark. Johnson replied and Jacob gave his answer. Johnson again took up the argument, and Jacob once more replied[1]. Finally, in 1599, this correspondence was published by "D. B." at Middelburg in a quarto volume bearing the title, "A Defence of the Chvrches and Ministery of Englande." The purpose of its publication was to prevent various English Puritans at Middelburg, and elsewhere in the Low Countries, from falling into separatism. In manuscript form it had already had satisfactory results in this direction. The initials of the publisher, "D. B." were erroneously taken to stand for Doctor (Richard) Bancroft.

In 1600 Francis Johnson published a book entitled, "An Answer to Maister H. Iacob his Defence of the Churches and Ministery of England". In this he gives an illuminating passage concerning the publisher of Jacob's work, in which he shows that the initials "D. B." do not stand for Doctor Bancroft, but for his own former co-sectary, Daniel Bucke[2], who had

---

[1] [Henry Iacob's] "A Defence of the Chvrches", Middelbvrgh, 1599, p. 3.

[2] It will be remembered that Bucke's deposition on March 9, 1592/93, gave very extended information concerning the Barrowist meetings and church officers. He was at this time a loyal separatist, and had been present at the organization of the congregation in September, 1592. Subsequently, however, he had changed his opinions, and we may now see what Johnson has to say about Bucke's later history :—

"These two letters, *D. B.* I fynd to be set for Doctor Bancroft of London in a * shameles book of his [From margin. "Geuev. (Genev. ?) Scot. (?) & Allobrog. Disc. Pag. 7."], not long synce sparsed abroad. In which respect, as also considering many as godles things here agayne published, albeit some might think it were therefore to be ascribed vnto him, yet

left the Barrowists, and evidently had now connected himself
with the Puritan congregation of the English Merchant Adventurers in Middelburg, of which Johnson had formerly been
pastor.

What effect this controversy with Johnson had on Jacob
is only indirectly indicated. It certainly did not convert
him to separatism, but it may have made him a little more
conscious of the defects in the Established Church, and the
more ready thereafter to take an advanced Puritan, non-
separatist, position. As is well known, Jacob appears[1] in
1603, as one of the Puritan leaders who drew up a so-called
Millenary Petition which was presented to King James I on his
accession to the throne. Fortunately several of Jacob's papers[2]

for other causes partly appearing in the book, partly knowen of the man,
I thinck this Preface [to Henry Jacob's "A Defence", 1599] was not
made by him: but rather by another "*D. B.* [From margin: "Daniel
Buck"] a Scrivener of London, a man that hath turned his coat and for-
saken the truth, as often as †D. P. [From margin: "†Doct. Perne"] the
old turncoat did, if not also oftener. He it was, that by letters desired of
me, to aunswer Mr Iacobs Argument, as here is said: being himself at
that tyme separated from the false worship and Ministery of England,
to which vomit he is now againe returned, wallowing in that myer from
which then he was washed. Then also he could say, himself thought
Mr. Iacobs Argument was frivolous and of no waight, and that his desier
with some others was to have it aunswered for the stopping of Mr Iacobs
mouth, who thought it vnaunswerable" (Francis Iohnson's "An Answer
to Maister H. Iacob his Defence of the Churches and Ministery of
England", 1600, 4º, Preface [p. v]).

[1] There is among the manuscripts preserved at Hatfield House,
Hertfordshire (Press-mark 72. 24.), a letter of W. Cholmley to Edward
Reynolds of the date, August 4, 1599, in which the following sentence
occurs: "My Lord has bestowed on me the office in the Tower [of London]
which Henry Jacob lately held." See the Reports of the Historical
Manuscripts Commission, Part IX., London, 1902, p. 27. Could this refer
to our Henry Jacob, or to any Henry Jacob closely related to him?

[2] MS. 113, fol. 242–53. The most important portions are given in
full in the volume of documents. These papers furnish various facts
concerning Jacob's life which have hitherto been little known in spite
of the probability that Dr John Waddington saw these same papers in
his earlier years, when, however, he made very poor use of the valuable
material therein contained. Strange to say, he appears either not to
have realized their value, or only to have glanced through them hastily, so

of the period 1603–5 have been preserved in Lambeth Palace Library where the author rediscovered them early in 1905.

From these papers it would appear that about the end of July, 1604, Jacob published his work entitled, " Reasons taken ovt of Gods Word and the best hvmane Testimonies proving a necessitie of reforming ovr Chvrches in England." The Bishop of London on hearing of the publication of the book sent a messenger, requesting Jacob to come to speak with him. A servant reported the message to Jacob, and he, not knowing, but possibly suspecting, the object of this invitation, called upon the Bishop, and was immediately made a prisoner and committed to the Clink[1]. After a time, as his imprisonment continued, Jacob's wife and four small children found themselves in much distress. He accordingly sent a request for his release, and explained that the publication of his book was really a very reasonable proceeding. In his conduct Jacob showed himself to be an entirely different type of person from Robert Browne, Henry Barrowe, and John Greenwood, all of whom were much more outspoken than he. They did not intend to show any respect to high clerical dignitaries. Jacob, on the contrary, was more politic, and well understood how to bear

that later when he wrote his extended history, he made little better use of them, and failed to state where they were to be found. The way in which he neglected these papers is all the more unaccountable, when one realizes that in the same volume which contains them are the two most extended manuscripts of Robert Browne's still extant. How Dr Dexter happened to miss this material is equally astonishing, for either he, or someone working for him, had certainly seen the contents of this volume as somewhat incorrectly described in the catalogue of the Lambeth Palace MSS., and as I have recently discovered, has even inserted in his Bibliography the following entry, "[1590.] [T. Cartwright.]—A Reproof of Certain Schismaticall persons, and their Doctrine concerning the Hearing and Preaching of the Word of God. fol. 32. [MS.]" ! He seems, however, to have sought to reproduce the original spelling of the title without consulting the manuscript itself !

The greater part of the Jacob papers was first published by the author in " The Review and Expositor" (Louisville, Kentucky) for October, 1907, pp. 489–513, under the title, " Lost Prison Papers of Henry Jacob".

[1] A citation by Dr R. W. Dale ("History of English Congregationalism", London, 1907, p. 215) suggests that this was not the first time that Jacob was imprisoned.

himself in the presence of superior ecclesiastics, so that their
displeasure would be somewhat mollified by his conciliatory
manner of speech and shrewd argument.

Not even his adroit pleading, however, availed at once to
move the Bishop of London to a display of leniency, though it
should be said that Jacob's previously mentioned request for
release may not have been written very long before he was
allowed to make a subscription to three articles. After this had
been signed, as he intimates in another place, during a private
interview with the Archbishop of Canterbury on April 4, 1605,
he was released on bail for half a year. It appears that Jacob
kept a copy of the text of this document, in order thereby, no
doubt, in case of necessity, to refresh his remembrance, or to
justify himself. To his private text he added various reservations and explanations, and says, "Whosoever do make any
other sense of my words they do me wrong. [Space.] Henry
Iacob." This subscription strikingly reminds one of Robert
Browne's signed in 1585, and of which the original manuscript
apparently no longer exists. Jacob's subscription is therefore
of unusual interest, as it not only gives us knowledge of a long-
forgotten event, but also makes his personality much more real.
Like Browne he evidently felt quite justified in giving his own
private interpretation to the text he was to subscribe, and in
signing it with that interpretation in mind. In fact, this seems
to have been the only way of dealing with the bishops of that
day, unless one wished to pass one's life in some dreary prison.

"A third humble Supplication" of the Puritans addressed
to the King in 1605, and corrected by Jacob[1], is to be found
among his papers. In this is a passage which well illustrates
the aims of the Puritans of that time. They request toleration,
and permission—

[1] This document is not that which Dr John Waddington in his account of Jacob ("Congregational History", 1567–1700, 1874, pp. 174–76)
mentions as being written by Jacob and annotated in King James I's
own handwriting, for this was not originally written by Jacob, and there
are no marginal annotations by the king. Jacob himself corrected this
document. The MS. to which Waddington here refers was described,
I believe, during the past year (1910) in "Blackwood's Magazine", as an
hitherto unnoticed Puritan document!

to Assemble togeather somwhere publikly to the Service & Worship of God, to vse & enioye peaceably among our selves alone the wholl exercyse of Gods worship and of Church Government viz. by a Pastor, Elder, & Deacons in our [?] severall Assemblie[s] without any tradicion of men whatsoeuer, according only to the specification of Gods written word and no otherwise, which hitherto as yet in this our present State we could never enjoye.

Provided alwayes, that whosoeuer will enter into this way, shall 1 before a Iustice of peace first take the oath of your Maiesties supremacy & royall authority as the Lawes of the Land at this 2 present do set forth the same; And shall also afterwards keepe brotherly communion with the rest of our English Churches as they are now established, according as the French and Dutch Churches 3 do; And shall truly pay all paymentes and dutyes both ecclesiasticall and civill, as at this present they stand bound to pay in 4 anie respect whatsoever; And if anie trespas be committed by anie of them whether Ecclesiastically or Civilly against good order and Christian obedience; That then the same person shalbe dealt withall therein by anie of your Maiestes Ciuill Magistrates, and by the same Ecclesiasticall government only wherevnto he ordinarily ioyneth him self, according as to Iustice apperteyneth, and not to be molested by anie other whomsoever.

This passage sums up what the Puritans of Jacob's type were seeking. In brief, they desire in their congregations a Pastor, Elder, and Deacons, and do not wish to be compelled to follow any human traditions. They are willing to take the Oath of Supremacy, to remain in " brotherly communion " with the Church of England, to pay all dues ecclesiastical and civil, and in case of any offence being committed by any of them, to be tried before any civil magistrate and also, evidently, by the governing body of the congregation to which they individually belong.

Certain opinions of Jacob's contained in a paper entitled, " Principles & Foundations of Christian Religion ", the entire text of which may be found in the volume of documents, show how far he had advanced in his Puritan, non-separatist, views before he left England in 1605. Here, for instance, is his definition of a true visible church :—

A true Visible or Ministeriall Church of Christ is a particular Congregation being a spirituall perfect Corporation of Believers, & having power in its selfe immediatly from Christ to administer all Religious meanes of faith to the members thereof.

As to the question of how such a true church is to be " constituted & gathered ", i.e., organized, he says :—

By a free mutuall [From margin: "Math. 18. 19, 20."] consent of Believers joyning & covenanting to live as Members of a holy Society togeather in all religious & vertuous duties as Christ & his Apostles did institute & practise in the Gospell. By such a free mutuall consent also all Civill perfect Corporations did first beginne.

As to church officers, he says they should be " A Pastor or Bishop, with Elders, & Deacons "[1].

From one of these citations we see that Jacob already advocated the employment of covenants among the Puritans, being thus early well advanced in his views as an Independent, or Congregational, non-separatist, Puritan, who believed that each congregation in the Church of England was sufficient to determine its own policy and manage its own affairs without the necessity of assistance from Archbishops and Bishops, or even from Classes, Synods, etc. It should especially be noticed that Jacob was not a separatist at this time, and he never became one. It is thus made evident that Puritans were already advocating views which hitherto have been ascribed only to the genius of separatists.

One of the first apparently to agree with, and to promulgate, the congregational Puritan views of Henry Jacob was William Bradshaw (1571–1618)[2]. In 1605 he stated these views with great clearness in an anonymous pamphlet, which, however, is well understood to have been written by him, entitled, *"ENGLISH PVRITANISME* | CONTAINE-|*NING.* | The maine opinions of the rigidest | *sort of those that are called Puritanes* | In the Realme of England. | ... | Printed *1605* ", 8°, pp. ii, 35. This title suggests that there was at that time more than one type of Puritan, and it seems possible after 1605, therefore, to separate the Puritans into two general divisions. First, there were those of the older Presbyterian non-separatist type, and secondly, after 1605, also those of the later "Jacobite", Bradshawian, Congregational, or Independent non-separatist type. Bradshaw's pamphlet is illuminating from an historical

---

[1] In one of his books published some years later, as is noticed hereafter, he speaks of the proper church officers as "Pastors, Teachers, Elders, and Deacons ".

[2] For Bradshaw's life see the excellent account of him in the "Dictionary of National Biography."

standpoint and should be read throughout.   Here are a few
specially pertinent passages[1] :—

1 T*HEY* [the "rigidest sort" of Puritans] hould and maintaine
*that euery Companie, Congregation or Assemblie of men,
ordinarilie ioyneing together in the true worship of God, is a true*
visible church *of Christ. and that the same title is improperlie
attributed to any other Conuocations, Synods Societies, combinations,
or assemblies whatsoeuer.*
2 They hould *that all such Churches or Congregations, communicating after that manner together, in diuine worship are in all
Ecclesiasticall matters cquall [equall], and of the same power cnd
authoritie, and that by the word and will of God they ought to haue
the same spirituall priuilidges, prerogatius, officers, administrations,
orders, and Formes of divine worship.*
3 They hould *that Christ Iesus hath not subiected any Church or
Congregation of his, to any other superior Ecclesiasticall Iurisdiction,
then vnto that which is within it self So that yf a wholl Churche or
Congregation shall erre, in any matters of faith or religion. noe other
Churches or Spirituall Church officers haue (by any warrant from the
word of God) power to censure, punish, or controule the same: but are
onely to counsell and aduise the same, and so to leaue their Soules to
the immediate Iudgment of Christ, and their bodies to the sword &
power of the Ciuill Magistrat, who alone vpon Earth hath power to
punish a whol Church or Congregation.*

In Bradshaw's exaltation of the civil magistrate to the
position of chief arbiter in all ecclesiastical matters we see
how the Congregational Puritans were planning to deal with
the practical problem of abolishing the offices of Archbishop,
Bishop, etc., how they would at the same time preserve the
Church of England intact as a National Church, and how they
would prevent the actual establishment of universal separatism
in England, should their ideal be realized.

I have not yet noticed that Bradshaw mentions the use of
covenants.   He is, however, emphasizing the external rather
than the internal policy of Puritan non-separatist, Congregationalism.   Hence his failure here to endorse the use of
covenants does not by any means indicate that he would not
advocate their employment.   The drawing up of covenants
by Congregational Puritans may not have been a frequent
occurrence in England before 1641, but the practice certainly

------

[1] Pp. 5–6.

increased as this type of Puritans became more common. John Robinson, for instance, was a Puritan of this kind and engaged in covenant with other Puritan members of the Church of England before he became a separatist, for he says[1]:—

We do with all thankfulnes to our God acknowledg, and with much comfort remember those lively feelings of Gods love, & former graces wrought in vs, & that one special grace amongst the rest by which we have been enabled to drawe our selves into visible Covenant, and holy communion. Yea with such comfort and assurance do we call to mynde the Lords work this way in vs, as we doubt not but our salvation was sealed vp vnto our consciences by most infallible marks and testimonyes (which could not deceave) before we conceaved the least thought of separation ; and so we hope it is with many others in the Church of Engl.[and] yea and of Rome too.

The employment of covenants may occasionally have been adopted by Puritans for some special reason. At any rate, it is well known that Richard Bernard in 1607, in order to counteract the influence of John Smyth, drew up a covenant with one hundred people in his parish at Worksop. This event is described as follows by Robinson[2]:—

Once you know Mr B.[ernard] you did separate from the rest an hundred voluntary professors into covenant with the Lord, sealed vp with the Lords supper, to forsake all knowne sinn, to hear no wicked or dumb Ministers, and the like, which covenant long since you have dissolved, not shaming to affirme you did it onely in policy to keepe your people from Mr Smyth....

This covenant engagement was evidently broken off when Smyth left England,—a fact which probably indicates that Bernard did not continue to maintain a Congregational Puritan position.

At a still later period, but some time before 1632, John Cotton, while at Boston in Lincolnshire, and holding office in the Church of England, "entred into a Covenant with the Lord", "with some scores of godly persons", "to follow after the Lord in the purity of his worship; which though it was defective, yet it was more then the Old Non-conformity"[3], or early Puritanism.

---

[1] "*A* Ivstification of *Separation*", 1610, p. 60.   [2] *Ibid.*, p. 94.

[3] John Cotton's "The Way of Congregational Churches Cleared", London, 1648, p. 20.

As has already been stated, Congregational Puritans who engaged in covenant were certainly not numerous in England before 1641, and even as late as 1648, when Governor Bradford refers to them in "A Dialogue, or the Sum of a Conference", he merely says: "there are some parish assemblies [in England] that are true churches by virtue of an implicit covenant amongst themselves, in which regard the Church of England may be held and called a true church."[1]

Thus far no reference has been made to John Robinson after his arrival in Holland, and as so much has already been written about him by others, only a few points relating to this part of his career will here be mentioned. As was pointed out in "The Christian Life" about five years ago[2], practically nothing was then known concerning the early life of Robinson. In an attempt to remedy this deficiency I have recently (1910) published "*A Tercentenary Memorial* New Facts concerning John Robinson Pastor of the Pilgrim Fathers"[3]. In addition to what is said there, it might now be suggested that up to the present time even his more public career in Holland has been much misunderstood. The Continental life of Robinson can best be studied in connection with that of Henry Jacob and William Bradshaw. The former came to Middelburg apparently some time about the summer of 1605, and if I am not mistaken, became the minister of the congregation of the English Merchant Adventurers in that city, over whom Johnson had ministered fifteen years or so before. We know that already in 1605 Jacob had well-defined Independent, or Congregational, Puritan (non-separatist) views as to church polity, and there is no reason to doubt that as soon as possible he endeavoured to put these ideas into practice in this Continental church. Jacob probably was well established in his position when Richard Clyfton and John Robinson, then a rigid separatist, arrived in Amsterdam about 1608.

[1] See Alexander Young's "Chronicles of the Pilgrim Fathers of the Colony of Plymouth, from 1602 to 1625...", Boston, 1841, 8°, p. 416.

[2] In a review of the late Rev. Morton Dexter's "The England and Holland of the Pilgrims", 1906.

[3] Oxford and London.

In 1609 Robinson and about one hundred of the original Scrooby company removed to Leyden, and in this year, I believe, as has been expressed in *"A Tercentenary Memorial"*, he became for the first time pastor of the church. According to the hitherto usually accepted traditional view Robinson met Jacob in 1610 and converted him to the ways of Independency. How baseless this tradition really is, though accepted by historians like Dr Dexter and others, will soon appear. In the first place, in 1610 John Robinson was not an Independent but a separatist, and in the same year he wrote his well-known work, entitled, "*A* | IVSTIFICATION | OF | *SEPARATION* from the Church of | England ", which teaches a doctrine that the early Independents never held. In the second place, as we have already seen earlier in this chapter, Jacob had been a leader in defining the opinions of the Independent, or Congregational, Puritans at least five years earlier than 1610, and even before he came to Holland. In the third place, the subsequent history of the lives of Jacob and Robinson clearly indicates that Jacob and other Puritans who more or less agreed with him converted Robinson to the ways of Independency, rather than *vice versa*. In the fourth place, the interviews between Robinson and Jacob are not dated 1610 in the earliest record we have of them.

A brief account of how the traditional view arose and has been perpetuated, may be instructive.—For this the so-called Jessey Records, preferably Memoranda, now transcribed into the Gould Manuscript (the text of a part of which is given in the volume of documents) seem to be primarily responsible, but it will be noticed on a careful examination of the text, that Jessey does not actually say that Jacob derived his opinions from Robinson, though such an impression might perhaps be made on the casual reader. The Memoranda read on this point as follows:—

He [Jacob] having had much conference about these things here [in England]; after that in the low Countries he had converse & discoursed much with Mr John Robinson late Pastor to the Church in Leyden & with others about them:...

The item is itself undated, but occurs between minutes dated respectively 1610 and 1616.

As is well known, the Rev. Daniel Neal was the first to use Benjamin Stinton's manuscripts, from one of which these words were copied into our present source, the Gould transcript. Neal decided that this passage meant that Jacob procured his views from Robinson—an interpretation which other evidence now appears to prove to be just the opposite of the truth, in spite of the fact that Neal's opinion has been perpetuated to the present day by an unbroken line of unsuspecting scholars.

Governor Bradford, who wrote about the same time that the sources used by Stinton were originally written, does not make any such claim for the influence of Robinson over Jacob. On the contrary Bradford merely mentions the fact that "some" of Robinson's congregation (probably Robinson, Brewster, Bradford, and perhaps others) "knew Mr. Parker, Doctor Ames, and Mr. Jacob in Holland, when they sojourned for a time in Leyden; and all three boarded together and had their victuals dressed by some of our acquaintance, and then they lived comfortable, and then they were provided for as became their persons "[1].

The reconstructed statement of the relationship in Holland between Jacob and Robinson, it would seem, ought to be somewhat as follows.—Robinson was a separatist, not an Independent, in 1610, and he published in that year his book already referred to justifying separation from the Church of England. In the same year Jacob brought out a work of considerably different import, in which he continued to advocate the congregational Puritan principles which he had championed in 1604. His treatise published at Leyden in 1610 is entitled, "THE | Divine Beginning | and Institution of Christs true | Visible or Ministeriall | Church. | ..." The appearance of these publications may naturally have led to conference on the subject of separation, when the Independent Puritans, Parker, Dr Ames, and Jacob were in Leyden some time

---

[1] Alexander Young's "Chronicles of the Pilgrim Fathers of the Colony of Plymouth, from 1602 to 1625", Boston, p. 439. Of course Parker, Ames, and Jacob did not maintain exactly the same views, but none of them believed in separatism.

between 1610 and 1616, and it seems very reasonable to
believe that Robinson, who in Leyden was removed from direct
contact with the more aggressive personalities of Johnson,
Ainsworth, Clyfton, and Smyth, was the more readily and the
more favourably impressed by these early Independent Puritan
leaders. Little by little and almost imperceptibly, it would
seem, Robinson now began to lay aside his more rigid separatist
views and to adopt those of the broader-minded, non-separatist
Independent Puritans. However this may be, it is evident that
by 1618[1] the pastor of the Pilgrim Fathers had become such an
Independent Puritan.

Not long before his death Robinson wrote the following
words, stating the position which he himself took in his later
life in relation to the Church of England, and which he would
advise his followers also to adopt toward it[2] :—

To conclude, For my selfe, thus I beleeue with my heart before
God, and professe with my tongue, and haue before the world, that
I haue one and the same faith, hope, spirit, baptism, and Lord
which I had in the church of England and none other : that I
esteem so many in that church, of what state, or order soeuer, as
are truly partakers of that faith (as I account many thousand to be)
for my christian brethren : and my selfe a fellow-member with them
of that one misticall body of Christ seatered [scatered] far and wide
throughout the world : that I haue alwaies in spirit, and affection
al christian fellowshippe, and communion with them, and am most
ready in all outward actions, & exercises of Religione lawfull &
lawfully done, to expresse the same: & withall, that I am perswaded
the hearing of the word of God there preached, in the manner, and
vpon the grounds formerly mentioned, both lawfull, and vpon

---

[1] John Paget in "An Arrovv *Against the Separation*", Amsterdam,
1618, p. 127, has the following passage:—

"5. Seing M^r. Robinson and his people do now (as divers of themselves confesse) receyve the members of the Church of England into
their congregation, and this without any renunciation of the Church of
England, without any repentance for their Idolatries committed in the
Church of England: how can you hold them to be a true Church and
communion with them lawfull: seing that by your reasoning they are
tyed in the cords of their sin, as well as we;..."

[2] "A Treatise of the Lawfvlnes of Hearing of the Ministers", 1634,
pp. 63–4.

occasion, necessary for me, & all true christians, with drawing from that Hierarchical order of church gouernement, and ministery, and the appartenances thereof: and vniting in the order, and ordinances instituted by Christ, the onely King, and Lord of his Church, and by all his disciples to be obserued : and lastly, that I cannot communicate with, or submit vnto the said [hierarchical] Church-order, and ordinances there established, either in state, or act, without being condemned of mine owne heart, and therein prouoking God, who is greater then my heart, to condemne me much more. And for my failings (which may easily be too many) one way, or other, of ignorance hearin, and so for all my other sinnes, I must humbly craue pardon first, and most at the hands of God. And so of all men, whom therein I offend, or haue offended any manner of way : euen as they desire, and look that God should pardon their offences.

Little more needs to be said here concerning Robinson. As is well known, he died in Leyden on March 1, 1625. After his death the congregation is said to have become so reduced in numbers as to have been only one fifth as large in 1634 as it had been in 1624. This diminution was partly due to the fact that some of the congregation, following and expanding Robinson's broader ideals, had "declined or apostated" from the church before 1631[1], but the falling off in membership seems to have occurred largely in 1634 through many of the members deserting their comrades, because two of their number, who had apparently been in England, had heard some of the clergymen of the Church of England preach[2]. Thus easily was Robinson's more charitable teaching forgotten and cast to the winds. How long this breach lasted is not apparent, but it is possible that some of the dissatisfied members may have gone to Amsterdam to join the congregation of John Canne, of whom, it is suggested, they had spoken in high terms. These deserters were evidently of an extremely narrow spirit, having even affirmed, as we are told, "that the verie speaking of a vvord through fraylty about worldly businesses vpon the Sabbaoth day, should haue as seuere a sentence, as he that

[1] A. T.'s "A Christian Reprofe", 1631, p. 20.
[2] See John Robinson's "A Treatise of the Lawfvlnes of Hearing of the Ministers", 1634, pp. iii–xii.

shall openly & prophanely transgresse against the 4. Commandement,..."

To counteract this more restricted view which had brought such disaster upon the church, those who remained firm in Robinson's opinions published in 1634 the following well-known treatise written by him, the manuscript of which was found in his study after his death, entitled, "A TREATISE | OF THE | LAWFVLNES | OF HEARING OF THE | Ministers in the church of England:..."

The material presented in the latter part of this chapter has been largely drawn from the Boswell Papers[1], extended texts of a number of which have been given in the volume of documents. It is sufficient here, therefore, to present only a brief summary of the chief contents of these papers.

In spite of the fact that the Puritans of the older type were never friendly to separatism, the various English Puritan churches on the Continent during the early years of the 17th century were on the whole not a hindrance to, but rather a help in, the development of such separatism. This undoubtedly was chiefly due to the fact, that the Puritan ministers, who went to Holland in search of greater religious freedom, were not all of the old type, some of the most influential, though apparently differing on particular points, being strong advocates of the new Puritan Congregationalism. Before the time of Charles I and the Primacy of Archbishop Laud, comparatively few English preachers seem to have fled to Holland, but we find a good number there in 1633.

From the Boswell Papers we learn the names of all the cities and towns in which the principal English congregations in Holland at this period were situated, whether such towns were garrisoned or not, and the names of all the ministers of these congregations in the year 1633. We are told the principal facts connected with the formation and early history of the

---

[1] Add. MS. 6394, in the British Museum, on the binding of which is stamped the words " Relative to the English Church in the Netherlands. 1600–1648".

English Classis in the Netherlands, also various points about the Brownists and their relation to the Classis, and many forgotten details concerning such men as John Paget, Hugh Peter, or Peters, Thomas Hooker, and John Davenport.

In 1621 Mr John Forbes, preacher to the English " Marchants adventurers" at Delft first obtained a commission for the English Classis in the Netherlands. Before that time Mr John Paget and Mr Potts had joined the Dutch Classis of Amsterdam, but when this new Classis was formed, they were urged by its members to associate themselves with it. Notice was accordingly given to the Dutch Classis, but its members were opposed to the English congregations having a separate classis, and also to the attempt thus made to draw away Mr Paget and Mr Potts, the former of whom, at least, appeared to have no desire for such a change. When further pressure was brought to bear on Paget's case, the Dutch Synod of North Holland confirmed the opinion of the Amsterdam Classis, and the "Burgomasters" at Amsterdam evidently took a like view.

The objections made to the English Classis were the following :—

the two maine reasons why the English Classis is condemned are these (as they may be seene vpon record) 1. Because the Ministers of England which come over hither are of severall & inconsistent opinions differing from one another & from all reformed churches. as expressely that some are Brownists. some Brownistically affected in particular opinions. as .1. in allowing private men to preach .2. In denijing [?] formes of praier. 3 In admitting Brownists to their Congregations not renouncing their Brownisme. Some are Iacobites who require a New Covenant for members of a church to make before they can be Communicants, 2. Condemne the Decisive & Iudging power of all Classes & Synods ; & that they have only a power of Counsailing & advising, because every particular Congregation is a church ; and that a Compleat church, and that it is Immediately given vnto every congregation from Christ to be a single & vncompounded policy ; (These are the very words of Mr Iacob, & Parker, & Baines,) And now the Dutch Classis & Synods conclude that such opinions as these do cleane overthrow the nature of their goverment ; and that amongst such diversity of opinions no true Classis can be....

2. Because of the Complaint of the french & wallons in those countries.. because they have a Classis graunted vnto them : It

were better (they say by experience) that they had no classis but were (as M[r] Paget is) mixed into the Dutch Classes. for by reason of the distan[ce ?] of their dwelling they cannot have Monthly or quarterly Meetings, as Classes have, but only annuall as Synods : and that then there[?] is such trouble in their gathering together some dwelling in one province & some in another at such great distance that they were never all...& by reason of their few meetings the[re ?] grow vp many Enormities in particular congregations vnpunished :...[1]

In 1633 Mr Forbes obtained a new commission for the English Classis, and once more tried to draw Paget into it, but he continued to have no desire to join, and knowing this, the members of the Dutch Classis promised him to do their utmost to prevent his removal from among them.

Evidently before 1628 some irregularities were known to exist in the English Classis. These seem to have consisted chiefly in the use of new liturgies and set forms of prayer, or of novelties in ceremonies, as of ordaining ministers without consulting other churches in the Classis, and in declining to suppress Brownist or Barrowist preachers. One may suspect that Paget had called the attention of Sir Dudley Carleton, the English Ambassador, to this state of affairs, and he seems to have reported it to King Charles I. At any rate, on May 19, 1628, certain articles were sent to the "Synod of the English & Scottish Ministers in the Netherlands, in the name of his Maiestie of Great Brittanie", by Sir Dudley, urging the correction of any such irregularities. This document the English and Scotch ministers answered in a very diplomatic manner, entirely defending their practice, and asking for his Majesty's favour in his consideration of their proceedings. The text of the articles and a large part of the answer to them are given in the volume of documents. Whatever may have been the result of their appeal, the irregularities still appear to have continued, for in 1633 some one, probably Stephen Goffe, wrote[2]:—

It is to be observed that of those Engl:[ish] Minister[s] [in the Netherlands] which vse not the English forme [of liturgy] 1. Some

---

[1] Add. MS. 6394, fol. 146 recto, in the British Museum.
[2] *Ibid.*, fol. 168.

vse the Dutch translated. as M[r] Paine. but yet that mended much left out, and some things added, as may appeare by M[r] Paines booke. /

2. Some vse none at all as M[r] Forbes. but every time they administer the sacraments a new. they[?] doe[?] not stand to one of their owne. /

3. Some vse another English forme putt out at Midleborough. 1586. This M[r] Goodyer saith he vseth at Leyden. and M[r] Peters saied to me that was the forme he found in his consistory. But whether he vse it or no I cannot tell, I beleive he goes the Forbesian way.

4. Some vse our English forme in the sacraments but mangle them Leaving out and putting in whole sentences....

Of the twenty-four preachers in the English congregations in the Netherlands in 1633[1] only Mr Forbes, Mr Peters, Mr Balmeford, Mr Paine, Mr Widdowes, and Mr Sibbald (a Scotchman) belonged to the English Classis. Of those who refused to join the English Classis, two were Dutchmen, who spoke English; some, including Mr Roe and Mr Drake, wished to belong to no Classis; three (Mr John Paget, Mr Fortree, and Mr Gribbins) were of the Dutch Classis; Mr Goodyer desired to join the Leyden Classis.

An extended history of the English church at Utrecht is given among the Boswell Papers in a manuscript written apparently not long after 1637. A considerable portion of this account has been given in the volume of documents, so that only a few of the principal facts need to be reproduced here.

In 1622, we find, Mr Thomas Scott became the first preacher of the English church in Utrecht then just organized. At that time, Mr Barkeley was the preacher of the English congregation at Rotterdam. On June 8, 1626, Mr Scott was murdered while on his way to church, and on Jan. 11, 1627, Mr Jeremy Elbrough took his place.

It is to be noted, that when Mr Scott became the preacher at Utrecht, the congregation were evidently "bound by couenant to pay" his salary. Possibly in some such way as this church

---

[1] Add. MS. 6394, fol. 175, in the British Museum.

covenants came little by little to be employed by Puritan congregations on the Continent. In 1629 Mr Elbrough became the minister of the English Merchants at Hamburg, and was succeeded at Utrecht by Dr Alexander Leighton, a Scotchman who joined the English Classis.

Reference may be made in passing to one other English Continental congregation not mentioned in the Boswell Papers, namely, that at Arnheim. Of this church one Robert Crane, in a letter dated, "Vtrecht the 16...1640", and addressed to his cousin, Sir Robert Crane of Chilton, Suffolk, has given the following description[1] :—

Since I came into these Countryes I haue bin in a perpetuall Motion, still rooleinge from Citye to Citye, so as yet I could not gather any thinge worth your notice, nor truly is there almost any discourse but of the lamented state of England. I meete here [in Holland] with many sects, but few Religions, and see more superstion [superstition] in theire houses then in theire Temples, 'tis vsuall to prophane the Churches without contradiction, whilst the very ground of their Chambers is held as holy; either wee must walke bare=foote, or else noe admission into theire Paradise, and if accidentally wee enter into a Garden, we find euery Tree bareth forbidden fruite; In Gelderland at the Citie of Arhnam [Arnheim] I receiued greate fauors from diuers worthy gentlemen of our Nation who haue theire seated themselfs, especially from these Sir William Constable, Sir Mathew Boynton, Sir Richard Saltingston of Yorkshire, as also from Mr Laurence who within few yeares liued neere Berrye [Bury St. Edmund's], They haue two Preachers, and this the discipline of theire Church; Vpon euery Sonday a Communion, a prayer before sermon & after, the like in the aftenoone, The Communion Table stands in the lower end of the Church (which hath no Chancell) Altar=wise, where the Cheifest sit & take notes, not a gentlewoman that thinkes her hand to faire to vse her pen & Inke, The Sermon, Prayer and psalme being ended, the greatest companie present theire offeringes, which amounte to about two or 3 hundred pounds a yeare Sterlinge. the Ministers content themselfs with a hundred pounds a man per Annum the Remainder is reserued for pious vses ;...

The name of John Robinson does not appear at all in the Boswell Papers, and that of Henry Jacob probably does not occur more than once or twice. This fact, however, is not

---

[1] Tanner MS. 65, fol. 24, in the Bodleian Library, Oxford.

surprising for two reasons,—in the first place, because the most
of the papers pertain to a time after 1630, though one or two
of them date back as far as 1622; and in the second place,
because Jacob had returned to England in 1616 and died
in 1624, while the Pilgrim Fathers, who formed the larger
portion of Robinson's congregation, had gone to America in
1620.

As we have already seen, however, Jacob had left such an
impression behind him, that the Independent Puritans were
evidently for some years known as 'Jacobites'. This fact is proved
by a passage, which, though it has been cited in another connection, may profitably be repeated here: "Some are Iacobites
who require a New Covenant for members of a church to make
before they can be Communicants, 2. Condemne the Decisive
& Iudging power of all Classes & Synods; & that they have
only a power of Counsailing & advising, because every particular Congregation is a church; and that a Compleat church,
and that it is Immediately given vnto every congregation from
Christ to be a single & vncompounded policy; (These are
the words of Mr Iacob, & Parker, & Baines,)..." The reader
will notice that the Independent Puritans are not here called
Robinsonians, as they probably would have been if, according to
tradition, Robinson had taught Jacob the views of congregational Puritanism.

From the Boswell Papers, as has already been indicated, a
good many facts may also be gathered concerning the lives of
various other notable Puritans. Among these Hugh Peters, the
Independent, or 'Jacobite' Puritan, may be first mentioned. He
seems to have been the assistant of Mr Forbes in the congregation of English Merchants at Delft in 1633, but he preached
his farewell sermon there on the last Sunday of October in
that year. On his arrival in Rotterdam, to which city he had
evidently been called to take charge of the local English church,
he appears at once to have drawn up the text of a very explicit
and extended covenant, and to have announced that no one,
not even old members of the congregation, who did not subscribe to that document, should be admitted to Communion.
At least one member, Alexander Browne, demurred at this

action on the new pastor's part and showed his deep feeling by writing: "what authoritie he haith to doe these thinges: I knowe not." Such a statement seems to indicate that this congregation had never before employed an explicit church covenant. Peters, however, was evidently successful in demanding the signing of the document, and the following vivid account of his ordination has been preserved[1] :—

Concerning Mr Peters ordinacion

1. There was a *New Covenant made* with[?] certaine precise & strict obligacions to which they should bind themselves. and he would be chosen by none but them that would put there[?] hands to that paper. This saith Mr Paget was a kind of Excommunicacion to above two parts of the congregacion in former times. & hath caused the difficulty of adminis[t]ering the sacrament because he will give it to none but them whose names are at his New Covenant. Those New Covenanted must choose & Call him. so before these a sermon was made by M^r forbes.

2. There was χειροτονεια. first by all the men, but said M^r forbes, I see what the men do : but what do the weomen do. Therevpon they fell a χειροτonising too & Lift vp their Hands.

3. There was χειροθεσία. The Imposing of all the hands of the present Ministers except Mr Daye who was not desired (*Mr Grim of weasell* [Wesel] *was present* and confirmes all this) and Mr Forbes held them above halfe an hower laijing [*sic*] his burthen vpon him in these words & manner, as if he had never beene made minister. /

The covenant prepared by Peters for this occasion, as has been said, is a remarkable document. No separatist before that time is now known to have drawn up one like it. Therefore, there is no probability that Peters borrowed this idea entirely from the Brownists. On the contrary, he needed only to follow in the footsteps of Henry Jacob, and at the same time to manifest his own genius. The complete text of the covenant, as given by Alexander Browne, reads as follows[2] :—

Articles or Couenant offered by M^r. Hugh Peters Minister, to the English Congregation at Rotterdam, to his Congregation before admission into it or to the Lords supper to be subscribed &c : 1633[3].

[1] Add. MS. 6394, fol. 146 verso, in the British Museum.
[2] *Ibid.*, fol. 161.
[3] This title is written on fol. 161 verso.

The 15 Artikells and Couenant of Mr Hugh Peter of Rotterdam[1]

1	To	Be Contented with meet triall for our ffittnes [Fittnes] to be members:
2	To	Cleaue in hart to to [sic] the truth and pure worship of God and to oppose all wayes of Innouation and Coruption.

[1] This copy of the covenant was apparently sent on Nov. 1, 1633. Later Sir William Boswell himself seems to have made an improved transcript of Alexander Browne's copy, and to have sent it to Archbishop Laud, who has endorsed it, "Received Decemb: 10. 1633." Boswell's version reads as follows:—

The 15. Articles & *Couenant* of Mr. Hugh Peter Minister of Rhotterdam.—

1. — Be contented with meet tryall for our fitnes to be members.—
2. — Cleaue in heart to the truth & pure worship of God & to oppose all wayes of Innouation & corruption.—
3. — Suffer the word to be the guider of all Controuersies.—
4. — Labour for growth of knowledge, & to that end to conferr, pray, heare, & meditate—
5. — Submitt to Brotherly admonicion & censure without enuie or anger.
6. — Be throughly reconciled one to another euen in iudgement before wee begin this work.—
7. — Walk in all kind of exactnes both in regard of our selues & others.—
8. — Forbeare clogging our selues & hearts with earthly cares, which is the bayn of Religion
9. To.- Labour to get a great measure of humilitie & meeknes & to bannish pride & hignes of Spirit.—
10. — Meditat the furthering of the Gospell at home & abroad aswell in our persons as with our purses:—
11. — Take nearly to heart our Brethrens condicion & to conforme our selues to these troublesome times. both in our dyett & apparell, that they be without excesse in necessitie.—
12. — Deale with all kind of wisdome & gentlenes towards those that are without.—
13. — Study amitie & brotherly loue.—
14. — Put one another in mind of this Couenant, & as occasion is offred to take an accompt of what is done in the premisses.—
15. — And for the furthering of the Kingdom of Christ: diligently to instruct children & seruants, yea & to look to our wayes and accompts daily.

·x·

This document is endorsed on the back as follows:—"The 15. Articles or Couenant of | Mr. Hu: Peters Minister of the | English Congregation in Rhoter|dam proposed to them befor[e] | their admission to the Communion | 1633." (S. P., Dom., Charles I, Vol. 252 (32).)

3	To	Suffer the word to be the guider of all Controuersies
4	To	Labor for growth of knowledge and to that end to Confer, pray, heare, and meditate:
5	To	Submitte to brotherly admonision and Censure with out enuie or anger
6	To	Be throughly reconciled one to a nother euen in Iudgment be fore wee begin this work
7	To	Walk in all kind of exactnes both in regard of our selues, and others
8	To	For bear Clogging our selues and harts with earthly Cares which is the bayn of religion
9	To	Labor to gett A great meassuer of humillitie and meeknes and to bannish pride and highnes of spirit
10	To	Med[i]tate the furthering of the gosspell at home and A braod[?] as well in our perssons as with our pursses
11	To	Take nearly to hart our bretherens Condition and to Conforme our selues to these troble same tymes both in in [*sic*] dyet and apparrell that thay be with out excesse in nessesitie
12	To	Deall with all kynd of wissdome and genttellnes towards those that are with out
13	To	Studie Amitie and brotherly loue
14	To	Put one and [*sic*] other in mynd of this *Couenant* and as occassion is offered to take an Acompte of what is done in the premisses
15		And for the furthering of the Kingdome of C[h]rist: dilligently to instruckt Chilldren & seruants: yea and to look to our wayes and accomptes dayley:

Finis

It should be noted that the arrival of Puritan ministers in Holland, and especially of 'Jacobites' who required church members to subscribe a covenant before they might partake of the Communion, early produced an effect. At Delft and Rotterdam in 1634, we are told, "many honest gentlemen" hoped to gain admittance to "the sacrament", but hearing of one case where it had been refused on the ground that the person who made the request had not signed the covenant, they "desisted in their suite. & complaine of the difficulty of the way to Heaven here [in Holland as being] more [difficult] then in England or the Gospell"[1].

In the Boswell Papers there are many references to John Paget. Of him, however, we perhaps learn less that is new than

[1] Add. MS. 6394, fol. 179 recto, in the British Museum.

of two other Puritans, Thomas Hooker and John Davenport, of whom he so bitterly complains, but it is almost certain that without his faultfinding we should know much less about these men. Paget was much of a busy-body, and he seems never to have been quite content either with his own affairs, or with those of other people. He was almost always at variance with some of the English clergymen who came over to Holland, and he evidently felt it to be his duty to spur up their hesitating orthodoxy whenever it was possible[1]. Thus apparently in 1633 after Hugh Peters had left Delft, and Thomas Hooker had taken his place as the assistant of Mr Forbes in the congregation of English Merchants, Paget propounded " 20 Proposicions to Mr Hooker " which the latter answered. As the first three of these have to do with the Brownists, they may be cited here. It will be noticed that Hooker had never before studied out a complete answer to the first point, but in all his replies he shows himself to have been a somewhat broad-minded, though also loyal, Puritan son of the Church. Hooker, it will be remembered, like Hugh Peters and John Davenport afterwards found his way to New England. The following are the three above-mentioned questions which Hooker was asked to answer[2]:—

Quest: 1 Whither it be lawfull for any to resort vnto the Publique Meetings of the Brownists, and to Communicate with them in the WORD of God. // Negatur
Answ: To separate from the faithfull Assemblies, and Churches in

---

[1] Even Paget, though not a Congregational Puritan, seems to have believed in the employment of simple covenants against evil, but of course not in the use of covenants of separation from the Church of England. Henry Ainsworth had no respect for such covenants, as appears in a letter of his published by Paget in his "Arrovv *Against the Separation*, Amsterdam, 1618, p. 121, where Ainsworth probably gives the text of the covenant employed in Paget's own church: "*As for your covenant which you mention, to separate from knowen evils, and to serve the Lord in the Gospel of his Son, so far as is revealed vnto you: they are but generals, such as Arians, Anabaptists Paptists, (and who not that professe Christ?) will make also:...*" Paget says elsewhere ("An Answer *To the unjust complaints* of William Best", Amsterdam, 1635, p. 145), that the Dutch Reformed churches also employed covenants such as was used in his church.

[2] Add. MS. 6394, fol. 67 recto and verso, in the British Museum.

England, as noe Churches is an error in Iudgment, and sinne in practize, held and mayntained by the Brownists, & therefore to Comunicate with them, either in this their opinion or practize, is sinnefull & vtterly vnlawfull, but for a Christian both their opinion, & practize, to heare occasionally amongst them, & so to Comunicate with them in that part of Gods worde (which I conceaue to be the meaning of the first Quære) is not so farre, as I yet see simply vnlawfull, but may prove occasionally offensiue, if either by goeing, wee should encourage them to goe on, in their Course of seperation, or els by our vnwise expressions, might serue to weaken ours, to like of it our selves, and so to drawe them to a farther approbation of that way, then was before meet, wherevpon it followes, if wee giue these occasions of offence, wee sinne if wee do not obstaine [*sic*], but if these occasions of offence may be remoued, by our Constant renouncing of their Course of [on] the one side, and by our free and open profession of our intents, on the other side. That wee goe only to heare some sauorie point opened, and to benefitt by the guifts of some able Minister, that may come amongst them, if I say the giving of any Iust offence by these, or any other meanes, may be avoided, I conceive then it is not a sinne to heare them occasionally, and that some men may prevent such occasions, it is to mee, it is to me [*sic*] a very disputable question not hauing euer studied this point before. /

Quærs [?] 2 Whether those Members of the Church [of England] which somtymes heare them, & stifly maintaine a Libertie therein are to be tollerated or rather censured. // censured

Respo: For the practise of members according to the former Caution & interpretation, being taken vp & mayntayned though stiffly, which Argumente, because it is but questionable and disputable before they be fully convicted of their sinne, they ought to be tollerated rather then censured: And this moderacion in things which are disputable, and not absolutely necessary to salvation....

Qu: 3 Whether such of the Brownists as haue not renounced their Seperation from the Church of England, Nor yett allow Comunion with the Puplique [*sic*] estate thereof may lawfully be receiued for members of our Church // Negatur.

Resp: The not renouncing seperacion from the faithfull assemblies in England and the not allowance of Comunion with the Publique state of the Church of England This meer opinion can in no wise make a man vnfitt to be receaved a member of this Congregation, vnlesse wee will say that such a man (being in his iudgment & life otherwise altogether vnblameable) in Iudicious Charitie is not a visible Christian, which is a more riged Censure then the wisest of the seperation would giue waie vnto, in a proportionable kinde, and I suppose a pious hart dare affirme,...

We now come to the experiences of John Davenport. In the first place, it should be said that the so-called Jessey Records throw a good deal of light on the beginnings of his Nonconformity. From these Memoranda it appears that during the year 1632, while John Lathrop's Independent Puritan congregation was suffering much from persecution, Davenport preached a sermon in condemnation of Independency. Some notes of what he had said were brought to Lathrop's people who were challenged for an answer. The challenge was accepted, but in order that any misconceptions might be avoided, a letter was sent to Davenport expressing the hope that he would send his own notes of his sermon for their perusal. This, we are told, he "loveingly" did. Lathrop's congregation accordingly studied what Davenport had written, and wrote thereto an extended answer, with the effect that he never again went to Communion in the Church of England, "but went away when the Sacrament day came, and afterward preached, publickly & privately for the truth, & soon afterward went to Holland, where he suffered somewhat for the truths sake,..."

Parts of three or four letters in the Boswell Papers relating to Davenport are given in the volume of documents. From these letters we may learn much concerning the Continental life of this man who later became so prominent in New England. It appears that Davenport came to Holland early in 1633/34 in order to escape persecution, and hoped to return to England after an absence of three or four months. He was now invited to become co-pastor with John Paget in the English congregation at Amsterdam, but unfortunately his views and Paget's were not entirely in harmony. The subject in regard to which they were chiefly at variance was the administration of baptism. It seems that Davenport objected to baptizing infants " vnles he approve [approved] the parents faith, and life ", while Paget would have him baptize any infant brought to him that had not already been baptized. The situation was made the more difficult because, according to the Dutch custom, both of the ministers in such a congregation, were supposed to be of equal authority, and were expected to join in baptizing every child, the " one reading the forme & explicacion of it. and the other

sprinkling the water with those words In the name &c."
Without a willingness for such co-operation, therefore, Paget
and Davenport could not be suitable colleagues "in that
pastorall charge". Davenport and his friends liked this arrangement so little, that they persuaded two of the Dutch ministers
to represent their point of view to Paget. He, however, could
not be prevailed upon to accept their standpoint, and thought
"that a more sollemne meeting should be had, & Damport
perswaded to a better sense, or else no admission." "Wherefore
shortly after", it is reported, "5 of the Dutch ministers came
vnto m^r Pagetts house, and there expected m^r Damport who
could not be brought to come vnto them." However, they held
a consultation, drew up a list of five conditions to which they
would require both Mr Paget and Mr Davenport to agree,
subscribed it with their five names, and sent the paper to
Davenport. He adroitly gave them to understand that he
was satisfied with the articles and accordingly preached before
Mr Paget, but at the close, on being requested formally to
accept the conditions which had been imposed upon him,
including those relating to the administration of baptism, he
drew back, and for some time no Dutch minister was able to
speak with him. After this event Davenport apparently went
to the Hague to consult the English Ambassador about his
difficulties. Two of the Elders of the church now suggested
that the Classis should allow Davenport to become Paget's
"Assistant in preaching", but should not urge him further to
become his co-pastor. They would recommend this course
because of "the excellency of his guifts, & his *discreet & peaceable*
carriage." Some members of the Dutch Classis, however, were
evidently becoming suspicious of Davenport's orthodoxy in other
respects. They said that Paget required a colleague, not merely
an assistant lecturer or preacher, and it was accordingly decided
that a deputation should be sent to Davenport to show their
disapproval of his refusal to accept their conditions concerning
the administration of baptism.

In a letter of Griffin Higgs to Sir William Boswell, dated
April 9 (Old Style), 1634, it is stated that Davenport was still
a [non-separatist] Nonconformist with regard to both the Dutch

and the English churches in Holland. The Dutch ministers had already silenced him, and unless he should conform before May 1, the church would reject him. The remark is also made, that the Dutch ministers disliked the English Nonconformists [Puritans], "and would more Easilie entertaine Conformable men of Learning, and good life, and moderation." Further, it was already being rumoured at Amsterdam, that thereafter financial support would not be given [by the city authorities] to any English clergyman who came thither contrary to "the King of Englands pleasure".

Unfavourable reports of Davenport's troubles in Amsterdam had apparently reached England before March 18, 1634, and had exasperated the "ArchBishop of Canterbury to reproachfull inuectiues, and bitter mena[ces?] against me [Davenport] in the [Court of] High Commission, whereby my [his] returne [to England] is [was] made much more difficult, and hazardous then I [he] could suspect". This sentence occurs in a letter of Davenport's to Boswell written on the above date, in which he shows that he did not maintain the views of Familists, Anabaptists, or Brownists, but was an opponent of them all, and that he would not have left England if he "could haue bene secure of a safe and quiett abode in my [his] deare natiue country". He says he is still a loyal subject of the king, and if his enemies continue to slander him, he feels it to be his duty to publish an "Apollogy" to the world, so that it may be generally known why he has changed his views and practice. "But", he adds, "it is not my purpose so to doe, vnles the continuance of iniurious aspersions make it necessary, in which case the law of God and of nature bindeth men to such a Vindicacion of theyre innocency as the Case requireth."

In spite of the opposition of Paget, and even without the consent of the Dutch Classis, the Elders of the English Puritan church at Amsterdam seem to have chosen Davenport to be assistant pastor of the congregation. Davenport was willing to recognize such a congregational election, and Paget says he had soon "gathered unto himself a great and solemne assembly apart, by preaching unto them at set times in a private house, without allowance of the Church "[1], which, of course, was also without the permission of the Dutch Classis. Davenport himself modestly describes these meetings as "*a Catechising the family where he lived, every Lords-day after the Sermons were ended at 5 a clock at night, where many receaved much edification*". Paget asks with some feeling if such a description of these catechisings is not a mockery, "when as the members of 30 or 40 families or more have bene reckoned to assemble together in that place ?..."

However, these meetings cannot have been held long. Paget did not like the way in which the church had supported Davenport contrary to his wishes, and accordingly seems to have complained to the Classis, with the result that the private meetings were stopped. This effectual boycotting of Davenport, and particularly the publication in 1634 of an anonymous pamphlet relating to him, which was written by William Best, and entitled, "A ivst Complaint against an univst Doer. Wherein Is declared the miserable slaverie & bondage that the English Church of Amsterdam is now in, by reason of the Tirannicall government and corrupt doctrine, of Mr. Iohn Pagett...", seem to have emboldened him to publish a defence of his cause in a book bearing the title, "A Protestation", etc., 1634. In 1635 Paget made reply to both these works in a book entitled, "*An* Answer *To the unjust complaints* of William Best,...*Also an Answer to* M^r. Iohn Davenport,...", Amsterdam, and in the following year, 1636, Davenport answered Paget in "An Apologeticall Reply..." With this work the published controversy appears to have ended.

Although it was said of Thomas Hooker and John Davenport, "that they were *such as abhorre all schisme*", the attitude which these early Independent Puritans took towards the separatists was somewhat different from that taken by the representatives of the older Puritanism, such as Thomas Cartwright, and later, John Paget. Paget says that Hooker, for instance, "maintayned that such of the Brownists, as persisted in their schisme or separation from the Church of England,

---

[1] John Paget's "*An* Answer *To the unjust complaints* of William Best", Amsterdam, 1635, p. 74.

might lawfully be receaved of us for members in our Church [which represented the Church of England in Amsterdam]"; that he continued to consider as members of the Church of England "such as went to heare the Brownists in their schismaticall assembly"; that he "maintyned that private men might preach and expound the Scriptures at set times and places, where the members of sundry families met together, and this without allowance of the Church"; and that he even asserted "that Churches combined together in the Classis, might choose a Minister, either without or against the consent of the Classis under which they stood"[1]. Both Hooker and Davenport appear to have been willing to consult the Classis in specially important, if not in all, matters, an attitude, however, for which Paget expressed his dislike by remarking "that this pretended reverence is [was] no more then that which M^r. *Iacob* & his company did give to Classes and Synods, for counsaile and advice". "Yea", says he, "the Brownists themselves doe seem to give as much"[2]. From these various statements it can readily be seen that the Independent Puritans evidently manifested at least a little more tolerance towards the Barrowists than was shown them by the Presbyterian Puritans,—a tolerance, which must have tended on the whole to the considerable increase of English separatism.

Henry Jacob returned to England in or about 1616, and in that year boldly instituted in London an Independent Puritan congregation. This was the first church organized on English soil to follow in general the principles enunciated several years before by Jacob and Bradshaw. The story of the organization and development of this congregation will be given in the next chapter. The growth of Independent, or Congregational, Puritanism in England at first appears to have been rather slow, but about 1640 it was evidently spreading in various parts of the country. As was not unnatural, these Independent Puritans were often confused with the Brownists or separatists, and were so called, though in reality not separatists. Such Independents,

---

[1] John Paget's "*An* Answer *To the unjust complaints* of William Best", Amsterdam, 1635, p. 74.

[2] *Ibid.*, p. 84.

I believe, were those persons who are referred to under the name of Brownists in a letter of Robert Abbot, Vicar of Cranford, written to Sir Edward Deering, and dated March 15, 1640. The passage to which reference is made, reads as follows[1] :—

These Brownists are not an inconsederable part. They growe in many parts of the kingdom, and in yowr deare cuntrey amongst the rest. And though it was thought that the high courses of some Bishops weare the cause of theire reuolt from vs : yet now they professe that weare Bishops remooued, the common prayer book, and Ceremonies taken away, they would not Ioyne with vs in communion. They stick not onely at our Bishops, seruice, and Ceremonies, but at our church. They would haue euery particular congregation to be independent, and neither to be kept in order (by rules giuen) by king, Bishops, Councels, or Synods. They would haue the votes, about euery matter of Iurisdiction, in cheefe [?], admission of members, and ministers, excommunication, and ab-solution, to be drawne vp from the whole body of the church in communion, both men, and women/. They would haue none enter communion but by solmne Couenant. Not that made in Baptisme, or renewed in the supper of the Lord, but another for reformation after theire owne way : and when they find it not to be so with vs, they keep aloofe, and prize [?] more their conuersion to theire owne opinions (which, mostly, are matters of fact not of faith) then theire conuersion from theire sinn[s ?] of nature and wickednese [?] of life which they receiued from vs [?].

Before 1645 neither separatism nor Independent Puritanism seems to have been really strong in London. Says Robert Baillie in 1645 : " for the...*Brownists*, their number at *London* or *Amsterdam* is but very small"[2]. The Independent Puritans of London he likewise reports "as yet to consist [of] much within One thousand persons; men, women, and all who to this day have put themselves in any known Congregation of that way, being reckoned. But setting aside number, for other respects they are of so eminent a condition, that not any nor all the rest of the Sects are comparable to them"[3].

[1] Stowe MS. 184, fol. 27 recto and verso, in the British Museum.

[2] In "A Disvasive from the Errours Of the Time", London, 1645, p. 17.

[3] *Ibid.*, p. 53.

CHAPTER XIII

THE HISTORY OF HENRY JACOB'S INDEPENDENT PURITAN
CONGREGATION IN LONDON; AND THE STORY OF THE
RISE OF THE ENGLISH PARTICULAR, OR CALVINISTIC,
ANABAPTISTS. WITH A CRITICAL EXAMINATION OF
THE GOULD MANUSCRIPT APPENDED

THE facts to be presented in this chapter must chiefly be
gleaned from the first two sections of the Gould Manuscript
preserved at Regent's Park College, London. These two sections are the so-called Jessey Records (preferably, Memoranda),
and the Kiffin Manuscript, which up to the year 1642 are
given in full in the volume of documents. A critical estimate
of the trustworthiness of the Gould Manuscript as an historical
source will be found appended to this chapter.

While the Jessey Memoranda and the Kiffin Manuscript, as
preserved in the Gould transcript, are undoubtedly to be regarded
as generally trustworthy historical documents, and while it is
certain that they were transcribed with great care from Benjamin
Stinton's now lost "Repository", it should not be thought that
every word in them is exact, or every statement true. The
early memoranda, however, to which Stinton was indebted for
the material he presents in these two first sections, were
evidently the work of persons who were well informed as to
the details of the events about which they wrote, but it is also
probable that they had to rely much on their memory, and that
their work, therefore, contains some, if not a good many, minor
inaccuracies. The mode of expression, also, is so obscure in
places, that it is difficult to ascertain the precise meaning.
In fact, this rambling style undoubtedly accounts for some of
the blunders of the Rev. Daniel Neal, which Thomas Crosby,
the Baptist historian, so much deplored. Some of the statements in Stinton's "Repository" must have seemed to Neal

a veritable labyrinth, and such they remain to-day as transcribed in the Gould Manuscript.

Out of these disordered, and not always exact, Memoranda it is the task of the historian to make a continuous and intelligible narrative. Fortunately, this can be very largely accomplished by a reconstruction of the facts contained in the Gould Manuscript based upon a study of the best available records and books, and a critical comparison of their contents with the account given in the manuscript.

1. *Henry Jacob's Independent Puritan Congregation in London.*

The history of the Independent Puritan congregation organized by Henry Jacob at London in 1616 is very fully given down to the year 1640 in the previously mentioned Jessey Memoranda. From this, and other sources, we learn, or infer, that Jacob returned to London from Holland in or about 1616, after having endured approximately ten years' exile, and having written several works relating to the reformation of the Church of England[1]; and that since 1603, in fact, he had discussed this subject both in England and in the Low Countries with various men including John Robinson, pastor of the Pilgrim Fathers. After his return to London, also, Jacob held many conferences with noted Puritan preachers, as Mr Throgmorton, Walter Travers, Mr Wing, Richard Maunsell, and John Dodd (but it is not reported that Jacob consulted with any separatists), in order to secure their opinions as to the advisability of organizing an Independent Puritan congregation in that city, such as he appears to have ministered to in Middelburg since 1605.

As an outcome of these conferences, which on the whole seem to have been encouraging, the church was "gathered" in 1616 in the following manner:—Henry Jacob, Sabine Staresmore (otherwise spelled Staesmore, Staismore, or Stasmore), Richard Browne, David Prior, Andrew Almey, William Throughton, John Allen, Mr Gibs, Edward Farre, Henry Goodall, and

---

[1] The titles of these books are not very accurately given in the Jessey Memoranda, but the original editions are all to be found in the Bodleian Library.

several others appointed a day of fasting and prayer, on which occasion the matter of the proposed organization of the congregation was chiefly considered. At the end of the day it was decided to institute the church, and those who wished to have a share in the undertaking "joyning togeather joyned both hands each with other Brother and stood in a Ringwise: their intent being declared, H. Jacob and each of the Rest made some confession or Profession of their Faith & Repentance, some were longer some were briefer, Then they Covenanted togeather to walk in all Gods Ways as he had revealed or should make known to them"[1]. This is the best extant text of the covenant of Jacob's church.

Within a few days, notice of the organization of the congregation was given "to the Brethren here of the Antient Church", or the London remnant of the church of Barrowe, Greenwood, and Johnson, which probably was now under the leadership of Mr (Nicholas) Lee. Perhaps Jacob thought that the members of Lee's congregation would join with him, but they did not, and although he maintained his friendly attitude towards the Barrowists, which they may have reciprocated for a time[2], they appear before long to have come to regard Mr "Iakobs people" as "Idolators in their going to the parish assemblies"[3].

After the organization had been effected, and that fact had been announced to the "Antient Church", Jacob "was Chosen & Ordained Pastor", "& many Saints were joyned to them". In the same year "with the advice & consent of the Church, & of some of those Reverend [Puritan] Preachers beforesaid",

[1] The spelling and punctuation of the quotations employed in this chapter have occasionally been somewhat altered when such changes seemed reasonable, or helpful to the understanding.

[2] As has already been seen in the preceding chapter, the Independent Puritans maintained a more lenient attitude towards the separatists than did the older Puritans, and subsequent events would seem to suggest that the London Barrowists may not fully have understood the status of Jacob's church. However, it should also be kept in mind that even Barrowe and Greenwood entertained a respect for the "Reformed" churches, after which, to some extent, the Independent Puritan congregations were modelled.

[3] John Robinson's "A Treatise of the Lawfvlnes of hearing of the Ministers in the church of England", 1634, p. 69.

he published a small work entitled, "*Anno Domini* 1616. | A | CONFESSION | AND PROTESTATION OF THE | *FAITH OF CERTAINE CHRISTIANS* | in England, holding it necessary to observe, & | keepe all Christes true substantiall Ordinances | for his Church visible and Politicall (that is, in-| dued with power of outward spirituall Govern-|ment) under the Gospel; though the same | doe differ from the common or-|der of the Land. | Published for the clearing of the said Christians | from the slaunder of Schisme, and Noveltie, | and also of Separation, & undutifull-|nes to the Magistrate, which their | rash Adversaries doe falsely | cast upon them. | Also an humble Petition to the K. Majestie for | Toleration there-in. | ...", 8°, 72 + 48 unnumbered pages. The last forty-eight pages have a separate title-page called, "A | COLLECTION | OF SUNDRY | matters;... | Anno Domini, MDCXVI." The Jessey Memoranda say that a portion of this last part was "made by Mr. Wring [? Wing[1]] the [Puritan] Preacher."

As was natural, Jacob's ideas seem to have changed some-what between the years 1604 and 1616. For instance, about 1605 he speaks of suitable church officers as being " A Pastor or Bishop, with Elders, & Deacons ". In a later undated work by him entitled, "A plaine and cleere Exposition of the 2^d. Commandement" a change is noticeable. The copy in the Bodleian Library lacks a special title-page, though it probably once had one. The work is mentioned in the Jessey Memoranda as having been published in 1610, which is apparently not far from the correct date. In this publication Jacob makes two statements that should be cited here :—

But alvvaies novv the ordinary Ministeries viz. *Pastors, Teachers, Elders,* and *Deacons* to particular Congregations, are to remaine both as only lavvfull, necessary, and sufficient for vs "[2].

Fourthly all religious Signes & Ceremonies in Scripture like-vvise commended vnto vs, are in this *Affirmative*; As *Baptisme,* and the *Lords Table,* vvith all theire proper appurtenances : as in Baptisme, *Dipping*[3];...Sitting in the eating and drinking togeather

---

[1] As suggested in the "Transactions of the Baptist Historical Society" for January, 1910, p. 212, note.

[2] Sig. E$_6$ recto and verso.

[3] In this statement Jacob follows the practice advocated as preferable

at the holy table.   Also *imposition of hands* (vvhere it is meete) by
the deputy or deputies of the Church &c[1].

In these last two citations Jacob advocates such officers for
a church as any Puritan of the older type, or a Barrowist, would
have recommended.   Later in 1616 he appears to have returned to his earlier and simpler views with regard to church
officers.   The following passages in Jacob's previously mentioned
work published in 1616 will repay examination :—

14.   Wee believe each Church ought to have one Pastor at
least : and that they may have moe then one, if the number of the
Church, and their meanes be fitt for it, and such plenty of choice
may be had.   Howbeit we judge that it is best, and most agreable
to the last Apostlelike practise, that even where many are, yet that
one have (during life) a precedencie and prioritie in order and place
(not in power) before the rest.   *Revel. 2. 1. &c.*   Touching their
power and authority in Church government, we believe (whether
they be in each Church single, or moe then one) they have all that
they have, and nothing more, then what the Congregation doth
commit unto them, and which they may (when need requireth)
againe take away from them ;...we judge each proper Pastor may
and ought to be trusted by the Congregation with the managing of
all points of their Ecclesiasticall affaires and government so farr,
that he with his assistants (when he hath any) doe execute and
administer the same : yet so, that in matters of waight the whole
Congregation doe first understand thereof before any thing be
finished, and the finall act be done in the presence of the whole
Congregation, and also that they (the sayd Congregation) doe not
manifestly dissent therefrom[2].

23.   Concerning making of mariage, and burying the dead, we
believe that they are no actions of a Church Minister (because they
are no actions spirituall) but civill.   Neither are Ministers called
to any such busines : Neither is there so much as one example of
any such practise in the whole book of God...[3]

Wherefore we humbly pray every upright-harted servant of God
to consider, that it is not possible for us (knowing that which we
know) to give this fore-rehearsed due obedience unto Christ, but by
walking in this way, which wee doe.   Which also cannot be but
first by eschewing the evill, and then by doing the good.   That

in the Book of Common Prayer, but sprinkling was about this time
becoming universal in England.

[1] Sig. E₆ verso.

[2] *"Anno Domini* 1616.   A Confession and Protestation...", sig. B₇
recto and verso.

[3] *Ibid.*, sig. C₅ recto.

is; first by renouncing to be ordinary and constant members of
any Diocesan, or Provinciall Church visible politicall. (Because the
forme of these is wholly without Gods word in the Gospell, yea
contrary to it.) And then also of the Parishes (as naturall parts)
depending on them, and on their Lord Bishops;...Wherefore thus
farr forth onely wee[?] leave our sayd parishes also: but no further.
That is, to be in them no ordinary and constant members; but
members in them occasionally we refuse not to be, seing in them we
finde (in many places) very many true visible christians, with whom
we cannot (as we believe) deny publike communion absolutely, and
therefore on occasion we offer to communicate with our sayd publike
congregations (or parishes)...[1]

Jacob may have readopted the above sensible view of the
number of church officers required by a congregation after
meditation on the criticism of such men as Matthew Sutcliffe,
who as early as 1590 aptly remarked concerning the Puritan
preachers: "can they all of them declare, how beside two
pastors and one doctor, a fraternitie of elders and deacons
may be mainteined in euery parish?"[2]   It was probably the
difficulty of properly supporting more than one principal church
officer that in time led to the abolition of Doctors or Teachers
among the Congregational Puritan churches both in England
and in America.

When Jacob's congregation was organized at London in
1616, it will be remembered that one of those whose advice
was sought concerning its organization, was a Puritan preacher
named Richard Mansell, or Maunsell. He appears to have been
in favour of the church when it was instituted, but in 1619 we
find that he had become Jacob's most dangerous opponent, and
in that year Sabine Staresmore, one of the leaders in the
organization of the congregation, published against Maunsell
a work, already mentioned in another chapter, entitled,
"THE | VNLAWFVLNES | OF READING IN | PRAYER. |
OR, | THE ANSWER OF Mr. RI-|CHARD MAVNSEL
PREACHER, | ... ", 1619, 8°, pp. viii, 48.

From this we learn that Jacob's church accounted the
Barrowists as "brethren in the common faith", and gave "the

---

[1] "*Anno Domini* 1616. A Confession and Protestation...", sig. D₅
recto and verso.

[2] In his "A Treatise of Ecclesiasticall Discipline :...", London, 1590,
p. 103.

members of their Churches" communion[1]; that formerly
Maunsell had strongly recommended John Robinson's congregation at Leyden to some who were fleeing to Holland, but
that later he quite changed his attitude. With the lapse of
time Maunsell had evidently become much opposed to the
"matter of prophesie", and, says Staresmore, had "taken
occasion to disgrace not onely all our brethren, but also our
teacher himselfe, whereby his ministery to some is made unprofitable, and divers of the brethren are of late so shaken by
you [Maunsell], that I feare their sincerities, and some have
also turned back upon us, yea head against us: which damage
I know not how you [he] can possibly recompence. You were
[He was] once a help to the building of Gods house, but now
behold your [his] endevours are to pull down and destroy; so
that of a loving friend you are [he is] become the most
dangerous and bitter opposite this poore Church hath met
with: for had you [he] been an enemy, we could have hid
our selves from you [him]: but since you were [he was] our
familiar friend, of whom we took counsell for our guidance to
the house of God, your [his] retirings are the more dangerous,
and your [his] speeches against us the more pernitious; especially
to unstable men that are not grounded in the truth, which are
ready to be caried away with every wind of doctrine, by the
deceits of men,...."[2]

The second source used in the compilation of the Jessey
Memoranda, which begins with the year 1622 and ends with the
year 1639, is particularly aggravating, because it contains important details which are so lacking in clearness as to be almost
unintelligible. Thus in 1620 Jacob's church appears to have
had additions of several persons who came from Colchester, in
spite of the fact that "an old Church of the Separation was
there", meaning probably that of John Wilkinson. Those
who left Colchester were probably not real separatists, but only
Independent Puritans, and that may explain why they were not
satisfied to remain there. Their names, so far as they have

---

[1] This report, of course, comes from Jacob's, not from the Barrowist,
side. See, however, p. 314 above, text and note 2.

[2] P. 47.

come down to us, were Joshua Warren, Henry January, St[ephen?] Puckle, Manasses Kenton, Lemuel Tuke, and others. These later by consent of Jacob's church became a separate, and possibly a separatist, congregation. Tuke went with them, but perhaps becoming dissatisfied with any tendencies towards separatism, left them, and about 1640 is said to have been a [Puritan] preacher at Dry.

"About eight Years", runs the record, "H. Jacob was Pastor of the said Church [in London, during which time "much trouble attended that State & People, within & without"] & when upon his importunity to go to Virginia, to which he had been engaged before by their consent, he was remitted from his said office, & dismissed the Congregation [in "1624"] to go thither, wherein after [blank] Years he ended his Dayes". There has been a persistent tradition that Jacob went to Virginia. Anthony à Wood knew of it, and in his "Athenae Oxonienses" mentions Jacob's journeying thither. The writer of the article on Jacob in the "Dictionary of National Biography" has repeated Wood's assertion, and closes with these notable words :—

In order to disseminate his views among the colonists of Virginia, he removed thither with some of his children in October 1622, and formed a settlement, which was named after him 'Jacobopolis'. He died in April or May 1624 in the parish of St Andrew Hubbard, London.

It will thus be seen that the Jessey Memoranda and Wood concur in the statement that Jacob went to Virginia, but further particulars on which we can rely concerning the latter part of his life, are almost entirely wanting. After some critical study of the subject it seems to me probable that this journey took place in 1622, but that Jacob died in Virginia in April or May, 1624. It should be added here that the part of the Jessey Memoranda which relates to this matter appears to have been written about 1641 or later, and that Jessey probably never knew Jacob and evidently had to rely entirely on tradition for the information he gives about him. In any good tradition, however, there is almost certain to be a kernel of truth, and I believe there is in this. But what is to be said of the settlement which Jacob is definitely stated to have founded called "Jacobopolis" in Virginia, or city of the faithful? Perhaps some one will suggest that it was actually established but dwindled away after Jacob's death. Before deciding the point, however, let us first examine this name "Jacobopolis". Is it not manifestly a compound of *Jacobus* = James and *polis* = city, in popular language Jamestown, a city founded in Virginia in 1607, and which in 1907 was celebrating its Tercentenary? This is certainly a blunder on the pages of the "Dictionary of National Biography" which ought to be remedied. But is it a fact that Jamestown was ever known as Jacobopolis? In answer we turn to Michael Antonius Baudrand's enlarged edition of Philippus Ferrarius' "Lexicon Geographicvm", published at Paris in 1670, in which the following entry occurs:—"[*Iacobi-polis*, Iamestowne, *urbs Americæ septentrionalis, in Virginia, ab Anglis excitata, & sic dicta à Iacobo Rege magnæ Britanniæ, juxta fluvium Pouvatanium, aliquot milliaribus à mari remota.*]"[1] We may, therefore, certainly conclude that Henry Jacob did not found a "Jacobopolis" in Virginia, and that if he ever lived in a locality of that name, it was probably historic Jamestown!

After Jacob's departure the congregation managed as best it could without a pastor until about 1624, when John Lathrop[2], who had formerly been a Puritan preacher at Cheriton[3] in Kent, and who evidently was still an Independent Puritan, joined the church. He was chosen pastor in 1625, and is said to have been "a Man of a tender heart and a humble and meek Spirit". In 1630 it was urged upon Lathrop's congregation to separate from the Church of England. Up to this time it seems probable that both Independent Puritans and separatists had mingled in peaceful union in this church, but the matter of separation was now specially forced upon their attention

---

[1] P. 365. A similar view has been independently expressed by Dr W. T. Whitley ("Transactions of the Baptist Historical Society" for January, 1910, pp. 212–13, notes 9 and 10).

[2] In Rawl. MS. A. 128, in the Bodleian Library, which consists partly of reports of cases tried in the Court of High Commission, it is hinted under the date, May 3, 1632, that Lathrop had been "Doctor King the Bishop of Londons Sizer in Oxford"!

[3] Henry Jacob is also said to have been settled at Cheriton some time before 1603,—a point worth noticing.

owing to the fact that some one associated with the congregation, possibly Sabine Staresmore, had had his child baptized in a parish church during that year. About this time separatism was gaining ground in London, and John Canne, who had been pastor of Mr Hubbard's church, and was about to sail to Holland, sought to persuade Lathrop's congregation also to become separatist, and in renewing their covenant to renounce the Church of England. Samuel Howe, who had been one of Lathrop's followers, but who had now taken Canne's place as pastor of his separatist church in London, as well as Canne, would then have communion with them. Mr Dupper especially approved of this separatist attitude, and requested the congregation " to Detest & Protest against the Parish Churches ", but the church as a whole declined to be tied by covenant to declare that the parish churches either were, or were not, true churches, for they said they did not know " what in time to come God might further manifest to them thereabout[.] Yet for peace sake all Yelded to renew their Covenant in these Words

"To walke togeather in all the Ways of God so farr as he hath made known to Us, or shall make known to us, & to forsake all false Ways, & to this the several Members subscribed their hands".

It was apparently after this decision in 1630 that Mr Dupper and Thomas Dyer joined with Daniel Chidley the elder, and some others in organizing a separatist congregation. Still others united with them, as Mr Boy, Mr Stanmore [? could this be Staismore], Benjamin Wilkins, Hugh Vesse, John Flower, Brother and Mrs Morton [? a son of John Murton, and his wife], and John Jerrow.

On Sunday, April 29, 1632, Tomlinson, the Pursuivant of the Bishop of London, captured about forty-two of the church members in the house of Humphrey Barnet, a brewer's clerk in " Black Fryers"[1]. Barnet was not then a member of the con-

[1] Rawlinson MS. A. 128 in the Bodleian Library gives extensive reports relating to the appearance of members of Lathrop's congregation, taken captive on April 29, 1632, before the Court of High Commission on May 3, 8, and June 7, etc., in that year. These reports may be seen in full in

gregation and was out of the house at the time, while eighteen members either escaped or were not present. "Some were not committed, as Mrs. Barnet, Mr. Lathrop, W. Parker, Mrs. Allen &c. Several were committed to the Bishops Prison called then the New Prison (in —— Crow a merchants house again) & thence some to the Clink, some to the Gate House, & some that thought to have escaped he joyned to them, being in Prison togeather viz"

John Lathrop [Lathorp]

Samuel Howes [House]

John Woddin [Wodwin]

William Granger

[Sara ?] Barbone

Mr Sergeant

Pennina Howes

John ⎰Melborne ⎱Milburn

Henry Parker

[Mrs Sara ?] Jacob

Joane Ferne, widow

Brother Arnold

Marke Lucar

[Sara ?] Jones

Elizabeth ⎰Milburn ⎱Melborne

Samuel How

[Phillis ?] Wilson

Ralfe Grafton

Henry Dod, deceased a Prisoner

[Abigal Delamar]

S. R. Gardiner's "Reports of Cases in the Courts of Star Chamber and High Commission", Camden Society, 1886, pp. 278–80, 281, 284–86, 292–95, 300–2, 307, 308–10, 315. The names of the prisoners here given are important since they have enabled us, as indicated above in the text, to correct some of the mistakes in the names found in the Jessey Memoranda, as well as to add some names to the list. From the High Commission reports the following names have been collected :—

Thomas Arundell of St Olave's parish.

William Attwood.

Sara Barbon.

Humphrey Barnett, or Bernard.

Abigal Delamar.

Elizabeth Denne.

Henry Dod.

Samuel Eaton.

John Egge.

Joane Ferne.

Ralfe Grafton "an Vpholster dwellinge in Cornehill", London.

William Granger of "St. Margarettes" in Westminster.

Samuel How.

Pennina Howse, or Howes.

John Ireland of "Mary Maudlins Church", Surrey.

Sara Jacob [undoubtedly Henry Jacob's widow].

Sara Jones of Lambeth.

John Latroppe their minister.

Marke Lucar of no parish.

Elizabeth Melborne.

Mabell Milborne.

Henry Packer [Parker].

William Pickering.

Robert Reignoldes of Thistleworth.

Elizabeth Sargeant.

Toby Talbot.

Susan Wilson.

John Woodwyne.

On Sunday, May 12 of the same year, twenty-six members were captured and committed to prison, and on May 26, just a fortnight after, the "Antient Church" of Barrowe, Greenwood, Johnson, and Lee was surprised, and two of its members were committed as their fellow-prisoners. Thus for about two years they gained "experience", some being only under bail, some "in Hold".

The prison experiences of Lathrop's followers during these two years are summarized as follows :—

1. In that time the Lord opened their mouths so to speak at the [Court of] High Commission & Pauls & in private even the weake Women as their Subtill & malicious Adversarys were not able to resist but were ashamed.

2. In this Space the Lord gave them so great faviour in the Eyes of their Keepers that they suffered any friends to come to them and they edifyed & comforted one another on the Lords Days, breaking bread &c.

3. By their Holy & Gratious carriage in their Sufferings, he so convinced others that they obtained much more faviour in the Eyes of all Such generally as feared God then formerly, so that many were very kind & helpfull to them, contributing to their Necessities, some weekly sending Meat &c. to them.

4. Their Keepers found [them] so sure in their promises that they had freedom to go home, or about their Trades, or buisness whensoever they desired, & [the keepers having?] set their time, & [they having?] sayd they would then returne, it was enough without the charges of one to attend them.

5. In this very time of their restraint the Word was so farr from [being] bound [i.e., kept from the people], & the Saints so farr from being scared from the Ways of God that even then many were in Prison added to the Church, viz.

John Ravenscroft	William [blank]
Widdow Harvey	Thomas⎫ Harris
Mary Atkin	Jane ⎭
Thomas Wilson	Widdow White.
Sara........	Ailce [Alice]⎫
Humphrey Bernard	Elizabeth ⎬Wincop.
[Barnet]	Rebecca ⎭
G. Wiffield	

6. Not one of those that were taken did recant or turne back from the truth through fear or through flattery or cunning slights, but all were the more strengthened thereby.

21—2

It will be seen by comparing these impressions of Lathrop's company with the reports of the Court of High Commission given in Rawlinson MS. A. 128 in the Bodleian Library[1], that the Jessey Memoranda give on the whole a very fair representation of the experiences of the prisoners, although the Commissioners certainly made some fun of them.

During this period of imprisonment Mrs Sara Jones and others spent some time in writing. The following manuscripts were produced by them, and about the time of the Commonwealth were probably still extant[2]:—

1. "The Answers of M$_{\frac{rs}{7}}$ [Sara] Jones & Some others" before the Court of High Commission.

2. Their Petitions to the king.

3. Mrs Jones' "Grievances", the manuscript of which was given into the hands of the Commissioners and read before them.

4. Mrs Jones' "Cronicle of Gods remarkable Judgments & dealings that Year [1632] &c   wonderfull are the Lords works its meet he should have all ye Praise."

In 1632, also, many of Lathrop's followers were manifestly not separatists, as appears in the examination of Samuel Eaton before the Court of High Commission on May 3, 1632. The report reads[3]:—

Samuell Eaton and two women & a maid appeared, who were demaunded why they were assembled in that Conventicle when others were at church? Eaton. we were not assembled in contempt of the Magistrate. London. Noe? it was in contempt of the church of England. Eaton. it was in conscience to God (may it please this honorable Court) and we were kept from Church, for we were confyned in the house together by those that besett the house, els divers would haue gone to Church and manie came in after the sermons were done.

During 1633, while a number of Lathrop's church were in prison, the membership had evidently increased so much as to be a real disadvantage to the welfare of the congregation. On

---

[1] These reports were published by S. R. Gardiner for the Camden Society in 1886, as previously stated in a note.

[2] I here follow the emendation of Dr Whitley ("Transactions of the Baptist Historical Society" for January, 1910, p. 217, note 16).

[3] Rawl. MS. A. 128, under the date May 3, 1632.

September 12 of this year, accordingly, after certain members had expressed dissatisfaction with the non-separatist position of the church, permission was granted to them to form a separatist congregation of their own, of which we shall hear more later.

Those of Lathrop's company who had been imprisoned, with the exception of Lathrop and Grafton, were all released upon bail after two years' confinement. These two, however, were to be kept indefinitely in prison. Consequently after the death of his wife, seeing that he could accomplish nothing by spending his life as a prisoner, Lathrop petitioned that he might be relieved of the responsibilities of his office as pastor of the congregation. This request was granted, and about June, 1634, he was released from prison to go to New England. He was accompanied by about thirty members, among whom were,—Samuel Howse; John Wodwin; Goodwives Woodwin, elder and younger; Widow Norton; and afterwards Robert Linel and wife, Mr and Mrs Laberton, Mrs Hammond, and Mrs Swinerton. During the years 1636–1637 after Lathrop's departure the remnant of the congregation were somewhat troubled by persecution, but on the whole they seem to have lived in comparative peace, and in the summer of 1637[1] Henry Jessey became pastor in Lathrop's place. In 1638 some others forsook the church, of whom we shall hear again later.

Still further changes were in store for Jessey's followers, as is made plain in the following statement[2]:—

This Congregation being at this time grown so numerous that they could not well meet together in any one place, without being discovered by the *Nimrods* of the Earth; after many consultations among themselves, and advice taken with others, but especially asking councel from above; Upon the 18*th* day of the third Month called *May*, 1640. they divided themselves equally, and became two Congregations, the one whereof continued with Mr. *Iessey*, the other joyned themselves to Mr. *Praise God Barebone*. each of the Churches renewing their *Covenant* and choosing distinct *Officers* of their own from among themselves;...

---

[1] "The Life and Death of Mr. *Henry Iessey*", 1671, p. 9.
[2] *Ibid.*, pp. 10–11.

With this citation we may leave Jessey's congregation[1], though it should be added, that he and his followers continued to be persecuted during the years 1638–1641, in spite of the fact that up to the end of this period Jessey does not appear to have been a separatist, but an Independent Puritan.

2. *The Rise of the English Particular Anabaptists.*

We may now turn to the rise of the English Particular Anabaptists, who first appear in a separatist church which broke away from Lathrop's congregation in 1633. While some facts relating to the evolution of the Particular Anabaptists are given in the Jessey Memoranda as well as in the Kiffin Manuscript, the latter seems to have been specially written to trace the development of the earliest English Particular Anabaptist congregations, and on that account is of more value for our purposes here.

Among those dismissed by Lathrop's church on Sept. 12, 1633, whose names have come down to our time, were,— Mr and Mrs Henry Parker, Thomas Shepard, Samuel Eaton, Marke Lucar or Luker, Mr Wilson, Joane Ferne, widow, Mary or Mabel Milburn or Milborne, John Milburn, one Arnold, Thomas Allen, one Hatmaker, and probably two or three others. "To these" in the same year "Ioyned Richard Blunt, Thomas Hubert, Richard Tredwell & his Wife Katherine, Iohn Trimber, William Iennings, & Samuel Eaton, Mary Greenway —— Mr. Eaton with some others receiving a further Baptism" evidently administered by sprinkling[2]. Eaton and "some

---

[1] Between 1636 and 1641 the following members among others appear to have been added:—Iohn Trash, Mr Glover, Mr Eldred, R. [? Br.] Smith, Sister Dry, Br. Russell, Br. Cradock, Mrs Lovel, Mrs Chitwood, Br. Golding, Iohn Stoneard, Mr Shambrook, Sister Nowel, Mr Nowel, and Mrs Berry. Mr Brown and Mr Puckle should perhaps be included in this number.

[2] On Jan. 11, 1635/36, one Francis Jones, of Ratcliff, Middlesex, basket-maker, was accused before the Court of High Commission of being accustomed to keep "private conventicles and exercises of religion", and of being an Anabaptist. He admitted that he had been rebaptized. He "was committed to Newgate" ("Calendar of State Papers, Domestic

others", therefore, were "Anabaptists", while the rest of the congregation were not. In other words, this new church was a mixed separatist congregation composed partly of Paedobaptists and partly of Antipaedobaptists. "Others joyned to them", we are told, and about 1638, but certainly not earlier, William Kiffin became a member.

Some time in the spring of 1638 still others in Lathrop's, now Jessey's, church, who had become convinced that baptism should not be administered to infants, but only to professed believers, deserted the congregation and joined with John Spilsbury who seems to have become pastor of Eaton's mixed church. Later, the deserters requested that Jessey should not censure them for their too hasty action, and their wish was granted on June 8, 1638. The following are reported to have been the names of those who made this application,—Mr Peti [? John[1]] Fenner, Henry Pen, Thomas Wilson, William Batty or Battee, Mrs Allen who died in 1639, and Mrs Norwood[2].

Eight women of Spilsbury's church were apparently taken prisoners not long before April 23, 1640, and on that date were brought before the Court of High Commission. Their names were Magdalen Spilsbury (probably the wife of John Spilsbury), Anne Pawle, Grace Dicks, Catherine Tredwell, Mary Evans, Anne Dunkley, Anne Goring, and Anne Gell. Their case was handed over "to the secular power of quarter sessions", as "these were poor women, schismatics, lately taken at a conventicle "[3].

Series, of the Reign of Charles I. 1635-1636 ", London, 1866, p. 468). It would be interesting to know whether Francis Jones was in any way connected with this London congregation of Particular Anabaptists, and also whether he was related to Mrs Sara Jones who was a member of Lathrop's congregation and appeared before the Court of High Commission in 1632.

[1] See the "Transactions of the Baptist Historical Society" for January, 1910, p. 231, note 3.

[2] The Kiffin Manuscript mentions a Mr Pen besides H. Pen, but like the Jessey Memoranda makes the total number of applicants six. Probably Kiffin made a mistake in inserting the name "Pen" twice. A " Mr. Wilson" and Thomas Allen were among the original members of this church in 1633.

[3] "Calendar of State Papers, Domestic Series,...1640", London, 1880, p. 406.

Concerning one of the characters with whom we are now concerned, namely Samuel Eaton, there has been more or less conjecture. For instance, Dr George A. Lofton[1] speaks of Eaton as if he were alive in 1641, and even Dr Dexter, I think, has somewhere queried whether this same Samuel Eaton was not later the pastor of the Congregational Church in Duckinfield. There is a passage in a pamphlet entitled, "The Brownists Conventicle", 1641, which seems to clear up the difficulty. From this work it seems that there had been two Samuel Eatons in England about this time. The first was the separatist who had evidently died before 1641, and the second was the Independent Puritan who was still living. The first is called " Eaton, the famous Button-maker in Saint Martins". The second is spoken of more at length as follows[2]:—

And now of late lest these supermysticall Sectists should be wanting in the Land, there is lately come over from New England, as from a New Hierusalem, one Samuel Eaton a Minister, who preached at Saint Iohns Church in Chester, that the very names of Parsons and Vicars were Antichristian, that Pastours and Teachers of particular Congregations, must be chosen by the people,...

These statements agree well with facts which prove beyond doubt that the separatist Samuel Eaton was not the Independent Puritan of the same name[3]. In the first place, in the Public Record Office is a paper[4] giving a description of the funeral of the separatist Samuel Eaton on Aug. 25, 1639, a copy of which may be found in the volume of documents; and in the second place, there is a passage in the fourth volume of the publications of the Chetham Society, published in 1845[5], which shows that Samuel Eaton of Duckinfield was the son of Mr Richard Eaton, Vicar of Great Budsworth, Cheshire, and that on returning from New England at the beginning of the Civil Wars he gathered a [Congregational Puritan] church at Duckinfield in the Cheshire

---

[1] "English Baptist Reformation", Louisville, Kentucky, 1899, p. 150.

[2] [P. 3.]

[3] Since the above account was written Dr Whitley has independently reached a similar conclusion ("Transactions of the Baptist Historical Society" for January, 1910, p. 221, note).

[4] S. P., Dom., Charles I, Vol. 427 (No. 107).

[5] P. 61 and note.

parish of Stockport. He had much trouble with the Presbyterian Puritans (now usually termed Presbyterians) and died in 1664.

With these facts before us, we may turn to what is known of the Brownist-Anabaptist, Samuel Eaton after 1633. From the Acts of the Court of High Commission he appears to have been taken prisoner again on or before May 5, 1636, on which date he was referred to the Commissioners. He is called a button-maker of St Giles's without Cripplegate, London. In 1638, not 1633 as given by Dr Waddington, he was in Newgate, committed by Archbishop Laud " for a Schismaticall and dangerous Fellowe ". He is reported by Frauncis Tucker, B.D., to have held " diverse Conventicles in the said Gaole ", at which seventy or even more persons had been present with permission of the prison keeper, and often to have affirmed in his sermons that " Baptisme [probably meaning, as administered to infants in the Church of England] was the Doctrine of Devills "[1]. It appears that the prison keeper was so much of a friend to Eaton, that he allowed him sometimes to leave the prison in order to preach at meetings for which he had arranged, and when Mr Tucker expressed surprise that a schismatic should be so handsomely treated, the keeper solemnly told him that he " had a strict Charge from the highe Commission to haue a speciall Care of the said Eaton &c ". Very natural instructions these, to be sure, but what a novel interpretation for a prison keeper in those dangerous times to have given to them!

How long Eaton received such favours we are not told, but he died in prison just before Aug. 31, 1639. We also do not know what caused his death. Probably he was more closely confined after Tucker had complained to the Archbishop. Some one saw Eaton's funeral procession, and out of curiosity followed the body to the grave " in the new Church yard neere Bethelem ". His popularity is attested by the fact that at least two hundred Brownists and Anabaptists are said to have been in the funeral procession. When they reached the churchyard " they like so many Bedlams cast the corpes in ; & with their feet, in stead of spades cast & thrust in the mould till the grave was allmost full : then they paid the grave maker for his paines,

[1] S. P., Dom., Charles I, Vol. 406 (No. 64).

who told them that he must fetch a minister, but they said, he might spare his labour." This is evidently a good illustration of the way in which the separatists were obliged to act under the trying conditions imposed upon them by unsympathetic Church and State officials.

In the Kiffin Manuscript under the date 1640, between the names, "Mr H. Iessey" and "Mr Richard Blunt", there is manifestly a break in the text. This defect may have been caused by an imperfection in the original document, or it may be due to a lack of care taken, or to some mistake made, by Stinton while originally copying his historical sources into the "Repository"[1], or finally to the unintentional omission of a portion of Stinton's copy made during the transcription of the "Repository" into the Gould Manuscript. In 1640, as the Kiffin Manuscript now reads, Henry Jessey and Richard Blunt would appear to have been convinced together of the truth of believers', or adult, baptism by immersion. We know, however, from document No. 4 in the Gould transcript, that Jessey was not so convinced until June, 1645. Hence we must infer that at least some words are missing at this point. Fortunately the most important facts do not seem to be lost.

As nearly as I can judge, the narrative should here continue somewhat in this way.—During 1640 Richard Blunt and certain other members of Spilsbury's, and perhaps a few of Jessey's, church, became convinced that baptism by sprinkling or pouring, whether administered to believers or adults, or to infants, was not the form of baptism employed in the time of the apostles, but that true baptism "ought to be by diping the Body into the Water, resembling Burial & riseing again". "Sober conferance" was accordingly held over this new matter which had been brought to their attention, but Spilsbury, the pastor, was evidently not convinced at this time of the position taken by Blunt. Thereupon, those who favoured the administration of baptism by dipping or immersion conferred among themselves as to what should be done. For one thing, they seem to have determined to separate from Spilsbury and to meet together in two companies. They also appear to have realized the difficulty before

---

[1] This second alternative seems to me the most probable.

them in the fact that immersion had been so long in disuse in England, for to whom should they go for this new baptism by "dipping" which they held to be necessary for their salvation, "none haveing then [in 1640] so so practised[1] in England to professed Believers"[2]?

Hearing, however, that some in the Netherlands, namely the Rynsburgers or Collegiants, practised immersion, they sent over to them "Richard Blunt (who understood Dutch)

[1] As is well known, by 1600 the administration of baptism by dipping or immersion had been practically discontinued in the Church of England. However, in literature mention was occasionally made of dipping as being the proper form of baptism, though it does not seem to have been pressed as the only form until about 1635. Henry Jacob, it is true, in one of his pamphlets, as has already been mentioned, alludes to dipping as the correct form of baptism, but he is, of course, referring to the immersion of infants and not of grown people, nor does he emphasize the point.

It appears from Giles Widdoes' "Schismatical Pvritan", Oxford, 1631 [p. 21], that as early as that date there were some in England who administered baptism "in Wells, in Brookes, in Rivers, &c. to defend, to vphold a factious spirit". These offenders were probably Puritans in the Church of England, and the subjects of baptism in such cases must have been infants, while the form of baptism employed may have been sprinkling or pouring. The fault that was found with those who so administered baptism in 1631, was that they did not baptize in the font, which "is the commanded place for baptisme", not because they administered a second baptism, or employed immersion. These irregular baptisms were evidently administered in a river, well, or brook in the same manner in which they would have been in the font.

In 1635 Daniel Rogers in "A Treatise of the two Sacraments", made a strong plea for the use of baptism by dipping in the Church of England. His view as expressed on pages 70–1 may even have made some impression upon the English Particular Anabaptists, who first began to employ immersion about 1641, while some of the baptismal irregularities which appeared in early New England were probably suggested by this work.

[2] The writer, of course, means that the people with whom he associated had never heard of any English Anabaptists, who had practised immersion before 1640. Perhaps the name of Leonard Busher was quite unknown to him, and though Busher certainly seems to have advocated the immersion of believers in 1614, yet it should be remembered that we have no evidence whatever that he was able to put his views into practice, nor do we know that he had any followers in England or in Holland. As has already been said, he appears to have been in Holland, not in England, when he wrote and published his "Religions Peace".

with Letters of Commendation who was kindly accepted there, & returned with Letters from...Iohn Batte [Batten][1]

[1] In the original record supposed to have been written by Kiffin from which Stinton copied this name into his "Repository", Batte was probably spelled Battĕ, i.e., Batten, but the line over the "e" has been lost in the Gould Manuscript.

A quaint and instructive, but rather extended, "*Account of the Rise and Progress of the Sect of* Rynsburgers, Collegiants, *or* Prophets" is given in Gerard Brandt's "The History of the Reformation...in and about the *Low-Countries*", 1720–23, Vol. IV., pp. 49–59. On page 53 occurs the following illuminating passage, in which "*John Batten of Leyden*" is mentioned as one of the five leading Rynsburgers :—

"They [the Rynsburgers] observed the following method in their Assembly : *First*, somebody among them read several chapters out of the New Testament ; then the Reader, or any other person pray'd ; and after the Prayer, it was asked, according to the Text in 1 Cor. xiv. 26. *Whether any man in the Assembly had any prophecy or spiritual gift for the edification of the people? Or whether any one had any doctrine, consolation, or exhortation, that so he might bring it forth.* Sometimes they made use of the very words of the aforesaid Text of the Apostle. Upon which one or other of the company arose, and read a Text or Sentence out of the Bible, which he had throughly meditated on before hand, and made a kind of Sermon, or Discourse upon it, which lasted sometimes an hour, or longer. This being ended, it was asked again, whether any body else had any thing to offer for the edification of the Assembly? And then up stood another, who read and spoke as before. This man having done, asked the same question as the other had done ; upon which a third man stood up : Nay, *Paschier* says, that he himself had seen four of them preaching, or, as they stiled it, *prophesying* one after another, and that it lasted from the evening till it was full day, the next morning ; and that some sate and slept in the mean while so heartily, that in the morning they knew as little of what had been said as the evening before. He further says, that the Speakers were commonly the same persons, though they invited, and gave every man free leave to prophesy. These Speakers were *Gilbert vander Kodde*, with his Brothers, *John* and *Adrian*, *Antony Cornelison*, and *John Batten* of *Leyden:* And though some others might now and then put in a word, yet the above-mentioned persons, or some of them were always of the number of the monthly *Holders-forth.*"

I have published the whole of Brandt's "Account" of the Rynsburgers with some comments in "The Review and Expositor", Louisville, Kentucky, for October, 1910, pp. 526–47. The article is entitled, "The Collegiants or Rynsburgers of Holland : Through whose Co-operation the Members of the first Immersionist English Anabaptist Congregation in London Procured their Baptism in 1641."

a Teacher there, & from that Church to such as sent him [Blunt]".

This is the story as slightly reconstructed from the Kiffin Manuscript. Is it trustworthy? Most assuredly, but before considering that point, we should notice that this account does not say that Blunt was immersed by John Batten, but only that he was kindly received and returned with letters for his church in London, which we may surmise contained with other information suggestions as to how the administration of immersion should be commenced and conducted by the English Particular Anabaptists[1]. There is, therefore, in this narrative nothing which it is impossible for us to believe, and even the statement that there were no immersionist Anabaptists in England before 1640 would not have seemed remarkable, if it had not been so difficult in certain quarters to believe that Thomas Crosby could have made a mistake!

The Kiffin Manuscript continues the story by pointing out that the immersionist Anabaptists, who had been meeting in two companies by themselves, intended so to meet in the future. On Blunt's return they evidently came together and agreed "to proceed alike togeather" to organize an immersionist church, "And then Manifesting (not by any formal Words a Covenant) which word was scrupled by some of them, but by mutual desires & agreement each Testified". Then, we are told, the two companies appointed "one to Baptize the rest; so it was solemnly performed by them". Next comes the following sentence which does not seem exactly to agree with the preceding statement, but which with it may give a very good idea of certain particulars observed in this first administration of immersion by English Anabaptists :—

Mr Blunt Baptized Mr [? Laur.(ence)[2]] Blacklock that was a Teacher amongst them, & Mr Blunt being [i.e., now having been?] Baptized [by Blacklock?], he & Mr Blacklock Baptized the rest of their friends that were so minded,...

[1] This, in my opinion, was the extent of the Rynsburgers' co-operation with the first congregation of English immersionist Anabaptists.

[2] The Gould transcript reads Sam.(uel) Blacklock and may be correct, but a mistake might easily have been made in copying. Laurence Blacklock appears to be rather better known than Samuel Blacklock.

From these two statements we may draw the following description as perhaps in accord with the intention of the original writer.—Some time in 1641 Richard Blunt was appointed to begin the administration of baptism, since he had been in Holland, and had learned there how immersion was administered among the Rynsburgers, but apparently not on the ground that he had been immersed by them. Their practice of baptizing by dipping or plunging he now faithfully reproduced in England, where it soon received the nickname of "ducking over head and ears". Blunt immersed Blacklock, who was evidently their leader, and Blunt (having afterwards been baptized by Blacklock[1]) together with Blacklock baptized the rest.

Many were now added to the church, or rather to the

[1] The record itself is extremely obscure as to Blunt's baptism, for it does not directly state that he was immersed in Holland, though that might be inferred ; nor can it be maintained with certainty from the text alone that he was not baptized by Blacklock. Accordingly, if we had only this record to fall back upon, we would be left in a hopeless dilemma, but fortunately for other reasons we may definitely conclude, contrary to all that has been written on the subject during the past thirty years, that Blacklock, and not Batten, baptized Blunt.

In the first place, it is quite unthinkable that the Calvinistic, or Particular Baptist, Blunt would accept baptism at the hands of the Arminian Collegiants, any more than John Smyth thirty years earlier would have been baptized by the Mennonites.

In the second place, since it is well known that Blunt did not baptize himself, it is evident from the following important statement that Blacklock immersed Blunt :—

"He [Shem Acher, i.e., Francis Bampfield] has been credibly informed by two yet alive in this City of *London*, who were Members of the first Church of Baptized [i.e., immersed] Believers here, that their first Administrator [of immersion] was one who baptized himself, or else he and another baptized one another, and so gathered a Church ; which was so opposed in Publick and in Private, that they were disputed out of their Church-State and Constitution, out of their Call to Office ; that not being able to justify their Principle and Practice by the Word, they were broken and scattered." ("שם אחר | A NAME, an After-one", London, 1681, p. 16.)

In an article which I have recently prepared, and shortly hope to have published, this whole subject has been much more fully treated than here seems advisable.

two divisions of it, so that its joint membership in January, 1641/42, is said to have been fifty-three. The first section of the congregation seems to have been under the leadership of Blunt, the second under that of Blacklock. This church as a whole became known later as that of Blunt, Emmes, and Wrighter[1], and in the first column of the list of members in January, 1641/42, the signatures of Richard Blunt and Samuel Eames [Emmes] appear. Wrighter evidently joined the congregation at a later date than January 9. The entire list of the names of the fifty-three members may be seen in the volume of documents, and may be consulted as a natural conclusion to this review of the rise of the first church of English immersionist Particular Anabaptists.

[1] Thomas Edwards' "The third Part of Gangræna", London, 1646, p. 112.

APPENDIX TO CHAPTER XIII

A CRITICAL EXAMINATION OF THE GOULD
MANUSCRIPT

This appendix is a corrected and considerably abbreviated text of an article published six years ago in America[1]. It is repeated here because the historical trustworthiness of the preceding chapter largely depends on the truth of the facts herein contained.

The reader is already aware from what has been said in the Introduction to this volume, that a discovery was made in 1880 which leads us to believe that the English Anabaptists began only about 1641 to practise immersion. During the past quarter of a century a very considerable, if not an absolutely exhaustive, body of evidence has been gathered in support of the new view. Since 1896 the Gould Manuscript, prepared for the late Rev. George Gould of Norwich[2] in connection with the "St. Mary's Norwich Chapel Case" of 1860, has been located and carefully examined, and the literature of the period before and after 1641, also, has been critically explored. In a word, before 1900, about everything possible had been done to establish the

---

[1] In "The Baptist Review and Expositor", Louisville, Kentucky, for October, 1905, pp. 445–71.

[2] In this connection a few words concerning the Rev. George Gould may be of interest. Mr Gould was not a university graduate, but the "Introduction" to his book, "Open Communion and the Baptists of Norwich", shows him to have been a man of unusual scholarly ability and critical insight, qualities nowhere manifested more conspicuously than in the transcription of the manuscript known by his name, since this volume has preserved for the Baptist denomination certain very important documents which otherwise might have been almost totally lost.

general truth of the new theory with the exception of determining a few points, one of which concerning Blunt's immersion has been briefly treated at the close of the preceding chapter, and another of which up to 1900 had apparently been beyond the range of definite and final solution, namely, Who was the original compiler of the material contained in the Gould transcript ? In an attempt to settle this second point and certain others relating to it the author gathered the facts presented in the following pages.

In the summer of 1901 the writer obtained his first opportunity of examining the Gould Manuscript, now in the possession of the Rev. George P. Gould, M.A., Principal of Regent's Park College, London, and a son of the late Rev. George Gould of Norwich. In the autumn of 1902 a second thorough examination was granted, as well as the opportunity to inspect certain original manuscripts, which had been in the possession of the Rev. George Gould, and carefully preserved by Principal Gould, but which had apparently not been used in recent times.

Though frequent reference of late has been made to the Gould Manuscript, and its contents, the following description of it may be given. It is a good-sized folio of somewhat over four hundred pages, half-bound, and contains transcripts of a considerable number of documents pertaining to the history of the early English Baptists. The manuscript begins with thirty numbered sections covering one hundred and thirty-eight pages, which are followed by eighteen pages of unnumbered documents, then by a long section of forty-four pages which contains several subdivisions and bears the general title, " Records of the Barkshire Association", and finally by a short note concerning William Turner's "A preseruatiue" [1551]. The work of transcription, with the exception of about a page and a half copied by Mr Gould himself, was entirely done by the elderly Mr William Keymer, a Master in Grey Friars' Priory School, Norwich, who wrote a very beautiful hand, and whom Mr Gould could trust to make a scrupulously accurate copy. The volume, therefore, makes an excellent impression in general, but strange to say, it does not bear the name of the original compiler, and this fact has been used to disparage its historical value.

Indeed, at first sight, the absence of the compiler's name

seems to be a serious defect, but ultimately proves to be none at all; for the manuscript from which it was transcribed was evidently itself anonymous. In spite of this fact, however, in the new light which during 1902–5 was brought to bear on the material contained in the Gould volume, the author finally succeeded not only in determining beyond all doubt the original compiler of the first thirty and most important documents contained in the Gould manuscript, but also in elucidating various other problems that had arisen concerning it.

On the back of the binding of the Gould Manuscript are stamped the words, "Notices of the Early Baptists". The first words within the volume are almost as anonymous,—"A RE-POSITORY of Divers Historical Matters relating | to the English Antipedobaptists. Collected from Original Papers | or Faithfull Extracts. | ANNO 1712. | I began to make this Collection in Ian: 1710–11. | Numb: 1. | The Records of An Antient Congregation of Dissenters | from wch many of ye Independant & Baptist Churches in London | took their first rise: ex MSS of m^r. H. Iessey, wch I rec^d. of M^r. Rich*a*rd | Adams." With these few words for his chief guide to the solution of the problem as to the name of the original compiler, the author set himself to the task. It first occurred to him that the Rev. John Lewis of Margate might possibly have been the original collector of the various documents included in the Gould transcript; but it was found necessary to abandon this theory at once, for Lewis in one place[1] quotes Crosby's version of the so-called Kiffin Manuscript (No. 2 of the Gould MS.) in such a way as plainly to show that he (Lewis) had never seen the original and had to take Crosby's statement concerning it for what it was worth. Now if the Rev. John Lewis was not the compiler of the material at present comprised in the Gould transcript, it seemed to the writer that there was only one other person at all likely to have collected these documents. That was Benjamin Stinton[2], whose manuscripts, Crosby says

---

[1] In his "Brief History of the English Anabaptists", "a 2^d. Edition prepared for the Press", fol. 41. This edition was never printed, but exists in manuscript.

[2] The writer is not the first to suggest Stinton as the original collector

(Vol. I., p. i), furnished a large proportion of the material used in the preparation of [volumes I. and II. of] "The History of the English Baptists". But would Stinton meet all the requirements of the case? The writer began to look carefully into the matter. He found that Crosby says (Vol. IV., p. 363) that Benjamin Stinton died "on the 11th of *Feb.* 1718. in the *forty-third* year of his age". He was living then in 1712. Thus far well. But who was the Mr Richard Adams mentioned in sections 1 and 2 of the Gould Manuscript, and was there a person of that name living in 1710, who would have been likely to possess such important Baptist documents, and especially to have given them to Benjamin Stinton about this time?

On looking at Crosby (Vol. III., pp. 37–8) the author found the description of just such a man, who, about 1676, came to London, and who " 'was', says Dr. *Calamy*, 'an *Anabaptist,* and succeeded Mr. *Daniel Dyke,* in the care of the congregation at *Devonshire-square,* a man of great piety and integrity'. He lived to a very great age, by reason of which, he could not preach some years before his death". Now William Kiffin had been an earlier pastor at Devonshire square, and it would seem extremely likely that Mr Adams might have secured these important documents and later have given them to the prospective author of a Baptist History, Benjamin Stinton, who in 1710 was pastor of the Baptist Church "upon Horsely-down", London, having succeeded his father-in-law, the well known Benjamin Keach, in the pastoral office, and concerning whom, Crosby says (Vol. IV., p. 365), "had the providence of God continued his life, till he had accomplished his intended design [of writing a complete Baptist history], I doubt not, but the

of the material now embraced in the Gould MS. Dr Geo. A. Lofton had made the same suggestion in 1899, but the writer, before reading his works, independently came to this same conclusion, and is the first, he believes, *definitely to prove* that Stinton was the compiler *only of the first thirty sections* of the Gould MS. The two works of Dr Lofton, published in 1899 and entitled, "English Baptist Reformation. (From 1609 to 1641 A.D.)...", Louisville, Kentucky, and "Defense of the Jessey Records and Kiffin Manuscript...Appendix to English Baptist Reformation from 1609 to 1641 A.D.", Nashville, Tenn., deserve a wider circulation and contain much interesting critical information closely related to the present subject.

learned would have readily born a testimony to him, and have rank'd him amongst the greatest men of his time." Crosby does not say in what year Richard Adams died, but in the "Baptist Year-Book" he is reported to have died in 1716. Thus the probable original compiler of the material now found in the Gould Manuscript had evidently been discovered. Still the writer naturally desired more definite evidence.

In the autumn of 1902 he one day fortunately noticed a reference to a Stinton manuscript[1]. When the opportunity came to examine it, it proved to be a small quarto in its original binding with the title, " A | IOURNALL | Of the Affairs | of the | ANTIPÆDOBAPTIS^ts | Beginning with the Reign of King | George, whose Accession to ye Throne | was on ye First of August, 1714. | As the same was kept, | By Beniamin Stinton ". For convenience we will call this manuscript *A*. On the back of the volume was written in ink, " N^o : IV." An examination of the manuscript showed that it contained the original text of only a considerable part of the fourth volume of Crosby's " History of the English Baptists ". This was rather disappointing, yet even such a discovery was a distinct advance toward the solution of the problem undertaken, for it now appeared probable that Crosby embodied in his work more than one volume written by Stinton.

Not long after the writer began to make a transcript of the documents found in the Gould Manuscript, and to study the contents of two other early manuscripts collected by the Rev. George Gould. One of these latter was a small quarto, evidently of the early eighteenth century, bound in its original green binding, entitled, "An Account of Some | of the | Most Eminent & Leading Men | among the | English Antipædo-baptists. | Eccles: 44. 8. | There be of Them that have left a Name behind | them, that their Praises might be reported. | In Epistola Bezæ Scripta. 1566. | Quosdam inter Anabaptistas esse bonos, veros Servos | Dei, Christi Martyros, & charissimos Fratres Nostros." No author, no place, and no date of writing are given. For convenience we will call this manuscript *B*.

---

[1] In Dr Williams's Library, London.

Here certainly was something interesting. The manuscript was written in two different hands, and from the general appearance of the volume, the material in it, and the characteristics of the first hand, it appeared to be nothing less than an anonymous work of Benjamin Stinton's, to which later additions had been made by some one, supposedly, Thomas Crosby, —a conclusion that has since been verified beyond all doubt. Almost every important item in the volume was printed somewhere by Crosby, but some paragraphs had been omitted by him and some parts improved, and the ordering of the material, except that apparently written by Stinton, had been greatly changed. Here, indeed, was a "find" in the right direction, that later might profitably be more closely examined. The other original manuscript was of special importance, a thin folio bound in limp vellum, which we may call *H*. It had no title-page, but two or three of its sections bore the date 1652. It did not, however, contain any of the first numbered documents in the Gould transcript.

As the author continued his study of the Gould volume, a new point of interest occasionally came to his notice. One day he discovered that this manuscript contained in reality at least two main divisions, and probably an intermediate section originally not belonging to either, and that this material seemed to have been transcribed from two or more distinct manuscripts. He came to this conclusion by finding that the original of the entire latter part of the Gould transcript, with the exception of the final note in the Rev. George Gould's own hand concerning William Turner's "A preseruatiue, or triacle, agaynst the poyson of Pelagius" [1551], was to be found in the old manuscript bound in limp vellum (i.e., *H*). This discovery appeared[1] to be of two-fold importance,—first, as helping to

---

[1] In reality the discovery was of but little value, for it now seems that Crosby copied the Berkshire Records as well as the intermediate sections into Stinton's "Repository", so that Mr Keymer made his copy not from the original, but from Crosby's transcript. Without the Stinton-Crosby original, therefore, it is at present impossible to say with certainty whether the divergencies between the Gould transcript of the Berkshire Records and the original manuscripts were due to Crosby or to Mr Keymer, but probability points to Crosby as their almost certain source.

determine more exactly the contents of the volume from which the first thirty sections had been transcribed ; and secondly, as serving by comparison to give an accurate idea of the care which Mr Keymer had taken in preparing this transcript.

Later the writer undertook to make a copy of the contents of the previously mentioned anonymous and undated green quarto, *B*; but it proved too extensive a task and was shortly abandoned. At the bottom of page 11, however, he met with an important statement, in which reference is made to a letter signed " H. H." (to be found in "I. P. Anabaptismes Mystry of Iniquity "), concerning which the anonymous author of the manuscript says, "I have therefore putt it into yᵉ Collection of Originals Numb. 7."

Turning at once in the Gould volume to "Numb: 7:" the author found a copy of this very letter signed "H. H." Thus, a direct relationship between the lost original of the first thirty numbers of the Gould transcript and the first sixty-six pages of the anonymous green quarto, *B*, had evidently been found. They were undoubtedly the work of the same man, and that man must be Stinton. But now the question arose, How, beyond all doubt, could these manuscripts be linked with the name of Benjamin Stinton? It will be remembered that reference has previously been made to a manuscript, *A*, on the title-page of which Stinton's name is directly given as the author. On examining the contents of this, the writer found that in one place six pages (pp. 93–98) had providentially been left blank where a letter from "the Elders & Churches of Iesus Christ at Pensilvania in America " " of the 20ᵗʰ of Iuly" [1715], should have been inserted. This contained a "particular account...of the begining & Progress of the Gosple in those parts of the World, and of the Number and present State of the Churches,... " Now a copy of this very document forms "Numb: 26 " of the Gould Manuscript, where the date "1715 " is also given. Here, then, was the last link of the chain that would bind these three volumes together and make Stinton, therefore, the original compiler of at least the first thirty numbered sections in the Gould transcript.

A further discovery confirmed this conclusion, for still

another Stinton original was found in the Angus Collection at Regent's Park College. This was a small quarto in modern binding, which we will call *C*. The first part is in the handwriting of Stinton and the latter part in that of Crosby. The volume contains autographs of both of these men, and the title-page reads:—" A | Iournal | of the | Affairs of yᵉ Antipædobaptists; | begining with yᵉ Reign of King George, | whose Accession to the Throne was on the | first of August: *1714.* | Kept by me, Benja: Stinton." This is almost exactly the title of the other Stinton manuscript signed with his name, *A*, but the other, *A*, is much more finished and complete than this, *C*, while this is certainly written in his own hand.

Now this Angus copy, *C*, has the following important statement on page 59: "Towards yᵉ latter end of this year [1716] we received a letter from yᵉ Baptist Ministers & Churches in Pensilvania in America, where in they gave us a large & particular Account of yᵉ Begining & progress of the Gospel in those Parts, the Present Number of their Churches yᵉ Names & Curcomstances of their Ministers, wᵗʰ several other particulars, a Copy of wᶜʰ I have put in my Collection of Historical Matters…" A transcript of this forms " Numb: 26 " of the Gould Manuscript, as previously mentioned.

Here, then, was confirmation of the evidence placing it beyond all doubt that Stinton was at any rate the original compiler of the first thirty sections of the Gould transcript, which (thirty sections) evidently in this passage he calls his " Collection of Historical Matters", and in the green quarto, *B*, "yᵉ Collection of Originals ". This Angus Stinton original, *C*, also served to establish the writer's belief, that the first sixty-six pages of the anonymous, undated green quarto, *B*, were written in Stinton's own hand and the remainder in Crosby's own hand, for a comparison of these two manuscripts made the truth of that supposition unquestionable.

It will have been noticed that the writer has limited Stinton's work in the original volume from which the Gould Manuscript was transcribed to merely the thirty numbered sections, thus not including the two or three unnumbered sections immediately following. This seemed necessary for three reasons:—1. Stinton cannot possibly have written *some* of the material between "Numb: 30 " and the beginning of the "Records of the Barkshire Association ", for at least one dated section is years too late for Stinton ever to have seen. 2. If Stinton had written the intermediate sections after "Numb: 30" he would probably have numbered them also. 3. One of these later unnumbered sections has reference to "Mr Crosby's History of the Baptists sufferings", and is largely quoted by him in his third volume. Judging from these facts and the contents of the known Stinton originals, the writer concludes that Stinton was the original compiler of only the thirty numbered sections, and that all the material found in the Gould transcript after "Numb: 30 ", with the probable exception of the final note concerning Turner's "A preseruatiue", was added by Crosby on succeeding blank pages of the now lost Stinton manuscript. The fact that the Berkshire Records are called "Records of the Barkshire Association" suggests that Crosby transcribed them into Stinton's "Repository".

Still later the writer also made a further discovery in regard to the lost original of the first main division of the Gould transcript, which it seems strange that he had not made long before. He had been puzzling over the question as to what this lost manuscript which Stinton in one place calls "ye Collection of Originals" and in another "my Collection of Historical Matters", had as its actual title, and whether it was dated and signed with his name. As the writer glanced over the first page of the Gould volume, the answer came unexpectedly, for in the first four lines of the transcript he saw that the Rev. George Gould had fortunately preserved the exact title of the lost Stinton original. It was anonymous, and probably Mr Gould himself did not know who was the actual compiler of the first thirty sections, but he evidently did know with certainty that Crosby used the volume from which he had the transcript made[1], and this was the title of the original,— "A REPOSITORY of Divers Historical Matters relating to the English Antipedobaptists. Collected from Original Papers

---

[1] See his "Open Communion and the Baptists of Norwich", 1860, pp. cxxiii–cxxiv.

or Faithfull Extracts. ANNO 1712." This lost original of the
" Repository " we will call *D*.

It may be safely said, then, that we now know three original
manuscripts of Benjamin Stinton, and the copy of a fourth. It
is to be hoped that others may also be found, as others undoubtedly were written. Indeed, of at least one other we have
probably the entire contents given in the Preface to Vol. I. of
Crosby's " History of the English Baptists "[1]. Most of all, however, let us hope that the original " Repository ", *D*, may be
located, for it contains the now well-known statement, which
has helped to revolutionize early English Anabaptist history.
In case, however, that the original should never be found, let
us be thankful that by means of the Gould copy, the veil of
tradition, which has concealed a point in the history of the
early English Anabaptists for two hundred years, has at last
been removed.

These discoveries naturally have an important bearing on
our understanding of the Gould Manuscript. They show that
this volume is not a unit in the sense that all the material
now contained in it was *originally* collected by one man, though
it is now evident that the whole text with the possible exception of the final note was copied from one volume by Mr
Gould and Mr Keymer.

The discovery of the three previously mentioned Stinton
manuscripts also helps to answer certain other questions that
either have been, or may be, raised in relation to the lost
Stinton " Repository " which we have called *D*, or to the
Gould copy of it. Among others the following may be mentioned :—

1. Did this lost Stinton manuscript, transcribed by Mr
Gould and the old school-master, contain the Jessey Records,
or Memoranda ("Numb: 1"), and the Kiffin Manuscript
("Numb: 2"), in their original documentary form, or copies of
them made by Stinton, and written on the pages of the
manuscript ? Judging from the three Stinton originals, with

---

[1] Pp. xviii–lxi. See also Vol. I., pp. i–ii, and Vol. IV., p. 365.

which the writer is now acquainted, he would say without hesitation that it contained transcripts of the original documents, not the originals themselves.

2. How perfectly did Mr Keymer transcribe these copies of the original documents made by Stinton? In the main apparently with very great accuracy, but still there may have been certain words, which he was not able to read, and which at any rate are omitted in the Gould Manuscript[1]; there may also have been some words, usually names, that he slightly misread, and occasional letters, which he changed from capitals to small letters, or *vice versa*; but in spite of these comparatively insignificant defects, which after all may not have been due to Mr Keymer, the transcript as a whole seems to be not only trustworthy, but accurate in a minute degree. The old schoolmaster has left us no merely modernized text, though he may occasionally have forgotten to retain the original spelling. Furthermore, Stinton's own transcripts were without doubt more or less modernized, for in his day little, if any, attention was paid to peculiarities of spelling. Everyone spelled as one pleased. Therefore, in this case we may suppose that Stinton copied these documents *verbatim*, but not *literatim*.

One curious mistake the old school-master possibly made. Throughout the first twenty-one sections of the Gould Manuscript, but not later, one very frequently meets with the word "ware" for "were". This looks like an early spelling, but as the word is found in the documents transcribed from printed books, where of course no such spelling is used, as well as in the Jessey Memoranda and Kiffin Manuscript, and further as "ware" occurs in the heading to document "Numb: 12" which probably was added by Stinton himself, the spelling "ware" in the Gould volume cannot so easily be referred back to a writer earlier than Stinton[2]. In no original manuscript of his now known to

---

[1] Some of these words and names were probably omitted, or misread, by Stinton himself in his transcript because of their illegibility, or the names may even have been omitted in the original documents, as having been forgotten by their respective writers.

[2] I have seen one letter in print signed by Will. Kiffin, John Spilsbery, and Joseph Fansom, and probably written by Kiffin, in which "ware"

the writer, however, does Stinton appear to use the word
" ware ", though he very frequently employs the old form of
" e " for the first " e " in " were ".   Now this old form of " e ",
when poorly or hastily written, somewhat resembles an " a ",
and Mr Keymer, while he was transcribing the first twenty-one
sections may have mistaken " were ", when thus written, for
" ware ".   Later, however, having perceived that this old form
of " e " was not " a ", he repeated the mistake no more, but
always transcribed " were " as " were ", whether the old form of
" e " was employed, or the new.   This view accounts for the
spelling " were " occasionally occurring in the first twenty-one
sections amid many instances of " ware ", for Stinton sometimes
wrote the word as we write it to-day, when it naturally caused
Mr Keymer no difficulty.

The really minute accuracy, however, with which the Gould
Manuscript was transcribed in general, may be illustrated by
the reference " 2 Col. 2. 12." found in " Numb: 2 " (the Kiffin
Manuscript) under the date 1640.   Of course Mr Keymer knew
there was no II Colossians, but he retained the error.   The
Rev. George Gould in his introduction to " Open Communion
and the Baptists of Nowich " corrected it.   Crosby, however,
printed the error[1], and the Rev. John Lewis of Margate, in his
" Brief History of the English Anabaptists ", " a 2ᵈ. Edition
prepared for the Press ", 1741, in manuscript, stars this reference and remarks in the margin, "a blunder, I suppose, of the
press".   In passing, however, it is to be noticed that the Kiffin
Manuscript used by Crosby, and that before the old schoolmaster, absolutely agree in this incorrect reference.   Mr Gould
in his published work evidently corrected insignificant im-
perfections in the manuscript, but Mr Keymer seems to have
made no intentional corrections or additions to the text before
him.

3.   If Mr Keymer intentionally added nothing to the text, who
probably originally wrote in " Numb: 2 " (the Kiffin Manuscript)

occurs at least twice (see John Nickolls' " Original Letters and Papers of
State, Addressed to Oliver Cromwell ", London, 1743, pp. 159–160).
Nevertheless I am inclined to favour the view expressed in the text.

[1] Vol. I., p. 102.

the suggestive words, "none haveing then [1640] so so [*sic*] practiced [dipping] in England to professed Believers"? Certainly not Crosby, and Crosby merely followed Stinton, so far as can be judged from an hitherto unpublished section of the green quarto, *B*. But Crosby says[1] that Stinton "did not live to digest in order even those [materials for "an History of the *English Baptists*"] he had collected, except the *Introduction*", which doubtless accounts in part for the fact, that he made this mistake in regard to the use of immersion among the earliest English Anabaptists, in spite of his having collected sufficient material pointing to an entirely different conclusion. Crosby evidently never went much deeper into this matter than Stinton, with the result than an error, which it has taken half a century of criticism to remove and explain, crept into Baptist history. Crosby seems to have omitted as much as possible of Stinton's work which would have tended to bring any uncertainty into the reader's mind, and this is doubtless the reason why he omits the previously mentioned section; for one can easily see, that while Stinton here makes one or two strong statements, he has nevertheless not thought the problem really through. The passage reads[2]:—

This Man [John Smyth] is by Some of y[e] Zealous writers against the Anabaptists called y[e] beginer of Baptism by Dipping, & the Captain of that & other Errors. [Note: "Walls plain discovery, &c pref. & p 44."] & they affirm that from him y[e] English Anabaptists have Successively received their New Administration of Baptism, But this must be a very great mistake, nothing is more evident in History than that there were many who rejected ye Baptism of Infants longe before this Man : several of whom were put to death both in England & other parts, & some for the very Crime of Dipping also : Tis probable indeed y[t] he was ye first from among The English Brownists y[t] ever Embrased ye Opinion of Antipædobaptism : & in the History of that People, when mention is made of one Sort of Brownists that deny ye Baptism of Infants & seperated from ye other who retained it [Note : "Hereseo. p. 87."], it seems to referre to this Smith & his followers : S[r] In[o] Floyer also observes that ye Practice of Immersion was vniversally left of in England

---

[1] Vol. IV., p. 365.
[2] Stinton MS. *B*. "An Account...", pp. 3–4. In place of this section a list of John Smyth's works has been substituted by Crosby, Vol. I., p. 268.

about ye begining of K. Iames ye 1st. so that he might be ye first y^t revived that manner of Administration among ye English in those times :...

Thus it appears that Stinton also could hardly have written the words in the Kiffin Manuscript to which reference has been made, and if neither Crosby nor he could have written them, they must have been the work either of Kiffin himself, or of Richard Adams (who was pastor of the same church of which Kiffin had formerly been in charge, and to whose care some of Kiffin's papers had evidently been intrusted), a man who lived to a great age, and who, in order to make clear to a later generation a fact that was all but lost, might possibly have inserted the words in question. The writer, however, inclines to the view that these words were a part of the original document, but if they were not it would make no real difference, for Richard Adams could surely be quite as much trusted as Kiffin in making such a simple addition.

4. Is there longer any hope that the original Stinton "Repository", *D*, will be found? Certainly. It must be in existence somewhere, very probably in some old Baptist family, or college library, and diligent search should be made to locate the volume. It will doubtless be found to be a small quarto, very likely in its original binding, and containing about two hundred or more pages of manuscript written in two different hands. The title-page will bear no author's name, but the following title,—"A REPOSITORY of Divers Historical Matters relating to the English Antipedobaptists. Collected from Original Papers or Faithfull Extracts. ANNO 1712."

Before concluding these remarks it will be well to note the important bearing the discovery of these four Stinton manuscripts (in this number is included the Gould copy) has on a thorough understanding of early English Anabaptist history. At last after the lapse of two hundred years, we are beginning to obtain a glimpse of the lights and shades of this history, to look upon these early writers as not infallible, and persistently to endeavour to get behind them to their sources in order to try every statement of importance at the bar of criticism. To be sure, the results are not always flattering to the correctness of preconceived views, but after all the truth is approximated, if not completely reached, and it is truth, of course, not fable, or tradition, which is the object of all real historical research.

The discovery of these four manuscripts, also, makes Crosby's "History of the English Baptists" a new book, and possibly, though not necessarily, takes away some of its lustre. We can now definitely locate in these Stinton writings perhaps one fourth, or possibly even more, of the contents of Crosby's four volumes excluding the Appendices, and thus we can approximately determine the proportion of the work done by Stinton. Further, by an examination of these manuscripts, we are the better enabled to appreciate Crosby's modest remark[1], that "Had the ingenious collector [Stinton] of them [" the materials, of which a great part of this treatise is formed "] lived to digest them in their proper order, according to his design, they would have appeared much more beautiful and correct, than now they do." Crosby, however, did his best, and when we rightly estimate the work which he accomplished, we cannot but do him honour. The fair and generous spirit that he shows throughout these four volumes must make his work a model in that respect at least for any future English Baptist history, which though it may settle some problems he left untouched or unsolved, yet can hardly hope to surpass his work in fairness and conscientiousness of aim.

As a complete list of the various documents contained in the Gould Manuscript may be of interest, the following extended description of its contents has been prepared.

"NOTICES OF THE EARLY [ENGLISH] BAPTISTS."

[Title stamped on the back of the MS. which was probably found on the back of Stinton's "Repository".]

---

[1] Vol. i., p. i.

[First Main Division.]

A REPOSITORY of Divers Historical Matters relating | to the English Antipedobaptists. Collected from Original Papers | or Faithfull Extracts. | ANNO 1712. [By Benjamin Stinton.]

[First item.]

I [Benjamin Stinton] began to make this Collection in Ian: 1710–11.

[The Jessey Records, or Memoranda.]

Numb: 1. | The Records of An Antient Congregation of Dissenters | from wch many of ye Independant & Baptist Churches in London | took their first rise: ex MSS of M^r. H. Iessey, wch I rec^d. of M^r. Rich*ard* | Adams.

[The Kiffin Manuscript.]

Numb: 2 | An Old MSS, giveing some Acco^tt_ of those Baptists | who first formed themselves into distinct Congregations, or | Churches in London. [Space] found among certain Paper given me | by Mr Adams.

Numb: 3. | The confession of Faith of Those Churches wch are | comonly (though falsly) called Anabaptists. | Subscribed by them in ye behalfe of Seven Congregations or | Churches of Christ in London.

[Text not given.]

Numb: 4 | An Account of divers Conferances, held in ye Congre-|gation of wch Mr Henry Iessey was Pastor, about Infant-|baptism, by wch Mr H. Iessey & ye greatest part of that Congre|gation ware proselited to Y^e Opinion & Practice of ye Antipedo-|babtists. | being an old M.S.S. wch I rec^d of Mr Adams, supposed | to be written by Mr Iessey, or transcribed from his Iurnal.

Numb: 5. | The Oath taken by Midwives when they ware | allowed in case of Necessity to Administer Baptism.

Numb: 6: | The Abjuration taken of 4 Dutch Anabaptists | in y^[e] Reign of Q. Elizabeth.

Numb: 7: | A Copie rightly related of An Anabaptists | Letter written to his sometimes Accounted Christian | Brethren showing y° Cause of his Seperation from y° Church | of England, indited by a Principle Elder in & of that | Seperation.
[In the margin.] from a Treatise | intituled Anabap-|tismes Mysterie | of Iniquity un-|masked, by I. P. | Anno 1623.
[The signature of the letter is given as " H. H."]

Numb: 8. | Two Orders of y° Parliament of y° Com̄on Wealth | of England, Scotland & Ireland concerning | the Anabaptists. | Tombes⁸ Reven [Review]. pᵗ 3ᵈ dedication

---

Numb: 9. | The Copy of A Letter written by y° Revᵈ Dʳ Barlow | afterwards Lord Bishop of Lincoln to Mʳ In° Tombs. Anno. 1636.
[In margin.] Tombes⁸ Reven [Review]. Prefac: 3 Vol.

Numb: 10. | An Account of y° Sufferings of Mʳ Laurence Clarkson | for Anabaptism, in y° Year 1645, & his recantation of y° Same. | taken out of Mʳ Edwards Gangræna, pg 72.

Numb: 11. | A Collectioň of y° Opinions of y° Old Lollards, New | Reformers & Anabaptists, complained of By y° Convocation in | the Reign of Henry y° 8ᵗʰ. wᵗʰ y° Articles of Religion agreed upon | & published by y° Kings Authority in opposition to y° Same. | Ex, Fullers Church History, Lib 5. Sec. 3ᵈ. pg 208

Numb: 12. | Dʳ̤ Burnets Account of y° Anabaptists yᵗ lived in y° Reign of | Edward the Sixth, & of y° Punishments yᵗ ware then Inflicted upon some of | them, particularly of y° Burning of Ioan of Kent, an English woman, | & George Van Parre, a Dutchman. | His: Refor: Vol 2ᵈ. part 2ᵈ. pg 110. 111. 112. 113.

Numb: 13. | Mʳ Iohn Fox's Letter to Q: Elizabeth in Faviour of two | Dutch Anabaptists condemned to be burnt in Smithfield. | Ex Fullers Church Hist: Cent 16. pg. 104.

Numb: 14. | The Address of y⁰ Anabaptists to King Charles II^d. before | his Restoration wth their Propositions annexed to it, & the Let-|ter sent along with it to his Majesty then at Bruges in y⁰ Year | 1658. [Space] Ex. Lord Clarendons His. Rebellion. Vol 3. p. 625. | Fo. Edit: 1719. Vo. 3. p. 359.

Numb: 15. | Two Apologys of y⁰ People called Anabaptists, | published presently after y⁰ Insurrection of Venner & his Accomplacies. | wherein they protest both against y⁰ Principles & Practices of | that Rebellious Party. Anno 1660. | ex Granthams Chris: Prin: [Christianismus Primitivus] Lib 2. [III.] pg 7. [Text not given.]

Numb: 16. | Mr Fuller's account of y⁰ Begining of y⁰ Anabaptists | in England: wth a discovery of his Mistake therein. | from his Church His: Book 5. pg 229.

Numb: 17. | Mrs Hutchinsons Account of y⁰ Revival of Antipædobaptism | towards y⁰ latter end of the Reign of King Charles y⁰ First.

Numb: 18. | An Account [by "Mr Francis Bampfield"] of y⁰ Methods taken by y⁰ Baptists to obtain | a proper Administrator of Baptism by Immersion, when that | practice had been so long disused, y^t there was no one who had been so | baptized to be found. wth y⁰ Opinion of Henry Lawrence, | Lord President, on y⁰ Case.

Numb: 19. | A brief Account of the Sufferings of y⁰ People called | Anabaptis [sic], in & about London, in y⁰ two first Years after | y⁰ Restoration of King Charles II^d. [Space] Anno 1661. 1662.

Numb: 20. | Several Antipædobaptists taken up for Preaching against | y⁰ Act of Uniformity made y⁰ 35. Eliz, & against y⁰ Kings Supremacy | in Ecclesiastical Matters. Ex Fullers Au: Hist: Book 11. pg. 172.

Numb: 21. | The Tryall of M^r. Benja: Keach who was prose-cuted | for Wrighting against Infant Baptism &c, with an Account of y^e | Punishment inflicted on him for ye Same. [Space] Anno 1664. | Taken from a Manuscript found among Mr Keachs Papers after his Death, | which as he informed me when alive [Stinton married a daughter of Keach, and so obtained first-hand information.] was sent him from one in y^t Country | who was present both at his tryall & Punishment, & took what passed in | Wrighting.

Numb: 22. | An Address of y^e Baptist Ministers in & about the | City of London, presented to his Majesty King William 3$^{rd}_{\overline{w}}$ | upon y^e French Kings proclaming y^e Pretended Prince of Wales, | King of England, &c.   from y^e London Gazette of Decem^r 29th. 1701. | Hampton Court. Dec^m 27. The following Address from y^e Baptist | Ministers in & about y^e City of London was presented to his Majesty by Mr Stanet [Mr. Stennett], | introduced by y^e R^t: Hon. y^e Earl of Peterborough.

Numb: 23. | An Account of A Church that usually met in | Southwark near S$^t_{\overline{n}}$ Mary Overys Church, consisting partly | of Pædobaptists, & partly of Antipædobaptists, from their first Con-|stitution in y^e Reign of K. Iames I, to their Dissolu-tion in 1705. | taken out of their Church Book, &c. [Supposed to have been written by " old Mr Webb ".]

Numb: 24. | An Acco$^{tt}_{\overline{w}}$ of 12. Anabaptists who were Sentanced | to dye at Ailesbury for their Nonconformity in 1669.
['At end: "This relation I received from M$^{rs}_{\overline{w}}$ Bowles, daughter to Mary Iackman y^e Widd y^t was condemn'd according to y^e best of her Rem(em)berance, Apr: 10. 1715."]

Numb: 25. | A Letter from y^e Baptist's Church at Waterford, | in Ireland, to some of y^e Same Perswasion at Dublin to dis-swade | them from haveing Com̄union wth Persons not regularly Baptized.

Numb: 26. | A Letter from Pensilvania giveing an Account of yᵉ State | & Number of yᵉ Baptized Churches in that Province in the Year 1715. | Philad: Aug. 12,,1714.
[There is evidently a mistake in this second date. The letter is clearly signed "Abell Morgan" and dated, "Philad: Iuly 20. 1715." Crosby's interpretation of the meaning of the second date in the heading may be seen in Vol. ɪ., p. 122. In his Vol. ɪv., p. 162, is further evidence that July 20, 1715, is the true date, whatever that in the heading ought to be, or may mean. "Mʳ B. Stinton of London" is mentioned in this letter.]

Numb: 27. | A Confession of yᵉ Faith of Several Churches | of Christ, in yᵉ County of Somerset, & Some Churches | in yᵉ Countyes neer adjacent. | ... | London....1656.
[The whole title, but not the text, is given in the Gould MS.]

Numb: 28. | Part of a Narrative & Complaint, that by yᵉ help of an | Honourable Parliament Man was presented to yᵉ King yᵉ 26 of | yᵉ 5ᵗʰ͞ Month, Iuly 1660. wᵗʰ the Kings Answer thereunto.

Numb: 29. | Some Parts of A Confession of Faith published by Certain | Persons term'd Anabaptists about 1611.

Numb: 30. | Two Sad Instances of the Persecution practiced by the | Protestants themselves in the Reign of King Edward yᵉ 6ᵗʰ͞, | against yᵉ Anabaptists met with in Fox's Latin Book of Martyrs, | but left out in his English, out of a tender regard, it is supposed, to the | Reputation of the Martyrs in Q. Maries Reign; translated by Mʳ Peirce, | in his Answer to Nichols, pg 33. wᵗʰ Mʳ Peirces remarkes on yᵉ Same.

[These preceding thirty sections evidently constituted Stinton's "Repository", or "Collection of Originals". To these, however, Crosby added some pages giving the titles of various early Baptist books with citations from them, and one letter signed, "Benjⁿ Miller" and dated "Downton, Ianʸ 14,,173⅞". The letter is preceded by these words: "The Copy of a Letter which I [Crosby] received from Mr Randall, | and was sent to him from a County Gen^t." This is an answer to a letter from Mr Randall evidently requesting information concerning the early General Baptists in Somerset and Dorset to be inserted in "Mr Crosbys History of the Baptists sufferings". Crosby printed a considerable part of this letter in Vol. III., pp. 121–4 and 126–7.]

[Second Main Division.]

[We now come to the second main division of the Gould volume, and have to deal with a manuscript which Stinton probably never saw, but which Crosby evidently copied into Stinton's "Repository". The original, *H*, from which Crosby made his copy is the thin folio volume already mentioned, bound in limp vellum. It has no title, but Crosby in his transcript fortunately indicated it by the words " Records of the Barkshire Association". Its records go back as far as "octob: 1652" and the latest record is of a "Meeting at Abingdon the Twenty third day of September *1708*". About thirty-five pages of records, evidently not the earliest, have been torn out of the original, but that must have been done many years ago, probably before 1700. Between the year 1659 and the year 1705, meetings may not have been held very regularly, and of the meetings that were held no account remains. The later records seem to have been written by Thomas Barfote, "Messenger from Witney". The name of "Ios: Stennett", also, is on the fly-leaf of the original under the date "1747". The contents of this thin folio makes in the Gould volume forty-four closely written pages, and with this material and the closing note on Turner's "A preseruatiue" [1551] the transcript ends.

It may be added in closing that if the English Baptists of to-day have a greater knowledge of their history than they have had since Stinton's time, it is to the Rev. George Gould of Norwich that they are first indebted for preserving the at present only known first-hand copy of this valuable and long lost Stinton-Crosby Manuscript.]

CHAPTER XIV

THE CHURCHES OF NEW ENGLAND UNTIL
ABOUT 1641

THE English congregations established in New England
before 1641 naturally deserve some notice in this work. That
field, however, has already been so thoroughly, and on the whole
so scientifically, studied, that there is little need for us to
devote to it more than a passing glance. We will, therefore,
only touch upon certain general features of early New England
religious history, which seem thus far to have been more or
less unnoticed, but which nevertheless should be very helpful in
determining the true ecclesiastical situation in that territory
during this period.

When the Pilgrim Fathers landed at Plymouth in 1620
under the leadership of Elder William Brewster, they did not
establish a new congregation, but until John Robinson's death
in 1625, and perhaps even later, remained a branch of the
parent church back in Leyden. It should also be kept in mind
that the members of Robinson's congregation who became the
Pilgrim Fathers were probably no longer strict separatists, but
seem to have been in the process of becoming non-separatist
Independent Puritans, who though they may not as a whole
up to this time have been quite so broad-minded as more
professed followers of Henry Jacob, must nevertheless have
been well leavened with 'Jacobite' doctrine[1].

---

[1] In spite of the tradition that the Puritan church at Boston was
modelled after that at Plymouth, there curiously seems at the first to have
been a considerable difference between the views maintained by these two
congregations. At Boston apparently little distinction was originally
made between the church-members and those who merely attended the
services. At Plymouth a more evident separation between the world and
the church was discernible. In fact, for a time the church at Plymouth

It was several years after 1620 before the next successful colony landed on the shores of Massachusetts Bay not far distant. Those who now began to frequent this territory were for the most part either Presbyterian, or Independent Puritans, who were not separatists, but denied that they had any thought of separation from the Church of England, a fact hitherto too much overlooked.

Dr Dexter has given the impression that these Puritans were ready to accept Plymouth Congregationalism (he means by this separatist Congregationalism) as soon as they reached American shores, and that under the influence of the Plymouth congregation they at once adopted a sort of Puritanized Congregationalism, or Congregationalized Puritanism. Several years of study in the source literature of early English and American Separatism has convinced me that there is nothing further from the truth. If the Plymouth congregation as such had any influence at all in shaping the church polity of the Puritan churches in Massachusetts Bay taken as a whole, it was evidently infinitesimal, and it seems exceedingly strange that this fact does not appear to have been recognized by one so learned as Dr Dexter.

Indeed, there seems to be nothing in the church organization and practice of the early New England Puritan congregations for which they were necessarily indebted to John Robinson, nor do these churches as a whole appear particularly to have studied the Plymouth congregation as a model. Certainly, too, they did not at once become separatist, but on the contrary looked

may even have maintained a moderately separatist attitude towards the Church of England. This appears to be suggested in a letter of Roger Williams to John Cotton cited by Benjamin Scott, F.R.A.S., in a pamphlet entitled, "The Pilgrim Fathers neither Puritans nor Persecutors" (third edition, London, 1891, p. 43), where he (Williams) says : ' "In New England, being unanimously chosen teacher at Boston before your dear father came, divers years, I conscientiously refused, and I withdrew to Plymouth, because I durst not officiate to an UNSEPARATING people, as upon examination and conference I found them (i.e., of Boston) to be."' But if the Pilgrim Fathers at first really maintained such an attitude, a decided change must have taken place before 1647, as we shall see later in this chapter.

upon themselves as true congregations of the Church of England. In fact, so much impressed with this idea was one " A. T.", who wrote in 1631, and whose work has been previously mentioned, that he suggests that some English people in Holland even then were migrating to New England in order to join the Church of England[1]!

But if this is true, how and when did these Puritan churches become separatist? One might think that this question could be answered by suggesting that the change occurred at the time of their arrival on American soil, and through the direct and immediate influence of the congregation of the Pilgrim Fathers at Plymouth. That this is not the true explanation, however, is perfectly apparent from John Higginson's " Attestation " in Cotton Mather's " *Magnalia* " cited in the note at the bottom of this page, as well as from evidence which will be presented later. On the contrary, in so far as the traditional dominating influence of the congregation of the Pilgrim Fathers is concerned, history appears to tell us quite another story, namely, that the early Puritan congregations in New England were principally, if not wholly, organized after

---

[1] See " A.T.'"s " A | CHRISTIAN REPROFE | AGAINST | CONTENTION. | ...", 1631, p. 40 : "some declining to the Church of England, & their liuing, other going a great compasse to new England to communicat with the Church of England :..."

This view is confirmed in John Higginson's " Attestation " at the beginning of Cotton Mather's " *Magnalia Christi Americana*", London, 1702 [p. viii], where the following passage occurs :—

" *Ninthly*, That the Little Daughter of *New-England* in *America*, may bow down her self to her Mother *England* in *Europe*, presenting this *Memorial* unto her ; assuring her, that tho' by some of her *Angry Brethren*, she was forced to make a *Local Secession*, yet not a *Separation*, but hath always retained a Dutiful Respect to the *Church of God in* England ;..."

These early Puritan Congregational churches steadily denied that they were composed of separatists, and their friends supported them in this contention. Such well-informed men as Gov. Winthrop, Gov. Bradford, John Cotton, and John Higginson all agree in denying that the Puritan churches of New England were separatist. It was only their enemies, or those who were jealous of New England, that sought to foist upon these Puritans the odious name of separatists, while others in England outside their circle, persisted in terming them semi-separatists.

their own ideals, while the Plymouth congregation with the passing years seems gradually to have become more and more like them, and finally to have lost altogether any distinctive character, which it may originally have possessed[1].   Only as the result of many changes which have taken place during the period of time intervening between that day and our own, have these Puritan congregations gradually, and by a practically unnoticed evolution, come to be separatist as they now are.

Hence it may be said that the origin of what is to-day termed Congregationalism both in England and America cannot be traced back, except indirectly, either to Robert Browne or to Henry Barrowe.   It had quite another source, namely, the Independent Puritanism which was first developed on the Continent by such men as Henry Jacob, Hugh Peters, Thomas Hooker, John Davenport, and others[2].   Nevertheless, while Browne had no direct connection with this later development in the organization of Congregational churches, yet both because of his early proclaiming of the principles of Congregationalism, and because of the change which with time has come over churches which were of Puritan origin, we may still look upon Browne as in a very real sense the father of modern Congregationalism.

The truth of what has thus far been said is borne out by the statements both of Governor Bradford and of John Cotton, two writers as trustworthy as any produced by early New England, who fortunately represent respectively the point of view of the Plymouth congregation and that of the New England Puritan churches.

The charge that the American Puritans had patterned their

---

[1] That the Plymouth congregation about the middle of the seventeenth century was in no important degree different from the well-known Puritan (Presbyterian) churches in New England, is made manifest by the fact that in the list of the New England ministers who belonged to the first Classis, the ministers of the church at Plymouth are given without any distinction being made between them and the ministers of well-known Puritan (Presbyterian) settlements.   See Cotton Mather's "*Magnalia*", 1702, Book III., pp. 2–3.

[2] Francis Johnson, before he became a separatist, might be named as one of this number.

A discourse of some troubles/

and excommunications in the banished English Church at Amsterdam.

Published for sundry causes declared in the preface to the Pastour of the sayd Church.

¶ Isah. 66. 5.

Heare the worde of the Lord all yee that tremble at his worde, your brethren that hated you, and cast you out for my names sake, sayd, let the Lord be glorified, but hee shall appeare to your ioy, and they shalbe ashamed.

¶ Psal. 55. 12. 13. 14.

Surely mine enemy did not diffame mee, for I could have borne it: neyther did myne adversarie exalt himselfe against mee: I would have hid mee from him. 13. But it was thou a man even mio compaiuon, my guyde, and my familiar. 14. Which delighted in consulting together, and went into the house of God as companions.

¶ 1. Pet. 3. 15. 16. 17.

Sanctifie the Lorde God in your hearts, and be redie alwaies to give an answer to every man that asketh you a reason of the hope that is in you. 16. And that with meeknes and reverence, that when they speake evill of you as of evill doers, they may be ashamed, which blame your good conversation in Chiist. 17. For it is better (if the will of God be so) that yee suffer for well doing, then for evill doing.

¶ 3. Iohn. vers. 9. 10.

I wrote vnto the Church, but Diotrephes, which loveth to have the preeminence among them, receiveth vs not. 10. Wherefore if I come, I will declare his deedes which hee doeth, prating against vs with malicious wordes, and not therewith content, neither hee himselfe receiveth the brethren, but forbiddeth them that would, and casteth them out of the Church.

¶ Printed at Amsterdam.

1 6 0 3.

TITLE-PAGE OF GEORGE JOHNSON'S "DISCOURSE OF SOME TROUBLES", 1603.
(Size of original $7\frac{5}{8}$ in. × $5\frac{1}{2}$ in.) See Vol. I., pages 158–9.

church government after that of the Pilgrim Fathers seems to
have been first made by William Rathband in "A Briefe
Narration of some Church Courses", 1644[1], and repeated by
Robert Baillie in "A Dissvasive from the Errours Of the Time",
London, 1645, where he says:—

"Master *Robinson* did derive his way to his separate Congregation at *Leyden*; a part of them did carry it over to
Plymouth in *New-England*; here Master *Cotton* did take it
up,"[2] and again, "the most who settled their habitations in
that Land [of New England], did agree to model themselves
in Churches after *Robinsons* patern."[3]

To this charge John Cotton replied that it was true that
the Puritans in New England did establish churches of the
same pattern [i.e., Presbyterian, or Congregational, Puritan
Churches, which however were not separatist], "one like to
another [though "I do not know, that they agreed upon
it by any common consultation"]. But whether it was after
Mr. *Robinsons* pattern, is spoken *gratis*: for I beleeve most
of them knew not what it was, if any at all."[4]

Cotton, further, says distinctly that he himself did not obtain
his views from Robinson, but from three [Independent] Puritans,
namely, Robert Parker, Mr Baynes, and Dr Ames, who, it will
be remembered, were friends of Jacob. These taught Cotton
that "the matter of the visible Church" consisted in "visible
Saints"; that "the form of it" was "a mutuall Covenant,
whether an explicite or implicite Profession of Faith, and
subjection to the Gospel of Christ in the society of the Church,
or Presbytery thereof"; and that "the power of the Keyes",
i.e., of excommunication, etc., belonged to each particular
"visible" congregation. Even rigid separatists could not have
presented these views to him more clearly.

Cotton and the early New England Puritans, however,
were never separatists from the Church of England. Says he:
"No marvail, if Independents [Puritan Congregationalists]
take it ill to bee called Brownists, in whole, or in part. For

---

[1] P. 1.   [2] P. 54.   [3] P. 55.
[4] In "The Way of Congregational Churches *Cleared*", London, 1648,
p. 17.

neither in whole, nor in part doe we partake in his Schism. He
separated from Churches and from Saints: we, onely from the
world, ..."[1], as was the custom of all Puritans, and again: "It is
an unjust and unworthy calumny to call either *Cotton* or the
Apologers, the children of...Brownists [Barrowists].   They
never begot us, either to God, or to the Church, or to their
Schism:...so we have ever born witnesse against it [separatism],
since our first knowledg of it."[2]

Not only does Cotton disclaim that the Puritans took their
views from John Robinson, but Governor Bradford admits that
what Cotton says is true[3]:—

And whereas Mr. Baylie affirmeth that, however it was, in a
few years the most who settled in the land [New England] did
agree to model themselves after Mr. Robinson's pattern, we agree
with reverend Mr. Cotton, that 'there was no agreement by any
solemn or common consultation; but that it is true they did, as
if they had agreed, by the same spirit of truth and unity, set up,
by the help of Christ, the same model of churches, one like to
another; and if they of Plymouth have helped any of the first
comers in their theory, by hearing and discerning their practices,
therein the Scripture is fulfilled that the kingdom of heaven is like
unto leaven which a woman took '...

Now John Cotton, like Governor Bradford, was not only
a very prominent and much respected man, but he also arrived
in New England at a very early period, and it is significant that
he came with the Independent Puritan Thomas Hooker, who
had previously been in Holland. This is what Cotton says
concerning his arrival:—

It was [in September] in the yeare 1633. when Mr. *Hooker*,
Mr. *Stone*, with my self arrived in the same Ship together: and
being come, we found severall Churches gathered, and standing in
the same Order, and way, wherein they now walke: at *Salem*, at
Boston, at *Water-Towne*, at *Charle-* [*Charles-*]*Towne*, (which issued
out of *Boston*) at *Dorchester* and *Rockesbury* [*Roxbury*]...[4]

These churches he looks upon as quite distinct from that at
Plymouth, but adds "that some of the first commers might helpe

---

[1] "The Way of Congregational Churches *Cleared*", London, 1648, p. 9.
[2] *Ibid.*, p. 10.
[3] Alexander Young's "Chronicles of the Pilgrim Fathers of the Colony
of Plymouth, from 1602 to 1625 ", Boston, p. 426.
[4] "The Way of Congregational Churches *Cleared*", London, 1648, p. 16.

[might have improved] their [own] Theory by hearing and discerning their practice at *Plymmouth*:..."[1] However, later on the same page he gives the passage cited earlier in this chapter, where he says he doubts if most of the Puritans even knew what John Robinson's congregation was like.

That these early New England churches were considered by their organizers as Puritan congregations of the Church of England, is made plain by Cotton's own statements as follows:—

Nor doe I yet understand why he [Robert Baillie] should account the Religion of *New-England* another Religion, then that of *England* and *Scotland* and other Reformed Churches[2].
the form of Church-government wherein we walk doth not differ in substance from that which Mr. *Cartwright* pleaded[3].
hee [Roger Williams] su[s]pected all the *Statos conventus* of the Elders [in New England] to bee unwarrantable, and such as might in time make way to a Presbyteriall government [i.e., of a State Church][4].

To be sure, the church at Salem asked the Plymouth congregation for its approval of their church organization, but perhaps chiefly after the organization had been effected, as may be inferred from the following letter to Governor Bradford concerning the formation of the Salem congregation[5]:—

The . 20 . of Iuly [1629], It pleased the lord to moue the hart [?] of[?] our God[?] to set it aparte for a sollemne day of humilliation, for the choyce of a pastor, & Teacher　The former parte of the day being spente, in praier. & teaching ; the later parte about the Election, which was after this maner　The persons thought on (who had been ministe[rs] in England) were demanded concerning their callings, they acknowledged ther was a towfould calling, the one an Inward calling, when the lord moued the harte of a man to take that calling vpon him,...The second wa[s?] an outward calling which was from the people, when a Company of beleeuers are Ioyned togither in Couenante, to walke togither in all the ways of God.　And euery member (being men) are to haue a free voyce, in the choyce of their officers, &c　Now we being perswaded that these . 2 . men, were so quallified,...we saw noe reason but we might

---

[1] "The Way of Congregational Churches *Cleared*", London, 1648, p. 16.
[2] *Ibid.*, p. 25.
[3] *Ibid.*, p. 27.　　　　[4] *Ibid.*, p. 55.
[5] "History of the Plimoth Plantation...Written by William Bradford", London, 1896, p. 173.

freely giue our voyces, for their Election,…So m^r Skelton was
chosen pastor, and m^r Higgison to be teacher;…
And now good S^r. I hope that you, & the rest of gods people…with
you, will say that hear was a right foundation layed,…

It is true also that the congregation which was organized at
Charlestown on July 30, 1630, and which was at once divided
into three distinct churches (at Charlestown, Watertown, and
Dorchester), asked the interest and prayers of the congregation
at Plymouth, and the advice of Samuel Fuller, Allerton, and
Winslow as to church government[1].

We may accordingly admit that four of the many New
England churches organized before 1642 possibly received some
slight help from the congregation at Plymouth at the time of
their organization.   There, however, the direct influence of the
Plymouth church seems to have ceased, and we do not believe
that its indirect influence extended much further, because of the
extreme probability that the views of the Independent Puritans
concerning church polity were either well formulated before
they ever crossed the ocean, or may have been gained from
other Puritan congregations already established in New England.   Furthermore, as the Plymouth church itself was probably
not rigidly separatist at this time, even those Puritan churches
which received advice from its members could not logically
trace their origin through it back to strict separatism.

Indeed, it is clearly noticeable that most of the early
settlers of New England were Puritans, not separatists.   Thus,
for instance, came John Cotton in 1633 and was chosen pastor
of the Charlestown-Boston church.   In the same way came
Hugh Peters in 1635, while John Davenport arrived less
than two years later.   Even Roger Williams on his arrival,
though perhaps less settled in his convictions than the average
Puritan, it should be remembered, was not a close separatist.
One might almost say that he was exiled into rigid separatism.
It was also practically an Established Church which expelled

---

[1] See a letter of Samuel Fuller and Edward Winslow to William
Bradford, Ralph Smith, and William Brewster, dated Salem, July 26,
1630, contained in "Governour Bradford's Letter Book" ("Collections of
the Massachusetts Historical Society, *For the Year* 1794", Vol. III., Boston,
1810, 8°, p. 75).

him, a Church of England which, to be sure, lacked the dis-
advantages of the hierarchy of archbishops and bishops, but
which well illustrated the relentless bigotry of a fully developed Puritanism.   Years before, Robert Browne had fore-
seen the evil possibilities of Puritan ambition, and here in New
England, and during the Commonwealth in Old England, his
estimate was amply proved to be just.

Roger Williams seems to have been the first New England
separatist of any importance.   He is supposed to have become
an Anabaptist, but apparently not an immersionist, in 1638,
or early in 1639, when he was converted to Anabaptist views,
and was evidently rebaptized by sprinkling or pouring through
the agency of one Holyman.   Then Williams "rebaptized him,
and some ten more."   Thus was organized at Providence, Rhode
Island, what is now supposed to have been the first non-
immersionist Anabaptist church in America.   Williams, however, had no sooner been thus baptized than he became doubtful
of the validity of his baptism, and three months later is said
to have withdrawn from the congregation, and to have become a
Seeker.   So potent did he deem the obstacles, which presented
themselves to all people who desired a complete Reformation
and the institution of new churches.

Once more we may turn to John Cotton[1]:—

And for *New-England*, there is no such Church of the [rigid]
Separation at al that I know of.   That separate Church (if it
may be called a Church) which separated with Mr. *Williams*, first
broke into a division about a small occasion (as I have heard) and
then broke forth into *Anabaptisme*, and then into *Antibaptisme*,
and *Familisme*, and now finally [in 1647] into no Church at all.

This citation, if true, and I know of no reason for doubting
it, makes at least three points plain:—(1) that in 1647, after
the dissolution of Williams' church, there was no rigid separatist
congregation in all New England (This statement includes of
course the church of the Pilgrim Fathers at Plymouth);
(2) that the continuous history of the present immersionist
First Baptist Church in Providence, R. I., cannot begin earlier
than 1647, while it probably commences somewhat later; and

[1] "The Bloudy Tenent, *Washed*", London, 1647 [second section],
p. 121.

(3) that the present First Baptist Church at Newport, R. I., cannot have been a separatist, or an Anabaptist congregation before 1647.

From another source we may also draw two further inferences, viz., that the Baptist Church at Newport, R. I., is probably the oldest Baptist church in America, having evidently begun to practise immersion about 1648 after the arrival of Marke Lucar from England; and that the present immersionist First Baptist Church of Providence probably dates back to the same year, when baptism by "dipping" may have been procured through the agency of the church at Newport[1].

Williams, however, though disturbed about the whole subject of baptism was not satisfied either in the authority for, or in the manner of, dipping :—

At Seekonk [he says[2]] a great many have lately concurred with Mr. John Clarke and our Providence men about the point of a new Baptism, and the manner by dipping: and Mr. John Clarke hath been there lately (and Mr. Lucar) and hath dipped them.   I believe their practice comes nearer the first practice of our great Founder Christ Jesus, then other practices of religion do, and yet I have not satisfaction neither in the authority by which it is done, nor in the manner; nor in the prophecies concerning the rising of Christ's Kingdom after the desolations by Rome, &c.[3]   It is here said that the Bay hath lately decreed to prosecute such, and hath writ to Plymouth to prosecute at Seekonk, with overtures that if Plymouth do not, &c...[4]

[1] W. H. Whitsitt's "A Question in Baptist History", Louisville, Kentucky, 1896, pp. 156–8, etc.

[2] "Publications of the Narragansett Club. (First Series.) Vol. VI", Providence, R.I., 1874, p. 188.

[3] These words show that already Fifth Monarchy views were being propagated among the early American Anabaptists.

[4] This last sentence is suggestive. It well illustrates the coercive methods which might be used upon the Plymouth Colonists by the Presbyterian Puritans of Massachusetts Bay to force them into line, so to speak, with the majority of New England settlers. In ways like this, no doubt, the people of Plymouth in time lost any individuality which they may originally have had. Perhaps, however, not much coercion was sometimes required. In another letter of Roger Williams, contained in the volume of Narragansett Club Publications mentioned above, p. 336, Williams says that he was "as good as banished from Plymouth as from the Massachusetts".

Williams is said never to have joined, or organized, another church, but to have kept the faith of a Seeker to the end, patiently waiting for the arrival of the special prophets or apostles, who alone, he considered, might usher in the much desired new Ecclesiastical era, but who in his opinion never came.

With this glimpse of the views held by the founders of New England we may pause in our study of the evolution of English Dissent before 1641. That this evolution was on the whole very gradual, appears not only directly from the testimony of the conventiclers themselves, but also from that of others who were familiar with their thoughts and activities. Many surprises await the investigator, for there are retrogressions as well as advances recorded in this period. Only in a later volume, unfortunately, can we illustrate the rapid expansion and the approximate completion of the evolution of the early English separatist movement. We may close our present study with a noteworthy passage[1] from John Bastwick's "THE | UTTER ROUTING | Of the whole Army of all the | INDEPENDENTS & SECTARIES, | ...", London, 1646, 4°:—

It is well knowne that in the time of the Prelats power, the removall of a very few things would have given great content unto the most scrupulous consciences: for I my selfe can speake thus much, not only concerning the conscientious Professors here in *England*, but the most rigid Separatists beyond the Seas, with many of which I had familiar acquaintance at home and abroad, and amongst all that ever I conversed with, I never heard them till within these twenty yeares desire any other thing in Reformation, but that the Ceremonies might be removed with their Innovations, and that Episcopacy might be regulated, and their boundlesse power and authority taken from them, and that the extravagances of the High Commission Court might be anihilated, and made void, and that there mightthrough [*sic*] the Kingdom be a preaching Ministery every where set up. This was all that the most that I was then acquainted with desired in the Reformation of Church matters. Indeed within this sixteene yeares I met with some that desired a more full Reformation, and yet if they might have injoyed but that I now mentioned, they would

---

[1] In "The Antiloqvie", sigs. f verso and f₂ recto.

have beene very thankfull to God and authority, and have sate downe quietly. But yet I say the extreamest extent of their desires, reached but to the removall of all the Ceremonies and Innovations, the taking away of the Service Booke, and the putting downe of the High Commission Court (which was called the court Christian, though it was rather Pagan) and the removall of the Hierarchy, root and branch, and the setting up, and establishing of a godly Presbyterie through the Kingdome; this was I say *all and the uttermost Reformation that was required by the most scrupulous men then living that I knew*; yea, I can speake thus much in the presence of God, *that Master* Robinson *of* Leiden, *the Pastor of the Brownist Church, there told mee and others, who are yet living to witnesse the truth of what I now say, that if hee might in* England *have injoyed but the liberty of his Ministry there, with an immunity but from the very Ceremonies, and that they had not forced him to a subscription to them, and imposed upon him the observation of them, that hee had never separated from it, or left that Church*...[1]

[1] For further information on Robinson's separation from the Church of England see the author's "*A Tercentenary Memorial* New Facts concerning John Robinson Pastor of the Pilgrim Fathers", Oxford and London, 1910, pp. 16–31.

APPENDIX A

AN ADDITIONAL NOTE CONCERNING THE BOOK
ENTITLED, "TRUTH'S CHAMPION"

THUS far my search for a copy of "Truth's Champion" has been in vain. Fortunately, however, I have noticed that both Stinton and Crosby give more complete descriptions of this work than I had obtained elsewhere, and accordingly, the original statement by Stinton may here be cited as follows[1]:—

"Altho' this Man [Iohn Morton] might after his return from Holland, stay sometime at London wth Mr Helwisse & his Church. Yet there appears a probability of his Setling afterwards in ye Country & preaching to Some People there: for at ye begining [?] of ye Civil Warrs, when they were demolishing au old Wall near Colchester, there was found hid in it ye Copye of a Book, writen by I. Morton supposed to be ye Same Person; The General Baptists were very fond of it, soon got it printed, & it has since received several Impressions: ye Author of this book appears to have been a Man of Considerable Learning & Parts, One y^t Understood ye Oriental Languages & was acquainted wth ye Wrightings of ye Fathers; but a very Zealous Remonstrant or Armenian: its intituled Truths Champion, & contains 13. Chapters on ye following heads. (1.) of Christs dying for all. (2). of his dying for all to save all. (3.) of ye Power of God in Christ given out unto all Men. (4) of Predestination. (5) of Election. (6) of Free-will. (7) of Falling away (8) of Original Sin (9) of Baptism. (10) of ye Ministry (11) of Love. (12) of those that hold that God hath appointed all ye Actions of Men, and ye sad Effects y^t follow. (13) of ye Man Adam and ye Man Christ. It is writ in a very good stile, & the Arguments are managed wth a great deal of Art & Insinuation, So that those who follow ye Remonstrant's scheem of Doctrines did not value it without a Cause."

Crosby published this passage with a few slight changes in *The History of the English Baptists*, Vol. I., pp. 277–8. Stinton had evidently seen the book. His description appears to me to make our Murton's authorship rather improbable. Evidently the problem can only be solved after a copy of "Truth's Champion" has been found.

[1] "An Account of Some | of the | Most Eminent & Leading Men among the | English Antipædobaptists. | ...", pp. 12–13.

APPENDIX B

AN ADDITIONAL NOTE RELATING TO "A VERY PLAIN AND WELL GROUNDED TREATISE CONCERNING BAPTISME"

RECENTLY I have fortunately come across a passage which seems to contain a reference to an earlier edition of this work than I have seen, published in or before 1620, and accordingly 1618 may after all have been the definite date of the edition which Dr William Wall saw two hundred years ago. The words to which I refer are the following : "*besides all which I haue not long since, seene a Booke translated out of* Duch *and Printed in* English, *proouing that the inuention of Infants baptisme, was brought in; and Decreed by diuers* Emperors, Popes, *and* Counsels;..."[1] In case this passage does have reference to such an earlier edition of this work, the edition of which I give a facsimile was really a later reprint, in which that fact is not mentioned. There is apparently no doubt that the pamphlet which I have seen was published after 1640. To make perfectly certain of this point, I have submitted my facsimile to an expert bibliographer, Mr Alfred W. Pollard, who agrees with me herein. That there were two editions of this work, I believe, has been hitherto unsuspected. This theory very readily explains how Dr Wall came to assign a definite date to the pamphlet which he saw, and also how it happened that Thomas Cobbet did not reply to the work until 1648. In reality he seems to have replied promptly to the second impression. I now know of four copies of the reprint, to one of which the date 1645 and to another of which a date between 1645 and 1650, if I remember correctly, had already been assigned.

APPENDIX C

THE LATEST DISCOVERY RELATING TO JOHN WILKINSON

Mr Walter H. Burgess in his recently published "John Smith the Se-Baptist", London, 1911, mentions the existence of a posthumous pamphlet of John Wilkinson's, which on examination I have found to contain more interesting views of his than have thus far been discovered. The book appears to be an unique copy. Wilkinson's style of expression as here exemplified is less vehement than that of Browne, Barrowe, and some other early separatists, but some

---

[1] [John Murton's] "A | DISCRIPTION | OF WHAT *GOD* | hath *Predestinated* | ...", 1620, 8°, p. 154. Mr Burgess in his "John Smith the Se-Baptist", London, 1911, pp. 310-11, has independently noticed this same reference.

of the positions maintained distinctly remind one of passages which occur in Browne's books. As the writings of John Wilkinson are less known than those of practically any other of the prominent early Brownist or Barrowist leaders, the following title of this work and a few of the best citations from it should prove of interest and value :—

"*AN* | EXPOSITION | OF THE 13. CHAPTER OF THE | REVELATION OF IESVS | CHRIST. | By *Iohn Wilkinson.* | [Device] | Revelation 14. 9. | *AND the 3. Angel followed them, saying with a lowd* | *voice, If any man worship the beast and his image, and* re-|*ceive his marke in his forehead, or in his hand,* | V. 10. *The same shall drink of the wine of the wrath of God,* | *which is powred out without mixture into the cup of his indig-*|*nation, and he shalbe tormented with fire and brimstone in the* | *presence of the holy Angels, and in the presence of the Lamb:* | V. 11. *And the smoake of their torment ascendeth up for ever* | *and ever.* | [Device] | Imprinted in the yere, 1619." 4º, pp. 37.

" *I*T was the purpose and desire of the Authour of this Treatise to haue published his Iudgment of the whole booke of the Revelation, But through the malice of the Prelates who divers times spoyled him of his goods, and kept him many yeres in prison; he was prevented of his purpose. After his death some of his labours comming to the hands of his friends, in scattred and unperfect papers; they laboured with the help of others that heard him declare his judgement herein, to set forth this little treatise, wherin they have not varied from the Authours Iudgement, but onely in one point in the 3. verse,...the which should not haue been altered, if the worke had been left perfect."[1]

"As the mouth is the meanes and instrument whereby men do declare their mindes, so this Beast had a mouth to declare and utter her minde; by which mouth was signified a Ministerie of false Prophets, and lying Spirits, namely, Doctors, Schoole-men, Monkes, Fryars, and all sorts of their Preachers, who teach for doctrines the commandements of the Beast, and declare and utter the minde and will of the Beast as being equall to Gods Word, this their Canons, Lawes, Books and Monuments, do manifestly witnesse: The effect of that which this mouth uttereth is noted to be, *great things, and blasphemies.* They boast of this Beast that she is the holy Catholick Church Militant, the Mother of all true beleevers, the chaste Spouse of Christ, the Pillar and ground of Truth, that it cannot erre, &c, And that all which will have God to be their Father, must haue her to be their Mother; Finally, that out of her lap and communion there is no saluation. These, and many other such great things speaketh the mouth of this Beast, which are indeed great things,

---

[1] Verso of the title-page.

and being so spoken are great blasphemies: For is it not great blasphemy to call that Holy, which is most abominable? To call her the Mother of all true Beleevers, which is the Mother of fornications, and of all abominations? To call that the Pillar and ground of Truth, which hath corrupted the earth with her errours and fornications and caused all Nations to drinke of the wine of the wrath thereof? To say there is no saluation but in her fellowship whose end and iudgement is to go to destruction? Beware of false Prophets, and teachers of lyes, for such are the mouth of this Beast." [1]

"And as they blaspheme the name of God; So likewise they blaspheme his Tabernacle, That is to say, the true visible Church of Christ vnder the Gospel, which is the place of Gods presence, which he hath chosen to put his name there, *[From margin: *Math. 18.] where two or three or more are gathered together in the name of Christ, there is Christ present, and where Christ is present there hath God put his name, there he is to be sought; and there hee may bee found, and there is his Tabernacle. To come together in the name of Christ, is when Gods people ioyne themselues together in a spirituall body politicke, separated from the common multitudes of knowne unbeleevers, to the end to meete together for the mutuall edification and comfort one of another, by doctrine, breaking of bread and prayer, and to practise all other Ordinances of Christ set downe in his Testament, as they shall haue occasion: and to companies of Beleeuers, hauing such fellowship and communion one with another, the title of the Churches of Christ doth (in our use of speech) properly and of right belong: but for beleevers to doe this apart by themselues is adiudged contempt of authority, factious, novelty, making of Conventicles and unlawfull Assemblies, dangerous to the State, and not to be suffered in any Kingdome or Commonwealth, and so they blaspheme the Tabernacle of God in a high degree, as if Gods people were a company of ungodly rebels, and wicked conspirators; but the righteous Lord will in due time visit his people, & rebuke his enemies.

"And on the other side, for Gods people now to deny the kingdome of the Beast; that is, (as they call it) the holy Catholick church Militant, to be the true Church of Christ: To refuse to partake and communicate with them in their abominations, delusions, and unfruitfull workes of darknesse, is adjudged disobedience, schisme and contempt of the power and authoritie of the Church: To speak against their proceedings, sedition, disturbance of the peace of the Church, heresie, impietie, and what not? Thus they adorne the Harlott, which corrupteth the earth with her fornications, with the title of the Church, and spouse of Christ, and Tabernacle of God; And so blaspheme the Tabernacle of God, as if it were not a communion of Saincts by calling and profession, but an habitation

[1] P. 12.

of Divells, an hold of Fowle spirits, and a cage of every uncleane & hatefull bird."[1]

"The ‡ [From margin: "‡ *For proofe of this looke no further then in the* 36. *Canon of the Church of Eng. made An.* 1603."] Prelacye and Clergy being as hath been before shewed, assembled with authority to make lawes, did ordeyne that every Bishop in his diocesse should carefully observe that none should preach or execute the function of a parish Parson, Vicar or Curat in any parish, but he that should sweare to observe their Lawes & Canons,...and therfore to what parish soever these tryed Lads are sent to doe service, upon sight of this Marke [the Bishop's "Letters of Orders"] they must be received without any opposition, upon penaltie of the Law upon those that shall refuse them.

"Here may be objected, that this Marke is onely received by the Clergie, and not by the people of all sorts, rich and poore, bond and free, according to the Text. I answer, that all persons which receiue these false Priests doe likewise receiue, and submit to that authority which sent them, and also the Marke by which they are sent, as is evident, when a Priest commeth to take possession of a Parish to which he is by the Bishop appointed; he is not received upon his word, nor because he tolleth the Bell, and putteth on the Surplice, and useth other Ceremonies inioyned him by the Prelate: But, shewing the fore-said Marke of the Beast they receiue both him and it, and communicate with him: Thus all, both small and great, rich and poore, bond and free, that receiue and submit unto their appointed Priest, receiue a marke in their foreheads,...those that receiue, heare, and ioyne in fellowship with these false Ministers, doe heare, receiue, and ioyne to the false power which sent them, and the marke by which they are sent."[2]

"As for the best sort of their parish Preists which are men of learning and gifts, they must also be confined within their limitts, they must worship God according to the rules prescribed them by these their spirituall Fathers, as in the 38. Canon. *If any minister shall omitt to use the forme of Prayer, or any of the orders or Ceremonies prescribed in the Communion Booke, let him be suspended, and if he doe not conforme within the space of a moneth, let him be deposed.* The absurdities and blasphemies conteyned in that Comon prayer Booke are many, which having been discovered and layd open by divers treatises already published in print, I will omit, onely this I will add, that in the imposing of that service Booke, or any other, this great iniquitie is committed by the imposers therof; That they doe exalt themselves both against Christ,...and also...against the holy Ghost,...Further their preachers may not teach against their corrupt Church state and Ministrie, though they know it to be Antichristian, nor against the forme of worship

---

[1] Pp. 15–16.   [2] Pp. 24–25.

prescribed in the said comon prayer Booke, nor against the ceremonies, nor the goverment of the church of England by Archbishops, Bishops, Deanes, Archdeacons, and the rest that beare office in the same, nor against the manner and forme of making and consecrating Bishops Preists or Deacons, nor against the Lawes and Ordinances *Ecclesiasticall* established in the sayd Church, whosoever transgresseth in these things, shalbe excommunicated *ipso facto*, as is playne in the 4 6. 7. 8. & 54. Canons. Thus by excommunicating and cursing they labour to mainteine and defend their corruptions, but not one iote of Scripture dare they shew, and no marvell; seeing the whole scriptures are against mens inventions and traditions, of which nature these abuses are, being left here by the Pope, and reteyned and renewed by his Prelates As they may not teach against these things, so on the contrarie, they may not teach the true and right way which Christ hath prescribed in his Testament, how we must worship God, nor how the true Church of Christ ought to be gathered and constituted, the Ministers thereof ordained, nor the manner how it ought to bee governed, as appeareth in the 9. 10. 11. and 12. Canons. By which we may see in what bondage their Preachers are kept, they must hide their Talent in the earth, and put their candle under a Bushell, lest men by the light thereof should come to the knowledge of the truth and beleeue it. Also it is to be observed as a generall rule, that none, good or bad, learned or unlearned, can be suffered to receiue their Orders of Priesthood or Deaconship, or be admitted to preach, or execute a Ministerie in their Parish Churches, unlesse they sweare to conforme to the worship and ceremonies prescribed by these Prelates, and also submit to their Antichristian rule and governement, which they challenge to themselues, as being Lords over all: Thus by swearing they make their inferiour Priests to sell themselues to work wickednesse; which trick they haue cunningly devised to bring the Land in subjection to their Antichristian yoke: And upon the taking of this Oath they receiue the Prelates Marke, which is called in this Chapter, *the Marke of the Beast;* which is understood to be the Letters of Orders under the Prelates hand and seale to testifie that they are made Priests or Deacons, according to the order and canons prescribed in that behalfe in this their Convocation, as wee may see in the 36. 48. and 50. Canons: And for refusing to worship them in these things, many are put back, and those that formerly haue been ordeyned, for refusing so to doe (which they call revolting) haue had their penall Lawes executed upon them, which is Suspension, Degredation, and Excommunication, and after these many other afflictions in body, goods and name; being accounted factious and seditious persons, that haue no right to buy or sell their wares." [1]

"Now if we compare the Church of England with these Scriptures, we shall finde that the practise and proceedings thereof, hath been,

---

[1] Pp. 32–33.

and is contrary. The people thereof (for the most part) are such as visibly and apparently liue in all kinde of licentiousnesse, and in their workes deny God, being abominable and disobedient. For these Lordly Prelates being armed with the sword of Civill authority, and hauing the Law of [on] their side, they haue not laboured by painefull preaching to draw men to the obedience of the faith, and to the fellowship of the Gospell apart from the prophane and wicked, that speake evill of the wayes of the Lord, but they haue compelled and inforced all sorts of people, both religious and prophane, not onely such as feare God, but also such as feare him not, by bodily punishments to be conformable to the profession which is by their Canon Law established in this Church: As if the Word of God, that Sword of the Spirit were not mighty enough in operation for the gathering together of the Saints. That this is their practise is plaine by the 90. and 114. Canons, where it is said, that Ministers and Church-wardens must present all persons aboue the age of 13. yeeres, that come not to the Church and receiue the Sacraments; after which presentation, if they doe not conforme they shall bee ex-communicated, imprisoned, and haue their goods attached: This is the meanes which hath been used for the gathering of this Church of England, whereby they haue confounded and mingled them together whom God hath commanded to be separated:...But this hath been the manner of gathering the Church of England, and therefore it is unworthy to be adorned with the title of the Church of Christ, but ought to be accounted the Image of the first Beast before spoken of,....

"And for confirmation hereof by the testimonie of their own mouthes, let us but consider the estimation which the members of this Church haue one of another: Some there are amongst them, who for making more conscience of their waies then the rest, are in derision called *Puritans* or *Precisians;* these on the contrary seeing the ungodly conuersation of the rest of their brethren, esteeme them as wicked, prophane, carnall and unregenerate men, such as (for the most part) are mockers, contemners, and evill speakers of the Truth, and in whom is no appearance of Religion and the feare of God; and therefore they distinguish the better sort from these prophane persons by the name of *Professors.*....I deny not but there are many amongst them, that are the Saints and Servants of Christ, that are godly and zealous people,...Such persons (I say) are fit stones for the building of the Church of Christ, but so long as they remaine in this confusion, they can no more bee said to be the true visible Church of Christ, then a heape of stones fitted for a building can bee said to be a house; therefore they must be separated from the wicked, and placed together according to the order prescribed by Christ Iesus, and practised by his Apostles, as in the new Testament, before they can be so esteemed."[1]

[1] Pp. 34–35.

APPENDIX D

THE WILL OF ANN ROBINSON, MOTHER OF JOHN ROBINSON, PASTOR OF THE PILGRIM FATHERS

"In[1] the name of God Amen the sixtenth day of October in the yeare of our Lord God 1616 I Ann Robinson of Sturton [le Steeple] in the Countye of Nottingham widdowe beinge aged and weake in bodye but whole and sound in mynd but of good and perfect remembrance thankes be to Allmightye God And prayeinge and consideringe the instabilitye of this vaine and transatorye world and the shortnesse of mannes liefe therein Doe ordaine and make this my laste Will and Testament clearly revokeinge and absolutely admyttinge hereby all and everye former will and testament by me in any wise heretofore made in manner and forme followinge That is to saye firste and principally into the hand*es* of allmightye Godd my creator Redemer and Sanctifier I commend my soule assurdly hopeinge and trustinge in and by the meritt*es* death and passion of his deare sonne Jesus Christ my onely lord and saviour to be one of his electe and blessed companye in the Kingdom of heaven and by noe other waye or means whatsoev*er* And my body I committ to the earth to be interred or buried in the p*a*rishe churche of Sturton aforesaid or elsewheare it shall please god to call me to his mercye Item I give and bequeathe unto the poore peorple [*sic*] of Sturton and Ferton forty shillings of lawful money of England to be given and bestowed at my funerall at the disposeinge of my son in law William Pearte Item I give unto my sonne Iohn my sonne and heire apparent the some of forty shilling*es* of lyke lawfull money of England Item I give and bequeathe unto Bridgett Robinson Wife to my said sonne John one paire of lynneinge sheets and one silver spoone Item I give and bequeath to Iohn Robinson sonne of my said sonne John the some of forty shilling*es* and to every one of my said sonne John his children the some of xx*s* Item I give and bequeathe unto my

---

[1] At the District Probate Registry, York, Vol. 34. This will was recently discovered by Rev. Walter H. Burgess, B.A("John Smith the Se-Baptist", London, 1911, p. 317). It finally and definitely locates the home and probable birthplace of John Robinson, and indicates the kind of family in which he grew up, viz., that of a modest gentleman farmer of the period. Mr Burgess deserves much credit for making this interesting discovery, since the difficulties which beset any investigator were very great and indeed appeared almost insurmountable. The finding of this definite information disposes of the conjectures of over half a century.

said sonne John Robinson all the pailes Railes stoupes gates [?] and
all fences round about the messuage or Coftestad wherein I now
dwell w*ith* [?] all and singular rackes and mainger*es* beast*es* houses
and ploucher*es* w*ith* [?] all the glass about the said messuage to remain
and be to him and his heires for ever Item I give and bequeath unto
Ellen my sonne William his Wife one paire of lynninge sheets and
a silver spoone and to every one of his children Twenty shilling*es*
Item I give unto foure of the children of my sonne in lawe William
Pearte that is to say to William Thomas Originall and John Pearte
every of them the some of xx^s Item I give and bequeathe unto
Mr Charles White of Sturton ten shilling*es* And I appoint and make
him (as I trust he will be) to be Super*intendent* and overseer of this
my said last Will and Testament Item I give and bequeathe to Mary
my daughter and Wife to the said William Pearte all my weareinge
app*a*rell wolle*n* and lynnen Item I give and bequeath to John
Robson ii^s and vj^d Item unto Jone Green's Servant*es* other two
shilling*es* and six pence Item I give and bequeath unto my saide
sonne William Robinson my debt*es* legacies and funerall expenses
p*ai*d and discharged and all and singular the moyte and halfe p*a*rte
of all my good*es* cattall*es* and chattlles quicke and deade moveable
and unmoveable of what kynde quantitye or qualitye soev*er* [?] they
be and unbequeathed And I make and ordaine my said sonne in
lawe William Pearte my sole Executor of this my last Will and
Testament And doe give and bequeathe unto the said William Pearte
all and singular the other moyte and halfe of all my said Good*es*
Cattells and chattells quicke and deade moveable and unmovable
of what kynde [?] quantitye or qualitye soev*er* [?] they be and
unbequeathed In Witnesse whereoff I have hereunto set my hand
and seale the daye and yeare first above written These beinge
Witnesses George Dickons Robt Byshoppe George Halton.

10.   "On the Sixteenth day of Ianuary 1616[/17]
                         Probate of this Will was granted by
                         the Exchequer Court of York to
                         William Pearte the sole Executor" [1]

[1] The text of this will here given was made for me at the District
Probate Registry, York.

APPENDIX E

DID ANY ENGLISH GENERAL ANABAPTIST PRACTISE IMMERSION BEFORE 1641 ?

This question, I think, must be answered in the affirmative, but thus far only one passage has been found to demonstrate that fact. This information is found in the second part of William Britten's "Moderate Baptist"[1], 1654, and reads in its context as follows[2]:—

"Βαπτισ[τ]ήριον, *Baptisterium*, that vessel for sprinkling or washing, callad [called] a Font, wee read not of in Scripture, it being another of their inventions. And for the further information of the manner, note the word Βαπτίζω, *immergo*, to plunge, dip, in, or overwhelm ;...Thus in the command of Christ they forsake him the fountain, and hew to themselves a broken Cistern.

"*Object.* Some object, that now there ought to be no water-baptism, neither of Infants nor Beleevers, alledging that the Ordinance is ceased, for want of a succession of Administrators from the Primitive times; in which they produce the Churches flight into the wildernesse [*Rev.* 13. 6], to be fed there one thousand two hundred and threescore dayes, which are taken Prophetically for so many yeares, and that time Antichrist had the power, when Popes, Popish Bishops, and Priests tyrannized over the Saints, who then solely exercised the Authority of Church-administration in publike, not suffering a Saint to appeare in a right Gospel-manner; and then the holy City (being the Church of Christ) to be troden under foot.

"Before I answer this, note thus much ; That these Objecters doe not all of them deny Baptism to beleevers with water, but say the way to Baptism is cut off, by means a succession of Baptizers did not continue in those persecuting times, and so no man hath that Authority to baptize with water, until Christ restores the same by such a messenger as shall be immediately called by himselfe.

"*Ans.* It is hard to prove a succession of Administrators in a Gospel-way; for the enemy having power a long time, then the poore Saints durst write little to keep it upon records, when themselves were persecuted from City to City,...Yet I question not but there was a Church continued under the same ordinances, although obscure and hid from the eyes of the world, as you may see, although the woman (the Church) was in the wildernesse [*Rev.* 12. 6], yet she dyed not there, but was fed of God ;...So it appeares God had a Church then.

....

[1] What is believed to be an unique copy of this work is in the author's collection.

[2] Pp. 65–67.

"Although the right Gospel frame did not visibly appeare to the world in the time of Popery, Prelacy and Presbytery, so that great Congregations could not be gathered ; yet if but two or three, Christ hath promised to be amongst them, (as a Church in his name) …yet this woman (the Church) was nourished from the face of the Serpent (those persecutors) during which wildernesse estate of Gods people, they had comfort and light in their dwellings,…

"In the yeare 1635. when Prelacy had so great power that it overtopt the tender plants, yet then I found one Baptist, who declared so much unto me, that I perceived in those tyrannical times there was a Church of Christ under his Ordinances accorinding to Gospel manner[1]; and why not formerly under other persecutors also ? for we never read of a total cutting off the Church of Christ, but a wildernesse estate, and how the witnesses shall prophecy in sackcloth [*Rev.* 11. 3.], which sets forth that mournful condition of the Church then ; yet all this while as the word was preserved, so I question not but the Saints were hidden in that measure whereby God had alwayes a Church upon the Earth, from Christ unto this present ;…"

[1] This sentence without doubt means that this anonymous (English) Anabaptist in 1635 baptized his converts by immersion, or "dipping". Evidently he was an Arminian, with whom or whose converts the Particular Anabaptists would have nothing to do, when they later adopted this mode of baptism. More probably, however, they had not heard of him.

END OF VOLUME I.

CAMBRIDGE: PRINTED BY JOHN CLAY, M.A. AT THE UNIVERSITY PRESS.

THE BAPTIST STANDARD BEARER, INC.

A non-profit, tax-exempt corporation
committed to the Publication & Preservation
of The Baptist Heritage.

SAMPLE TITLES FOR PUBLICATIONS AVAILABLE
IN OUR VARIOUS SERIES:

THE BAPTIST *COMMENTARY* SERIES
Sample of authors/works in or near republication:
John Gill - *Exposition of the Old & New Testaments (9 & 18 Vol. Sets)*
(Volumes from the 18 vol. set can be purchased individually)

THE BAPTIST *FAITH* SERIES:
Sample of authors/works in or near republication:
Abraham Booth - *The Reign of Grace*
Abraham Booth - *Paedobaptism Examined (3 Vols.)*
John Gill - *A Complete Body of Doctrinal Divinity*

THE BAPTIST *HISTORY* SERIES:
Sample of authors/works in or near republication:
Thomas Armitage - *A History of the Baptists (2 Vols.)*
Isaac Backus - *History of the New England Baptists (2 Vols.)*
William Cathcart - *The Baptist Encyclopaedia (3 Vols.)*
J. M. Cramp - *Baptist History*

THE BAPTIST *DISTINCTIVES* SERIES:
Sample of authors/works in or near republication:
Alexander Carson - *Ecclesiastical Polity of the New Testament Churches*
E.C. Dargan - *Ecclesiology: A Study of the Churches*
J. M. Frost - *Paedobaptism: Is It From Heaven?*
R. B. C. Howell - *The Evils of Infant Baptism*

THE *DISSENT & NONCONFORMITY* SERIES:
Sample of authors/works in or near republication:
Champlin Burrage - *The Early English Dissenters (2 Vols.)*
Franklin H. Littell - *The Anabaptist View of the Church*
Albert H. Newman - *History of Anti-Pedobaptism*
Walter Wilson - *History & Antiquities of the Dissenting Churches (4 Vols.)*

For a complete list of current authors/titles, visit our internet site at
www.standardbearer.com or write us at:

he Baptist Standard Bearer, Inc.

No. 1 Iron Oaks Drive • Paris, Arkansas 72855

Telephone: (501) 963-3831   Fax: (501) 963-8083
E-mail: baptist@arkansas.net
Internet: http://www.standardbearer.com

Specialists in Baptist Reprints and Rare Books

Thou hast given a *standard* to them that fear thee; that it may be displayed because of the truth. -- *Psalm 60:4*

Printed in the United States
4225